**Ninth Edition**

# 100
# BEST
# Family Resorts
# in North America

## 100 QUALITY RESORTS WITH LEISURE ACTIVITIES FOR CHILDREN AND ADULTS

W9-BXY-700

# JANET TICE AND JANE WILFORD

**INSIDERS'** GUIDE®

GUILFORD, CONNECTICUT

AN IMPRINT OF THE GLOBE PEQUOT PRESS

**INSIDERS' GUIDE**®

Text design: Mary Ballachino

ISSN 1536-6170
ISBN 978-0-7627-4529-6

Manufactured in the United States of America
Ninth Edition/First Printing

The prices and rates listed in this guidebook were confirmed at press time. We recommend, however, that you call establishments to obtain current information before traveling.

TO FABIANA AND SYKES,
WHO FIRST PROVIDED THE INSPIRATION,
AND TO PAUL AND SARAH,
WHO CONTINUED THE ADVENTURE.
OUR WONDERFUL CHILDREN
AND OUR BEST FAMILY TRAVEL CRITICS!

# CONTENTS

# PREFACE

"Best" is a curious adjective, one that is entirely subjective. So let us define our sense of best—both what it does and what it doesn't mean.

Best is not necessarily the fanciest, the biggest, or the most expensive.

Best is not always the sleekest, the poshest, or the newest.

Best, in the context of this book, is what is best for families.

Best is variety in setting and atmosphere.

Best is variety in recreational interests and in prices.

Best is variety in geographic location. A broad selection allows you to have choices whether you want to travel far or near.

We searched for the most extensive children's programs, yet balanced this with an interest in presenting a good cross section of North America. If we have overlooked your favorite, let us know. Please write to us in care of The Globe Pequot Press, P.O. Box 480, Guilford, CT 06437.

Janet Tice
Jane Wilford

# INTRODUCTION

Although traveling with children is not a new phenomenon, many Americans these days are viewing the traditional family vacation in a different light. In past decades family vacations most frequently have been determined by the needs and wants of the children. Planning the entire vacation around the kids often left Mom and Dad feeling that they had not had a vacation at all but, rather, a trial by fire. The only option was to leave Junior behind in the care of grandparents or close family friends while the parents ventured off on their own. In an attempt to share experiences with their children, many parents, seeking middle ground, are adjusting the focus of their leisure-time plans.

Vacations these days often mean shorter and more frequent jaunts. Increasingly, they involve flying rather than loading up the family car and driving. Minivacations are becoming popular and are frequently planned to coincide with one or the other parent's business trips. On the philosophical side, current trends in child care emphasize the importance of a parent's presence, especially for the first three years, and many parents are reluctant to leave their infants and toddlers for extended periods.

The intent of this book is to identify those places where adults and children can enjoy interesting and age-appropriate activities. Babysitting services for infants, a ski school for three-year-olds, and a supervised recreational program for older children are some of the possibilities explored. In selecting resorts, we have taken into consideration different styles, price ranges, and diverse geographic locations. It is a representative sampling rather than an all-inclusive listing. Often we have been limited by lack of space

and lack of information. This book does not highlight every Disney and Six Flags Over Somewhere establishment in the United States. While these certainly serve an important educational function in a pleasant and exciting atmosphere for children, therein lies the catch: They are directed primarily toward children. But parents deserve vacations, too—adult vacations with grown-up activities.

This is not, then, a book about vacations *for* kids. Rather, it is a book about vacations *with* kids, about family adventures in which adults can be adults and children can be children and in which there is common ground for sharing. Our original concept of "time together and time apart" remains valid.

In general we are pleased with the progress we've noted in the resorts we have chosen from our previous editions. They are not resting on their laurels but seem to be enthusiastic and dedicated to making more and more improvements and providing better and better facilities and programs for families. In addition, new resorts developing exciting programs are constantly entering this family-oriented market.

If we've left out your favorite family spot, or if you own a resort and feel slighted, please write to us in care of The Globe Pequot Press. We're always glad to know of places where families find special treatment.

## Costs and Caveats

Prices are noted throughout the book in the accommodations section of each resort's description. They are current as of 2007. Inflation and the Internet both play a major role in the accuracy of prices—the former makes prices go up, while the latter causes them to go down. However, the prices quoted here can serve as a basis for comparison among resorts regardless of when you consult this guide.

The problem most commonly caused by prices is sorting out just what a given price includes. In the travel industry, various pricing schedules are frequently used to identify the relationship between lodging and meals. For example:

**European Plan** means the rate quoted is for lodging only.

**Modified American Plan** means two meals a day (usually breakfast and dinner) as well as lodging are included in the daily rate.

**Full American Plan** means three meals a day and lodging are covered in the daily rate.

**All-inclusive** means that all meals, generally all activities, and other extras are included in one price.

The extent of what else is included in the daily room rate, such as use of the recreational facilities, varies widely from one resort to another. Every effort has been made to identify the extras for which no additional charge is required. If "complimentary" or "free" is not clearly stated for a service or activity, you can safely assume that there is a fee.

Certain other things may come as a shock when you check out, so be sure to investigate beforehand. For example, we have not included taxes in the rates. This varies from state to state and will be 7–17 percent additional. Sometimes occupancy taxes are also added, based on the room or on the number of people.

Recently, it's become a common practice for hotels to add a "resort fee" or "amenity fee" of $5 to $25 per night. This fee covers things that previously were "free" or

included in the rate: in-room coffee and tea, daily newspapers, Internet access, or telephone charges for local or toll-free numbers, and so on. Often, resorts will add this fee to include "use of the facilities"—fitness rooms, swimming pool, beach chairs—any number of things. We've tried to identify these charges, but they're not always easy to find. You'll want to read the fine print, so to speak, and ask, ask, ask. No one wants a nasty shock at the end of a lovely vacation.

Although we've already discussed rates, it's a complicated issue and bears repeating, so please forgive us if you already know this. The rates that we list will not be exact. Sometimes they may be more; often they may be less. Rates depend on many things—size of the room, day of the week, location and view, season of the year, number of adults and children—the list goes on and on. Especially now that technology is so prevalent, hotels are following the airlines' examples and using yield management techniques. This simply means that a hotel will look at its past booking patterns and its current occupancy rate (how many empty rooms are sitting there) and adjust its rates accordingly, sometimes day by day. And competition is fierce: A resort may lower or raise its rates based on what its neighbors are doing. Also, many resorts, again like the airlines, are putting lower rates on the Internet. While we often give a sample package rate in the descriptions, there may be more packages available. Sometimes it may not be labeled a family package, so don't limit yourself. The resort may be marketing the spa or other recreation, with very good rates.

Besides lodging, prices are specifically noted for children's programs. As a well-seasoned traveler, you already have a ballpark idea of the prices of lift tickets for skiing and greens fees for golf. Emphasis here is on costs of the children's activities because now you're beginning to become well seasoned as a traveling parent.

Most children's programs, even if it's not stated in the descriptive entry, require children to be potty-trained. Those programs specifically for infants and toddlers, of course, do not. However, they usually do require parents to supply diapers and baby food or formula.

Reservations, reservations, reservations!! Again, we may not always list this in the entry, but it's safer to assume that reservations are required. If staffing is limited, the program may fill up—many parents plan months in advance via phone or Internet. Most resorts plan their staffing ahead of time, and if no children are signed up, there may be no program. Another caveat: Many hotels are now charging a fee if you cancel your child within twenty-four hours. Illness might not count, but capriciousness would. Advance planning may limit the spontaneity, but ultimately it makes life, and certainly family vacations, smoother.

# PLANNING FAMILY VACATIONS

## How This Book Can Help You

As your vacation rolls around, you start weighing the pros and cons of bringing the children along. You feel that you desperately need exclusive time for adult conversation with your spouse or other grown-ups. Yet you wonder if following through on that idea is fair to your kids. Vacations need not be an either/or proposition—either resigning yourself to a week or two of nonstop "Sesame Street" activities with no relief in sight or excluding the children from the few leisure weeks you have away from a demanding career. The former scenario almost always requires relinquishing your own interests, while the latter is complicated by worry and guilt over leaving the kids behind at Grandma's as you're off footloose and fancy-free. It is possible, however, to have a vacation that is fair to both you and your children.

So you're ready to plan a vacation with the kids. Though this sounds like what parents have been doing for generations, you're different from previous generations. You're better educated and fairly well traveled; you've delayed getting married and having children until your career was launched; and most likely you're older as you reach this phase of family life than were your parents. In addition, you probably have different expectations for both yourself and your children, expectations that influence how you want to spend your leisure time. While you're devoted to your children and conscious of the importance of your input into their intellectual, emotional, and social growth, you also realize that part of being a good parent is tending to your own physical and psychological well-being. At the same time, children today are also more accustomed to structured social activities and interaction with their peers. You imagine that it must be feasible to share a pleasurable vacation experience with your children without denying your own interests and concerns. Well, it is!

When you've made the decision that the kids should come along and you know that one more carousel or one more pair of Mickey Mouse ears just might drive you crazy, then let this book help you discover the perfect vacation spot, where the whole family can be happy together.

Whether you are considering a few relaxing days at a country hideaway or a week of fun in the sun on a beach, rest assured that there are accommodations with facilities and activities that will delight both you and your children. A family vacation doesn't have to mean settling for renting the same house at the nearest beach each season for the next several years or the proverbial visit to Grandma's house year after year. Variety can be found, and if you're itching for a good game of golf, you don't have to fret over whether your three-year-old can manage walking eighteen holes or what antics he'll perform along the way. These concerns can be resolved by choosing the proper surroundings and conditions.

When we once inquired about children's activities at a resort, the staff member replied, "I can probably find a bottle of bubbles." That would last about thirty seconds, right? Thank goodness many resorts are more enlightened, and you'll find those here.

Explore in the following pages a selection of hotels and resorts that offer conveniences to accommodate the needs and wishes of both adults and children. So that you can gratify your diverse and periodically changing geographic interests, you will discover that this guide includes establishments throughout the United States, with a few in Canada.

In compiling this collection, several criteria were considered: attractive surroundings; good dining facilities, including comfortable lounges and bars; babysitting services; and recreational activities for both parents and children. Needless to say, some of the establishments listed here meet more of the criteria or meet them better than others. But then, your wishes and requirements may vary from one trip to the next. One year you may need just a competent babysitter to stay in your hotel room with your infant while you enjoy an elegant, leisurely dinner, and the next year you may need a complete day-care center/nursery school for your energetic toddler while you spend the day out on the slopes. This book does not rank resorts on how well the criteria are met; it simply describes them and all their available services. You can then pick and choose according to your personal preferences and current needs.

To make it easier to find your ideal vacation spot, the descriptive entries are grouped by geographic location, then alphabetically within these divisions; addresses, telephone numbers, and Web sites are included in the descriptions.

Following the descriptions is a standard alphabetical index of resort names to help you pull out the perfect place that a friend recently mentioned at a dinner party, the location of which eludes your recollective powers. We've also included an alphabetical index by state and province. This arrangement should afford you easy access to the required information regardless of your perspective when designing your vacation.

Finally, a special categories index is given that lists resorts by the seasonal schedule of the children's programs.

While probably the foremost concern for your next trip is simply to make that perfect match between your personal circumstances and the most suitable resort, you may occasionally feel a bit nervous about some of the practical logistics of traveling with kids. The next section, on helpful hints when traveling with children, may forestall a few inconveniences that can arise when away from home; the medical information should allay some fears about illnesses and emergencies; and the segments on educating yourself and the advantages of a specialized travel agent may help in ironing out the details of your vacation arrangements. In any case, they will stimulate you to analyze your own and your children's habits so that you can anticipate some of the problems and joys of traveling with youngsters.

So you're off. Good luck and have a happy vacation!

## Helpful Hints for Traveling with Children

It can be a joy to travel with children. Sure, sometimes the preparations may seem exhausting, and spurts of parental anxiety en route may be tiring as well, but the excitement and wonder of children as they encounter new experiences are worth the price of admission.

On the following pages you'll find some helpful hints for traveling with kids. Many of these suggestions may seem incredibly obvious, but stating the obvious is not always a disadvantage. And a little repetitive reinforcement may help you react more quickly or think better on your feet. One easy-to-read and practical resource book is *Trouble-Free Travel with Children: Over 700 Helpful Hints for Parents on the Go* (Book Peddlers,

2004) by Vicki Lansky, author of more than twenty-five books for new parents.

Preparation, preparation, preparation! The first trick to traveling with kids is preparing them for the adventure. Talk to your child in advance; advise her where you're going and what you'll be doing. Infants (in spite of the mounds of diapers you must tote) are very portable. Even toddlers whose whole world revolves around Mom and Dad are happy as long as familiar faces are near at hand. But as a child's world expands to include friends and a wider realm of belongings, verbal preparation becomes very important. Sometimes it's easy to assume that your youngster will pick up on things by osmosis, but children don't always assimilate information about vacation plans that floats around the house in chitchat. It's necessary to explain directly to them what is in store.

Many families like to spend time together planning vacations. Encouraging participation from all family members and allowing children to help plan the trip makes them feel like "shareholders," creating cooperation and increasing satisfaction for everyone. Books and maps about your destination and route can be shared; even for very young children, maps translate the excitement of travel into a tangible form. Participation easily continues throughout the vacation when you assist children with keeping a "journal" (drawings, pictures, flowers, poems, ticket stubs, whatever!); allow them their own camera (inexpensive, of course); or encourage them to collect postcards, or badges for their backpack, or to follow any theme that appeals to them.

Besides detailing the fun of this new experience, reassure your child that you'll be returning home; that although your daughter may not bring along every Barbie doll and Raggedy Ann, her dolls will still be here when she gets back; and that even though your son may miss his best friends, they won't forget him. Even three- and four-year-olds can "write" postcards along the way as a means of staying connected with friends back home. A time and stress saver is to address stick-on mailing labels before you leave home, preventing frantic searches and disappointment.

As an experienced traveler, you know the ropes of appropriate packing for trips. As a conscientious parent, you are most familiar with what your child will want or need away from home. The standard rule of thumb—don't overpack—applies just as well for children as it does for adults. The length of the trip adjusted for the dirt factor of your own child (how many outfits can he go through in a day?) should give you a reasonable handle on the amount of clothes to pack. Laundromats are never that far away, many hotels have laundry services, and kids' clothes (just by virtue of their size) are fairly easy to hand wash in a hotel bathroom. And don't take along what your child isn't happy with. No matter how much time dear Aunt Josie spent crocheting that sweet little dress, if your daughter doesn't like it, if it's uncomfortable, it will be nothing more than an unnecessary bulge in your suitcase. We've developed a couple of packing "rules" over the years. Rule #1: Take half as many clothes and twice as much money as you think you need; and Rule #2: Pack your bag and then walk around the block with it to test it before departure!

If your child uses a bottle, a trip may not be the best time to nudge him out of it; a bottle may provide a bit of security in unfamiliar surroundings. Just be sure to pack a bottle brush: If a bottle gets lost at the bottom of a travel bag for a day or two, new life forms may be discovered.

Toys, too, have to fall under the "don't overpack" rule. Remember that for children, seemingly mundane objects in new surroundings often provide considerable amusement. It's a good idea to stash away a couple of new attention-getters, but don't forget the tried-and-true. A cuddly doll, even if it is beginning to look somewhat old and ratty, or a special pillow is often very comforting for a little one sleeping in a strange bed for the first time. Age-appropriate books, a small ball, crayons, coloring books, scissors, construction paper, a beanbag (remember them from when you were a kid?), and small games such as a pint-size checkerboard are all packable items. Even blocks like Duplos or Legos, if arranged in one compact cube, can be packed fairly easily. Some parents cherish a CD player (with earphones, please) as something akin to a gift from the gods. Terrifically totable and accompanied by a selection of CDs, this can effectively hold a child's attention. According to your tastes and budget, many compact electronics for children are also on the market now.

For the preschooler or older child, consider investing in a backpack or small wheeled case. Set down the rules with your child when packing: She can bring along whatever fits, and she has to carry it. This way you give your child a sense of participating in the preparations and obviate the almost inevitable whine about something Mom didn't include. And you can sneak in a little lesson in responsibility practically unnoticed. Just make sure enough room is left for new additions along the way.

A "surprise box" is a fun way to keep children interested and amused. Without divulging details, prepare "surprises" such as snacks, small toys, or other things you know your child will like. Then watch the fun as he delves into the goodies when the vacation adventure begins. A surprise box can entertain your youngster anywhere from two minutes to two hours; if you're clever, you'll be on the upper end of the spectrum.

When making plane reservations, try to secure seat assignments at the same time. Indicate the age of your young traveler, and request the bulkhead seats. These seats afford a little extra legroom and can be padded with blankets and pillows if your child decides to snooze (lucky you!). It may mean that your feet will be struck by paralysis if she nestles down on her pillow and curls up on your toes, but it is an improvement over having her elbow in your drink. Also, without passengers in front of you in this seating arrangement, you won't fret over a rambunctious child's kicks disturbing other people. Try to avoid placing children in aisle seats, as little arms and legs can get bumped and escape is too easy.

If two parents are flying with a lap child (under two years old), try to reserve an aisle seat and a window seat. Regular air travelers never request a center seat, so if the plane is not full, you'll wind up with that third seat in which to spread out; if a stranger does venture into your row, it's simple enough for one parent to move over a notch. Often parents opt to purchase a ticket for the child, bringing their own safety seat.

In the past, airlines stocked onboard activity packs, and even special meals for their younger travelers. These days, you need to pack your own. Bringing a mostly disposable picnic lunch on board can keep the whole family happy. Do take advantage of the early boarding that airlines provide for families with small children—it helps to "settle in" before the crowd arrives.

Airplanes pose additional problems: Small children often have greater difficulty than adults in adjusting to altitude changes. During takeoffs and landings, infants should be encouraged to nurse or drink a bottle; the sucking action combats blocked ear and painful sinus problems. Older children can use the same techniques as adults—yawning and chewing gum or candy.

If you plan to rent a car during your vacation, be sure to request a car seat for a child four years old and younger. While many rental agencies take this in stride, the number of car seats is usually limited, so it's important to make a reservation for this accessory in advance. Whether your mode of transportation is your own car or a rental, plan frequent stops. Cramped legs and fidgetiness set in fast for youngsters. These factors are not unknown in air travel either; even a walk down the aisle of the plane to the bathroom is a change of pace for a child.

In car travel, a small ice chest in the backseat can be a real boon. Filled with milk, juice, and fruit, it provides a source of ready refreshment and relieves frantic searches for a fast-food stop or a corner grocery. Even when traveling by air, if your luggage allotment permits, check a small ice chest (empty) along with your other bags. Once you arrive at your hotel, it can be filled with ice and drinks and can be taken along in a rental car on side trips. Or, upon arrival at your destination, make one of your first stops at a grocery, drug, or discount store and pick up an inexpensive Styrofoam cooler that can be left behind. Many accommodations include small refrigerators in the rooms, and some are equipped with kitchens, but if not, you've solved a problem before it arises. It's much easier to dig into an ice chest for a drink than to track down juice somewhere in the hotel facilities at nine o'clock at night. But if this seems too cumbersome and your child desperately needs something late at night, remember the hotel bar—it is the best place to hit, for it always has orange juice (for Screwdrivers), tomato juice (for Bloody Marys), and milk (for White Russians). It may be more expensive, but can you really afford to count pennies when Johnny refuses to go to sleep without his nightly cup of milk? It's an investment in your peace of mind.

When stocking up on drinks, buy the variety in cardboard cartons. Since they are unbreakable and need no refrigeration, they can be squirreled away in a suitcase or even tossed into a purse. On an airplane, the flight attendants never seem to pass by soon enough or often enough to satisfy little ones.

For edibles, small boxes of raisins, granola bars, and individually wrapped cheese chunks such as The Laughing Cow (what child can resist a silly laughing cow in a red net bag?) make good nourishing snacks. Good old clever Mom can rack up some kudos when she pulls one of these treats from her bag before Susie even thinks about getting antsy.

Once you arrive at your destination and settle into your hotel, turn over an area, even if just a corner, to your child. Having his own space filled with his own stuff may mean a lot in terms of a sense of belonging, and with a bit of prodding, you may avoid having toys strewn all about.

Collecting souvenirs on a trip can be a time-consuming process or maybe even cause a headache or two. Either Joey wants everything in sight or he chooses the most inappropriate piece of junk you've ever seen. Sure, certain limits on buying have to be set, but who cares if he chooses the made-in-Japan pencil sharpener in the shape of a cannon during a visit to Valley Forge? Just as a cookbook containing three wonderful meat-pie recipes from Nova Scotia or an artistic ceramic tile made in the Southwest is something that you must have, there are special reminders of a trip that a child feels he needs. They're just different. A few neat rocks and a couple of sticks may be the only things Joey wants to show off to his best buddy back home. Or if your little girl wants to take home a shiny red coin purse to her best friend, she doesn't care (and neither does her friend) that the same item is on the shelves in every chain store across the country, so why should you? A smattering of understanding and patience can go a long way.

Recreational activities in your new surroundings must be evaluated with a clear head and a sharp eye. Most of the resorts included here offer organized children's activities or babysitting services, so it may not be necessary to drag kids along on every adult event you want to investigate. Antiques hunting and long museum visits are usually not first-rate attractions for members of the kiddie league. Plan on a babysitter or a group activity for an afternoon that you want to spend on a grown-up outing.

And for those days that are devoted entirely to being together, alternate grown-up pursuits with juvenile ones. Remember that a child's attention span is not as refined or sophisticated as an adult's; variety is more than the spice of life—it's the key to sanity in some cases. Climbing on the cannons at an old fort is much more fun for a child than reading every historical marker; a mixture of both keeps everyone happy. All day on the beach may be too much for a three- or four-year-old, and you can take ten-to-one odds that he won't be content following your lead to relax and soak up the sunshine. Bargain with your child: a run on the beach and a few splashes in the waves, then quiet time building a sand castle; an hour of shopping or sightseeing for two hours in the swimming pool.

Many resorts have lodging with fully equipped kitchens so that you can cook family meals in a homelike setting. Many resort restaurants make an attentive effort to please children; a special dining hour for families or a children's menu certainly helps make life more pleasant. And when you grow weary of dining in restaurants, a picnic may be a reasonable alternative. Many hotels can prepare box lunches, or you can pick up some cold cuts at a small grocery for a do-it-yourself picnic. Ordering a meal through room service is often a special treat for a child.

As you skim the descriptive entries of the resorts that follow, you'll realize that most are self-contained vacation spots. Each offers a place to sleep, a place to eat, and something to do. This is intentional, as children seem to function best staying in one place. Establishing a home base, exploring the setting, and taking afternoon side trips are often preferable to being on the road constantly. Besides negating all the packing and unpacking of a traditional road trip, having a home base helps a child develop a sense of security as the new surroundings become familiar.

With a few tricks up your sleeve, some understanding, and forethought, traveling with kids can be a fun-filled family adventure. Your well-considered plans make the whole process workable and buy a lot of happiness for both you and your child. With solid preplanning there's space for those spontaneous "happenings" that make a vacation memorable.

## Medical Information

Unless you can take your own family doctor or pediatrician with you, the best advice to follow is the old Girl Scout motto "Be Prepared." Keep in mind: (1) This adventure you're about to embark upon is not a trek along the shores of the East Siberian Sea, and (2) you are not the sole custodian of Band-Aids. As amazing as it may seem, doctors and pharmacies do exist out there in that twilight zone called family vacations.

Before starting your trip, consult your pediatrician for advice; she may even be able to supply the names of colleagues where you'll be visiting. If you fear that your child is coming down with something as you depart on your vacation, or if he's particularly accident-prone, you can check with the resort staff upon arrival about the location of the nearest hospital and pharmacy and the availability of doctors and nurses (many resorts have medical personnel on call). Sometimes the best recommendations come from other parents, wherever you may find them. If the need is immediate, don't hesitate to ask a likely looking parent working in a car rental agency, a restaurant, a shop, or the airport. And without seeming alarmist, look up the telephone number of the local poison control center; anticipating the slim chance of ever needing it, you'll be gratified that it's handy should your child ingest a handful of your brightly colored vitamin pills. It is also a good idea to check with your medical insurance provider before you leave home for out-of-state or -country authorization/billing procedures.

Pack a medical emergency kit and try to envision the unexpected. If your child scrapes a knee at a playground or develops an earache in the middle of the night, you won't want to take time tracking down a drugstore to relieve his discomfort. You can purchase a ready-made medical kit that fits compactly in a car's glove compartment or carry-on bag, or you may prefer the do-it-yourself variety. The following list is merely suggestive; review your own medicine cabinet to fill in the gaps.
- vitamins and medications your child normally takes
- a thermometer
- children's anti-inflammatory
- children's cough syrup
- adhesive strips
- nose drops (though most kids hate them)
- a decongestant
- an aspirator

- ear drops
- suppositories and antidiarrheal medicine (change in water and altitude or sheer excitement can affect a child's system)
- Desitin, A&D, or calendula ointment
- antibiotic ointment or spray (for cuts and scrapes)
- tweezers and a sterile needle (to remove splinters)
- ipecac (to induce vomiting if your child overdoses on peculiar substances)
- Q-Tips and cotton balls
- sterile gauze pads (for applying direct pressure to cuts)
- insect repellent
- Band-Aids (of course)
- sunblock

Though this list seems long, the items take up very little space in a suitcase. Remember, you don't have to pack a lifetime supply of any of these things. A small supply will meet the immediate need and buy you time to find a drugstore.

## Knowing What Questions to Ask

Sometimes it seems as if there are almost as many pricing schedules, package plans, and special programs as there are stars in the sky. There are EP, MAP, FAP, golf and tennis packages, weekend specials, and midweek discounts. Depending on geographic location, high season is winter at one resort and summer at another. Even the seasons are defined arbitrarily. Summer may be the end of June through Labor Day or, perhaps, Memorial Day through August. Christmas season starts December 15 at some places and a week later at others. All the jargon and variations on a theme can make you feel like a babe in the woods when contacting a resort about your plans. To avoid arriving someplace and getting halfway through your stay only to find out that you should have taken advantage of some special offer, you have to be savvy in the possibilities and the vocabulary. Even if you aren't familiar with the latest buzzwords, just knowing that different vacation configurations exist puts you a leg up; you can at least ask, "Are there any family discounts or package plans for _____ (fill in the blank—golf, tennis, skiing, etc.)?"

At some resorts, you walk in and pay one price. At others, every hour on the tennis court or every bicycle ride around the block is charged separately. Both approaches have redeeming aspects. To some folks, it's downright annoying to have to constantly reach for a wallet. After all, this is a vacation, and they don't want to be troubled with mundane monetary matters. On the other hand, some people would rather pay as they go, laying down the cash for only the services they use. If you've had aquaphobia since childhood and don't care to be within 10 feet of a lake, much less out in the middle rocking a canoe, free boating privileges are worthless. As long as you're in the know as to a resort's practices and policies beforehand, you'll suffer no surprises and no aggravation or disappointment during your visit.

Much of a resort's terminology is self-explanatory, and acronyms may or may not be a mystery to you. The most commonly used abbreviations are EP for European Plan, meaning lodging only; MAP for Modified American Plan, which includes two meals a day in the room rate; and FAP for Full American Plan, which includes three meals a day.

Knowing a resort's designation of low and high season is also crucial to your planning. If you're not absolutely wedded to certain dates and you can juggle your schedule on the home front, you might land in the low season simply by altering your plans by a week.

Moving to more detailed information, you may want to ask a resort certain specific questions. The questions outlined here can be used on the resorts described in this book for elaboration on particular points, or you can test them out on places that you discover on your own.

## Lodging

Are the accommodations hotel rooms, condominium units, or cottages with kitchens?

If they are hotel rooms:

- Are there connecting rooms? Do you offer a discount on the second room?
- Is there a refrigerator in the room?
- What is the range of prices, and is there a reduced rate for children?
- Is there a charge for a crib or rollaway bed?
- Are strollers available?
- Do you have child-proofing kits?

## Dining

- What types of dining areas are there? Is there a spot to get the kids a hot dog as well as a place that tantalizes more refined taste buds?
- Is there a dress requirement? (What a disappointment to venture into a tempting restaurant only to learn that gentlemen are required to wear jackets and you packed nothing but golf shirts!)
- Is there a meal plan? Is it mandatory or optional?
- Is there a children's menu?

## Kids

Is there a supervised program for children?

- What are the planned activities, and what are the ages of the children who participate?
- When is it held—times of the year, days of the week, and hours of the day? (The level of specificity may

seem a little overboard, but consider a Monday-through-Friday-morning program: It's not going to be much help if you pull in at 1:00 p.m. on Friday and leave at 10:00 a.m. Tuesday.)
- What is the daily or hourly fee?
- What are the qualifications of the staff? What is the ratio of caregivers to children?

Is there a playground or game room? (Even if you're doing the supervision, if there's something amusing for the kids, they can release some energy, and you can sit on the sidelines and read the newspaper.)

Is there a wading or kiddie pool? Is it enclosed by a fence?

Are babysitting services available?
- Who makes the arrangements—you or the resort staff?
- What is the average rate? (You may linger a bit longer over that fine cabernet if your babysitter receives $6 an hour rather than $15 an hour.)
- What are the babysitter's qualifications? Are references available?

And if you're skittish about your kid's health or proclivity toward disaster, inquire about local medical facilities.
- Is there a doctor or nurse in residence or on call?
- Where are the nearest hospital and pharmacy?

**For You**
If you're investigating a resort or have chosen it as a vacation destination, you no doubt have an inkling as to its recreational facilities. You're looking at it because of its beach, golf course, tennis center, or ski mountain. Besides its main attraction, you'll also want to know what secondary diversions are possible. You can't play golf sixteen hours a day—not even Tiger Woods does that. So ask:
- Is there a jogging path? Parcourse fitness trail? Hiking trails?
- Is there a spa or exercise room? Sauna, steam room, whirlpool?
- Does the tennis complex also house racquetball courts? Indoor courts?
- For golf, tennis, and fishing, is it possible to rent equipment, or is it necessary to bring your own?
- Are there any concerts, lectures, or classes?

Your interests will determine which questions to ask. Once you get a handle on what to ask, you'll find planning a vacation a lot more fun and a lot less time-consuming. You don't have to have all the answers; just being able to pose a few intelligent questions sets the ball in motion and can generate maybe even more information than you thought you wanted. As a knowledgeable consumer, you can pursue plans on your own or you can work quite effectively with a travel agent. In either case, a little self-education can certainly enhance the preparation and the end product: your leisure-time pleasure.

## Information, Please

Travel, like so much else today, has become increasingly complicated. Since the deregulation of the airlines, the proliferation of airfares has been phenomenal. Any given pair of cities has up to one hundred different fares, with as many rules and regulations. While this ultimately benefits the pleasure traveler, it also creates a certain amount of chaos. On a trip from New York to San Francisco, for example, the same seat in the airplane can cost anything between $299 and $1,499, depending on how far in advance you book, how long you're staying, and the promotional needs of the air carrier. When one adds other factors such as the day of the week, certain airports, one-stop versus nonstop flights, or whether you're wearing polka dots, more complications arise. While airlines generally give you their own lowest fares, they do not necessarily tell you about a competitor who may have even lower fares or more convenient flights.

The Internet provides what seems like an unlimited amount of information, as well as a direct and efficient system for travel suppliers to market their wares. Airlines constantly evaluate their "load factors"—how many empty seats remain on each flight. Once that airplane takes off, each empty seat is "dead" and has earned no revenue. The same is true of hotels—an empty room cannot be profitable. Therefore, more and more, airlines are offering last-minute flights, particularly on weekends, in an effort to fill those seats. They are also offering lower fares, additional frequent-flier miles, and other incentives to encourage travelers to directly book online. Hotels and car-rental companies are following suit and wooing travelers with free nights, upgrades, and special offers. Developing "brand loyalty" has long been a goal of travel suppliers; the advent of the Internet has intensified that process.

Incredible amounts of information exist in cyberspace. You can get lost for hours, sometimes pleasurably, sometimes not. Most airlines, hotels, car-rental companies, tour companies, and cruise lines have their own Web sites. Tourist offices in many states and countries offer virtual tours. Newsletters, chat rooms, and articles abound. A search for "travel with children" quickly gets you started. Each entry in the book has an Internet site listed, on which you'll find photos, detailed descriptions and hours, and the latest prices and packages. It's an invaluable adjunct to planning.

Not comfortable with surfing the Web? Ask your ten-year-old to help! Start with Family Travel Forum (www.familytravel forum.com, 888–FT–FORUM), a comprehensive site for family travel information. The site offers lots of news, deals, and ideas for free; flexible membership plans begin at $3.95 a month for "armchair travelers" and include savings and discount coupons from family-friendly suppliers. Three-month ($10) and one-year ($38) plans include custom trip planning. Encourage your children to share their travel experiences by submitting articles to FTF for publication on their affiliate site, www.kidtravels.com. Another affiliate site, www.tinytravelers.net, lists tips and articles on trips, health, gear, and keeping baby safe.

Familytravel.com (www.familytravel.com) is an excellent site with tons of information for traveling families. It offers lots and lots of details and good firsthand experiences.

Family Travel Network (www.familytravel network.com) is another extensive site for talking online with other parents and kids and finding tons of information, hot deals, links, and travel tips—all free.

Dorothy Jordon, one of the acknowledged pioneers of family travel, offers advice and a quarterly newsletter, *Family Travel Times,* at www.familytraveltimes.com. The site is fairly simple, and Jordon's approach is straightforward and no-nonsense. As she says, it's "an honest publication—written by parents, for parents—based on firsthand research." Subscription information is found on the Web site or call (212) 477-5524.

We live in an age of information overkill; managing this information, sorting through the myriad possibilities, can be mind-boggling. Working with a professional travel agent or tour operator can add several dimensions to this information process. An agent is a bountiful source of books, brochures, and maps; but also important are the agent's personal experience, the client base that gives feedback on pros and cons of trips, and close contact with colleagues who have traveled extensively. Even something as seemingly straightforward as a hotel reservation can be complicated by weekend specials, golf or tennis packages, seasons, midweek, and family offers. A good agent is a whiz at interpreting brochures and deciphering the fine print. "Ocean view" does not mean on the beach; in fact, you may have to hang over the balcony with a pair of binoculars to see the ocean. "Secluded" may mean private, or it may mean you have to go 10 miles to find any other signs of life. Finally, you can capitalize on an agent's knowledge of the fares and facilities that each airline provides for children and of any special family-travel offers, such as "kids fly free" and discounts for spouses. A good agent can pull all of this together, analyze your needs, and help make your vacation dream become a coherent reality.

If you work with an agent or tour operator, certain considerations are basic. What are their policies on service charges, refunds, and payments? Are they an appointed agency of the airlines, Amtrak, and the cruise lines? Airline appointments or tour operator licenses indicate a certain basic financial investment and preparation. Ask if they hold your money in an escrow account until your travel date. What insurance do they provide? What is their responsibility to you if the hotel/cruise/tour reservation is canceled or not properly delivered? In short, be proactive. This is your vacation; you should feel comfortable and ask questions—even the same one repeatedly and especially the ones you're afraid may sound dumb.

Whether you use a travel agent or tour operator or do it yourself, the higher your level of involvement in planning, the more satisfaction you stand to gain from your trip. A good agent should be able to determine the broad outlines of your trip, to respond and listen to your ideas and needs, and to fill in with specific suggestions. The agent should have an idea of your lifestyle, your ideal vacation, and your budget. Your agent should ask, or you should volunteer, what seems to be personal information: How do you like to spend your days? Is shopping important to you? If you have a beach, are you happy? Will you die if you have no evening entertainment, or do you prefer a quiet stroll and a good book? What are your hobbies or special interests? Again, do not be afraid to discuss financial expectations. This can avoid a few nasty surprises—such as having to ransom one of the kids to pay for the trip!

Two established tour operators specialize in family travel, working with both travel agents and individual clients. In Chevy Chase, Maryland, Grandtravel provides escorted tours for grandparents and grandchildren, both in the United States and abroad (800-247-7651; www.grandtrvl.com). In San Francisco, California, Rascals in Paradise (800-U-RASCAL; www.rascalsinparadise.com) offers resorts and tours all over the world. Many local agencies are becoming aware of the family market and are beginning to specialize in this field; check your local parents' paper or the travel section of the local Sunday paper for agencies in your area. Several agencies are listed on Family Travel Forum's Web site, www.familytravelforum.com.

No one knows your expectations as well as you, so assume some of the legwork for detailed information yourself. Check with the tourist offices of the state or country you plan to visit for brochures and information on special events and attractions. The American Automobile Association (AAA) is an excellent resource for maps and detailed information if you're a member and are driving for part or all of the trip. Travel books and articles are fun for the family and often have good advice on extras or little-known attractions in the area; check your local library for these. Chinaberry Book Service, in San Diego, California, is committed to conscious parenting and has well-selected general books, CDs, and tapes cataloged for various ages and interests (800-776-2242; www.chinaberry.com). Also, talk to your friends who have been there, for those real inside tips.

Finally, close your suitcase, lock the door, and take off—secure in the knowledge that your advance planning, plus professional help, will make this the best trip ever!

# NEW ENGLAND

Maine
Massachusetts
New Hampshire
Rhode Island
Vermont

# THE BALSAMS GRAND RESORT HOTEL

Dixville Notch, New Hampshire

In the fine tradition of grand old hotels, The Balsams, a 15,000-acre private estate located high in the White Mountains, has been graciously welcoming guests since 1866. The three main buildings are interconnected and quite impressive, with their white facades and red-tiled roofs. Two date from the late 1800s—the Dixville House and The Balsams Inn—and the "new" wing, the Hampshire House, was added in 1917. At the foot of three very precipitous mountains—almost entirely surrounded by steep, 1,000-foot cliffs with the Notch Road the only way in or out—and overlooking Lake Gloriette, The Balsams offers a relaxed escape in a charming atmosphere. In summer Dixville Notch is a refreshing mountain retreat; in winter, a delightful getaway for skiers.

The Balsams' all-inclusive American Plan adds all the amenities for a fun-filled vacation in a worry-free atmosphere. Golf, tennis, swimming, hiking, mountain biking, lawn games, children's day camp, fine dining, and nightly entertainment are available and—an increasingly rare practice these days—at no additional charges for use of any of the facilities. Spring and fall seem to be the seasons for groups and conventions, while the Summer Social Season (late June to early September) and winter (mid-December to late March) are geared toward individuals and families. The resort is open year-round.

**Accommodations:** The Balsams has 204 rooms, many with views of the mountains or the lake. Select family suites (connecting bedrooms with one bath) and parlor suites (sitting room and bedroom) offer ample room for youngsters; these are quite popular, so early booking is advised. The Hampshire House is configured to provide convenient adjoining rooms for family accommodation but is substantially higher in cost. Each room has a unique decor and character, creating a comfortable ambience. Rates depend on the size of the room, its location and view, and the time of the year. The Balsams offers a Full American Plan that includes three meals in summer, two in winter; all activities and sports (but not equipment rental); and children's programs and entertainment. Rates are per person, per night, and range from $189 to $299 for ages seventeen and older; children ages five to twelve pay $100 each. Rates may be slightly lower in winter. European Plan and Bed-and-Breakfast are available, but these rates are variable and therefore not for publication; check with the hotel directly for more information as well as holiday rates. Cribs are provided.

**Dining:** The main dining room serves breakfast, lunch, and dinner during the summer season and only breakfast and dinner during the winter season. The summertime luncheon buffet is a sumptuous display of hot and cold entrees, cheeses, fruit, and desserts; you might sample the fried Maine shrimp or the Atlantic salmon. At dinner an Edwardian ambience prevails as guests enjoy stupendous mountain or lake views from the twenty picture windows, with elegant table d'hôte service featuring draped linen, silver settings, and waiters in bow ties. The Balsams achieved the *Condé Nast Gold List* in 2007, with a rating of 100 percent for food and 97 percent for overall service. The menu offers an entirely different selection every evening, featuring seafood dishes as well as Long Island duckling, beef, and chicken. At the dinner hour jackets for men are required. Parents are advised to bring appropriate dinner clothes for older children as well.

In the summer you might try The Panorama Golf Clubhouse Grille or the poolside bar for refreshments; both offer delightful views and a chance to soak up the beautiful scenery. In winter you'll be shuttling over to The Balsams/Wilderness Ski Area, where breakfast and lunch are served at the base lodge. Back at the hotel, evening entertainment means cocktails and floor shows in the Switzerland of America Ballroom or dancing and drinks at The Tavern. Typical pub fare is served until 8:00 p.m.

**Children's World:** The Balsams is interested in providing excellent service for its younger guests as well as its adult visitors. For children this translates into a busy schedule of fun activities. Camp Wind Whistle is available from late June through Labor Day, seven days a week; here children five through ten-plus meet with counselors in The Balsams Playroom for sports, games, picnics, swimming, nature walks, arts and crafts, fishing, farm visits, and movies. Outdoor activities are emphasized. Children have lunch with their counselors, and then, after linking up with Mom and Dad around 4:00 p.m. to share their day's experiences, they can rejoin their young group for dinner at 6:30 p.m. Age groups are divided as follows: five to six years, seven to nine years, and ten and above, with age-appropriate activities.

The outdoor children's area features a state-of-the art fiberglass and stainless steel play structure. The indoor game room (supervised) has an array of board games, video games, and table tennis and pool

tables. Open daily from 9:00 a.m. to midnight, the game room is a popular spot for youngsters to gather and make friends during both summer and winter seasons.

In winter children ages three to five can enroll in the Wee Whistle Ski School. Older children have their own morning and afternoon lessons. The cost is approximately $40 for 1 to 1½ hours. Wintertime room rates for children at The Balsams include ski privileges, but not lessons.

From December through March a well-equipped nursery/play area in the Alpine Base Lodge welcomes children ages six months to five years. The experienced staff amuses children with a selection of games and toys from 9:00 a.m. to 4:00 p.m.; parents may want to join their children for lunch. Costs for Camp Wind Whistle in summer and the Alpine Lodge Nursery in winter are included in the Full American Plan and ski packages. For older kids winter fun brings some organized events such as skating parties and broomball games; all the sports, recreational, and entertainment facilities are available with appropriate levels of adult supervision.

Individual babysitters can be arranged for $7 per hour, with a $20 minimum (cash payment expected); sitters should be requested when lodging reservations are made or forty-eight hours in advance.

**Recreation:** At The Balsams you can spend busy days of back-to-back events from morning to night or just relax, set an unhurried pace, and enjoy the peace and beauty of the mountains. Five major garden areas with over 35,000 flowers and plants please both guests and local hummingbirds.

Two golf courses await golfers. The Panorama, an eighteen-hole championship course, was designed by Donald Ross, a Scottish golf course architect famous during the early twentieth century. Set in the mountains, the undulating terrain can be challenging and the views truly stunning. The nine-hole executive course, the Coashau-kee, is just right for beginners or those who haven't tested their clubs in a while. There are pro shops at each course, putting greens, a practice fairway, and a pro staff on hand to help you polish your swing. The Centennial Golf School operates in June and features individualized coaching by PGA profession-als. The Balsams is the only resort in New England to be named "One of the Nation's Finest Golf Courses" by *Golf Magazine*.

Tennis enthusiasts can choose to play on either red-clay courts (three) or all-weather courts (three). Improve your skills at the Tennis Tune-Up and Tennis Camp clinics, sign up with the pro for group or private les-sons, and stop by the tennis shop to pick up those indispensable accessories.

Swim a few laps in the Olympic-size heated swimming pool overlooking Lake Gloriette. With the mountains in the back-ground, this is an idyllic spot for sun-bathing. You might try a refreshing dip in the lake or a relaxing excursion in a pad-dleboat, canoe, or rowboat. Fish in a crystal-clear mountain stream, hike in the wilderness (solo or with a guided group), or take a nature walk with the staff naturalist. The hotel's natural-history program com-bines tours, hikes, and discussions for a good introduction to the flora and fauna of the area. The mountain biking trails are well marked and offer fun at every level. Mountain bike rentals and repairs are available.

Lawn sports include badminton, horse-shoes, croquet, volleyball, and shuffle-board; when you head indoors, there are billiards, table tennis, bingo, an aerobic-exercise room, and a movie theater. Take to the library/card room to snuggle up with a good book or play a few hands of bridge, or

view wide-screen films in the movie theater. To track down that essential souvenir, drop in at the gift shop, craft shop, gallery, bal-loon store, and fashion boutique.

In the wintertime this wonderland is draped in snow, and The Balsams/Wilder-ness Ski Area (located on the property) is just a short shuttle ride from the hotel. There are sixteen tree-lined downhill trails and 95 kilometers of packed and groomed trails for cross-country, ranked among the top ten in North America. Wintertime also means ice-skating or snowshoeing on dedi-cated trails. Like to stay inside? Enroll in the three-day culinary cooking class and prepare a sumptuous four-course meal for family and friends.

Nearby attractions include a "Watchable Wildlife Corridor" along Route 26 with view-ing stations for watching moose and pere-grine falcons; an American bald eagle nesting site on Lake Umbagog; the Poore Family Homestead, a farm dating back to the 1820s; the 45th Parallel, marking the latitude equidistant from the North Pole and the Equator; and Magnetic Hill, where cars facing downhill seem to mysteriously roll backward up the hill. You may also find a visit to the Ballot Room in Dixville Notch interesting. Here the first-in-the-nation vot-ers cast their ballots at midnight in all pres-idential primaries and general elections.

Whether you're seeking an escape from city crowds or want an active sports-oriented vacation, The Balsams makes it all possible.

---

**1000 Cold Springs Road**
**Dixville Notch, New Hampshire 03576**
**(603) 255-3400, (877) 225-7267**
**www.thebalsams.com**

# HIGHLAND LODGE

## Greensboro, Vermont

Need a break from big and glitzy? Then step out of the fast lane into a small, quaint family-owned inn set on the edge of a crystal-clear lake in the Northeast Kingdom of Vermont. The fact that it is also a top-notch cross-country ski center and extremely family-friendly is simply icing on the cake. The Highland Lodge began as a farmhouse/boardinghouse in the 1920s, and the Smith family is now in their fifty-third year of innkeeping here—they are certainly doing something right! A lovely old white-frame building with a comfortable front porch, the lodge is set on 160 acres bordering Caspian Lake. Open from Christmas to mid-March, the lodge facilities make it easy to enjoy wintertime sports; open again from Memorial Day weekend until mid-October, the lodge is a perfect spot for viewing the fall foliage colors or for enjoying a summer trip in the mountains. Step back in time, relax, and enjoy.

**Accommodations:** Choose one of the eleven guest rooms in the lodge or one of the ten cottages on the hillside just behind the main building. Tastefully decorated with nice furnishings and old-fashioned wallpaper, these accommodations can house approximately sixty guests. Organdy curtains, armchairs, and rockers invite you to linger. The cottages feature a living room, porch, bath, and one to three bedrooms; nine cottages include kitchenettes. Based on a Modified American Plan and double occupancy, room rates are $227 to $285. One- to four-bedroom cottages range from $255 to $530 per night. Children sharing a room or cottage with their parents are charged according to their ages: Infants are free (cribs provided), toddlers (two to four

years) are $35, kids four to seven years are $60, eight to eleven years are $70, twelve to fifteen years are $75, and sixteen to twenty years are $90. Summer rates are $5 to $20 more.

**Dining:** Included in the rates, breakfast and dinner are served in the dining room, overlooking either garden or lake. A la carte lunch is also available in the summer and fall, except on Mondays. On summer Mondays guests enjoy a beach cookout. At dinner an elegant four-course meal is served; for entrees you may select fresh fish, lamb, duck, veal, or prime rib with vegetables from a local farm. Sample the homemade soups and breads, but be sure to save room for what the staff boasts are sinful desserts. You might sit near the fireplace in the dining room or by the large windows to take in the view; weather permitting, dining tables are set up on the porch. Children's portions and special items for youngsters tempt the pickiest palate. Box lunches may be requested.

**Children's World:** A swing set and a sandbox stocked with toys attract little ones. There are tennis and hiking for older children. For children of all ages, swimming at the private beach is a great way to spend the afternoon. After a busy day kids may settle into the children's library, where they'll find books, games, and puzzles. A separate room with table tennis and foosball is a popular spot for kids to "hang" and socialize. In the mornings during July and August, youngsters four to nine link up with the Play Lady, who devises programs of crafts, games, and nature hikes; this is free of charge to guests. Two or three times weekly the inn arranges special programs for ages six and up in the afternoon—perhaps a children's hike or nature or art programs. There's a nominal charge (from $5) for these activities. In addition, the staff can make arrangements for individual babysitters.

**Recreation:** Thirty miles of groomed cross-country ski trails meander through fields and forests and across frozen lakes, linking to the Craftsbury Outdoor Center Trail System. You can line up a guided tour or pick up a little instruction. Bring your own equipment or rent the necessary paraphernalia at the ski/snowboard shop. Sledding, tobogganing, and snowshoe trails wind through the property.

Enjoy the sights and sounds of nature in both summer and winter with a resident naturalist on guided nature walks. In warmer weather hike or jog in the adjoining Barr Hill Nature Preserve, walk the lodge's nature trail, rent a bicycle, or take to the water. Cross the road and follow a short trail through the woods to Caspian Lake. Swim at the beach or head out on the lake in a canoe, kayak, or paddleboat provided by the lodge; sailboats are available to rent. The lake also means good fishing, particularly in early summer and fall; set your line for salmon, trout, or perch.

Back on land, challenge another guest to a tennis match on the clay court and then round up a game of badminton, volleyball, horseshoes, or croquet on the lawn. Golf is accessible at the nearby Mountain View Country Club. The Green Mountains lure guests into afternoon driving and hiking excursions. Or simply sit on the wide veranda and let it all come to you.

------

**Caspian Lake**
**1608 Craftsburg Road**
**Greensboro, Vermont 05841**
**(802) 533-2647**
**www.highlandlodge.com**

# KILLINGTON SKI AND SUMMER RESORT
### Killington, Vermont

------

Killington is the largest ski area in the eastern United States, and its vital statistics are indeed impressive: 200 runs on six interconnected mountains, plus Pico Mountain at Killington; more than 3,000 vertical feet; and a ski season that starts in mid-October and continues to June. Killington boasts an average annual snowfall of 250 inches. To ensure it has the earliest opening date and latest closing date in the East, sophisticated snowmaking techniques assist Mother Nature. Thirty-three lifts, including an eight-passenger heated gondola, get you quickly to the top.

A year-round resort, Killington is cradled in the Green Mountains of central Vermont, a setting whose beauty does not wane with the melting snow; in late spring and summer, the lush green landscape is the backdrop for tennis and golf holidays; in autumn the fall foliage colors take over.

**Accommodations:** There are almost 200 properties at Killington, ranging from small inns and lodges to condominium complexes and private houses. Killington Central Reservations (800-621-6867) lists more than 115 of these and publishes helpful, descriptive information clearly outlining the many package plans available. Ski-in locations include Trailside Lodge, with standard rooms/bunk beds; Trailside Village; Sunrise Village; and Spruce Glen condos. Rates are lower in summer and higher at holiday periods. Call or check the Web site for the latest rates.

Killington Resort Villages (800-343-0762) offers hotel-style and one-, two-, and three-bedroom condos, some within walking distance of the slopes, plus several other condominium complexes. The Grand Resort Hotel is 50 yards from the lift, while Sunrise Mountain Village in Bear Mountain Base Lodge has its own lift and trails. Condominiums not within walking distance but right at the base of Killington Mountain include Edgemont, Whiffletree, Highridge, Mountain Green, and Pinnacle. Studio to four-bedroom units have fully equipped kitchens and fireplaces. Some condominiums have special features, such as indoor pools or spa/exercise facilities (if you don't get enough on the slopes!). Shuttles run every fifteen to twenty minutes in winter.

Lodgings near the Snowshed Base Lodge may be the most convenient location for families, as this is one of the main lodges for adult lessons/activities and is also located across the street (connected by an underground passageway) from the Rams Head Base Lodge, where children's activities and day care are held. Packages begin at $97 per person for four people in the most economical lodging.

**Dining:** In addition to the half dozen cafeterias at the bases of and on the mountains, in the area you'll find Italian, Chinese, Mexican, and German restaurants, or you can sample French country dinners at the Red Clover Inn, typical New England dishes at the Vermont Inn, or continental cuisine at the Casa Bella. Especially fun for families is Casey's Caboose, where model trains circle the room, and dining is done on the floor, in odd nooks and crannies, or up a ladder in a boxcar. Peppers, Peppino's, Charity's, and the Santa Fe Steakhouse are good choices for families, as is Johnny Boy's Breakfast, one of Killington's most popular eating places for breakfast and lunch. For that romantic, haute cuisine dinner for adults only, Hemingway's is the place. Pubs and nightclubs provide late-evening entertainment in winter and summer.

**Children's World:** Whether your child is six weeks old or twelve years old, a first-time skier or a veteran, he or she will find a niche at Killington's Children's Center. Friendly Penguins Day Care provides for infants six weeks to twenty-three months at the Ramshead Base Lodge Family Center from 8:30 a.m. to 3:15 p.m. Monday through Friday (from 8:00 a.m. on weekends and holidays). Program includes indoor/outdoor play, stories and art, free play, movies, nap, and snacks. Parents are not encouraged to "drop in" as this disrupts the children, but they may check at any time with the counselors and view their wee ones through the one-way mirror. The First Tracks program combines the Friendly Penguin day care with outdoor on-snow sessions to introduce toddlers twenty-three months to four years old to skiing and is customized to each child's developmental levels and enthusiasm in one or two one-hour sessions, with lift tickets, equipment, and lunch included. Four- to six-year-olds enjoy the Ministar (skiing) and Lowrider (snowboarding) programs from 8:30 a.m. to 3:15 p.m.; indoor play and two-hour outdoor sessions, in the morning and afternoon, include lunch and lift tickets. The Superstars Program groups experienced seven- to twelve-year-olds by ability for a full day of ski or snowboard play, including lunch. Camp Free Ride is a new program geared toward those kids with skill enough to be ready for a new adventure and to hang out with Killington's best free-ride pros; no formal lessons, just new school skiing and riding. Ages seven to twelve who are first-timers can join the new Learn-to-Ski or -Ride one-day program. SnowZone, for ages thirteen to eighteen, is designed to engage teens in on-snow learning while providing an opportunity for them to interact with their peers. The winter children's program runs from November through the first week of April. Cost ranges from $80 to $103 for a full day and $47 for a half day (ages seven and up only). Check to make sure exactly what is included in the cost.

In the past the Grand Resort Hotel has offered a summer kids' program in July and August for ages two to ten, with indoor and outdoor activities. It is unclear at press time if this will continue. Please check directly with the hotel when you're ready to travel. Johnson Recreation Center on River Road in Killington offers weekly or daily summer programs for youngsters. From late June to mid-August, programs run from 8:30 a.m. to 4:30 p.m. Monday through Friday. Camp Loads of Fun, for five- to nine-year-olds, utilizes the Town of Killington playgrounds and swimming pool, along with arts and crafts, field trips to the library, quiet time, and afternoon free swims. Adventure Camp, for ten- to thirteen-year-olds, ventures further afield for horseback riding, spelunking in local caves, hikes, and swimming in state parks or on Mount Tom. Cost is approximately $85 per week or $25 per day. Call (802) 422-3932 or go to www.killington town.com for more information and registration forms.

**Recreation:** Start your visit with a Meet the Mountain tour; skiers are grouped by ability and guided through a complimentary two-hour introduction to Killington's mountains. All seven mountains are accessed by the same lift ticket. All have beginner runs from their summits so that even novices can enjoy top-of-the-mountain views. From long lazy runs (one beginner's trail is 10 miles long) to steeply pitched expert terrain, every skier finds the appropriate challenge. This goes for ski and snowboard clinics too, from classes for the newest beginner to workshops in racing for the advanced skier.

When you tire of the slopes, head to the Snowshed Adventure Center, hub of winter activities. Outdoor fun continues at the Snow Action Park, with a snow-skate park, four-lane tubing hill, Jib Park, and Snowdeck. Discover indoor fun at Kid Zone, with bounce houses, Velcro and climbing walls, air hockey, arcade games, and billiards. Address your hunger at Bennedito's Bistro, with a full family menu. Dogsledding, cross-country skiing, snowshoeing, snowmobiling, and ice-skating are just a few off-mountain adventures to tempt you. Killington has partnered with Nickelodeon for the Family Winter Festival, a series of fun-filled events.

Après-ski activities include movies in the village, ice-skating, rock climbing, snowmobiles, puppet and magic shows, and ice-cream socials. Or maybe most appropriate for the end of an active day is a quiet rest in a sauna or a massage at the Grand Resort Hotel.

Summertime brings golf on an eighteen-hole course (actually, there are 270 holes of golf in the area); tennis at the Killington School for Tennis; fishing, hiking, mountain biking, and horseback riding in the mountains. Killington's Adventure Center specializes in—you guessed it—adventures; try water slides, a skateboard park, and climbing wall for starters. Another center at Pico adds minigolf, an Alpine Slide, and the Bungee Thing. There's something for everyone, from scenic chair rides to art and antiquing.

**4763 Killington Road**
**Killington, Vermont 05751**
**(800) 621-MTNS**
**www.Killington.com**

# THE LIGHTHOUSE INN
## West Dennis, Massachusetts

An old-fashioned country inn, The Lighthouse Inn sits on the shores of Nantucket Sound on Cape Cod. It was originally constructed in 1854 as a lighthouse called the Bass River Light, which was operative until 1914. In 1938 the Stone family purchased the Lighthouse property, and three generations later they still own and operate the inn. After being dark for seventy-five years, the light was relit in 1989 and is the only privately owned, privately maintained working lighthouse in the country, now recognized by the Coast Guard as the West Dennis Light. The classic Cape Cod–style main house provides a beautiful view of the ocean; sprawling out behind are nine secluded acres with additional accommodations and recreational facilities. The inn, which could house 25 guests in 1938, has grown to have room for more than 150 guests.

**Accommodations:** A wide selection of accommodations exists: rooms, family suites, and oceanview and oceanfront cottages with one to three bedrooms. The Main House, Lookout, and Carriage House offer family suites. Daily rates include either full breakfast or breakfast and dinner (MAP). Based on two adults, family suites are $291/$352. Based on three adults, two-bedroom cottages are $483/$573; ocean-front cottages are $535/$625; adjustments are made for families. Children sharing a room or cottage with their parents are charged a graduated daily rate based on age. The rate for ages three through twelve is $40/$50 and for thirteen and over is $45/$75. Mid-May through June and early September to mid-October, deduct $40 per person from all rates.

**Dining:** The dining room in the Main House entices guests with a varied menu, including fresh fish and lobster dinners and lovely views over the water. Outdoors, the oceanside deck is the setting for a la carte lunches. A snack bar adjoins the pool, serving light lunches and beverages during July and August. Once a week a poolside cook-out is planned.

A really nice touch is that all children are welcomed to a special InnKids Dinner offered each evening from 5:30 to 8:30 p.m. They may order their favorite meal in advance, eat, and play with their peers—all in a separate area from the more formal Main Dining Room, where proper attire is requested, and parents can tarry over a relaxed dinner. Evening entertainment in the Sand Bar ranges from boogie-woogie piano to jazz saxophones.

**Children's World:** Games, swimming, arts and crafts, sand-castle building, kite flying, miniature golf, and nature walks fill the days for InnKids. Three- and four-year-olds participate from 9:30 a.m. to noon, while children ages five and older carry on until 3:00 p.m. In the evening both groups are invited to get together from 5:30 to 8:30 p.m. for dinner and entertainment—perhaps a movie, a magician's show, puppets, clowns, and sing-alongs. Children under three are welcome to participate if accompanied by a babysitter. The InnKids program runs from late June through Labor Day and is included in the fees for children noted above. Individual babysitting is available on request.

**Recreation:** Enjoying the soft ocean breezes may be all the activity you want during your first couple of days at The Lighthouse Inn. Renewed and refreshed, you can then jump into the swimming pool, splash in the gentle waters of Nantucket Sound, and stroll along the beach. The outdoor tennis court awaits you when you turn energetic, golfing is available at one of five nearby eighteen-hole courses, or fishing can be a pleasant morning outing. You may choose to play table tennis, pool, and shuffleboard or pursue quieter interests in the library/game room. The inn is also in a great location for exploring Cape Cod. For off-site activities try whale watching or an "ice-cream float" narrated cruise of Hyannis Harbor; more active pursuits might include renting Jet Skis, kayaks, or paddleboats or hiking or biking at Nickerson State Park, the Cape Cod Bike Trail, the National Seashore, Salt Pond, or one of several conservation areas. For quieter amusements take a trip to another town and explore any of the dozen or so art, natural history, or historical museums, such as Plimoth Plantation (Plymouth), the Glass Museum (Sandwich), or the John F. Kennedy Museum (Hyannis). And, as the old song by Patti Page says, "If you're fond of sand dunes and salty air, quaint little villages here and there, you're sure to fall in love with old Cape Cod."

---

**1 Lighthouse Inn Road**
**West Dennis, Massachusetts 02670**
**(508) 398-2244**
**www.lighthouseinn.com**

# MOUNT SNOW
West Dover, Vermont

---

Over fifty years ago, Walter Schoenknecht decided that music, barbecues, and outrageous special events would liven up his ski area. Since other resorts weren't even serving food, he was deemed rather eccentric. But sure enough, old Walt was right, and today that same infectious, creative spirit is not only encouraged but is one of the core values of the resort.

A very popular New England ski resort, Mount Snow is situated in the beautiful Green Mountains of southern Vermont. Much of its popularity is, no doubt, due to its accessibility and proximity to major Northeast metropolitan areas: A four-and-a-half-hour drive from New York and a two-and-a-half-hour drive from Boston make this a very manageable weekend trip for residents of these cities. But Mount Snow's size and variety also account for its appeal. From gentle beginner and broad intermediate slopes to some of the steepest expert runs in the Northeast, a total of 106 trails drop down from a 3,600-foot summit for 1,700 vertical feet, served by nineteen lifts. The average annual snowfall is about 156 inches. It is supplemented by sophisticated snowmaking that covers 80 percent of the 590-acre skiable terrain; the ski season runs from about early November to late April.

**Accommodations:** Lodging runs the gamut of possibilities in atmosphere, style, price, and location. From modern condominium complexes to quaint country inns, more than fifty options are within 10 miles of the mountain base. The lodging bureau (800-451-4211) will help you choose the right spot, and various package plans for lodging and lift tickets are offered. The following are best suggestions for families.

A full-service hotel at the edge of a small lake with grand views of the mountain, Snow Lake Lodge runs free shuttles to and from the slopes. With its own restaurant, game room, and spa, it's also within walking distance to evening entertainment at the Snowbarn. Seasons and Snow Mountain Village are condominiums near the base, with kitchens and fireplaces; some have balconies and mountain views.

The 200-room Grand Summit Resort Hotel is located slopeside in Mount Snow's main base area and offers a variety of rooms, ranging from standard hotel-style rooms to multiroom suites with kitchenettes. Amenities include ski-in/ski-out accommodations, valet parking, a health club, spa and fitness programs, and a year-round heated outdoor pool. Rates vary widely, as much as $200 from one week to the next, so factor dates and number of days into your inquiry. For lodging only, a two-night weekend in mid-season, Snow

Lake Lodge averages $370 with continental breakfast; Snow Mountain Condominium is $850; and a studio at the Grand Summit is $825.

**Dining:** Loads of good eating awaits you on the mountain. At the Main Base Lodge, choose the Marketplace Café or Fresh Tracks for breakfast and lunch, Cuzzins Bar & Grill for lunch and the best après-ski, and Tony's for huge slices of pizza. Waffle Haus entices with Belgian goodies, and Timber House Grill serves up barbecue and Austin Blues. You'll find cafeterias in the Sundance and Carinthia areas, and at the very top you can sit on the outdoor deck of the Summit Lodge & Double Diamond Bar and view the world from over 3,000 feet. More options for casual dining are the Lakeside Bar and Grill in the Snow Lake Lodge; Harriman's at the Grand Summit; or the Snow Barn, on the edge of Snow Lake. The Grand Country Deli & Store is a great place for a box lunch, snacks, wine, beer, chocolate, and other goodies to take with you and is also a quiet place for breakfast and quick lunch. Most of the inns and lodges of the area have their own restaurants and feature a variety, from hearty home-style cooking to continental cuisine. Venture into Wilmington or West Dover for family dining at Dot's Restaurant or TC's Family Restaurant. For more upscale dining, visit Deegan's Tavern or Dover Forge Restaurant & Billiard Sanctuary. Unusual dining venues in Wilmington include Ravello's, in a restored farmhouse; The Vermont House, a hotel that began as a stagecoach stop in the heart of downtown; and the nautically themed Ponchos Wreck. Many restaurants have children's menus.

**Children's World:** Throughout the year, kids have a place at Mount Snow. Child Care, a quality program for ages six weeks to six years, is located in the heart of the main base area. The program is fully licensed by the state of Vermont and is designed to be interactive, fun, and developmentally appropriate for each child's needs. Playrooms are designated as Baby Bears (six weeks to twelve months), Magical Forest (thirteen months to twenty-three months), Furry Friends (twenty-four months to thirty-five months), and Bears Den (three years and up). Child Care is open weekdays from 8:30 a.m. to 4:30 p.m.; weekends and holidays, 8:00 a.m. to 4:30 p.m. Reservations are required (800-889-4411). A full day is $75; snacks and lunch are provided, but you must supply diapers and infant food. A list of babysitters is available through Child Care.

Cub Camp allows three-year-olds to experience the thrill of skiing through fun and games, combined with Child Care programs. A morning or afternoon one-and-a-half-hour on-snow session, including equipment, costs $62; Child Care add-on is an additional $50. For children four to twelve, Mount Snow offers Perfect Kids ski and snowboard clinics. Snow Camp is divided into full- and half-day sessions and is designed especially for children four through six years of age. Children are placed in small groups based on their age and ability levels, and groups ski, take breaks, and have fun together. Full-day programs include lunch and child lift ticket; cost is $97 for one day, $177 for two days. Half-day sessions include snack and lift ticket, $67 one session, $119 for two days. Multiday rates are available. Mountain Camp and Mountain Riders is for seven- to fourteen-year-olds; rates are $83 for a full day with lunch and $48 for half days. Rental equipment is not included and begins at $26 per day; junior lift tickets are also required. Children new to skiing or snowboarding can enjoy expanded, private learning terrain. All Perfect Kids programs are centrally located in the main base area.

Children five and under ski/ride free, while kids twelve and under ski/ride free when their parents purchase a three- to five-day nonholiday lift ticket. During "Kid's Adventure Weeks," three- to five-day vacation packages include lodging, lift tickets, and many fun family activities. The week is filled with games, activities, pizza parties, ice-cream parties, fun races, and free tubing. Mount Snow also offers a new lift-served snow-tubing park open every day and weekend nights. The Galaxy Arcade is open daily in the main base area and features video games, recreational games, a penny candy counter, and a lounge area.

Summer is in full swing from mid-June through August with Mount Snow's Kid's Adventure Camps. The Child Care program is available Monday through Friday, again offering individual playrooms and programs for ages six weeks to five years. Activities include arts and crafts, water play, puppet shows, mini–nature hikes, gardening, games, and music. Special rest areas are also provided for quiet time. Mount Snow's Summer Kid's Adventure Camps offer children from age six to twelve years a variety of activities and hands-on exploration. Kids are grouped according to age and enjoy swimming, hiking, mountain biking, creative arts and crafts, chairlift rides, and field trips around the Mount Snow area. Kid's Adventure Camps and child care are offered Monday through Friday mid-June through August. Operation times are from 9:00 a.m. to 4:00 p.m. Rates for both programs are $50 per day ($200 for five days). Lunch is not included, and bathing suits are part of the "uniform." Reservations are required and can be made by calling (800) 889-4411 or (802) 464-4152.

For dedicated golfers, Nike and Mount Snow have teamed up to offer four junior camps and two parent-child golf clinics from mid-June through early August. Junior

Residence Camps are five days, and the cost of $1,065 includes lodging, instruction, and all meals; an extended day rate of $975 includes lunch, dinner, instruction, and evening activities. Special lodging rates are available for campers' families. The three-day parent-child clinics are $475 per person and include instruction, course play, and lunch. Call (800) NIKE-CAMP or Mount Snow for details. Additionally, on one day weekly for approximately ten weeks during summer, the resort offers a one-day golf clinic for ages seven to sixteen for $12.

**Recreation:** Almost 70 percent of the runs at Mount Snow are ranked intermediate. The rest are just about evenly split between beginner and expert. The Main Mountain has forty beginner and intermediate trails; the North Face, with its steeper terrain and moguls, attracts advanced skiers; and the Sunbrook area, with sunny southern exposure, supports a couple of long lazy runs. Four terrain parks and a Super Pipe keep snowboarders happy. The teaching staff is prepared to show you the way to improved techniques, and you have your pick of packages for various combinations of lifts, lessons, and equipment.

For cross-country skiers, four touring centers are within 10 miles of Mount Snow at the Hermitage, Sitzmark, Timber Creek, and White House. Also within this distance are three stables—Beaver Brook, Flames, and Adams Farm—where you can arrange sleigh rides. Other winter sports include snowmobiling, a tubing park, and nearby snowshoeing and ice-skating. If your tastes run to being pampered, schedule a session at the Grand Summit Spa, or curl up in front of the fire with a hot drink.

When the mountains turn green, the big event is the Golf School, held on the championship Geoffrey Cornish course. More warm-weather activities include swimming, fishing, hiking, biking, and horseback riding. Sit back and enjoy the scenery from one of the scenic chairlift rides, or prowl through the unique shops that feature the crafts, pottery, wood carving, and antiques to be found only in Vermont. The whole family will love Adams Farm, a sixth-generation working farm with hands-on farm activities. Take a hayride, wander through the craft and quilt shops, enjoy just jumping in a haystack, or relax with a bonfire and marshmallow roast.

---

**Route 100**
**12 Pisgah Road**
**West Dover, Vermont 05356**
**(802) 464-3333, (800) 245-7669**
**www.mountsnow.com**

# THE MOUNT WASHINGTON RESORT AT BRETTON WOODS
### Bretton Woods, New Hampshire

Majestic Mount Washington presides over this resort, a massive complex of lodging, dining, and recreational facilities on 2,600 acres of wooded New Hampshire countryside in the White Mountains. Voted a *Better Homes and Gardens* "Favorite Family Resort," the architectural gem and focal point of this New England resort is the gracious and stately hotel. Built in 1902 by the industrialist and railroad tycoon Joseph

Stickney, the hotel began welcoming visitors to a lifestyle of classic elegance and soon claimed its status among prime vacation retreats of the Northeast.

International fame came to Bretton Woods in 1944 when the hotel hosted financiers from forty-four countries who created the World Bank and the International Monetary Fund and set the gold standard at $35 an ounce (ah—the good old days). In 1978 this fine old structure—with its wonderfully spacious veranda furnished with white wicker chairs and settees, and its 150-foot-long lobby—was added to the National Register of Historic Places. Since 1986 it has held the distinction of being a National Historic Landmark. With the purchase of Bretton Woods, Mount Washington became a year-round resort.

**Accommodations:** The 200-room hotel offers standard to deluxe lodging with a number of two-bedroom family suites. Nearly all have views of Mount Washington, the Willey-Rosebrook Mountain range, or the well-tended gardens. Most guests in the hotel participate in a Modified American Plan, and room rates per person, per night begin at $185, based on double occupancy. Children under age four stay for free, ages four to twelve are $35, and over twelve are $70. A two-room family suite joined by a central bathroom accommodates up to six guests. Family suite rates start at $570 per suite and include dinner and breakfast for up to four guests. European Plan (room only) rates begin at $99 per person, per night for rooms and $310 per night, per suite.

The thirty-four rooms and suites of the Bretton Arms Country Inn, also a National Historic Landmark, offer accommodations in the atmosphere of a Victorian inn. Guests here enjoy all the facilities of the main hotel. Rates are per person, per night and include breakfast; rooms start at $85 and suites at $130; children's rates are $10 per night for ages four to twelve, and $20 for thirteen and older. The Bretton Arms is open year-round.

Also open year-round, The Lodge at Bretton Woods, located across from the hotel's entrance, offers contemporary accommodations starting at $99 per night, with continental breakfast included.

For an economical alternative, the Townhomes at Bretton Woods provide ample space for parties of two to twelve people; situated on the mountainside, these one- to five-bedroom units (with full kitchens) start at $199 to $449 per night, accommodations only, depending on the size of the unit. All guests have access to all resort recreational facilities. Cribs are complimentary, and cots are available at $10 a night. Inquire also about special seven-day vacation packages.

**Dining:** With all the different dining arrangements, your biggest problem will be deciding where to pick up your napkin. From casual, light meals to gracious, formal dinners, it just depends on how the spirit moves you. The opulent three-diamond main dining room of the Mount Washington Hotel is a large octagonal space (heaven forbid anyone should be relegated to a corner!) glimmering with crystal chandeliers and stained-glass windows. The menu changes nightly and features continental cuisine and regional American dishes. In this elegant setting, with orchestra music and views of Mount Washington, guests are invited to regard dinner as a dress-up affair; jackets are required for men, and ladies and children should dress appropriately. Sumptuous breakfasts are also served in the dining room.

The Bretton Arms dining room is also open year-round for breakfast and dinner; here the evening meal features classic New England cuisine. For lunch and seasonal dinner, Stickney's Restaurant (located on the lower concourse of the hotel) has a cafe atmosphere with indoor and outdoor seating and specializes in lighter fare—salads, sandwiches, and light entrees; afternoon cocktails are also served here. Catalano's Main Street Pizzeria in the lodge serves seasonal dinner; guests enjoy family dining in a warm, rustic atmosphere, along with scenic views of the mountains and the hotel. For sandwiches, Italian fare, and seafood, Fabyan's Station is open year-round for lunch and dinner. A restored railroad depot from the Victorian era, Fabyan's is near the base of the ski area about a mile from the hotel. The Bretton Woods Alpine Base Lodge at the ski area offers full lunch at Slopeside. Quick breakfasts and lunches cafeteria-style for those eager to hit the slopes can be found at Lucy Crawford's Food Court. The midmountain Top O' Quad restaurant serves lunch with spectacular mountain views in winter.

For sipping cocktails, you may want to linger at Stickney's, the Conservatory, the Princess Lounge, or the Verandah. Try the unique Rosebrook Lounge, set behind the grand staircase and serving on the porch and veranda, weather permitting. The Cave Lounge, located in the lower lobby of the hotel, offers a speakeasy atmosphere and nightly live entertainment. The Pool Bar offers refreshments on warm summer days.

**Children's World:** Late June through Labor Day, and on holiday weekends/weeks, the hotel sponsors Kids Camp for children four to twelve. Enroll your child for a full- or half-day program with adventures like hiking in the woods, treks to the stables, swimming, tennis, "Cooking with the Chef," "Putting with the Pro," and crafts sessions. The program is from 9:00 a.m. to 3:00 p.m., and is complimentary for hotel guests except for lunch. For resort guests not staying in the hotel, the cost is $25 per three-hour session. Lunch is available for $10. There's also an evening program from 6:00 to 9:00 p.m. that includes dinner so that parents can dine

quietly alone. Babysitting can be arranged for children under the age of four. The resort charges a $10 processing fee; rates are $10 per hour with a three-hour minimum, plus $2 per hour for each additional child. Reservations are required for all programs (800-314-1752 ext. 8541).

In the wintertime, the Babes in the Woods nursery at the ski area lodge takes children from two months to five years for an indoor program costing $69 full day or $45 half day. Open 8:00 a.m. to 4:30 p.m., hourly rates ($12, with a two-hour minimum) are also an option. Children ages four to twelve participate in the Hobbit Children's Ski and Snowboard School; however, snowboarding is only for ages six to twelve. Rates for lifts, two lessons, equipment, and lunch are $95 a day. Half days are $69 (no lunch). Those children under age five and toilet trained, who are new to the slopes, can join a snow play and ski-readiness program at the same rates. For reservations call (800) 278-3345.

On Saturday evenings and select holidays during winter season, the resort hosts a supervised evening program from 6:00 to 9:00 p.m. for ages four to twelve years. Games, activities, and a kids-only dinner make these themed gatherings fun for all. Again, there is no charge for hotel guests, $25 for resort guests.

In 2002, *Ski Magazine* rated Bretton Woods number two in North America for family programs, and in 2003, number one in New Hampshire for family programs.

**Recreation:** All room rates at the Mount Washington Resort at Bretton Woods include an array of complimentary features. Summer offers court time, putting green, full use of Bretton Woods Sports Club, family lawn games, guided walks and mountain bike tours, and introductory clinics in golf, tennis, and fly fishing. In winter take part in ice-skating (with skates available), snowshoe tours, and ski clinics. Year-round enjoy music, culinary demonstrations, arts and crafts, and admission to special events. Check with Recreation, and ask for the special discounts on other activities.

You'll never be at a loss for things to do at Bretton Woods; your only dilemma may be trying to fit in all the activities. You may start your day jogging on one of the many marked trails, ranging from 1 to 11 miles in length and graded by levels of difficulty.

Then stroll over to the first tee for a match on the eighteen-hole Donald Ross–designed championship golf course or the challenging nine-hole Pleasant Course and take in the rolling terrain and mountain views, or sharpen your skills on the putting green and driving range. The Golf Club Pro Shop can meet all your needs for equipment and accessories (including attire) and can assist in scheduling lessons.

There are two heated pools (one outdoor and a smaller indoor one) at the hotel and another indoor heated pool at the lodge; both locations have a sauna, and the lodge facility includes a Jacuzzi as well. Or you can take a refreshing dip in the Ammonoosuc River.

Tennis buffs can head over to one of twelve well-groomed red-clay courts or join the tennis program for instruction (group and private lessons) at all levels of expertise.

The horseback-riding stables mean good fun for those who want their exercise sitting down. Set in an old Victorian building, the stables offer lessons and guided trail rides on the 50 miles of picturesque trails in the woods and fields. The woods are captivating whether you choose horseback riding or hiking (maybe you'll link up with a guided tour or a nature walk).

Other diversions include trout fishing; a game of badminton, croquet, volleyball, or horseshoes; an afternoon of bicycling; a sunset carriage ride; or an hour in the game room for billiards, table tennis, and video games (particularly big with the seven- to fourteen-

year-old group). Your interests may take you to a night at the movies, a fashion show, an aerobics class, a bridge tournament, or a presentation of fine culinary techniques (these often include a bit of wine, sampling a dish, and a tour of the kitchen). The activities staff is on hand full-time to plan interesting and varied events. For some private, quiet time, wander into the library or relax under the nimble fingers of an expert massage therapist.

Kids love an excursion on the Mount Washington Cog Railway, the original "little train that could." Built in 1869, it was the world's first mountain-climbing cog railroad, and it remains the only one still powered entirely by steam. The (breathtaking!) round-trip takes about three hours, and you can visit the mile-high park and observation center at the top.

Wintertime explodes in skiing events at Bretton Woods. The Bretton Woods Touring Center, housed in a Victorian-style building, is one of the finest cross-country skiing complexes in the East. There are approximately 100 kilometers (60 miles) of beautifully groomed trails among the 1,700 acres of firs and birches, scenic countryside, and the White Mountain National Forest; three different trail systems are ranked in difficulty. Head out on your own, enroll for instruction, or join a daytime guided tour or a moonlight trek. Alpine skiers and snowboarders are delighted with the expansion done in the past decade. This once modest ski area now boasts a 1,500-foot vertical drop, 101 trails, a terrain park, and nine lifts. The addition of West Mountain makes Bretton Woods the largest ski area in New Hampshire, and it's set to become even larger with the addition of Mount Stickney. The ski season lasts from late November to early May; the average annual snowfall is 200-plus inches, and 92 percent of the trails are covered by snowmaking equipment to assist Mother Nature.

In 2007 the excitement of dogsledding arrived at the resort. Add snowmobiling, snow tubing, ice-skating, snowshoeing, sleigh rides, and winter hiking trails, and there's enough to keep you busy for two vacations.

**Route 302**
**Bretton Woods, New Hampshire 03575**
**(603) 278-1000, (800) 314-1752**
**www.mtwashington.com**

# SMUGGLERS' NOTCH RESORT
## Smugglers' Notch, Vermont

The Green Mountains of Vermont are not just about beautiful foliage colors in the autumn and skiing fun in the winter. Smugglers' Notch Resort makes sure there's much more to enjoy all year long. This is our idea of a true "family resort." Tucked in the rolling hills and mountains of northern Vermont, Smugglers' Notch is a self-contained resort village with sports facilities and getaway relaxation potential for the whole family. In winter, when Mother Nature blankets the region in snow, skiing on the three interconnected mountains is the primary activity. Tennis, hiking, swimming, and horseback riding are favorite pastimes when the weather warms. Any time of year one can explore the natural beauty and charm surrounding this mountain village and experience family fun—guaranteed! Yes, the resort guarantees families will have fun, or it refunds the activity portion of their stay. Maybe that's why, for eight years in a row, Smugglers' Notch has been voted the number one family resort by *Ski Magazine,* and the number one family resort in the Northeast by *FamilyFun,* a Disney publication, for three years.

**Accommodations:** Almost 650 condominium units are arranged in five "communities" of two- and three-story, modern but rustic buildings. From these all the amenities of the village are accessible by foot or free shuttle service. Most of the units have fireplaces and private balconies, and all have completely equipped kitchens or kitchenettes. Size varies from studios to five-bedroom apartments.

The Club Smugglers' package plans cover lodging and most of the recreational activities. For example, the summertime FamilyFest program for seven days/seven nights includes accommodation in a one-bedroom condo (which sleeps four), full-day programs for children three to seventeen, guided walks and hikes, swimming and water sliding, evening entertainment for both families and adults, and much, much more; rates are from $1,759 to $3,049 (based on dates of stay). A winter five- to seven-day package in the same type of lodging costs $99 to $195 per adult per day and $85 to $195 for youths three to seventeen years, depending on the time period. This includes lift tickets, lessons (Nordic, Alpine, snowboard, cross-country, telemark, and shaped skis), ski camp, outdoor ice-skating, welcome parties, swimming pool, sauna, and après-ski activities. A crib or extra futon cot for two- to seven-year-olds can be provided for $20 for the entire stay.

**Dining:** Though you may opt to cook in your condo, there are several restaurants in the village when dining out seems better than facing a skillet. The Green Mountain Deli serves home-baked breakfast treats and hot lunches with fresh-roasted specialty coffees. Slopeside, with great mountain views, the Morse Mountain Grille is open for all three meals, including light fare available well into the evening and a special buffet for children. And for you snow bunnies, après-ski fun is available at The Pub from 11:00 a.m. to 10:00 p.m. In the heart of the village, casual family dining in the Hearth & Candle is complemented by white-tablecloth service for adults only in the Birch Room. Local organic vegetables, fresh fish and meat, homemade desserts, and a children's menu satisfy everyone. Save Tuesday evening for another adult-only treat, the Snowshoe Adventure Tour ($65 per person). Take the lift to the Top of the Notch and have a gourmet four-course meal without guilt, as you'll then work it off with a forty-minute snowshoe trek down to the Base Lodge!

In the Village Lodge, at Riga Bello's, all ages savor the ever-popular Italian favorites—pizza, calzones, salads, and beverages—to eat in or have delivered to their condo. For ice-cream treats, there's Ben and Jerry's Scoop Shop, or choose refreshing drinks at Bootlegger's Lounge, with its big-screen TV. At the foot of Madonna and Sterling Mountains, daytime eating options include the Base Lodge Cafeteria; Green Peppers for soups, salads, wraps, and panini; Snow's Chowder Pot or, weather permitting, the BBQ Bistro; and the Black Bear Tavern for drinks and pub food.

The Mountainside Cabana is a relaxing summertime spot for lunch and cocktails. For extras, snacks, and wines, stop by the Village Country Store.

**Children's World:** The Smugglers' Just for Kids program operates from early December to the beginning of April. Discovery Dynamos' three- to five-year-olds join their ski host for morning and afternoon ski les-sons (snowboards for four years and up), tractor rides, movies, and arts and crafts. Skiers and boarders ages six to ten meet with the Adventure Rangers Ski or Snowboard Camp for lessons, snow soccer, and races. The Notch Squad, for ages eleven to fourteen, increases the adventure with more emphasis on improving skills. Après-ski activities include a daily bonfire at 3:30 p.m. with hot chocolate for parents and children. With lunch included, the daily rate for these programs, 9:30 a.m. to 4:00 p.m., is $99, or $72 on a Club Smugglers' package.

For teens fifteen to seventeen, Mountain Explorers offers challenging instruction ($39) and techniques, racing development, and a great way to make new friends. With the Outer Limits and Teen Alley teen centers and scheduled daily activities at 7:00 and 9:00 p.m., teenagers have plenty to do.

Treasures Child Care Center is the fully certified, $1 million facility for children ages six weeks to three years, with special features like giant fish tanks in every room, one-way mirror viewing for parents, 5,400 square feet of indoor space, and over 4,000 square feet of outdoor playground.

Located in a quiet, sunlit slopeside area of the resort, Treasures offers ten rooms of real state-of-the-art facilities. There are kid-size bathrooms, a complete kitchen, an infant "crawler room" equipped with mirrors and soft-sculpture gym, a separate crib room for naps, a closet of costumes, radiant floor heating, and an indoor jungle gym. Little Rascals on Snow allows two-and-a-half-year-olds their first ski experience. Open from 8:30 a.m. to 4:30 p.m. during ski season, Treasures is staffed with professionals and boasts a ratio of one caretaker to four children. Rates are $72 per day, or $15 per hour for up to three hours.

If you prefer, individual babysitters are available in your condo at $10 per hour for one child, $1 per hour each additional child, plus a $4 finder's fee. Smugglers' has a great understanding of kids of all ages, and more options than it's possible to list. Check the Web site for all the details and watch your kids get super-excited.

During the summer season, from mid-June through Labor Day, days and nights are filled with fun events: outdoor games, fishing, arts and crafts, hiking, treasure hunts, and swimming. At the playground are swings, climbing equipment, and a sandbox. The day camps are included in the price of the FamilyFest vacation ($85 per day, regular rate). Summer Fun University allows kids to major in fun and minor in a variety of other activities like arts and crafts, nature and hiking, sound and stage, or adventure and games. So, they'll get the same great activities always offered in the all-day camps, plus a special focus of their own choosing. They'll join the Discovery Dynamos (ages three to five), Adventure Rangers (ages six to ten), The Notch Squad (ages eleven to fifteen), or Mountain Explorers (teens sixteen to seventeen)—all from 10:00 a.m. to 4:00 p.m. daily. Teen Alley (ages thirteen to fifteen) and the Outer Limits (ages sixteen and older) provide gathering centers with all those things dear to teens—video games, Internet access, music and dancing, and no parents! Optional programs, for extra fees, include tennis and golf camps; overnight hikes; "Wheels," clinics in mountain boarding (blending snowboard and skateboard) and "diggling" (a cross between a mountain bike and snowboard); and Video Camp, where kids learn the basics of camera operation, make their own video, and enjoy watching their directorial debut weekly at Smugglers' Vermont Country Fair. The fair is a taste of a small New England fair, with cotton candy, entertainers, and lots of family games and contests.

And talk about entertainment—try the Friendly Pirate Breakfast, where the pirate sings, tells jokes, and swashbuckles with the kids (cost of breakfast only). Another nice feature is Kids Night Out, when children ages three to eleven are invited to dinner and a fun evening from 6:00 to 10:00 p.m. The cost is $25 per child, and it operates on Tuesday, Wednesday, Thursday, and Saturday in summer and Wednesday, Thursday, and Saturday in winter.

The fun doesn't end in the fall. For families with children under five, AutumnFest packages provide morning programs for children six weeks to five years (all day on Wednesday and Friday) with family fun in the afternoons, amidst that gorgeous Vermont foliage—and at the lowest rates of the year.

**Recreation:** A network of seventy-eight trails on three interconnected mountains is the focus of wintertime play. The ski season runs from Thanksgiving to mid-April, and the average annual snowfall of 286 inches is supplemented by snowmaking equipment covering 62 percent of the terrain. The three mountains fall more or less into novice, intermediate, and advanced runs, but each mountain offers skiing for all levels of expertise. The total vertical drop is just over 2,600 feet, making it Northern Vermont's biggest. For the cross-country skier, 14 miles of trails roam through the mountains. Lessons in cross-country skiing, downhill skiing, and snowboarding can help you learn as a beginner or improve your skills. Smugglers' has four Learning and Fun Parks, geared from rank beginner to expert. You might also try ice-skating with the kids or snowshoeing, an increasingly popular sport. Experience the winter woods on your own two feet, with dedicated snowshoeing trails, guided family tours, or, for the more adventurous, a lift ride up the mountain, and a walk down. Add more winter fun with tube slides, snowmobiles, dogsledding, and the newest craze of airboards, plus all the daily family activities and the grand finale fireworks that light up the mountain on Thursday evenings—whew, just not enough time to do it all!

Turning indoors, you can enjoy the benefits of the Mountain Massage Center. The FunZone offers indoor play for all ages: inflatables, rolling in the ball slides, table tennis, basketball, jousts (very popular with teens), and even a little minigolf. Also in winter, the large, heated swimming pool is covered with a bubble, so pack your swimsuit along with your ski sweater.

In summer the bubble comes down. There's a water slide called the Flume, a baby wading pool, and a seventeen-person outdoor hot tub. Free swimming instruction is provided as part of the day-camp program, and adults can join the Aqua Aerobics class for a good workout. Lots of family activities are balanced by some evening adults-only programs, including improv comedy and Marko's Hypnosis Show.

Notchville Park, Smugglers' newest water playground, encompasses three acres with three pools in a unique, tiered hillside setting. In addition to 5,000 square feet of water, the park includes Raven's Roost Climbing Tower, Catbird's Croquet Court, Sand Swallow's Volleyball Court, Peregrine's Picnic Pavilion, and the Half-Moon Bath House. The Twister has 360-degree turns and twists, covering two swimming pools—not for the faint of heart.

The Mountainside Pools is a third, separate water facility that includes a turtle slide (for children ages three to eight years), the Little Smugglers' Lagoon (a large splash pool with waterfall, tunnels, fountains, and a lazy river ride), a lap pool, and every parent's delight, the Giant Rapid River Ride—306 feet of twists and thrills on an inner tube beginning 26 feet up in the air. Bathhouse, snack bar, and lounging deck with gorgeous mountain views help one recover.

Also a favorite with families is Rum Runner's Hideaway, a beautiful swimming lake tucked in the mountains, a short hike or drive away from the village. Access is free to resort guests for swimming, fishing, picnicking, and relaxing; canoes and paddleboats are available for rent. It's a great way to relive the old days and introduce your kids to the joys of summer days at the ole swimmin' hole, with updated trampoline, logroll, and aqua-jump.

In addition to two indoor tennis courts, there are eight outdoor clay courts; six are lighted for evening play. The Ten Pro Tennis School, which has videotape review, just about guarantees improvement in your game.

For those who can't possibly leave home without their golf clubs, courses in nearby Stowe and Morrisville are open to Smugglers' guests, or take a practice time with instruction on Smugglers' own driving range.

Hiking and biking are popular ways to enjoy the mountain countryside, or try jogging on one of the cross-country trails. Head to a mountain stream for perch, pike, and trout fishing. Outdoor lawn games include Frisbee, basketball, volleyball, soccer, and shuffleboard. Disc golf is quickly becoming a family favorite. If your inner artist is seeking expression, take a painting or sculpting workshop. And don't forget Vermont! Stowe is just across the Notch, and the surrounding area is filled with antiques, country shops, glorious scenery, and even the sound of music, as the Von Trapp family settled nearby. A cider mill, a teddy-bear factory, and Ben and Jerry's ice-cream factory just may be irresistible.

---

**4323 Vermont Route 108 South**
**Smugglers' Notch, Vermont 05464-9537**
**(802) 644-8851, (800) 419-4615**
**www.smuggs.com**

# SUGARLOAF/USA

## Carrabassett Valley, Maine

Traditional New England reserve seems to be missing at Sugarloaf/USA. The prevailing attitude is friendly, upbeat, and casually welcoming. While mainly associated with skiing and winter, Sugarloaf is fast becoming an all-season destination, with golf predominating in summer. All access is via Portland or Bangor, and once in western Maine, just about all roads lead to Sugarloaf. Route 27 is the main road to the ski area, and from the Carrabassett Valley, Sugarloaf literally stands out. You can distinguish the peak from 20 to 40 miles away, and once you leave the valley floor and start to climb, the panorama just gets better and better. Locals and repeat visitors have dubbed one particular spot "Oh-my-gosh corner," because it is so stunning as you round the corner and suddenly see the front of this impressive mountain with its 124 trails and an Alpine village set on the slope.

**Accommodations:** Sugarloaf has the capacity to sleep approximately 7,000 people on the mountainside. Nine hundred–plus condominiums are set in various clusters of two to twenty-eight units and offer a wide selection of design. Styles include hotel rooms, studios, lofts, and up to five-bedroom, three-bath complexes. The forty-two-room Sugarloaf Inn and the Sugarloaf Grand Summit Resort Hotel's 120-plus rooms and suites complete the lodging options. Custom packages are planned for each family's needs. Packages generally include a health club pass and group ski lessons. A complimentary shuttle system gets you around the resort with ease.

Rates range from $128 to $678 for a hotel room, from $135 to $745 for a one-bedroom unit, and from $370 for larger units. Cribs and rollaway beds are provided at a daily charge of $5.

Sugarloaf was one of the first ski areas to introduce the ski-in/ski-out concept; in fact, most accommodations are slopeside or within walking distance of a lift. This is great for older children, as it gives them a sense of independence and it gives everyone a sense of freedom. If you want to sleep late or linger over coffee, others in your party need not delay their skiing. Gondola Village, the largest condominium and the heart of the development, is where you will find the nursery.

**Dining:** Dining in the Sugarloaf area is a fun adventure that is taken quite seriously. With nine on-mountain restaurants, you can have everything from burgers to bouillabaisse to full meals.

Gepetto's is a slopeside restaurant with salad, pasta, soup, and steaks; a greenhouse addition; and a mini-arcade. The Double Diamond Steakhouse at the Grand Summit boasts good food, great drinks, and entertainment. For après-ski the Widowmaker Lounge offers cocktails and music you can hear yourself talk over. The Shipyard Brewhaus in the Sugarloaf Inn serves up Maine lobsters and microbrews, fried clams, and other seafood, creatively prepared. This casual pub has a living room with fireplace, TV, and pool tables and is a perfect place to relax at the end of the day. Hearty soups, pizza, and sandwiches can be found on the mountain at Bullwinkle's, Bull Moose Café, D' Ellie's, Sugarloaf Sports and Fitness Café, the Base Lodge, and the Bag & Kettle. During the summer six restaurants remain open, so there's still a wide choice.

**Children's World:** Sugarloaf has a terrific winter child-care program. A state-licensed child-care center at the base of the mountain accepts children from ten weeks to five years of age. Hours are from 8:30 a.m. to 4:00 p.m. Advance reservations are a must (207-237-6804). The charges are $58 for a full day or $40 for a half day. The night nursery is available from 6:00 to 9:00 p.m. on Thursday and Saturday for $25, $10 per additional sibling. A fenced-in outdoor play area adds to winter fun, and inside are toys, movies, story time, circle time, and arts and crafts—a developmentally appropriate program provided by caring professionals. The nap area is separate, with individual cribs, cots, and mats. A hot lunch is served, and snacks are given during the day. Mooseketeers for willing three-year-olds introduces them to skiing ($73/$57).

Mountain Magic teaches skiing to children ages three to six years and stresses independence, safety, and fun. The Perfect Kids system teaches walking on skis, wedge stops and turns, side-stepping, falling, and, of course, getting up. In fact, most first-timers will be skiing under their own power after the first day. Half- ($57) and full-day ($73) programs are available. The full-day program includes lots of skiing, indoor activities, a snack, and a hot lunch. Lift passes are included in both sessions. For three-year-olds, the morning half-day Mooseketeers session is recommended. This allows your youngest to acquaint themselves with skiing at a comfortable pace. Mountain Adventure is a program for ages seven to fourteen, in which skills are perfected. These programs run from 8:30 a.m. to 3:00 p.m.; half-day ($52) and full-day programs ($65) are available. The full-day program includes lots of skiing/riding, a snack, and a hot lunch. Mountain Teen provides group clinics for ages fifteen to eighteen. Lift tickets and equipment are not included for these age groups. Evenings offer free supervised games and movies for five- to twelve-year-olds on Tuesday, Thursday, and Saturday. Family Turbo Tubing is offered nightly Tuesday through Saturday. Reservations are required.

Summertime brings flowers and traditional July-to-mid-August day camps. A six-week program provided by Carrabassett Valley begins in the second week of July. Kids ages four to thirteen enjoy lessons in swimming, tennis, golf, and fly fishing, and an extensive arts program. Weekly themes cover environment, ecology, nature, and weather. At $140 for five days, $90 for three days, or $35 per day, it's a great deal. For little ones, Sugarloaf offers summer child care Monday through Friday from 8:00 a.m. to 4:00 p.m. for ages ten weeks to five years. Reservations are required (207-237-6959), and the cost is approximately $40 per day or $25 for a half day.

**Recreation:** The most impressive aspect of skiing Sugarloaf is that you are skiing a big mountain. It is a traditional mountain in that it begins gently, goes to intermediate in the middle, and gets "durn hard at the top," as a local might say. Sugarloaf has the most continuous vertical drop in the East. It is possible to come almost straight down the 2,820-foot vertical drop (and even do it in an upright position if you're good) having taken only two lifts. A good beginner or low intermediate skier can take Tote Road, a 3-mile trail from the top that follows the ridge and comes safely to the base but gives that exciting feeling of skiing at the top of the world and surviving it. A Super Pipe, Half Pipe, and three terrain parks add to the thrill. The Pipeline boasts hits so big you can see your house from there. At the Outdoor Center, cross-country skiers can explore 100 kilometers of trails, including some lighted for night skiing, or relax at the warm, comfortable lodge.

Other winter fun includes ice-skating, snowshoeing, turbo-tubing, and hockey. The three Family Theme weeks offer additional family activities, and Holiday Weeks are chock-full of entertainment opportunities, such as a free sleigh ride through the woods. At the foot of Sugarloaf/USA, the Carrabassett Valley Antigravity Recreational Complex is a 20,000-square-foot facility that boasts Maine's largest indoor skate bowl, trampolines with harness rigging, an indoor rock-climbing wall, and a multipurpose court with a running track, along with weight training and aerobics facilities. It's a favorite place for teens, both locals and guests, to gather.

Come summer, when there is no snow on the ground, the Sugarloaf Golf Club opens. Designed by Robert Trent Jones Jr., this course is one of the best for wilderness golf and is one of the top one hundred to play in the United States, according to *Golf Maga-*

*zine.* Every tee has a spectacular view, and the mountain air is always cool. Tennis is limited to outside play, with two courts on the mountain and four in the town. The village has indoor racquetball courts, a sauna, hot tubs, a steam room, tanning beds, a climbing wall, and two swimming pools. But probably the most exciting summer sport is white-water rafting on the Kennebeck River. Sugarloaf also has a concentrated mountain biking program, environmental programs, and guided adventures for the whole family.

RR 1, Box 5000
**5092 Access Road**
**Carrabassett Valley, Maine 04947**
**(207) 237-2000, (800) THE-LOAF**
**www.sugarloaf.com**

# THE TYLER PLACE FAMILY RESORT
## Highgate Springs, Vermont

Tucked away in the northwestern corner of Vermont, on Lake Champlain and just minutes away from the Canadian border, Tyler Place Family Resort rightly boasts of its beautiful setting and family-friendly atmosphere. Tyler Place was one of the first resorts to devote itself entirely to families, back in 1933. The original owners, Mr. and Mrs. Edward Tyler, developed a concept that includes family time as well as time for parents to rejuvenate as a couple. And for over seventy years, the Tyler family (now the fourth generation) has continued to carry on the resort's family philosophy. Open from late May to early September, it's the kind of place that families return to again and again.

Parents and even grandparents who came here as children now bring their own kids.

**Accommodations:** With an informal, down-home Vermont country feel, the inn is the main hub of activity. Here you'll find recreation rooms, main dining room, fireside lounge, deck, and glass-enclosed porches for visiting, relaxing, cocktails, and candlelight dining. Guest rooms—some are studios, some suites—are located in a separate wing. In addition, thirty cottages, most with a fireplace in the living room and two or more bedrooms, are situated on or near the lake; these have kitchenettes and can sleep up to eight people. Both cottages and suites feature a separate bedroom for parents—what luxury! These have one to four bedrooms for children, often with sleeping lofts or bunk beds, so it's not hard to get kids to settle into a new place. Cribs and high chairs for infants and toddlers are available at no extra charge.

In total, Tyler Place accommodates approximately sixty-five families. Tyler Place has an all-inclusive plan—and we mean ALL inclusive; the rates cover lodging, all meals, some snacks, sports, eight separate Toddlers to Teens programs, and more activities than we can list. Family Retreat Times (end of May to mid-June and the first week in September) are more flexible, and rates are lower. The rates per person, daily, based on two adults, are $90 to $254 for adults; $72 to $98 for children and teens; $51 to $85 for infants and toddlers. From June 9 to September 8, vacations are seven days only, generally from Saturday to Saturday. The daily per-person rates are $173 to $320 for adults and $108 for children and teens. Request the special brochure for infants and toddlers. There are some half sessions, as well as a special Memorial Day long weekend. If your dates don't match theirs, they'll make every effort to fit you in, space permitting. The resort is closed the rest of the year.

**Dining:** The main dining room in the inn serves a semibuffet breakfast, lunch, and dinner. New American country cuisine is the kitchen's specialty, with fresh, locally grown foods, and since a Full American Plan is in effect, you have only to decide which delicious entree to sample. Children have earlier dining hours with their counselors, allowing parents to relax over evening meals. Share breakfast with your children in the family breakfast room or request a family picnic lunch basket at no extra charge.

**Children's World:** Outstanding, individualized, and flexible describes the children's programs at the Tyler Place Family Resort. During the entire season there's an extensive program of events geared to eight different age groups, plus infant care. From the youngest Junior Toddlers (twelve to eighteen months) to Senior Teens (thirteen- to fifteen-year-olds), children are well entertained with morning and evening activities led by energetic and enthusiastic college students. Children take meals with their group leaders, and the hours between breakfast and lunch and after supper are filled with arts and crafts, nature walks, songs, games, storytime, volleyball, swimming, hayrides, fishing, movies, treasure hunts, sailing, tennis, sailboarding, kayaking, indoor pool parties—one gets out of breath just listing the activities! Busy and active, your child will no doubt be happy as well, with no chance of being "kid-starved." Afternoons (1:30 to 5:30 p.m.) are devoted to individual family time, with activities available if desired. If you can drag the kids away from friends and counselors, the staff will help you plan a day of sightseeing or fishing and send you off with a picnic lunch.

For the very young (newborns to two and a half years), the resort features one-on-one "Parents' Helpers" (from high-school-age to mature adult), who will care for your young child and even prepare meals. The standard fee is $5.50 to $7.50 per hour. This is a real vacation for Mom and Dad, a break from wet diapers and baby food. During Family Retreat Weeks, Parents' Helpers are available only in the evening. Mornings, the Infant Center provides care for the wee ones (with a 1:2 ratio of caregivers to children), and toddlers are looked after in the Toddler Center (with a 1:3 ratio).

During the first week of September, you're invited to bring a friend (ages six to fifteen) at no extra charge as long as the friend is in the same age group as your child.

**Recreation:** Beautiful Lake Champlain is the source of much of the recreation and relaxation of Tyler Place. Take off in one of the resort's sailboats, canoes, kayaks, pontoons, or sailboards. Try waterskiing, wind-surfing, guided canoe and bike trips, yoga, aerobics (step and water), and the workout facilities. Or bait your fishing line for bass and pike. The outdoor and indoor heated pools and Jacuzzi on the lakeshore provide hours of fun. Kids and adults both get a thrill from the "banana boat ride."

Retreats for the whole family feature hands-on activities for all ages, including such topics as gardening, nature and outdoor skills, lakeshore studies, rural and farm life, and family wellness.

On land, six tennis courts and a fleet of bikes (one-speed, mountain, children's, tri-cycle, and child seats, all with helmets) are at your disposal, and the nature trails beckon hikers and joggers. For a change of pace, challenge another guest to an old-fashioned game of horseshoes, or try your hand at archery. Maybe you'll join a soccer game or start up a tennis round-robin with the folks in the neighboring cottage. Golf privileges are available at three golf courses within a fifteen- to forty-five-minute drive of the resort. Recreation fees are applied only for golf, outboard motors for fishing, water-skiing, lake cruises, and mountain bikes.

Within an hour's drive you can get a taste of Europe by visiting cosmopolitan Montreal, or take a mountain hike and an aerial tram ride at Stowe or Jay Peak. Covered bridges, waterfalls, little New England towns, country auctions, and antiques shops are even closer. A plethora of working farms, state parks, and vineyards and wineries can make decisions difficult.

Nighttime brings other events, from dances and live jazz to guitar sing-alongs and Monte Carlo nights—pick your pleasure. What many guests like most is the hospitable atmosphere of the many and varied activities, with never any pressure to participate.

P.O. Box 254, Old Dock Road
**Highgate Springs, Vermont 05460**
**(802) 868-4000**
**www.tylerplace.com**

# WEEKAPAUG INN
### Weekapaug, Rhode Island

If you like lights, action, and lots going on, then just skip right over this entry. However, if you sometimes tire of the hectic, everyday insanity most of us call our ordinary lives, you may wish to read on. The story begins in 1899, when the Weekapaug Inn was simply another fashionable seaside resort, one of many strung along the length of the Atlantic coast. Frederick Buffum, the original owner, built it because he thought that "the view was just too gorgeous not to share with friends." It comes full circle to the present, with owner Jim Buffum, the fourth generation of his family to run the inn, delightedly accepting the Forbes.com declaration that the 108-year-old Weekapaug Inn is one of three best beach resorts in the United States and among the twenty-five best in the world. *Money* magazine ranked nearby Westerly as one of the top twelve vacation spots in North America. What's the attraction here? Perhaps the beautiful beach, the view across water and more water to distant Block Island, the stately edifice, or a sense of serenity and tradition, of time suspended? Perhaps it's the feeling of retreating to a lovely old summer house? It's really hard to say. It's not an easy place to find, it's not on many maps, and even if it is, it's so small that people often don't know they've arrived.

Weekapaug comes from a Niantic Indian word meaning "end of the pond," and that's exactly where it is. The mile-long expanse of sand is actually a barrier beach with the ocean on one side and saltwater ponds and marshes on the other. The inn was rebuilt in 1938, after a major hurricane destroyed everything on the beach, and, as *Forbes* observed, "it has remained true to its original conception." After that hurricane, the Buffum family was instrumental in getting agreement from all the neighboring landholders to prevent any future development on the beach, so the view remains perfect. Weekapaug is at the western end of Quonochontaug Pond—easy to say, right?

**Accommodations:** The sixty-five rooms are clean and comfortable, but rather plain. There are no telephones and no television in the rooms; pay phones are available, and hotel policy allows "discreet use of cell phones in designated areas." A story from a book commemorating the one-hundredth anniversary of the inn tells of the early guest who was puzzled by the fact that the inn was full, even though "the furnishings were poor, the beds hard, there was no running water in the room and the bath is at the end of the hall." The senior Buffum thought for a minute and said, "Frankly, I don't understand it either." The guest returned every year. All rooms now have private baths (and running water), and showers have been added to the claw-foot bathtubs. The inn is open from the third Thursday in June through Labor Day. The room rates are all-inclusive; all meals, amenities, and activities are included in the per-person rates of $225 daily. Children are "about" $150 daily, depending on their ages and the room. The inn does not accept credit cards.

**Dining:** Upon arrival, each family is assigned a table, and like a cruise ship, that's your table for the duration. You get to know your waiter and your neighbors. Mostly college students, the fifty-plus employees live on-site, as does the owner's family. Menus are mouthwatering, and anything but simple. You might choose from asparagus, Gorgonzola, and spinach strudel with yellow tomato coulis; smoked tomato risotto–stuffed calamari; coffee-crusted grilled filet mignon with a Venezuelan quasala sauce; roasted eggplant pancakes over a ratatouille sauce with garlic mascarpone cream; tandoori chicken; or poached salmon—and that is just a portion of the menu for one meal! It makes it worth getting dressed—tie and jacket are required for gentlemen and appropriate dress for women and children. Daytime attire can be "somewhat casual," but no bathing suits, please. Lunch is generally a buffet in the dining room; you may also order a picnic lunch delivered to the bathhouse. Sunday features a more elaborate buffet lunch, and a light dinner. Thursdays bring a casual cookout by the pond. Smoking is not permitted anywhere inside, and the inn does not sell alcohol. However, each room has an assigned cubby near the lounge for bottles, and self-serve ice and mixers are available for a small charge, on the honor system.

**Children's World:** The children's program is included in the rates and meets twice a day for ages three to ten years, from 10:30 a.m. to 1:30 p.m. and again from 5:30 to 8:30 p.m. Regular activities include playing at the beach, art, crafts, games, and nature hikes, and meals are taken as a group. Evenings bring movies or a theater excursion. The Children's Playroom has a television, but not for use during program hours. Babysitting can be arranged with twenty-four hours' advance notice.

**Recreation:** Bring all those books you haven't had time to read and correspondence you've been saving for the past year, as evenings are quiet and made for socializing or playing board games. There are two televisions, but it's interesting how boring they are compared to what's happening around you. Sometimes storytellers or guest speakers are on the agenda, as are dancing or movies. If golf is your game, local courses are nearby. Two tennis courts are on-site, and lawn bowling, shuffleboard, and croquet are popular pastimes. Your croquet not quite up to speed? Complimentary lessons are offered every Tuesday by the Weekapaug Croquet Club. Bicycles are a lovely way to get around. Sailing, canoeing, kayaking, and rowing on the pond are great fun—sign up for a boat at the front desk. Guests may use the Weekapaug Yacht Club Bathhouse at the private community beach, with attendant on duty from 9:00 a.m. to 5:00 p.m. for towels, chairs, and umbrellas. Fenway Beach, also private but open to guests, is good for children as it has a more protected area with gentle, sloped access into the water. Clamming in Mud Cove delights children and may bring back memories of your own earlier summers—or imagined ones!

---

**25 Spray Rock Road**
**Weekapaug, Rhode Island 02891**
**(401) 322-0301**
**www.weekapauginn.com**

# EAST

New York
Pennsylvania

# MOHONK MOUNTAIN HOUSE

### New Paltz, New York

The wholesome peace and serenity of Mohonk Mountain House are not merely by-products of its setting in 2,200 acres of the Shawangunk Mountains, 90 miles north of New York City. The resort was founded in 1869 by twin brothers, Albert and Alfred Smiley, who, following their Quaker upbringing, regarded drinking, dancing, smoking, and card playing as unacceptable activities. Rather, they emphasized spiritual renewal, as evidenced by the nature walks or prayer meetings planned for their proper clientele.

The times have indeed changed, but the gracious, quieter way of life of a bygone era still prevails at Mohonk. No discos swing until dawn here. Instead, you'll find cozy conversation lounges furnished with Victorian antiques, verandas lined with rocking chairs, miles of hiking trails, and extensive gardens. Open year-round, the rambling wood-and-stone Victorian structure appears almost like a castle, complete with turrets and towers, and sits on the edge of a clear mountain lake half a mile long. In fact, Mohonk means "lake in the sky" in Iroquois. Though physically isolated, guests want for nothing during a stay here.

**Accommodations:** The 251 guest rooms are spacious and tastefully and simply decorated with period furnishings. Some have fireplaces and private balconies overlooking the lake or looking across the valley to the mountains. Some connecting rooms share a bath. On a Full American Plan (mandatory), daily rates are from $415 to $565 for a standard double guest room. The special Victorian and tower rooms command higher rates. For children occupying a room with their parents, the charge is $146 a day for those over twelve

and $82 a day for four- to twelve-year-olds; children under age four are accommodated free. There is no charge for cribs or roll-away beds. Weekly rates and package plans are available. Ask about the "kids stay free" events held throughout the year.

**Dining:** Breakfast, lunch, and dinner are included in the rates. The main dining room is large and elegantly simple with highly polished woodwork and paneling rising 30 to 40 feet. The kitchen specializes in American cuisine and ingredients indigenous to America. "Sound Choice," vegetarian, and kosher menus are also available, and the spectacular natural setting adds to the dining experience. Jackets are standard attire for gentlemen age twelve and older at the evening meal. Cookouts and clambakes are occasionally planned; enjoy casual outdoor dining at Picnic Lodge or the Granary; and complimentary afternoon tea is served daily at 4:00 p.m. Refreshments are also available in the Ice Cream Parlor and Soda Fountain and the Tee Room on the golf course. The West Lounge is open from 5:00 to 11:00 p.m. for cocktails and light fare.

**Children's World:** On weekends and holidays throughout the year and daily from mid-June through Labor Day, Mohonk's Kids' Club divides children into three age groups: Tykes, two- to three-year-olds; Explorers, four- to six-year-olds; and Adventurers, seven- to twelve-year-olds. Groups have daily activities in the morning and again in the afternoon, after lunch with the family, and evening activities as well. Typical events on the agenda are hikes, nature walks, scavenger hunts, shuffleboard contests, swimming, pony rides, rock scrambles, and frog hunts. Movies, square dances, and campfires are frequently planned for evenings. During July and August, special activities for teens (ages twelve to eighteen years) are planned. From mountain biking, rock scrambles, tennis and golf clinics, and daylong hikes to just "hanging out" in the Teen Lounge for music, movies, and socializing, all activities are well supervised. Winter brings ice-skating, snow tubing, snowshoeing, and hot chocolate. Kids' Club is a complimentary service for hotel guests. Babysitters can be hired for younger children, with advance notice, and there are planned activities for the whole family to enjoy together.

**Recreation:** Discovering nature's beauty is at the core of Mohonk's recreational activities; with the exception of horseback riding, carriage rides, weekend golf, and massage, recreation is complimentary. More than 85 miles of hiking trails wind through the woods and along the lake; dotting the paths are one hundred gazebos where you can sit to take in the views. Explore the grounds on horseback (Western and English style), or leisurely meander through the award-winning gardens and Victorian maze. Lake Mohonk has a small sandy beach at the west end and is stocked with trout; it is the location for swimming, fishing, and boating. Try your hand at rock climbing on a truly spectacular cliff.

Traditional sports are tennis (lessons available) on six courts (two clay, four Har-Tru) plus two platform tennis courts, and golfing on the nine-hole course designed after St. Andrews in Scotland, or the put-ting green. Tennis and greens fees are complimentary midweek. There are tennis and golf pro shops for equipment and apparel. Lawn games include shuffleboard, croquet, and lawn bowling.

During the winter months, when the lake freezes, snow tubing and ice-skating are favorite sports. Mohonk's Victorian Skating Pavilion is host to skating parties on a refrigerated ice rink in fall and winter. And Mohonk maintains more than 35 miles of marked trails for snowshoeing and cross-country skiing, also included in the rates.

Throughout the year lectures, concerts, nature shows, movies, and dancing are scheduled in the evening. Several three-day to weeklong themed programs are planned, covering topics such as bird watching and identification, gardening, photography, foreign languages, cooking, music, mystery and sleuthing, and stargazing; professionals in the respective fields conduct these programs.

The Spa at Mohonk Mountain House, opened in 2005, prides itself on sixteen treatment rooms, all amenities, indoor and outdoor pools, and a state-of-the-art fitness room.

---

**Lake Mohonk**
**1000 Mountain Rest Road**
**New Paltz, New York 12561**
**(845) 255-1000, (800) 772-6646**
**www.mohonk.com**

# NEMACOLIN WOODLANDS RESORT

## Farmington, Pennsylvania

Nemacolin Woodlands Resort, set on 3,000 acres near Uniontown in the Laurel Highlands of southwest Pennsylvania, celebrated its twentieth year in 2007. It began in 1968 as a private game reserve, with a hunting lodge and golf course. Over the years two lakes were added, and Beaver Creek, now an excellent trout stream, was born. In 1987 Joseph Hardy purchased it for his daughter, Maggie, who loved fishing. Since then Nemacolin Woodlands has become a premier four-star, four-diamond resort, with many amenities and extensive programs. Maggie Hardy Magerko still serves as president and owner. Expansions and renovations continue, and in 2007 a Wildlife Academy opened, with buffaloes—including a rare white buffalo—joining the mix of wildlife.

**Accommodations:** The property has 335 guest rooms and suites, town houses, and private homes, plus two boutique hotels. The upscale Chateau LaFayette, in the classic European style, offers 124 guest rooms and a Club Level with twenty-four-hour butler service. Falling Rock, a five-diamond hotel and clubhouse inspired by Frank Lloyd Wright's architecture, is situated on the eighteenth green of the Mystic Rock golf course and is perfect for golfers; it has forty-two guest rooms and twenty-four-hour butler service. The Lodge is the original hotel, styled as a classic English country inn. Ninety-eight oversize guest rooms offer one king bed or two doubles. The Hardy family art collection, valued at $4.5 million, is here. It may seem strange to have a luxurious resort with a lodging option of bringing your RV—but somehow, Nemacolin makes it work. Maggie Valley RV Park is in a lovely wooded setting and features complimentary satellite TV; water, electric, and sewage hookups; telephone jacks; and even high-speed Internet access. Picnic tables and a fire pit are at each site. A shuttle service takes you to the resort, and room service will deliver meals if you desire! The RV park is open April through November. Rates are $100 to $150.

Lodge, Chateau, and one-bedroom town house rates are based on single or double occupancy; two-bedroom town house rates are based on quad occupancy; children under eighteen are free, and cribs are complimentary. Weekends have a two-night minimum stay; holidays require at least a three-night stay. Nightly rates average $305 to $330 at the Lodge and $370 to $425 at the Chateau. A one-bedroom town house is $195 to $210, and a two-bedroom town house is $380 to $410. With a three-night stay on the Kidz Rule package, the family receives a $300 activity credit to be used throughout the resort. A Summer Escape package with one activity per person may be a good deal. A winter bed-and-breakfast package is $135 to $215 per person at the Chateau and $115 to $170 at the Lodge. The rates for children are $12 for ages four to twelve and $23 for ages thirteen to seventeen.

**Dining:** Choices abound at Nemacolin, from haute cuisine to burgers. Lautrec is the most acclaimed, a AAA four-diamond restaurant offering French specialties as well as a seven- and twelve-course tasting menu. At Chateau LaFayette the setting is elegant and the food artistic. Jackets are requested, and children under twelve are discouraged. Aqueous, at Falling Rock, is another four-star restaurant. Open for breakfast, lunch, and dinner, Aqueous offers a menu centered on local meats and produce and takes "steakhouse" to a new level. It was voted one of Pittsburgh's Top 25 restaurants in 2005 and 2006, and attire is resort casual. In the Lodge, Autumn brings the taste of Italy and a relaxed atmosphere at breakfast and dinner daily. For casual dining you may choose from at least ten venues. Kids like the aquarium at the Tavern, an English-style pub; the Caddyshack is another favorite, with six TVs and an arcade with foosball; Elements, within the spa, offers healthy choices; at the Gazebo you can gaze at the mountains of three states. Or you can have a burger or sandwich at Orville's Pub & Grille at the Shooting Academy—but you may drink only *after* you've finished shooting! And finally, PJ's is a 1950s ice-cream and pizza parlor. Summer Saturdays bring a Family Steak Fry Safari near Lake PJ. Food, activities, an Animal Show, s'mores, and a movie are perfect for families. Weather permitting, Mulligans is open, and in winter the Hitchin' Post Saloon and Hungry Moose Café is open at the ski lodge. The Poolside Bar serves food and swim-up libations from 11:00 a.m. to 5:00 p.m., weather permitting. Seven bars and lounges and the largest wine cellar in Pennsylvania will ease you into evening socializing. At the Chateau you can enjoy the luxury of the lobby lounge or savor a traditional English Tea, with piano music. Amber Lounge at Falling Rock has wonderful hors d'oeuvres, and if cigars are your thing, the Cigar Bar offers a fireplace and an air filtration system. Diamond Lil's nightclub and lounge provides dance music and a party atmosphere until 2:00 a.m.

**Children's World:** "Wet, Wild, and WooHoo" is how the resort describes its Kidz Rule program, and there's something for everyone—from toddler to teenager. The program operates daily, year-round; activities vary based on season and attendance. From 9:00 a.m. to 4:00 p.m., Little Tykes entertains kids ages six months through three years in the state-of-the-art Hardy Learning Center. The cost is $60, with lunch, or $40 for a half day. Babysitting is also available through the concierge. Kidz Klub, for ages four through twelve, has the same hours and rates. Days are filled with things kids love, such as looking at bugs under a microscope, tracking animals and casting their prints, or making your own slime. The Krew provides an opportunity for tweens and teens (ages eleven and up) to meet with their peers and exercise their cool for more adventurous activities such as biking, climbing, ropes course, sporting clays, and fishing. A full day, from 10:00 a.m. to 5:00 p.m., costs $125.

Kidz Night Out (ages four to twelve) is scheduled every night from 5:00 to 10:00 p.m. when kids gather for dinner, themed games, swimming, or making their own snow. Cost is $55 per child. Sorry, Mom and Dad, it's kids only, so you're on your own!

**Recreation:** Thirty-six holes of excellent mountain golf await you here in the Highlands of Pennsylvania, with wonderful vistas and a top golf school. Pete Dye designed Mystic Rock, and the Falling Rock clubhouse is luxury personified. The more traditional Links course is Scottish-style, and it has some interesting terrain changes. Activities are organized by centers, each with their own locations. The Activities Center has lots for families, from video arcades to the family swimming pool and PJ's Ice Cream & Pizza. Families also have a year-round indoor pool here, only 3 feet deep. Table tennis, croquet, shuffleboard, and badminton are complimentary; tennis is $15 per hour on one of four lighted, omni-turf courts. Other activities are also fun for kids and families. The daily Arts in the Afternoon program allows families to be creative; minigolf at Fallingbrook, pedal boats at the Marina, pony rides, and tennis clinics can fill the day. The Hardy Girls Gymnasium is an Olympic-caliber facility with a variety of classes and clinics for both budding and more experienced gymnasts.

The Adventure Center organizes recreation for guests of all ages and is the center for paintball, archery, ropes course, minigolf, climbing wall, zip line, biking, and Quick Draw Alley; prices vary. The Equestrian Center offers both indoor and outdoor arenas, trail rides, in-depth encounters, and classes. Winter or summer, try a sleigh or surrey ride. The Shooting Academy is one of the best and most comprehensive. Clay shooting, woven throughout 140 acres, can be tailored to all skill levels. Accompanied by NSCA instructors, you travel from station to station; customized instruction begins at age ten. If fishing challenges you and you seek quiet and fresh air, fly fishing is for you. The resort offers trout fishing on Beaver Creek and bass fishing and also is an Orvis®-endorsed fly-fishing lodge. The Off-Road Driving Academy lets you ride along in a Hummer ($50 for thirty minutes) or take the driver's seat ($300 for ninety minutes), 365 days a year. On the quieter side, take an art tour of the Hardy collection, join a wine-tasting or cooking class, or take a Rolls Royce with chauffeur to tour the Frank Lloyd Wright houses in the Laurel Highlands. Stop by the Woodlands Spa for a game of squash or to rejuvenate and relax from all the fun. New in 2007 is The Marina at Paige's Beach, with lots of family activities, such as paddleboat, canoe, kayak, and sailboat rentals; pony rides; combat paintball; and, of course, the beach. Also new in 2007 is the Wildlife Academy, an activity location. Wildlife habitats are diverse and include black bears, zebras, and buffaloes. The emphasis is on education and interaction, with a petting zoo, Wild World of Animals, Fatbird Express Safari, and guided tours.

In the winter Mystic Mountain opens for downhill skiing on ten slopes and trails, with a half-pipe for snowboarding. Snow tubing, snowshoeing, and cross-country skiing add to the winter fun, and the Sundial Ski Lodge keeps you warm and well fed. Snow Monsters ski programs are available for kids. Mystic Mountain is open Friday through Monday, from late December until March. Whatever the season, there are lots of reasons to visit here.

**1001 LaFayette Drive**
**Farmington, Pennsylvania 15437**
**(724) 329-8555, (800) 422-2736**
**www.nemacolin.com**

# ROCKING HORSE RANCH

## Highland, New York

"Giddy-up, ole paint" and, with a tip of your ten-gallon hat, off you ride into the sunset. Located only 75 miles from New York City with a three-diamond rating by AAA, Rocking Horse Ranch has been owned and managed by the Turk family since 1958. They take pride in treating their guests as family; in fact, more than 80 percent of the guests are repeat clients. The 500 acres easily accommodate up to 450 guests while permitting a feeling of "wide-open spaces." With a stable of 120 horses, mainly quarterhorse stock, Rocking Horse stakes a claim to being one of the best family dude ranches in the East.

**Accommodations:** Rooms (120 in all) are located in either the main lodge or the Oklahoma Annex (motel-style units). The twenty-four connecting rooms and the ranchettes may be appropriate for large parties. The latter are similar to minisuites, with sitting areas and convertible sofa beds. Eighteen rooms have refrigerators. Summer daily all-inclusive package rates based on double occupancy are $250 to $330 per adult; children under four are free; ages four to fifteen are $115 for the first child and $110 for additional children. Less per day for longer stays! Weekly rates per adult are $1,220 to $1,425, first child is $580, additional children $545. Spring, fall, and winter feature weekend and midweek stays; during certain time periods, rates are further reduced by 10 to 25 percent. Winter weekends (Friday to Sunday) range from $340 to $420 per adult and $155 per child (ages four to fifteen years). Spring and fall rates are comparable, and holidays are more expensive.

**Dining:** Meals and entertainment are included in the resort's rates. Choose from the Longhorn Dining Room, The Cactus Grill, or, during summer, poolside parties and snack bar. Adults receive breakfast and dinner, while children have all three meals, enjoying lunch with the counselors. Meals are five to six courses, prepared by graduate chefs from the nearby Culinary Institute of America. Dinner selections include roast prime rib, barbecued steaks, or fillet of sole brought in fresh from a local market, com-plemented by a huge salad bar. At the dessert bar the chocolate blackout cake is not to be missed. The Round-Up Room Nightclub has floor shows and a live band. Two other cocktail lounges, each with a fireplace and a conversation area, are also quite inviting.

**Children's World:** The Fort Wilderness playground area, with swings and climbing equipment and the animal farm where Chewbacca the Camel lives, is a favorite with kids. Year-round, children have a planned, supervised program seven days a week. The 9:00 a.m. to 5:00 p.m. schedule is filled with horseback riding, swimming, waterskiing, crafts, and games. In the evening the family fun continues with pizza parties, dances, and cookouts. On weekends during the winter, kids turn to skiing and snow tubing.

There is no charge for the day's events, which include lunch and snacks with the counselors for ages four to twelve. Children are divided into small groups (ages four to six, seven to ten, and eleven to twelve) with age-appropriate activities. The under-four set is the only group with an extra charge ($7 per hour) either in the nursery or with an individual babysitter. Teens have evening programs and mixers, and plenty of opportunity to "meet and mingle" during daytime activities.

**Recreation:** You might start your day with an early-morning horseback ride; invigorated by the sweet mountain air, lead your horse down a quiet trail through the woods. If you're a novice, you can link up with the experienced ranch staff for some basic instruction.

The rest of your day may be filled with waterskiing (instruction is free), enjoying more than 150 feet of water slide, swimming, fishing, and boating (paddleboats and rowboats) on the ten-acre lake. Play a game of tennis and hike or jog along the nature trails. A relaxing swim in one of three heated pools (two are outdoors, with one just for kids) can revive your spirits for a workout in the exercise room or a rousing game of volleyball, softball, basketball, or badminton. The climbing wall is a popular place. For an easier pace, try a round of croquet, shuffleboard, bocci, or horseshoes. An archery field and an indoor shooting range are available for aspiring marksmen, and the eighteen holes of miniature golf are fun for kids and their parents. A Giant Fun Barn features interactive foam ball play at Ballocity and an indoor climbing wall.

In the fall the social director plans hayrides and cookouts; in winter add cross-country skiing, snow tubing, and horseback riding in the snow. The 300-foot vertical ski slope is modest but has two new trails. At Rocking Horse more than fifty activities are free; the horseback riding, the use of all the sports equipment and facilities, and the entertainment are all covered in the lodging rates.

---

**600 Route 44-55**
**Highland, New York 12528**
**(845) 691-2927, (800) 647-2624**
**www.rhranch.com**

# THE SAGAMORE
## Lake George at Bolton Landing, New York

The notion of an island hideaway usually involves images of thatch-roofed huts or oceanside condominiums, palm trees waving in a gentle breeze, miles of sandy beach, and golf, tennis, sailing, and swimming. The Sagamore will take you by surprise, for it is an island resort, and it grants its guests opportunities for golf, tennis, sailing, and swimming—and then it deviates from the traditional image. You see, The Sagamore is on a seventy-acre island in Lake George in upstate New York. Surrounded by clear lake waters and the Adirondack Mountains, the tall evergreen trees and the clean mountain air set the stage here, and Lake George and Bolton Landing are within the borders of the six-million-acre New York Adirondack State Park.

The Sagamore itself is different. Originally opened in 1883, it is part of another era, gracious and elegant. The main hotel building dates from 1930 and is listed on the National Register of Historic Places. It is a member of Preferred Hotels and Resorts Worldwide. Awards for this four-diamond, four-star hotel include "bests" for both tennis and golf.

The hotel's wings radiate from the main lobby and its semicircular, white-columned porch seems to embrace the lawns, gardens, and lake views. Down the wings are more porches for sitting, strolling, and catching a different view of the lake. In the center is the bell tower, topping off this Victorian showplace. The resort is open year-round.

**Accommodations:** The Sagamore's 350 rooms and suites are in the main hotel and distributed among the island's seven lodges. You will find attention to detail and historical accuracy in the decoration of the rooms and throughout the hotel. You'll think "charming, quaint, elegant, reserved" when you see Adirondack Stick or American Country furniture. Perhaps your room will be in mahogany, and you'll draw a Queen Anne–style chair up to the desk when writing postcards. Rocking chairs and quilted bedspreads complete the picture in some rooms. In others fireplaces or balconies capture a guest's eye. Even the bathrooms are special and true to a grand era, with their pedestal-base sinks and mahogany towel bars.

Rates vary within the main historic hotel and the lodges, depending on the season. Winter rates are the lowest, beginning at $185 nightly for a hotel room, or $295 for a suite. This rate goes from $410 to $549 from late June to early September, the Adirondack season. A lodge suite begins at $295 in winter and $499 in the Adirondack season. Children to age thirteen pay $25 daily, except in July and August, when that drops to age six. The Sagamore's rates do not include meals; there is an additional daily service charge of $9 per person.

**Dining:** For a casual afternoon by the pool, you can have a light lunch and beverages at the Cabana. For dinner the newly renovated Trillium serves French/American cuisine. In between these options are the Sagamore Dining Room near the lake, where regional favorites are served at breakfast and seasonal dinner, and the Club Grill on the mainland, where views stretch out over the golf course and the lake. During the Adirondack season, The Pavilion offers outside dining on the lake for lunch, and a Wednesday through Monday evening Lakeside Lobsterbake. At the glass-enclosed Verandah, in the lobby, guests can enjoy tea and finger sandwiches in the afternoon, and nightcaps before retiring. Mister Brown's Pub serves light meals in a publike setting and provides evening entertainment. All restaurants are family-friendly, with selections for children.

May through October, the 72-foot yacht *Morgan* cruises the lake during lunch and dinner, offering its diners constantly changing scenic views. It is suggested that you make your dinner reservations when you book your room.

**Children's World:** Under the cheerful and watchful direction of the activities counselor, Sagamore kids take swimming lessons, play lawn games, dance, do face painting, go on boat rides, see clown shows, and unveil their hidden talents in crafts classes. In this one area The Sagamore does not follow nineteenth-century practices, which were somewhat restrictive when it came to children. Instead, in keeping with modern philosophies, The Sagamore wants its energized children to have a fun, athletic, and creative visit. The authentic 16-foot tepee gives the program its name: The Tepee Club. It runs from 9:00 a.m. to 4:00 p.m. daily, July 1 through Labor Day for ages four through twelve; a modified program operates on holidays year-round. Costs are $25 for a half-day session (no lunch) or $65 for a full-day session (with lunch). From 5:00 to 9:00 p.m., children can have dinner together, play, and enjoy games such as dress-ups or clown parties ($45 per session). A game room offers table tennis, a pool table, video games, and a television. Babysitting is available for $15 an hour for the first child, $5 each additional child, with a three-hour minimum required. Children under four may participate in the programs, accompanied by a babysitter.

**Recreation:** Just across the bridge from The Sagamore's island, Donald Ross designed an eighteen-hole championship golf course in the Adirondack foothills near the lake's edge, complemented by the restaurant and pro shop facilities at the course's attractive Tudor-style clubhouse.

The indoor swimming pool, tennis courts, and racquetball courts help guests stay busy and active year-round. The complete fitness center offers its own form of indoor workout with its Nautilus equipment and then pampers with saunas, whirlpools, steam rooms, and massages. European-style full-service spa packages include special diets, herbal wraps, and aromatherapy.

In warm weather swim in the beautiful, clean, freshwater lake; skim across its surface sailing, waterskiing, or sailboarding; or gently stroke the waters in a rowboat or fishing boat. Sailing clinics are available for teens, women only, and new sailors. Jog on the trails around the island or hike the foothills around the golf course. Take a horse out for an hour-long jaunt or stay close to home for a Sunday afternoon concert on the lawn.

In the wintertime Lake George freezes; hearty souls go ice-fishing, while others snuggle together during a horse-drawn sleigh ride. Ice-skate over the frozen lake or go tobogganing and cross-country skiing on the snow-covered golf course. Downhill skiers can take advantage of nearby Gore Mountain and West Mountain, ski areas to which The Sagamore provides free bus transportation.

Saratoga is about 30 miles away and in summer shares its Performing Arts Center with interested visitors. Tour historic Fort Williams, the setting for *The Last of the Mohicans;* walk along the lake boardwalk for shopping and dining; or visit Great Escape Amusement Park, boasting one of the country's top ten roller coasters, The Steamin' Demon.

---

**110 Sagamore Road**
**P.O. Box 450**
**Bolton Landing, New York 12814**
**(518) 644-9400, (866) 385-6221**
**www.thesagamore.com**

# SCOTT'S OQUAGA LAKE HOUSE
## Deposit, New York

A reader shared this gem of a family resort with us and described it as "warm, friendly, hospitable, fun, down to earth, great for every age, and even enchanting." We tend to agree. Six generations of Scotts have created this lovely resort, beginning in 1869. Over the years the warmth of the welcome you receive and the sense of belonging to a family have not dimmed. Set on a clear, spring-fed lake amidst the hills and woods of beautiful New York State, it is truly run for families, by a family; Mom and Pop Scott (Ray and Doris) plus daughter Patty and her now-grown children and their spouses all work in different capacities at the resort. Reminiscent of the Von Trapp family, the "Singing Scotts" even present a Broadway musical review! An all-inclusive policy (you never see your wallet during your stay) adds to the old-fashioned charm of this country resort—and there's no tipping! Scott's is open late May to mid-October, so stroll up the flower-lined walk to the main house and into everyone's memory of a summer house on a lake—somewhere.

**Accommodations:** One hundred thirty-five rooms are set in the main lodge, various buildings, and cottages, some with two doubles or two twins, a few with king-size beds; all are simple, clean, and comfortable. Rates are per person and include room, three full meals, all recreation and entertainment, kids program, and unlimited golf, tennis, waterskiing, and all other sports and activities. The rates shown are for July and August high season; daily rates at other times are about $10 lower. Single parents pay only $30 to $40 more. Based on double occupancy, daily per-person rates range from $127 to $148; two-room suites are $188. Weekly rates are $785 to $904. Children's daily/weekly rates are based on age: Kids younger than three are complimentary; ages three to five are $58/$358; ages six to twelve pay $74/$448; and ages thirteen to nineteen are $88/$546.

**Dining:** Contrary to many times in our hectic lives, eating is a communal event here, showcased in the large dining room. Fresh, natural ingredients prepared simply and with care, shared family-style with fellow guests, make it easy to slow down and appreciate life and good food. Choices abound, and kids may even eat their vegetables! Twice a week you can bus or hike to a sheltered pavilion for a lavish cookout, with live music and dance and a spectacular view.

**Children's World:** Long summer days spent swimming in a lake or watching nature in the woods, lunch with friends, lots of adventures—it's great to give your kids a taste of a slower, relaxed time. Supervised activities from 9:30 a.m. to 12:30 p.m. and again from 2:00 to 4:30 p.m. provide just that, while keeping kids from three up busy and amused. Age groups are blended nicely, and it's secure enough for kids to strike out on their own yet still be safe. A large playhouse on the lakefront, which includes a nostalgic soda fountain, pool tables, table tennis, and some old-fashioned bowling

alleys, provides a focal point for fun. Teens can "hang" here, and while they'll laugh at having to set up their own pins, they'll probably secretly get a kick out of it.

**Recreation:** You'll experience no shortage of activities here, as the resort's nearly 1,100 acres are packed with things to do. Anything even remotely connected with sports is yours for the asking—volleyball, softball, bocci, table tennis, pool, bowling, two scenic nine-hole golf courses, a ninehole pitch-and-putt and a putting green, and one indoor and three outdoor tennis courts. On the water, row a boat, canoe, sail, take a speedboat ride, fish, or waterski. In the water, swim, splash, or simply lie on the floating raft and soak up the sun. For a different water experience, go on a canoe trip down the Delaware River—all included! Colorful Adirondack chairs line the lakefront beach, perfectly conducive to contemplating the green mountains while everyone else does all of that activity. Hike, bike, walk in the woods, or dance—your choice of ballroom, square, line, country, or folk dancing, all on a 3,200-square-foot hardwood dance floor on the lakefront. Enjoy live shows and family entertainment nightly. Ride the *Show Boat,* a tradition on Oquaga Lake for years, and you provide the singalong show! Most of all, experience summer as you like it.

---

**Oquaga Lake, Box 47**
**Deposit, New York 13754**
**(607) 467-3094**
**www.scottsfamilyresort.com**

# SKYTOP LODGE

### Skytop, Pennsylvania

The Pocono Mountains have long had a reputation as a romantic honeymoon destination. While this is certainly warranted, the Skytop Lodge will convince you that this area of northeast Pennsylvania is just right for a family vacation as well. Set on 5,500 acres of rolling hills, lakes, and rivers, the lodge is a large, rambling, stone building with a welcoming circular drive. Just 100 miles from either New York or Philadelphia, Skytop attracts many visitors with its relaxed atmosphere, hospitable charm, and recreational activities. One of the Historic Hotels of America, it is open year-round. Room, three gourmet meals, and countless activities—it's all included!

**Accommodations:** Most of the English country–style rooms in the historic stone manor house have views of the gardens and grounds; some will accommodate a family of four. If a large-enough room is not available, or if parents prefer, children are given their own room at $100 off the regular rate. This applies to two children only; additional children are $45 each. Based on double occupancy, Full American Plan high-season (May through October) rates begin at $535 per night; winter rates begin at $380. Children under sixteen sharing their parents' room pay $45.

Also available are ten cottages, each with four interconnecting bedrooms. Each room within the cottage can be occupied separately or together in suites from two to four. Midweek Family Fun packages, based on two adults in standard or cottage rooms, begin at $595 for one night, $983 for two nights, and include three meals, the children's program, and use of seasonal recreational facilities including golf, tennis, skiing, and ice-skating. May through October, rates change to $640 for one night, $1,113 for two nights. Midweek golf packages, including three meals, begin at $395 per night. Rates are higher in January, February, July, and August.

**Dining:** Skytop's Full American Plan includes a choice of meals in the Windsor Room in the Main Lodge and the Lake View at the Inn; both request that gentlemen wear jackets, although ties are not required. Also available, but not included in the dining plan, is the Deli, a seasonal lunch spot in warm weather. The Pine Room, an elegant and inviting area of the lobby with floor-to-ceiling windows, is the site of afternoon tea (part of the dining plan), with musical entertainment in the summer and cozy gatherings near the fireplace in the winter. The Tap Room, offering food, cocktails, and entertainment/dancing, and the Tea Room, with light fare such as soups and sandwiches, are not included in the dining plan.

**Children's World:** Camp-in-the-Clouds is in session for four- to ten-year-olds daily from mid-June to Labor Day. The morning program runs from 9:30 a.m. to 1:30 p.m., the afternoon program from 1:30 to 4:30 p.m. Each session is $15, or $30 for the full day, and covers a program of swimming, boating, hiking, soccer, golf and tennis lessons, games, and crafts. Young children also enjoy the playground and the kiddie pool, while the older ones make the most of pool, table tennis, and video games in the Recreation Room. Saturdays bring picnics for everyone and an evening dinner from 6:00 to 8:00 p.m. for children. The weekly Saturday night "Grand March" has become a tradition at Skytop. A combination parade, quadrille, and snake dance, it becomes hilarious at times, and guests and staff alike anticipate the fun. At holiday times during the rest of the year, the staff plans activities, dinners, and movies for children. Individual babysitters can be arranged for $12 an hour; $1 each additional child. Reservations must be made prior to arrival.

**Recreation:** The Poconos make a lovely setting for sports activities. The eighteen-hole championship golf course is a combination of lush fairways and beautiful old trees on a rolling terrain. Putting greens and a pro shop round out the golfing facility. Tennis players are invigorated by the clean mountain air; of the seven outdoor courts, five are Har-Tru and two have all-weather surfaces. Private lessons and clinics are offered.

Skytop's Fishing and Shooting Center provides fishermen with a trout-filled stream and three lakes full of bass and pickerel; novices will appreciate the Orvis School fly-fishing instruction. Others take to these waters for swimming, boating, and canoeing. There's an outdoor swimming pool, and in cool weather swimmers enjoy the large indoor pool in its solarium setting.

You can work out in the exercise room, but outdoors you can have beautiful scenery *and* all the exercise you want. Try lawn bowling on well-tended greens (tournaments are held during the summer), or practice more conventional sports like bad-minton, croquet, archery, shuffleboard, softball, and miniature golf. The 30 miles of trails through the woods are perfect for hiking, biking, and jogging, and the gardens are suitable for relaxing strolls. Naturalists conduct tours of the local wildlife and vegetation. In the evening you might find a bridge game, play a little pool or billiards, take in a movie, or relax in the library.

In the winter Skytop has a few gentle slopes for downhill skiing. Two poma lifts and four trails with a vertical drop of just 295 feet make it ideal for learning. A ski pro can help with lessons. Several well-groomed trails cover acres of attractive territory for cross-country skiing; or if you're daring, explore winter on snowshoes. Rental equipment is available, and larger ski areas are nearby at Alpine Mountain (8 miles) and Camelback (15 miles). Tobogganing, sledding, and ice-skating are also wintertime favorites. The Spa is always an option for facials, wraps, and massages that delight and relax you.

---

**One Skytop**
**Skytop, Pennsylvania 18357**
**(570) 595-7401, (800) 345-7759**
**www.skytop.com**

# MID-ATLANTIC

Maryland
North Carolina
South Carolina
Virginia
West Virginia

# THE GREENBRIER

## White Sulphur Springs, West Virginia

The Greenbrier is a 6,500-acre estate in the beautiful Allegheny Mountains. Its history dates back to just after the Revolutionary War, when early settlers discovered the sulfur springs of this area. The grand Georgian architecture of The Greenbrier, with its white columned porticoes, elaborate formal gardens, and friendly atmosphere, sets the scene for a memorable experience of fine dining, recreation, and relaxation.

The only problem at The Greenbrier may be deciding what to do first. With a list of more than fifty recreational and social activities, you may need a personal secretary to help you get organized. When planning events for your stay, though, save time for an escape to discover nature's charms along the enticing woodland trails, well marked for joggers and walkers alike. And pause among the twelve acres of formal gardens, tended meticulously from spring through fall. A National Historic Landmark with a reputation that has attracted presidents and royalty, The Greenbrier provides a level of elegant service and comfort that ensures an unforgettable vacation. It is open year-round.

**Accommodations:** With rooms and suites in the hotel as well as guesthouses and cottages, you have a wide choice of accommodations. The Greenbrier has recently undergone extensive renovation. Sixty-three main building guest rooms are completely new, while all 721 guest rooms have new bedding and linens. Rooms are large and bright, with comfortable, elegant furnishings, and each one is unique in both decor and configuration. April through October is high season, when a family vacation package (minimum two-night stay) begins at $379 ($429 on weekends) per room, per night in a traditional room; meals and a resort fee of $25 per room, per night are not included. Children seventeen and under stay free in the same room or may have their own room at half price. Cribs are complimentary. The guest cottages include one to four bedrooms, a living room, and a porch or patio; many have fireplaces. Per-room rates for the cottages are the same as for the hotel; cottages may not be split.

**Dining:** The Greenbrier boasts exciting culinary experiences. Regional Southern specialties, such as spoon bread and fresh trout from the nearby mountain streams, as well as continental dishes make dining a special part of a visit here. The sumptuous breakfasts, featuring homemade biscuits and country ham, are a real treat. A coat and tie are standard attire for gentlemen at dinner in the main dining room; live piano and violin music accompany dinner. Chef Peter Timmins is one of only fifty-nine certified master chefs in the world, so prepare your palate!

Sam Snead's at the Golf Club is a casual and seasonal dining option, showcasing panoramic golf course views and an open kitchen, where you can watch the food being prepared. Slammin' Sammy's is a sports lounge (with ultra-large TV and pocket billiards) and good-time entertainment spot with a daytime a la carte menu. Both are open only in summer. The Rhododendron Spa Cafe, located adjacent to the indoor pool, offers a light, spa cuisine lunch menu, smoothies, fresh juices, and snacks. Drapers Cafe—especially popular for its homemade ice cream—is convenient for lunch, snacks, and an impressive breakfast buffet. Complimentary afternoon tea is served daily with musical accompaniment, and the elegant Lobby Bar is where to meet for drinks. New in 2007, Hemisphere, under the direction of Chef Michael Voltaggio, allows you to choose from up to four tasting menus. Relax in an intimate, exotic setting and indulge yourself in innovative global cuisine. The new 38°80 is "the place" for evening entertainment. World lounge music and a floor plan that encourages you to sip, toast, watch, or dance create a dramatic yet intimate experience.

**Children's World:** From Memorial Day through Labor Day and at the holiday times of Thanksgiving, Christmas, and Easter, the Greenbrier Adventure Zone more than fills the days of three- to twelve-year-olds. During the summer elementary-school teachers and child-development specialists supervise full-day and evening programs for Discoverers (ages three to five), Explorers (ages six to eight), and Expeditioners (ages nine to twelve), combining intellectual enrichment with outdoor activities. Creative Classrooms, an innovative series of hands-on workshops designed with Carnegie Hall, West Virginia, include mask magic, puppet making, basketry, art history, and more; drama and stagecraft classes are taught by staff and performers of the Greenbrier Valley Theatre. Along with the usual swimming, tennis, golf, nature hikes, and fishing, children can experience falconry, carriage rides, or visits to the stables and fire station. Full-day programs run from 9:00 a.m. to 4:00 p.m. The fee is $58 a day for your first child and $48 a day for each additional child and includes lunch and a snack.

From 6:00 to 10:00 p.m. for $48 first child, $38 each additional child, children ages six to twelve years old can join their counselors for dinner and an evening of bowling, board games, or movies. Babysitting services for younger children are also available at an average hourly rate of $8 for the first child, $2 each additional child. So it's possible for grown-ups to arrange an evening or two for wining and dining. Teens have the option of hikes, kayak trips, mountain biking, and even spa treatments designed especially for them.

**Recreation:** Avid golf and tennis players are well served at The Greenbrier. The Allegheny hills provide the beauty and the challenge of three eighteen-hole championship golf courses, one of which was redesigned in 1979 by Jack Nicklaus. The Old White has been restored to its original 1914 elegance. The Greenbrier Golf Digest Academy provides golfers of all skill levels the opportunity to improve their game. The academy provides professional teaching staff and state-of-the-art equipment and services.

The staff at the tennis pro shop can assist in finding partners on one of the five outdoor or five indoor courts. You may also confront the idiosyncrasies of your swing during instructional videotaped replays of your performance.

Kate's Mountain is the picturesque site of the Gun Club, with trap and skeet fields and sporting clays. Game-bird hunting is available April through October. The Falconry Academy allows guests to interact with hawks and falcons and to taste this "sport of kings."

Fishing enthusiasts head for the well-stocked streams and lakes, while swimmers can work out in the indoor or outdoor pool or relax poolside. An exercise room is adjacent to the indoor swimming pool. The bowling center (eight lanes), table tennis, horseback riding, shuffleboard, horseshoes, croquet, bicycling, carriage rides, and movies offer additional diversions. The five hiking trails are graded by length and rise in elevation. One of the two jogging trails features twelve exercise stations. Winter brings snow hiking and sleigh rides.

Downhill skiing is ninety minutes away at the Snowshoe Ski Resort.

And when the body wearies and the spirits droop, the only respectable place to be is the Spa, which pampers guests with mineral baths, massage, steam, and sauna facilities. It was the sulfur water with its medicinal and recuperative powers that first attracted visitors to this region. At the Art Colony you can watch artisans work with metal, leather, brass, wood, glass, and pottery. View the Greenbrier's early history and memorable moments from the visits of twenty-six U.S. presidents at the Presidents' Cottage Museum or tour the Bunker, a former U.S. Government Relocation Facility now open to the public. If you're a fan of Christmas, experience it year-round at the Christmas Shop at the Depot.

---

**300 West Main Street**
**White Sulphur Springs, West Virginia 24986**
**(304) 536-1110, (800) 453-4858**
**www.greenbrier.com**

# THE GROVE PARK INN RESORT AND SPA

Asheville, North Carolina

---

The scenery and climate of the Blue Ridge Mountains have long attracted visitors to Asheville. The Grove Park Inn, located on the western slope of Sunset Mountain, opened its doors to guests in 1913 and gives a feeling of pure country in the midst of the city, with grand vistas of mountains and green golf courses. Built of granite from the nearby Sunset Mountain and dedicated to preserving a gracious early-twentieth-century atmosphere, the inn was added to the National Register of Historic Places in 1973. Its guest list over the years reads somewhat like a who's who: Thomas Edison, Henry Ford, Woodrow Wilson, Enrico Caruso, Béla Bartók, and President and Mrs. Franklin Roosevelt. History buffs will have a fine time wondering which room General Pershing slept in or if F. Scott Fitzgerald sat by the fireplace in the Great Hall sipping an after-dinner brandy. The Great Hall certainly deserves its name, with ceilings that soar 24 feet upward and two amazing 14-foot stone fireplaces whose chimneys hide a secret—elevators to guest rooms! Carved into wall stones scattered throughout the lobby are inspiring sayings by notable authors.

The resort's country club (originally the Swannanoa Hunt Club, which began in 1893) and the inn were renovated in the late 1980s, when two wings, which complement the architectural style and materials of the main building, were added. The Spa was built in 1998, the same year that more renovations were completed. The four-diamond, three-star Grove Park Inn is open year-round and, as William Jennings Bryan declared in 1913, "has been built for the ages."

**Accommodations:** Both the historic main inn and the wings house 510 guest rooms, all refurbished within 2003–2005; those offering panoramic mountain views enchant many a guest. There are theme suites and an exclusive club floor if your entourage warrants the space or additional amenities.

In the historic inn rooms, a small refrigerator keeps children's drinks and snacks chilled and close at hand. Panorama Corner rooms are more spacious, with superb views, and are ideal for families. Daily rates range from $310 to $395 for a double room; a one-bedroom suite is $625 to $1,250. Value season is January through March, while June through October is peak season, with the highest rates. Rates are EP. Various packages are also available. Children under sixteen stay free in their parents' room; cribs and rollaway beds are available at no cost. Again, check for packages and free-night offers.

**Dining:** A full range of refreshments, from snacks and sandwiches to full-course meals, is offered. Enjoy breakfast, lunch, and dinner in the glass-enclosed terrace of the Blue Ridge Dining Room. Casual attire can be worn during the day, but collared shirts and long pants are requested in the evening. One of the South's most famous and popular outdoor dining verandas, the Sunset Terrace offers majestic views and sunsets over the city skyline and mountains, serving prime rib and fresh seafood for lunch and dinner; in the evening dinner music and dancing are added. In the winter months, it simply moves inside, still with lovely views. Enjoy a casual lunch by the waterfall at the Spa Cafe or at the Pool Cabana, adjacent to the golf course and outdoor pool at the Country Club. Sample the award-winning gourmet cuisine at Horizons, a four-diamond-rated restaurant; jackets are required. In the evening you can enjoy your favorite beverage in the old-world charm of the Great Hall Bar, stop by Elaine's Piano Bar for lively dueling pianos and drinks, or sink into the soft couches and clublike setting of the Magnolia Lounge for cocktails and a delicious bite, along with spectacular mountain views.

**Children's World:** Monday through Friday from Memorial Day through Labor Day, and on Saturdays the rest of the year, the inn organizes children ages three to twelve in Cubs Adventure Camp, a fully supervised program. Usual activities include theme days, swimming, nature hikes, and arts and crafts. Full-day sessions are from 9:00 a.m. to 4:00 p.m., for ages six and up; the cost is $55 and includes lunch. For ages three to six, half-day sessions are available from 9:00 a.m. to 1:00 p.m. (including lunch, $40) or 1:00 to 4:00 p.m. ($35). Discounts for the second child are $10 full day/$5 half day.

"Kid's Night Out" provides a "night out" for kids and parents alike from 6:00 to 10:00 p.m. on Monday through Thursday during summer. Available Fridays and Saturdays year-round, activities include dinner, night swimming (there's an indoor pool), organized games, face-painting, campfires, and movies for $35. If you prefer, the concierge desk will provide a list of individual babysitters, with varying fees.

**Recreation:** An eighteen-hole Donald Ross championship golf course meanders down the gentle mountain slope. Practice your backhand on one of the six tennis courts (three outdoor, three indoor). The staff in the tennis and golf pro shops can assist you with your playing and fashion needs. Awards include being rated as Tennis Resorts Online's "Top 25 Tennis Resorts in the World," and one of "America's Best Resort Courses" in 2007 by *Golfweek.* In summer, half-hour tennis clinics for ages four to seven are scheduled Monday through Thursday. Junior Tennis Camps take place every Friday from 9:00 a.m. to 2:00 p.m. Inquire for exact times, reservations, and cost. An indoor Sports Complex has racquetball and tennis courts, weight and exercise rooms, and a fully equipped aerobics room with professionally taught classes. Indoor and outdoor pools are also available for hotel guests. And remember to make time for a walk down the garden paths and nature trails, also suitable when the urge to jog hits you. The Grove Park Inn was created as an idyllic retreat, a place for total relaxation; that lofty goal is enhanced by the Spa. Beautifully designed, it is open to the sun, yet protected, while waterfalls and pools add to the serenity. Allow yourself to just stop—and enjoy. Access is complimentary with a treatment; otherwise it is $55/day, $65 on weekends.

Nearby you can explore the lake or try your hand at fishing, horseback riding, cycling, mountain biking, white-water rafting, ballooning, or llama trekking. In the winter a day of skiing (cross-country or downhill) is a popular excursion. For souvenirs, you'll discover unique items at the resort's six gift shops as well as many crafts shops and potteries in the area. The Biltmore Estate is only 8 miles from the inn; an afternoon can be well spent discovering the art, antiques, winery, and formal gardens of this magnificent old estate. Strolling the streets and shops of Asheville provides hours of diversion.

---

**290 Macon Avenue**
**Asheville, North Carolina 28804**
**(828) 252-2711, (800) 438-5800**
**www.groveparkinn.com**

# HIGH HAMPTON INN & COUNTRY CLUB
### Cashiers, North Carolina

The verdant Blue Ridge Mountains provide a beautiful setting, and High Hampton Inn, located in the Cashiers Valley at an altitude of 3,600 feet, allows its guests an escape to clean, crisp air, clear mountain lakes, and tall pine trees. Some people like the ambience of a country inn—quiet, friendly, with rustic accommodations and good home-style cooking. Others like the atmosphere of a resort, with lots of activities and events and busy days and nights. Happily, High Hampton has managed to blend the best of both these worlds. Roam over the 1,400 acres and explore the beauties of nature in the southwest corner of North Carolina. Dating from the mid-nineteenth century, High Hampton was once the summer home of Confederate General Wade Hampton and remained in the Hampton family until the 1920s. The inn is on the National Register of Historic Places.

For more than eighty years, under the continuing ownership of the McKee family, the inn has welcomed guests to an informal atmosphere for golf, tennis, swimming, fishing, and simple relaxing. The architecture of the inn is charming and rustic, blending with the natural surroundings. The wide porches filled with plants and the lobby's stone chimney with four fireplaces hint at the warmth and friendly spirit within. The inn is in full swing from mid-April to mid-November, with a famous Thanksgiving Houseparty to close the season. For the first time, select winter packages (room and welcome basket) are available from November through April. No meals or activities are offered, as the inn remains closed.

**Accommodations:** The 117 rooms (some of which are suites) are simple, warm, and rustic; the knotty pine walls and mountain-style furniture echo the landscape and the crafts of the region. Many of the rooms have very pleasant views of the grounds, and there are no telephones or televisions in the rooms. What a way to relax! Several cottages are nestled into the mountain landscape. Rooms are divided into four categories, depending on size and location. Based on double occupancy, the per-room, per-night premium rates from mid-June to mid-August are $273 to $304, including Full American Plan. Children under four stay free; the rate for ages four to twelve is $42 and for ages thirteen and up is $71. Two- or three-night minimum stays are required during certain periods, especially fall. Cribs are available for infants and toddlers at no charge. A number of privately owned homes are also available; these are fully equipped, with fireplace, deck, laundry, and kitchen. Choose from two to four bedrooms with no meals, but with daily maid service, for $290 to $514 a day. If you choose not to cook, a la carte meals are available.

**Dining:** The one dining room at the inn specializes in regional Southern cooking, and service is buffet style. Imagine down-home favorites like country ham, fresh local trout, cream of peanut soup, homemade biscuits, and vegetables fresh from the garden. The Overlook Cafe, next to the Pro Shop, serves light lunches, continental breakfast for early birds, and everyone's favorite—ice cream and sweets. Coats and ties are standard attire for men in the evening, as High Hampton clings to traditional ways. Afternoon tea is served daily in the lobby with cakes and socializing.

Wine and beer only are served in the dining room, but mixed drinks are served at the Rock Mountain Tavern, a popular spot to gather, listen to music, meet other guests, and line up partners for bridge or tennis; coat and tie are required after 6:30 p.m.

**Children's World:** Kids have their own building at High Hampton, called Noah's Ark, where youngsters ages three to twelve meet with counselors for daily activities such as arts and crafts, games, tennis, nature studies, and hiking. Offered from June 1 through Labor Day, the program runs from 9:00 a.m. to 2:00 p.m. and includes lunch. After a free afternoon children can rejoin their group at 6:00 p.m. for dinner (sometimes a hayride and cookout!) and games, movies, and stories until 9:00 p.m. The fee is $4 an hour per child. Babysitters are available for wee ones and for nights after 9:00 p.m.

While there's no swimming pool, a restricted, shallow area of the lake with a sandy beach is especially designed for young children. The area includes a toddlers' play-house, swings, seesaw, and jungle gym, keeping the little ones amused for hours.

Rather than a teen club, High Hampton has the Gathering Place. Here, the next generation can gather to socialize and enjoy the pool table, table tennis, and video games. Outdoor activities such as volleyball, boating excursions, and picnics or mountain hikes are planned and enjoyed by all.

**Recreation:** The mountain terrain and picturesque scenery make golf a challenge and a pleasure. The eighteen-hole course, designed by George Cobb, is carved on a gently rolling plateau, skirting lakes and weaving through white pine and hemlock. There are two putting greens and a practice range; lessons are available.

The tennis center encompasses six outdoor clay courts, a pro shop, and a practice area; clinics and private lessons are offered. Hampton Health Club is the new workout space for weights, cardiovascular, yoga, and core training. It's also the place to relax with a lovely massage or facial.

There are three mountain lakes, but the thirty-five-acre Hampton Lake is the center of activity, where paddleboats, canoes, rowboats, and sailboats can be rented. Blissfully, motorboats are not allowed. These clear waters are not just for invigorating swims and peaceful excursions. When the fishing mood strikes, you'll be happy to know that one of the lakes has rainbow and brook trout; bass and bream can also be lured from the waters.

Discover the rich natural beauty of these surroundings on one of the eight major hiking trails. Or take to the mountain trails—in one and a half hours, you can climb to the 4,618-foot summit of Chimney Rock for absolutely spectacular views. Take the ten-station Fitness Trail to the base of Rock Mountain. Weekly guided half-day hikes with picnic lunch and walking sticks provide yet another diversion. In a more leisurely manner, lawn sports such as badminton, croquet, shuffleboard, and archery may attract you, or maybe you'll be drawn to the gardens for a stroll among the dahlias, mountain laurel, rhododendron, and azaleas. Movies, lobby games, bridge, and mountain hayrides fill the evening. Small groups of guests may gather on porches to compare notes, sip their own drinks, and talk about the day.

The inn occasionally holds workshops in such diverse areas as bridge, fly fishing, quilting, watercolor painting, and investments—what a pleasant way to glean helpful hints on a variety of topics! While proud of its facilities, the High Hampton Inn mostly boasts of its friendly atmosphere, its low-key pace, and the serenity and beauty of its natural setting. It is also proud that High Hampton "is not for everyone." But those who stay return year after year, and their children bring their own children. It's that kind of place.

**P.O. Box 338, 1525 Highway 107 South Cashiers, North Carolina 28717 (828) 743-2411, (800) 334-2551 www.highhamptoninn.com**

# THE HOMESTEAD
## Hot Springs, Virginia

Few classic institutions in the United States have captured the attention of vacationers for many centuries. With all its charm and grace, The Homestead ranks as one of these. Its fascinating history has roots in the 1700s, and yes, George Washington visited here (1755 and 1756), yet The Homestead has moved into this century with style, preserving an atmosphere of friendly Southern elegance. As with several fine old resorts in this country, the medicinal quality of mineral springs first attracted people to the site of The Homestead. In fact, the real history dates back to 7000 B.C. when prehistoric peoples began using the famous springs. While The Spa is still a captivating diversion for guests, many recreational facilities have been developed over the years, with golf being the premier sport here.

The current hotel was built in 1902, with additions continuing into the late 1920s. Despite almost three decades of construction, The Homestead is a cohesive, majestic structure of red brick and white columns in Georgian style. At an elevation of 2,300 feet, the estate sprawls over

15,000 acres (yes—15,000!) of the Allegheny Mountains in western Virginia. It is open year-round.

**Accommodations:** The Homestead boasts 486 bright and spacious rooms, all recently renovated. Almost every room offers views of the surrounding Allegheny Mountains. Each wing of this National Historic Monument has its own theme. Sizes vary from traditional rooms to parlor rooms and suites; the rate is determined by the size of the room and its location. Based on a Modified American Plan, the rate for a superior double room from May through July and September through October is $538 to $568 per person per day; weekend rates are the highest. The rates are slightly lower November through March and August ($330 to $410), except during the holiday seasons. There is no charge for children under five and no additional charge for cribs and rollaways. Children ages five to twelve pay $20 each for meals and ages thirteen and over pay $85. The Modified American Plan rates include the room, breakfast and dinner daily, valet parking, swimming, afternoon tea, evening movies, hiking trails, and the fitness center. Separate fees are charged for all other activities, and family packages are available.

**Dining:** Dining at The Homestead is special. Imagine baked apples and kippered herring for breakfast; consider lunches and dinners that feature local favorites such as Smithfield ham, rainbow trout from nearby mountain streams, and fresh turnip greens, as well as fine international cuisine. The sublime creations of pastries, sorbets, and fresh fruit tarts should not be missed.

The Dining Room is open year-round and requests jackets and ties for gentlemen in the evenings. During the April through October season, the 1766 Grille features fine dinner dining with French and American cuisine in an intimate atmosphere.

Jackets are required, and a $25 per person surcharge applies. Four miles south of The Homestead, the seasonal Rubino's at the Cascades Restaurant offers a casual lunch dining atmosphere for golfers just finishing their round. The Casino Club Restaurant, also seasonal, features a hearty lunch menu in a casual setting overlooking the swimming pool, tennis courts, and lawn game area. During the summer the Casino is also open on Friday and Saturday evenings for dinner. Sam Snead's Tavern serves history along with tavern favorites for lunch or dinner. Located across the street from the resort in a late-nineteenth-century building, it provides a bit of local color. In winter the Mountain Lodge Restaurant is a cozy getaway for skiers and nonskiers alike. Choose the elegant Presidents Lounge for pre- and post-dinner cocktails or The Players Pub for tuning in to all the sports action, darts, billiards, and dancing to Top 40 music while drinks and snacks are served continually. Or do both!

Picnic lunches can also be prepared if you choose to spend the day outdoors in the wooded mountains.

A time-honored custom at The Homestead is afternoon tea, served daily at 4:00 p.m. in the Great Hall. In an elegant setting graced by chandeliers and Corinthian columns, you can relax to soft piano music while sipping tea.

**Children's World:** Headquartered in their own Clubhouse on Cottage Row, The Homestead offers excellent daily year-round supervised activities for ages three to twelve. The Kids Club runs from 9:00 a.m. to 4:00 p.m. daily (only to 12:30 p.m. on winter Sundays); it is licensed through the Commonwealth of Virginia Department of Social Services and is a member of the National Association of the Education for Young Children and the Virginia Fine Arts Museum. "Learning through Fun" is the program's goal—kids love the "fun" aspect of the program, and parents (and kids!) like the "learning" part. Activities follow three areas: children's literary and storytelling, science and biology, and art and design. These themes weave through both indoor and outdoor activities and provide a seamless experience for kids.

The outdoor playground has been completely renovated, and children have their own fishing pond—great for kids of all ages. Other activities, even if children choose not to join Kids Club, include tennis on special minicourts, bowling, swimming, hiking, mountain biking, hand-led horseback rides, and exotic falconry demonstrations. In the winter, kids learn to ski at the Bunny School, and enjoy winter sports such as ice-skating, snowboarding, and snow tubing. Costs are $60 for a full day ($40 for additional children in the same family); $40 for a half day with lunch. On Saturday evenings Kids Night Out is held from 6:30 to 10:30 p.m.; the cost is $40 per child. Babysitting requires a two-hour minimum and is $12 an hour for the first child and $2 for each additional child in the immediate family.

**Recreation:** Even golf and tennis have hundred-year-old histories at The Homestead. There are three eighteen-hole golf courses, and the fact that native son Sam Snead started his golfing career here adds a certain panache to the atmosphere and lends credence to the caliber of play. The Old Course was opened in 1892 and revamped in the 1920s when a second course, the Cascades, was added. Robert Trent Jones designed the third course, the Lower Cascades, which opened in 1963. All three courses weave through a picturesque wooded landscape. With a putting green, a practice fairway, a pro shop, and lessons available, you have all the necessary ingredients to improve your game.

Tennis also got under way here in 1892. Today The Homestead has six courts, including two Har-Tru courts and four clay courts. Two tiers of courts are laid out to give your game privacy plus a spectacular view of The Homestead tower and the mountain valley. Tennis lessons can be scheduled, and the tennis shop is well equipped.

The facilities at The Spa include massage, aromatherapy, mineral baths, skin therapies, aerobics classes, and indoor and outdoor swimming pools. The beautiful indoor pool, built in 1903, is fed by the naturally warm mineral water of the nearby hot springs. There may be no proven miraculous powers in the famous mineral waters, but the benefits of a spa regimen to both body and spirit are not to be questioned.

For fans of trap and skeet, there are four fields; instruction is offered so that even novices can try this sport. Other outdoor sports include horseback riding in the wooded countryside, canoeing and kayaking, trout and fly fishing in the Cascades Stream, and hiking or biking on the 100 miles of mountain trails. A guided hike through the Cascades Gorge is very popular. Or you may prefer to enjoy the scenery during a carriage ride in an old-fashioned buckboard or a surrey with fringe. The tractor-driven hayride to a secluded bonfire is a great family activity.

Other interesting activities are paintball games for ages twelve and up, on a special course; mountain boarding; touring the unique caves in the area; a challenge course (see how much you trust your family members!); and falconry, with a history stretching back nearly 4,000 years. Lessons are available, and you even get a photograph with the hunting bird. Or opt for bowling, table tennis, billiards, or card and board games. In the evenings go dancing or take in a movie.

Winter sports are limited, but The Homestead does have ten downhill ski runs, open mid-December through March. With a vertical drop of just 700 feet, it cannot offer the diversity and challenge that a good skier or snowboarder seeks, but it may be a fun place for kids to learn, and it does provide an added dimension to a winter vacation. A ski school and bunny school get you started. Near the lodge, which houses a restaurant, the ski school, and ski shops, is an Olympic-size skating rink; skating lessons are offered. A snowboard park, with half-pipe, jumps, and moguls as well as tubing, offers more fun in the snow. Cross-country skiers can explore acres of mountain meadows and trails, weather permitting, of course.

Nearby explore Monticello, home of Thomas Jefferson, and Montpelier, home of James Madison. George Washington and Thomas Jefferson National Forests are also in the area.

---

**1766 Homestead Drive**
**Hot Springs, Virginia 24445**
**(540) 839-1766, (800) 838-1766**
**www.thehomestead.com**

# HYATT REGENCY CHESAPEAKE BAY

## Cambridge, Maryland

---

Hyatt's Golf Resort, Spa, and Marina fit beautifully on the Choptank River on Maryland's eastern shore. This is the perfect spot for visiting wildlife refuges with two nearby, and the Heron Point Wildlife Refuge on the resort property. Cambridge is Maryland's second-largest deepwater port, and 1,700 miles of shoreline wind around the area. It's only an hour from urban Baltimore, but the 342 landscaped acres and the river make it feel like the country.

**Accommodations:** Four hundred luxurious rooms, including sixteen suites, are available, all with balcony or patio area and minirefrigerators, and the style and amenities one expects from Hyatt. Winter is low season, when rates begin at $199. In summer, rates begin at $279 to $329. Packages are an excellent value; for example, the mid-week family special is $249 per night (two-night minimum) and includes breakfast for the adults, discounted golf, and a $50 activity credit. The Family Plan offers the second room at half price, year-round. Children under eighteen stay free in the room. When you reserve, you may request a pack-and-play crib. A $12 per day resort fee covers most activities, including tennis, miniature golf, and driving range.

**Dining:** Feasting on the local specialties is practically a requirement of your visit. Soft-shell crab, Maryland blue crab, Blue Pointe oysters, and rockfish are popular menu items, creatively prepared and presented. At Water's Edge Grill, enjoy breakfast, lunch, and dinner while watching it happen at the display kitchen. Outdoor dining may be enjoyed seasonally on the screened porch overlooking the crescent pool. At the far end of the resort overlooking the marina, sunsets and seafood specialties are equally famous at Blue Pointe Provision, a freestanding restaurant almost on the banks of the Choptank River. The Eagle's

Nest Bar and Grille, also on River Marsh Marina, is by the Golf Club, with scenic views of the greens. It's perfect for sandwiches, wraps, and salads as well as nineteenth-hole libations. Dock's poolside bar personally serves you refreshments at any of the four pools, the beach, or even the hot tub. Stock up on snacks and provisions at either the Bay Country Market or the Quarterdeck Marina Store. Mitchener's Library, in the lobby, would do the famous author of *Chesapeake* proud. Stone fireplaces border a two-story glass wall with spectacular views, and outside benches invite you to tarry amid fountains or warm yourself at the fire pit. Little nooks, named after people connected to Cambridge history, like Harriet Tubman, King Ababaco, and Annie Oakley, provide cozy spots for reading, billiards, or just curling up next to the fireplace.

**Children's World:** Camp Hyatt at Pirate's Cove offers fully supervised fun for kids ages four to twelve daily from Memorial Day to Labor Day and on holidays and weekends year-round. Kids have their own reception desk, activity room, a multimedia room, and even an enclosed outdoor playground adjacent to the center. A long list of activities includes crabbing (of course, this is Maryland!), building sand castles, treasure hunts, kite contests, tennis, golf, and nature hikes. Indoors, kids color, play board games, and participate in arts and crafts, shell art, and storytelling, just to mention a few activities. The Captain's Parlor is where you'll find table tennis, air hockey, foosball, and, more than likely, the kids. The split-level pool is always an attraction, and is partially indoors for inclement weather. A full day with lunch, from 9:00 a.m. to 4:00 p.m., is $75; half-day morning or afternoon is $40 per child. Evening sessions, Friday and Saturday year-round, run from 6:00 to 9:00 p.m. for $50 per child, so parents are able to have their own "night out." Sessions include dinner and are scheduled more often in summer. In addition to Camp Hyatt, Recreation plans activities hour by hour during the day for families to share fun experiences. Contests, crafts, and games, most complimentary, create memories to treasure.

**Recreation:** The Golf Club at River Marsh, an eighteen-hole championship course designed by Keith Foster, has an elaborate driving range, chipping and putting greens, and a pro shop. Don't know where to park your boat? The 150-slip marina should solve that problem. Don't have your own boat? Rent one from Chesapeake Outdoor Adventures and enjoy sailing, kayaking, paddleboats, or Hobie Cats. Relax by any of the four pools, both indoors or outdoors and on several levels. The Winter Garden pool is glass-enclosed, providing year-round enjoyment and views of the river. The volleyball court on the beach is fenced, so you don't have to chase those missed balls too far. The Stillwater European Health Spa offers thirteen treatment rooms with unique indigenous spa treatments, and you can get or stay in shape at the fitness and aerobics center. Four lighted tennis courts also give a good workout, and jogging and walking trails wend through the eighteen-acre Blue Heron Rookery, where you might see an American bald eagle or a blue heron. Nearby visit Taylor's Island Wildlife Refuge, Blackwater Wildlife Refuge, or the Harriet Tubman Museum for a bit of local history. If you have the time and inclination, you can enjoy all sorts of off-site activities coordinated by private companies: hiking, hunting, clay pigeons, fishing, crabbing charters, canoe and kayak tours, and even skydiving.

---

**100 Heron Boulevard
Cambridge, Maryland 21613
(410) 901-1234, (800) 233-1234
www.chesapeakebay.hyatt.com**

# KIAWAH ISLAND GOLF RESORT

Kiawah Island, South Carolina

In climate and scenery, the islands off the coast of the Carolinas offer some of the finest resort living. Set amid 10,000 acres, just 21 miles from Charleston, Kiawah Island Resorts offers the beauty of a natural setting that has been carefully respected, while man-made amenities have been added to provide visitors with the best in comfort, relaxation, recreation, and fun. The name Kiawah (KEE-a-wah) comes from the Indians who lived, hunted, and fished here prior to the 1600s when Charles Town (present-day Charleston) was settled. A barrier island with 10 miles of beach on the Atlantic Ocean, Kiawah is actually two resort villages, each with its own lodging and recreational facilities, and Night Heron Park, a twenty-one-acre recreation area that encompasses pools, a lake, playgrounds, and picnic sites. With the recent addition of an ultra-luxurious, oceanfront hotel, The Sanctuary, Kiawah is a truly unique getaway. The Sanctuary has achieved the coveted AAA·five-diamond award, was rated by *Travel + Leisure Family* as the Top Family Resort in the East/Southeast and ninth in the country, and has been listed among the Top 10 North American Resorts by *Condé Nast Traveler*—and this is in addition to countless golf and tennis resort awards.

All these conveniences and amenities, and yet you still have the opportunity to feel close to nature. The sound ecological planning at Kiawah preserves the lagoons and marshes and ensures homes for deer, raccoon, egrets, and brown pelicans; you might even get to see a loggerhead sea turtle, alligators, dolphins, or an eagle. As you enter the main gates to Kiawah, you're given a car registration pass that reads "Please respect the wildlife that inhabits Kiawah Island.

Alligators are potentially dangerous and extremely fast. They should never be fed or teased in any way." When you see alligators plying the lagoon waters, you'll understand this warning!

**Accommodations:** The Sanctuary (877-683-1234) is Kiawah's gem, a most luxurious oceanfront hotel with 255 rooms and suites, two elegant restaurants, and a nature-based spa. The hotel was built to resemble a Southern mansion; the lobby boasts walnut floors and Italian crystal chandeliers; live oaks dripping Spanish moss have been imported to frame the driveway. The staff is marvelously attentive, and rooms are spacious (520 to 560 square feet), with multiple amenities, such as balconies, marble baths, and custom bedding. Winter rates begin at $275 for scenic view, $400 for oceanfront; in summer those same room types start at $520 to $710. Club-level accommodations include more amenities; summer rates range from $650 to $940. There is no extra charge for up to five people of any age in the room.

If high-rise is not your style, choose from 600 villas or private homes. Cedar-shingled or natural-wood frame condominium villas are dispersed throughout the island in different settings appealing to all different interests. These may have an ocean view or be next door to the tennis courts, alongside the lush green fairways of a golf course, on a lake, or nestled among oaks and hickories and sweet gum trees. These one- to four-bedroom units have well-equipped kitchens, and most of them have sundecks or screened porches—terrific spots for having breakfast or just taking in the views. Villas have AAA four-diamond ratings. One- to seven-bedroom luxury homes are also available.

Rates vary depending on location and which of the eight seasons you choose. As an example, weekly rates for a one-bedroom villa·in winter are $625 to $1,035; in summer the range is $1,091 to $1,705. Daily rates are also available, and cribs are $20 per day or $100 per week. Guests renting villas and homes directly from Kiawah Island Golf Resort (800-576-1570) enjoy preferred access and pricing for all island amenities.

**Dining:** Shrimper's, in West Beach, is a casual dining spot that caters to families; it's open for lunch and dinner and features seafood and sandwiches. Nearby is Scooper's, where the ice cream and pastries are hard to resist (who can pass up an ice-cream flavor called Mississippi Mud?). The Market at Town Center, a casual market, is located in East Beach, offering a variety of quick meals, grocery items, newspapers, apparel, wine, and even take-out pizza.

On Monday evenings, families head to Mingo Point on the Kiawah River for an outdoor barbecue and oyster roast, followed by the down-home music of a bluegrass band. Another favorite is the Thursday Safari Night at Night Heron Park.

The four clubhouses are home to excellent restaurants as well. The Ocean Course Grille, Osprey Point Grill, and Haulover Creek Bar and Grill at Oakpoint serve breakfast and lunch; Turtle Point Sports Bar and Grill is also open for dinner. Salads, seafood, and sandwiches are to be found until 8:00 p.m. poolside at the Night Heron Grill, weather permitting.

The Sanctuary features signature dining in the Ocean Room, with spectacular views; it is open for dinner only, and jackets are required. The Jasmine Porch gives you a Southern experience of fresh local ingredients and traditional Low-Country favorites; it serves breakfast, lunch, and dinner in a casual atmosphere with terrace dining an

option. The Loggerhead Grill, steps away from the beach, and Beaches and Cream keep you from starvation while playing in the ocean waves or pool. The Morning Room serves afternoon tea (go figure!), and the Lobby Bar and the Bar at the Ocean Room invite you to relaxing drinks and live music in the evening.

Freshfields Village, outside the main gate of Kiawah at the crossroads of Kiawah, Seabrook, and Johns Islands, features a Main Street–like collection of more than twenty unique stores and services—from restaurants and a coffee shop to clothing boutiques, a gallery, a bookshop, a general store, a pharmacy, and more. Stop at Newton Farms, a full-service market, or try Hege's for cocktails and French-inspired cuisine made with local fresh ingredients.

**Children's World:** From early March through Labor Day and at Thanksgiving, Christmas, President's Day, and Easter, children and parents alike find Kiawah Island the perfect destination for a family vacation.

Energetic college students with training in sports and recreation supervise young visitors in activities designed to ensure happy, fun-filled days. In fact, there's much more to do than we have room to outline, so check the Web site for all the details and themed days such as circus, pirates, safari, icky sticky slimy, and more. Kamp Kiawah in the spring season runs Monday through Saturday in March, April, and May, and accepts ages three to eleven. Hours are 8:30 a.m. to 12:30 p.m. for $47, including lunch. As the day lengthens, so does camp. From Memorial Day through Labor Day, and during Easter/spring break week, Kamp Kiawah operates Monday through Friday all day. Half-day sessions are from 8:30 a.m. to 12:30 p.m. ($42) and 1:00 to 4:00 p.m. ($37); the full-day session ($62) includes lunch. Divided into three groups—three to four years, five to seven years, and eight to eleven years—kids enjoy swimming, treasure hunts, crabbing, storytime, and crafts.

Designed for children ages five to eleven, Kids Night Out is the perfect solution when grown-ups want to enjoy a night out themselves. On Monday and Friday evenings from March to September, kids enjoy dinner and supervised activities. The cost is $42, including dinner. During spring break week and summer, the hours are 6:00 to 9:00 p.m.; during other times of the year, the hours are 5:00 to 8:00 p.m.

Youth activities designed for ages nine to twelve are scheduled at various times; arts and crafts projects, capture the flag, bingo, three-on-three basketball, paint tag, scavenger hunts, and more occupy youngsters for an hour or two, and range from free to $10 in cost.

Kiawah has found that successful blend of teens' favorite things—sports, music, food, and loose structure. Similar to the youth activities, most are complimentary; additional activities include kayaking ($30), Survivor Night, black-light volleyball, pool parties, socials, dances, and cinema.

Children also enjoy the playgrounds filled with wooden climbing equipment, swings, and slides; the largest one at Night Heron Park is built in and among the trees, hardly disturbing the natural vegetation. The Night Heron Park Center features video games, live animals, and nature wear and gear, as well as a recreation concierge.

When you want to be together and join other families, afternoon and evening hours are filled with bingo, games, nature films, family movies, and cookouts; most of these activities are free. Particularly fun is the "dive-in movie"—movies shown at the pool, with swimming allowed. Babysitters are available.

**Recreation:** With five championship eighteen-hole championship golf courses and a twelve-month golfing season, golfers

think they've discovered a little bit of paradise at Kiawah. Host site of numerous and prestigious tournaments, the Ocean Course, designed by Pete Dye, is known worldwide. The Cougar Point Golf Course was designed by Gary Player, the Turtle Point Golf Course by Jack Nicklaus, the Osprey Point Golf Course by Tom Fazio, and Oak Point by Clyde Johnston; talent like this ensures challenge in a beautiful natural setting. You can enroll in group or private lessons or in a clinic and then practice newly acquired skills on the driving ranges and putting greens. The pro shops are well stocked with equipment, apparel, and accessories to enhance your game.

For tennis enthusiasts, the West Beach Tennis Club offers sixteen courts; the East Beach Tennis Club has twelve courts and a ball machine. Combined, Kiawah boasts twenty-three clay courts and five hard courts. Add a practice alley, resident pros, clinics, and group and private lessons and you have every opportunity to improve your game. Kiawah has been ranked number one on the "50 Greatest U.S. Tennis Resorts" list by *Tennis* magazine.

Swimmers take to the ocean from April through October or dip into one of the two pools located in Night Heron Park and East Beach Tennis Club. You can sign up for swimming lessons for yourself or your child (even an infant). The pool complex at The Sanctuary is for hotel guests only. Other water sports, such as sailing, canoeing, and sailboarding, are also popular. The Spa at The Sanctuary is a destination in itself. Designed with plants and trickling water, it brings to mind the tranquillity of a grand Southern porch and garden; treatment themes borrow from the ocean, maritime forests, and botanical gardens. It is sheer luxury and all for your pleasure.

Bicyclists have more than 10 miles of hard-packed beach and 30 miles of paved trails to explore (rentals, many with baby seats, are available). Joggers find a good workout on the 1.1-mile parcourse fitness trail with twenty exercise stations. Try your luck fishing in the lake or creek and surf casting in the ocean, or introduce your child to the fun of crabbing, where an old chicken neck can net beautiful blue-legged crabs. Adult exercise classes (aerobics and water exercise) are offered weekdays during the summer.

Special nature programs with a staff naturalist allow children, teens, and even adults to have a hands-on, fun experience with nature. Ocean seining with a huge 40-foot net, canoe trips through the marshes, pond exploration, night walks on the beach, bird watching—with more than 10,000 acres of marshland and five staff naturalists, the possibilities go on and on. Costs range from $3 to $15. The Discovery Room at The Sanctuary is an interactive environment that encourages children and adults to explore. Daily themes are enhanced by books, crafts, computer tracks, and even tours; and an on-duty naturalist answers all your questions.

Discovery Series, a free weekly program, features speakers accompanied by live snakes or alligators, fascinating historical tidbits, storytellers, and more.

Nature lovers can participate in numerous expeditions into wilderness areas and river tours for a close look at the Low-Country wildlife and vegetation and an education on barrier islands. The Nature Excursion Programs are unique to a barrier island, and more extensive than most resorts. Naturalists conduct marsh creek canoe trips, sea kayaking, birding walks, night beach walks, loggerhead turtle crawls, and even bird tours on bikes.

For unstructured fun, the twenty-one-acre Night Heron Park features basketball courts, a soccer field, swimming pools, a pavilion area, and a bicycle rental shop. Night Heron Park also serves as a popular gathering spot for special events, such as symphony concerts, family park cookouts, and beach music parties.

More than fifteen family activities are scheduled; crafts involve a small fee, but others like sand sculpting, poolside games, bingo, and basketball are free. If shopping entices you, the Shops at Kiawah Island and the Town Center at East Beach Village beckon. And nearby Charleston can charm you with historic houses and antiques shopping. With all it places at your disposal, Kiawah may tempt you back for many return visits.

---

**1 Sanctuary Beach Drive**
**Kiawah Island, South Carolina 29455**
**(843) 768-2121, (800) 654-2924**
**www.kiawahresort.com**

# KINGSMILL RESORT
## Williamsburg, Virginia

In 1736 Richard Kingsmill was granted land along the James River near the new town of Williamsburg, Virginia. Centuries later, much remains the same—deer and waterfowl still live in the unspoiled forest, some of the original plantation buildings still exist near prehistoric Native American sites, and nearby Colonial Williamsburg remains as a unique example of eighteenth-century America. Some things, however, have changed. Developed by Anheuser-Busch Companies, the Kingsmill of today shares its natural beauty and sense of history with both a modern-day resort and a separate thriving community of 5,000 people. The 3,900-acre site was originally selected for a new brewery, and part of the agreement was the construction of a theme park, Busch Gardens. Development has been well planned, and none of this impinges on the resort itself.

Environmental awareness is also a priority as 40 percent of the area remains green space, and future expansion of one area currently depends on a bald eagle nesting in the treetops of fifty-two prime acres near the river, which Kingsmill is preserving. No wonder it has the Audubon International Certification!

**Accommodations:** Kingsmill offers 435 accommodations, including hotel rooms and one- to three-bedroom villa suites. Organized into villa-style clusters around the Resort Center, all are within walking distance of resort facilities. Each suite contains a complete kitchen and living room; many feature fireplace and balcony. Guestroom rates begin at $129 in winter (December, January, February); $229 to $299 March through November. Weekend rates are slightly higher. One-bedroom suites range from $259 to $449; two-bedroom suites are $399 to $729. Look into a package that includes activities you'll probably do anyway. Starting at $999, Family Vacation Packages (late March through Labor Day) include three nights/four days of lodging, unlimited and VIP admissions to Busch Gardens and Water Country USA, golf and tennis discounts, and daily breakfast. The Discovery Package, available late May through Labor Day, begins at $599 and offers two nights/three days of lodging, admission to theme parks, and more sports options at the resort. Be sure to check the theme parks' opening/closing dates. Children under eighteen stay free in the room; roll-aways are not available. A shuttle operates throughout the property, as well as to the local attractions of Busch Gardens, Water Country USA, and Colonial Williamsburg.

**Dining:** Six restaurants and lounges offer a variety of styles and menus. Eagles, an authentic steak- and chophouse, features exclusive beechwood-smoked cooking and hearty meals for breakfast, lunch, and dinner, along with panoramic views of the beautifully landscaped grounds and the river. The Bray Bistro, also serving breakfast, lunch, and dinner, brings past and present together in modern American cuisine served with indigenous ingredients and generous views of the James River. The most casual venue is Regatta's Café and Market, with its open kitchen and fun foods; it also has a deli, to-go selections, and convenience items. For afternoon socializing the Marina Bar & Grille is right on the river, with outside dining and a fireplace for cool weather, a seafood bar, sandwiches, drinks, and live entertainment. Bray Landing is the spot to relax for coffee or a drink, while Moody's Tavern is the nighttime gathering place.

**Children's World:** Make your first stop the sports concierge desk for Junior Guest Registration and everything you need to know about kids at Kingsmill.

Kingsmill Kamp uses the entire resort as a playground for five- to twelve-year-olds. Beach fun, limbo, and tug-of-war at the Marina; sports of all kinds; tennis and golf (including one-half-hour instruction); carnival games; picnics; hiking; crabbing; and even building a bird feeder are some of the activities kids enjoy. Operating Monday through Saturday from mid-June to Labor

Day, programs include lunch and snacks. A full day (9:00 a.m. to 4:00 p.m.) costs $50; a half day is $30. As a special treat, Spa Kamp is ninety minutes of magic manicures, terrific toes, and mini-facials; at $40, it's sure to attract the young females of the species. For ages five to twelve, Kids Night Out is offered Thursday through Saturday in summer and on select Friday nights in spring. It starts with pizza, is filled with fun, games, and crafts, and ends on a tired but happy note at bedtime. Kids Night Out costs $40 per child and runs from 6:00 to 10:00 p.m.

During the rest of the year, supervised programs are available on Friday and Saturday if requested in advance, and if enough children participate. Special activities are planned around holiday periods.

**Recreation:** Golfers are happy with three eighteen-hole championship courses and a nine-hole par 3 course. Awards are numerous, including *Golf Magazine*'s Silver Medal, *Condé Nast*'s Top 50 Golf Resorts, and *Golf for Women*'s Top 50 Fairways. Pete Dye designed the River Course to challenge professionals but be enjoyable to the average golfer as well; it's characterized by rolling hills, thick woods, and water everywhere. The Plantation Course by Arnold Palmer and Ed Seay is a little more forgiving, but no pushover. The Woods Course, by Curtis Strange and Tom Clark, is a parkland-style course stashed in its own private corner of the resort. The Golf Academy has an extensive program of instruction with a maximum 1:5 teacher-student ratio.

Voted one of the World's Top 75 Tennis Resorts by Tennis Resorts Online, Kingsmill Tennis Club offers instruction academies, events, and packages. Fifteen courts include two lighted stadium courts, two Deco-Turf all-weather courts, and six hydro courts; court time is $8 to $16 per adult for the day.

The one-hundred-slip (fifteen are transient) Marina boasts a store, the Deck for dining, a small beach area, and the possibility of meeting visiting boat owners. The Sports Club is where you'll find the indoor and outdoor swimming pools, exercise classes, fully equipped fitness room, whirlpool, steam room and sauna, and 4-mile jogging course. Arrange a personal training session, work out, or simply play in the Game Room with billiards, table tennis, and video games. Stop by the concierge desk for the self-guided walking tour that includes all the plants and flowers. The Spa at Kingsmill is a welcoming place for massage, body treatments and wraps, facials, and even a special golfer's manicure.

And, of course, you'll need time for Busch Gardens, Water Country USA, and Colonial Williamsburg. Kingsmill runs frequent shuttles to all of these destinations. All different and all fun for families, these destinations have more information on their Web sites. And remember to search for packages that include these attractions, which may be a value for your particular family needs.

**1010 Kingsmill Road**
**Williamsburg, Virginia 23185**
**(757) 253-1703, (800) 832-5665**
**www.kingsmill.com**

# SEABROOK ISLAND CLUB

Seabrook Island, South Carolina

Sunshine and sandy beaches; lazy strolls under moss-draped oaks; palmettos waving in the breeze; enough fresh crabs, shrimp, and oysters to make your mouth water; golf, tennis, horseback riding, marina, fitness center, and water sports—is this a little bit of paradise? Visitors to this unique, private island believe so. Seabrook has the feel of a country club—no neon, no high-rises, not even any hotels! Share nature in harmony with eagles, dolphins, and bobcats, in a place where the beach is private and nothing is higher than two stories. All this is only about thirty minutes from beautiful, historic Charleston; it almost seems as though you can have your cake and eat it too. Activities and events for every member of the family support Seabrook's "something for everyone" philosophy. The resort is open year-round.

**Accommodations:** The one- to three-bedroom villas—all with fully equipped kitchens, many with sundecks or balconies—are distributed throughout the 2,200 acres of Seabrook Island property. Some are ocean-side, with expansive views of the Atlantic and close to the Beach Club; some line the scenic fairways of the golf courses; and some overlook the racquet club, marshlands, and tidal creeks. Some villa clusters have their own swimming pools. Rates depend on size, location, and time of year. During low season, December through mid-February, one-bedroom villa rates are $143 to $160. The weeks around Easter and early June through early September are high season; rates are $195 to $310. A two-bedroom villa in summer ranges from $240 to $370. A three-night minimum stay is required. Rates are for villa accommodations only; most recre-

ational activities have separate charges. Weekly rates provide a savings, as do tennis, golf, honeymoon, or getaway packages. A family recreation package during June, July, and August is a good value, with 20 percent discounts on most things, including golf.

**Dining:** Restaurants are seasonal at Seabrook, so be sure to check specifically during your stay. The Island House Restaurant is elegant and offers traditional Southern cuisine and tempting seafood specialties; jackets are preferred for men at dinner. Here you might choose a sweet-potato soufflé or prawns stuffed with crabmeat. Bohickets Lounge has a more casual atmosphere overlooking the golf course—you can watch the greens and eat them at the same time! Try the famous Seabrook Sunday Brunch at the Island House, a lavish buffet with live entertainment, and the Friday seafood buffet is a real extravaganza. All restaurants have children's menus. Pelican's Nest is the perfect spot for ocean-side lunch or light dinner. At the Beach Club, Cap'n Sam's is the choice for quick and casual lunches. A friendly atmosphere in which to sip a drink and discuss the day's events is provided at the outdoor Pelican's Nest Bar, Half Shell Lounge, and Bohickets Lounge.

**Children's World:** From Memorial Day to Labor Day, children ages four to twelve have their own daily "Koastal Kids" supervised program. Meeting from 9:00 a.m. to 4:00 p.m. in the Kids Club, supervised activities include alligator "hunting," beach walks, pony rides, crabbing adventures, swimming, treasure hunts, nature hikes, puppet shows, storytelling, and arts and crafts. The cost is $55 including lunch; a half day (9:00 a.m. to noon) is $27, including lunch. A children's playground offers lots of equipment for the younger set. Junior Olympic swim clinics and Munchkins Tennis clinics give the chance for more focused instruction. Poolside Pandemonium is for the whole family and in summer keeps everybody busy having fun. Activities last about thirty minutes, and different ones are scheduled hourly between noon and 4:00 p.m. Most are free.

Kids Night Out, daily during summer, features sunset beach walks, games, crafts, and alligator or turtle hunts for four- to twelve-year-olds. Program runs from 6:00 to 10:00 p.m.; cost is $35 and includes dinner. The Teen Center is a spot for ages thirteen to seventeen to "just hang out" with their favorite things—video games, pool, table tennis, foosball, air hockey, and socializing. Special nights are also planned for the entire family at a small cost.

The fun keeps on rolling at holiday times like Christmas, Thanksgiving, and Easter. Added to the regular activities may be Christmas caroling and a visit from Santa, The Little Pilgrims Program, or an Easter decorations crafts class and an Easter egg hunt. With all of this, normal babysitters may seem a bit of a letdown, but they are available.

**Recreation:** With average midday temperatures of sixty degrees in January and eighty-nine degrees in August, golfing's fine in the Carolinas. Seabrook has two vastly different eighteen-hole courses; Crooked Oaks was designed by Robert Trent Jones Sr. and meanders through majestic oaks and dips along the sea marshes. Ocean Winds, designed by Willard Byrd, catches some of the tricky ocean breezes that make the play challenging and interesting. A fine teaching staff can help you smooth out the rough spots of your game, and the pro shop can fill in the gaps for clothing, equipment, and accessories. Seabrook is the first golf facility in South

Carolina recognized as a certified member of the Audubon Cooperative Sanctuary Program for golf courses.

Enjoy one of fifteen clay tennis courts at the Raquet Club. The Raquet Club offers a pro shop and a staff of pros who can do wonders for your backhand in individual or group lessons, camps, and clinics.

With 3½ miles of glorious private ocean beach, you might suspect that water sports tempt many visitors here. There are sunbathing, swimming, ocean fishing, and shelling. Canter along the beach at the edge of the surf or take a leisurely ride through the forests—both are possible at Seabrook, one of the few resorts with an on-site Equestrian Center. The center offers trained instructors who can give you tips to improve your technique. Parent-led pony rides create lots of excitement in the under-eight crowd. A junior Olympic pool, a heated pool, and a wading pool for children more than accommodate both serious swimmers and sun lovers. There's fun for the whole family with Poolside Pandemonium, as well as water basketball and volleyball. With their palm trees, gardens, and lovely surroundings, the pools also charm serious loungers in for just a quick splash. Perhaps you don't want to sing for your supper, but if you want to *catch* your supper, try fishing (in the ocean or the creeks) or crabbing and shrimping in the tidal marshes. Bicycle along the island's 10 miles of roads—many rental bikes come equipped with baby seats—or join the current craze for in-line skating.

The Recreation Pavilion, open year-round, takes care of a lot of your needs (rental beach chairs, in-line skates, bikes, and fishing and crabbing equipment) and is the focus of the Family Fun Program—activities that all the family members can enjoy together, like nature walks, family games, cookouts, bingo, and water volleyball. You may even challenge your child to an evening of video games.

Within 1 mile of Seabrook's gate, stroll the Bohicket Marina for chartered deep-sea fishing, creek fishing, and three family-style restaurants and shops. For the essentials and the fun of shopping, Seabrook has several stores: the Village Market for groceries; the Seabrook Shoppe for gifts, clothing, souvenirs, and sundries; and the golf and tennis shops for the latest fashions and equipment.

Freshfields Village, outside the main gate of Kiawah at the crossroads of Kiawah, Seabrook, and Johns Islands, features a Main Street–like collection of more than twenty unique stores and services—from restaurants and a coffee shop to clothing boutiques, a gallery, a bookshop, a general store, a pharmacy, and more. Stop at Newton Farms, a full-service market, or try Hege's for cocktails and French-inspired cuisine made with local fresh ingredients.

---

**3772 Seabrook Island Road**
**Seabrook Island, South Carolina 29455**
**(843) 768-1000, (800) 341-4248**
**www.discoverseabrook.com**

# THE TIDES INN
Irvington, Virginia

In eastern Virginia, peninsulas of land reach out like fingers between the many rivers heading into the Chesapeake. It is a region steeped in history, from the early-seventeenth-century settlements of Jamestown and Yorktown to the family homestead of Robert E. Lee. Its people have always had close ties to the water, originally for commerce and travel and today for recreation.

The northernmost of these peninsulas, bounded by the Potomac River and the Rappahannock River, is known as the Northern Neck. On its southern shore, on a bluff overlooking Carter's Creek, sits the Tides Inn. The hotel is surrounded by water, and yachts literally dock in the front yard. A member of the Leading Small Hotels of the World, the Tides emphasizes uncrowded luxury and informal elegance in a leisurely atmosphere. Among other accolades the Tides Inn is ranked among the world's best 500 hotels and number 8 among the "50 Best Kid-Friendly Resorts in the U.S. and Canada" (*Travel + Leisure,* 2006), as well as one of the "Top 20 Hotels" in the United States, as identified by *Zagat*. Originally a stop for the steamboat lines between Baltimore and Norfolk in the late 1800s, the nearby small community of Irvington remains a quaint, picture-perfect town with friendly smiles for everyone.

**Accommodations:** All 106 rooms and suites are newly renovated; many have balconies or terraces, and almost all have great views of Carter's Creek. Rooms are located in the Main Building, the Garden House, the Windsor House, and the Lancaster House. Choose from deluxe rooms or premium rooms ($160 to $365), or Vista Suites ($260 to $465). Four luxury suites are also available. Children stay free in the room with parents if beds are adequate; cots are $25; cribs are complimentary. A meal plan (breakfast and dinner) is available for $99 per adult, $50 for children ages ten through fifteen, and children under ten are free per one paying adult. The high season at the Tides is May to October; the inn is closed for six weeks from January to mid-February.

**Dining:** Breakfast and dinner are served in the East Room. Breakfast is from 6:30 to 10:30 a.m., with an "early bird" continental breakfast or a "sleepyhead" breakfast later in the morning. At dinner jackets are appreciated after 5:30 p.m. Just off the main lobby, the Chesapeake Club is open from 11:00 a.m. to 11:00 p.m., serving lunch, dinner, lounge food, and cocktails. Sit inside or out and enjoy the casual setting with nightly entertainment. Creekside, Commodore's is a casual summer restaurant for enjoying lunch and sunset drinks overlooking the pool and beach; late dinners are served on weekends. Also seasonal, Cap'n B's on the Golden Eagle Golf Course is open from lunch to sunset. It's a popular spot even with nongolfers, as the 400 rolling acres with lovely lakes and unspoiled woodlands add an extra dimension of pleasure to the New Orleans–style dining. On Saturdays in summer, splurge on a dinner cruise on the Rappahannock River on the historic yacht *Miss Ann*. And finally, if it fits your schedule or your mood, room service or picnic lunches are always options.

**Children's World:** In addition to the beach and swimming pool, a grassy playground with slides, swings, climbing bars, and the Chesapeake Bay Lighthouse attract young guests. From Memorial Day to Labor Day, the Crab Net Kids children's program is in session daily from 9:30 a.m. to 3:30 p.m., with lunch at the pool and swimming twice a day. All activities are covered for $65 per child per day. Morning sessions with lunch and snack are $40; afternoon sessions with snack only are $35. Crafts and games, scavenger hunts, sand sculpting, tennis, pitch and putt golf, bicycling, boating, and, of course, crabbing keep youngsters from four to twelve years old busy. On Friday and Saturday evenings from 5:00 to 8:00 p.m., children meet as a group for dinner and evening activities, such as a "coketails and pizza party," followed by a movie; cost is $40. Babysitting is available at $10 an hour for one child with a three-hour minimum; add $1 an hour for each additional child.

**Recreation:** With water on practically all sides of the inn, boating is a natural sport here. The Premier Sailing School offers classes for all ages and experience levels. You can take off in a small craft like a sailboat, canoe, or paddleboat, or check out the yacht program and cruise the creek, the river, and the bay. The weekly routine schedules varied yachts for luncheon cruises, cove cruises, and bay-shore picnics. No additional fees are charged for use, of the paddleboats, canoes, kayaks, or some of the yacht programs. In fact, rates include almost all activities—tennis, nine-hole par 3 golf course, bicycles to explore scenic Irvington, evening music and dancing, and the fitness and health facility. Treat yourself to a classic treatment at The Calming Waters Spa.

For golfers, a nine-hole par 3 complimentary course on the main grounds is just right to brush up on your short game or enjoy a family outing. The Tides Inn's eighteen-hole Golden Eagle has been described as "magnificent," and *Golf* magazine calls it "the toughest course no one's ever heard of."

Many of the ponds along the golf courses are well stocked for the fisherman, who may also, in search of a saltwater catch, line up a trip with the dockmaster. A saltwater pool overlooks a small sandy beach, and table tennis, a pool table, video arcade, croquet, basketball, and shuffle-board are available in the activities cottage. For your evening entertainment, enjoy dancing, movies, bingo, or a pleasant stroll. The Chesapeake Club features live entertainment nightly.

For history buffs, nearby sightseeing excursions lead to Stratford Hall Plantation (the birthplace of Robert E. Lee), Wakefield (George Washington's birthplace), Christ Church, and Epping Forest, where George Washington's mother lived. Colonial Williamsburg is just an hour and fifteen minutes away and makes a nice day excursion.

---

**480 King Carter Drive**
**Irvington, Virginia 22480**
**(804) 438-5000, (800) 843-3746**
**www.tidesinn.com**

# WILD DUNES RESORT
## Isle of Palms, South Carolina

Have you ever watched a three-year-old scamper across a sandy beach to the ocean? A biker pedal down paths through the marshes? A fishing boat return to harbor after a successful day's mission? A sailboat catch the sun and the wind in one skillful motion? An ace serve zing across the net? Or a golf ball soar over the fairway and over grand oaks on its way to a perfectly manicured green? Award-winning Wild Dunes can package all of these images into quite a family vacation for you.

Wild Dunes has garnered some of the best features of the Carolina coastal islands and wrapped them up into a fine year-round resort. It is recognized by *Better Homes and Gardens* as one of thirty "Favorite Family Resorts" and one of the "Top 50 Best Family Resorts" by *Travel + Leisure Family*. This relaxed and gracious community occupies 1,600 acres of the northern tip of the Isle of Palms, just thirty minutes from historic Charleston. Bounded by the Atlantic Ocean on the east and the Intracoastal Waterway on the west, Wild Dunes delights in mild temperatures, soft ocean breezes, and fresh salt air. Relax and rejuvenate your spirits here in South Carolina's Low Country.

**Accommodations:** Wild Dunes offers AAA four-diamond accommodations with the new ninety-three-room Boardwalk Inn, located in the heart of the resort. These luxurious accommodations combine the charm and elegance of Charleston with the casual ambience of the beach. From June until mid-August, daily rates are $225 to $425; junior suites are $100 more, all based on double occupancy. A Victorian-style boardwalk leads from the inn to the villas and the Grand Pavilion with its open-air gazebo, two oceanfront pools, and 2 miles of sandy beach. The 365 one- to four-bedroom villas are grouped in two- to five-story buildings. Many are arranged along the beach, some border the tennis center, others look out on the fairways of the golf course, and still more enjoy the seclusion of the woods and marshland scenery. Inside decor ranges from dramatic, bold interiors to soft pastel furnishings that reflect nature's seaside colors; a fully equipped kitchen is standard in every unit. Cribs can be provided for infants and toddlers.

Summer rates for a one-bedroom villa range from $290 to $440; two-bedroom villas range from $340 to $515. Ask about weekly rates and special packages.

Private homes are also available. Included with all rentals are one hour of tennis court time per bedroom per day, priority golf tee times, Island Adventures (the resort's Family Recreation Program), access to the Fitness Center, Grand Pavilion, and the Sports Pavilion Swim Center, local phone calls, and on-property transportation.

**Dining:** It is not surprising that seafood is highlighted on the menus of Wild Dunes's restaurants; gumbo and she-crab soup are favorite Low-Country dishes. But beef eaters can find tasty, tender selections here too. With the opening of the Boardwalk Inn, Wild Dunes gained a luxurious restaurant. The Sea Island Grill, serving breakfast, lunch, and dinner, features the freshest seafood available, prepared in myriad ways. Guests may dine in the casually elegant dining room or alfresco on the piazza overlooking a lush tropical environment. Casual dining for breakfast, lunch, and dinner is found at Edgar's on the Links. Both restaurants have children's menus. Entertainment is offered in Edgar's Bar five nights a week, and summer Mondays are Family Nights, when kids are supervised on the patio for dinner, allowing parents to enjoy quiet dining inside. The Grand Pavilion, open only in summer, has early-twentieth-century architecture, an old-fashioned boardwalk, Coney Island–style food, and an airy gazebo. Duney's serves sandwiches, snacks, ice cream, and cocktails by the sea. If you have a hunger attack on either golf course, you're in luck. Hot dogs, sandwiches, and drinks are to be found at the Half-Way House, on the Links. The Dunes Deli & Pizzeria features light fare for breakfast and lunch, as well as limited grocery items, on the Harbor Course. Both are open year-round. At least twelve restaurants offer a variety of dining on nearby Sullivan's Island and the Isle of Palms.

**Children's World:** Ranked one of the top five by *Tennis* magazine for having the "Best Kids' Program," Wild Dunes knows just how to make your little ones' vacation special. Using college students majoring in recreation and child development, the scheduled activities are both impressive and nonstop. Fun begins in early April to mid-May with special activities. Wild Dunes's summer program for kids runs from the end of May through Labor Day, when the fun really kicks in. Dunes Discovery Club for ages three to five provides structured, themed activities on Monday, Tuesday, Thursday, and Friday. Full-day sessions run from 9:00 a.m. to 3:00 p.m. ($50, including lunch); half-day sessions run from 9:00 a.m. to noon ($30). Themes include Island Exploration, Wet 'N' Wild, Pirate Day, and Go Wild Day. Older children, from six to ten years, are part of the Wild Adventure Club, where they enjoy beach games, swimming, crabbing, scavenger hunts, putt-putt golf, and other "wild" adventures, including field trips to local parks. The full-day session runs from 9:00 a.m. to 3:00 p.m. and costs $50.

Teens gather on the beach for volleyball or at the Grand Pavilion for live music, participate in a weekly three-on-three basketball tournament, or play Capture the Flag. Summer nights glow with black-light volleyball or putt-putt ($5). More intense adventures include a kayaking challenge or Thursday's 9:00 a.m. to 2:00 p.m. "Salt Marsh Survivor" experience on a barrier island ($75). Video movies, special pool games, and sports allow teens to socialize informally.

Li'l Dune Bug Club allows younger kids (ages three to ten) to leave their parents at home for a night out to play games, watch movies, and munch goodies. These sessions are held Wednesday and Friday from 5:00 to 9:00 p.m.; the cost is $50 and includes dinner.

Special programs incorporate the natural surroundings—such as the Barrier Island Marine Bio-Camp for ages five to twelve presented on Wednesday and Friday from 9:00 a.m. to 1:00 p.m. ($50, plus $8 for lunch). Visit a barrier island; throw a cast net; crab, fish, and catch animals to make a touch-tank; use found items in arts and crafts. And bathing suits are required!

Kids and parents both can participate in at least twenty crafts and games for an hour or two—make scrapbooks, T-shirts, suncatchers, and birdhouses; check the schedule for your favorite. Some activities are complimentary; some have a small materials fee.

**Recreation:** A day of golf can begin on one of the two eighteen-hole golf courses designed by Tom Fazio. The older course, the Wild Dunes Links, is on the resort's ocean side and provides interesting play with its many water hazards. Two holes edge by the sand dunes of the beach and are dramatically beautiful as well as challenging. The newer Harbor Course is across the island, surrounding the marina and harbor, and has its own fair share of demanding water hazards. One example? Check out the photo of a twelve-foot alligator, surrounded by a dozen golf balls! We swear he's smiling. A driving range, putting green, professional instruction, and a pro shop can help you over the hurdles with improved style and equipment. Wild Dunes received four stars as one of the "Best Places to Play" by *Golf Digest*.

In addition to golf, Wild Dunes offers tennis facilities, which have received numerous awards, including the "Top 10 Greatest U.S. Tennis Resorts" by *Tennis* magazine. Guests receive one hour of free court time per day per bedroom. With a total of seventeen Har-Tru courts, including five lighted for night play and one stadium court, tennis players might not want to go home. Tennis instruction can take the form of private or group lessons, clinics, and camps for a week, a weekend, or an intensive one-day session. Along with its well-stocked pro shop, this tennis facility leaves you very few excuses for not improving your game. Wild Dunes is one of the first resorts to feature beach tennis—try this newest fad.

The Isle of Palms Marina has 200 boat slips. Here you can dock your own vessel or rent a boat for fishing in the Gulf Stream. Join a charter if you need an experienced captain's guidance in snagging the big ones, or finish off a day with a cruise in Charleston's harbor. Besides taking deep-sea excursions, fishermen can cast their lines in the ocean's surf, the creek, and the lagoons.

Swimmers have pools at most of the villa complexes, the main pool at the Swim Center, two oceanfront pools on the Grand Pavilion, the pool at the Boardwalk Inn, and, of course, the beautiful Atlantic Ocean. Joggers and bikers share the nature trails, where pine, oak, and magnolia trees grow; the hard-packed sand beach is also suitable for running and biking. Along the 2-mile stretch of beach, you'll find sunbathers, strollers, and seashell collectors, and just offshore, sailors and sailboarders. At the beachfront picnic area, the kids' playground consists of natural-wood climbing equipment under the trees. For a close look at the egrets, herons, and pelicans of Wild Dunes, take a canoe trip through the creeks and marshes.

Indulge in head-to-toe "therapies" at the spa and salon, or have a relaxing massage. Take a yoga or Pilates class, try a personal trainer, or get a physical fitness or sports training assessment.

Wild Dunes has one of the most extensive family programs we've seen, and is rated in the top five in the country. Check their Web site, and you can be busy probably more than twenty-four hours a day. We encourage you to make your camp and activity reservations at the same time you reserve lodging. The program is that popular! Eco-sunset tours, sailing and dolphin viewing, creek fishing, kayak adventures, or watching the River Dogs, a minor-league baseball team, are just a start, and charges vary for these activities; complimentary fun encompasses putt-putt, sand soccer, cookouts, treasure hunts, and much, much more.

Nighttime comes alive at Wild Dunes with live music five nights a week at Edgar's Bar. The Grand Pavilion swings with live music, tennis exhibitions, a Low-Country luau, and more.

From mid-June to mid-August the resort features weekly entertainment such as a Sunday welcome party, "Shaggin' at the Beach" (with Shag lessons!), karaoke, steel calypso music, and much more.

And when you decide to take a break from the fun and recreation, don't forget how close Charleston is. In a day of sightseeing, you can enjoy a historic Charleston tour of antebellum houses, fine restaurants, and shopping for antiques or at more modern boutiques.

---

**5757 Palm Boulevard
Isle of Palms, South Carolina 29451
(843) 886-6000, (800) 845-8880,
(888) 845-8926, (888) 778-1876
www.wilddunes.com**

# SOUTHEAST

Alabama
Florida
Georgia

# AMELIA ISLAND PLANTATION
## Amelia Island, Florida

Driving into Amelia Island Plantation, amidst the live oaks dripping Spanish moss, one immediately feels encircled and welcomed. With a sigh of relief, you can just sink into that lush vegetation and Southern hospitality. Like many of its counterparts along the coasts of the Carolinas and Georgia, Amelia Island Plantation is a well-planned and carefully executed development that combines resort living with an appreciation for natural beauty.

Amelia Island Plantation, which opened in 1974, occupies 1,350 acres of the southernmost island in the Golden Isle chain along the eastern seaboard of the United States. Open year-round, it is on the coast of northeast Florida, about a forty-five-minute drive from Jacksonville. Besides palmettos and oak trees, a 4-mile sandy beach, marshlands, and lagoons, this corner of paradise is blessed with mild temperatures year-round and balmy ocean breezes. Amelia Island Resort has won *Family Circle* magazine's "Best Family Beach Resort" award, AAA four diamonds, and *Southern Living*'s Reader's Choice award for "Best Resort."

**Accommodations:** You can lodge in one of 249 oceanfront hotel rooms at the Amelia Inn and Beach Club—all with private balconies—or in a villa or hotel room overlooking the ocean or a lagoon, bordering the tennis complex, or along one of the fairways of three golf courses. The one- to three-bedroom villas have complete kitchens; many have private patios, balconies, or screened porches. Architecturally, the multilevel accommodation buildings arranged throughout the property are of various contemporary styles, with stucco or natural-wood facades. Each villa complex has its own swimming pool.

Rates vary according to size, location, and category. Packages are plentiful and suit every need imaginable. Be sure to ask when you call for reservations, as Amelia Island practices yield control—if your dates fit a time when they have vacancies, the price will be even better. Some all-inclusive packages that feature family weeks or recreation and the children's program can be very cost-effective. Regular daily rates in the Amelia Inn range from $166 to $298 resort view and $226 to $366 ocean view, double occupancy. Children under age sixteen stay free in the room; cribs are available. Daily rates for a one-bedroom resort villa range from $206 to $348, while an ocean villa costs from $256 to $436. Weekly rates range from $1,092 to $2,002.

**Dining:** When cooking in your villa seems just too strenuous after a day of sunbathing, gather the family at the Verandah in Racquet Park. Located in a building tucked among old oak trees, the dining room has large windows overlooking the tennis courts. Sample such fresh seafood from the Atlantic as sea bass, flounder, shrimp, and crab in the family-style atmosphere. The Amelia Island Mud Pie is not to be missed!

More elegant dining is available in the Ocean Grill. With expansive views of the ocean, this restaurant features mouthwatering selections such as Lobster Velouté with caramelized apples and leeks or Chilean sea bass with Swiss chard and caviar enveloped in a white truffle parsnip sauce. Children are not left out and may even eat their vegetables happily when it's Ants on a Log (celery and peanut butter with dried cherries) or Snow Peas and Carrot Spiders. Daily breakfast is offered in the Sunrise Café. PLAE, People Laughing and Eating, showcases innovative cuisine at the spa and shops, plus an intimate lounge with fireplace and live entertainment.

Stop by the Marché Burette, an old-fashioned fresh-food market, for fruits, vegetables, meats, and fresh-baked breads. You may be tempted by the delicious aroma to stay for a sandwich and coffee. Also appropriate for breakfast and lunch is the Golf Shop Restaurant at Amelia Links or the Longpoint Clubhouse, about a mile and a half south. At the Beach Club Grille, burgers, wings, and ribs are served; TVs add action to a meal or dine outside. The Dunes Club Bar serves light lunches and tropical drinks poolside (seasonally) between Sea and Turtle Dunes. Roberto's will deliver pizza to your door. Relax with a drink at the Lobby Lounge or "fly by" the Falcon's Nest, a combination of aviation history/memorabilia and the island's hottest nightspot. The Cessna flown by Sky King, that icon of 1950s television fame, may be a replica, but the drinks and entertainment are the real thing!

**Children's World:** Kids' Camp Amelia children's program entertains three- to ten-year-olds daily, year-round. Three- and four-year-olds attend the morning camp only. Activities include swimming, crabbing, sports, and arts and crafts, all with a daily theme. Take nature walks and enjoy many activities with the resident naturalist for a small fee. June through August, golf and tennis clinics and field trips are offered at special rates.

The cost for the full-day kids' program (8:30 a.m. to 4:00 p.m.) with lunch is $55, the morning session (8:30 a.m. to 1:00 p.m.) with lunch is $40, and the afternoon session (12:45 to 4:00 p.m.) is $30. The Kids' Camp is included in the recreation package.

Teen Explorers has just the kind of loosely structured activities that older children (eleven and up) prefer. Minigolf, basketball, scavenger hunts, bowling, barbecues, and bonfires provide a chance to socialize while participating in fun activities. Programs and costs vary (from free to $50), so check with the recreation department for details and to register.

Just for Kids presents themed dinner parties for ages three to ten. Hours are from 6:00 to 9:30 p.m. Wednesday through Saturday from March 1 to Labor Day, when a buffet dinner is served; it drops to Thursday through Saturday (room service menu) for the rest of the year. The cost is $40, but only $30 if parents are dining at the Ocean Grill or Verandah Restaurant.

At Aury Island a tree house and a dock for fishing and crabbing are reserved just for the twelve-and-under set. At the Beach Club little ones have their own wading pool and a playground filled with wooden climbing equipment. To find a babysitter, you can pick up a list of names and numbers at the main registration desk; rates begin at $15 per hour, with a four-hour minimum.

Daily at 2:00 p.m. the whole family can join in poolside activities such as trivia, volleyball, games, and contests. At 3:00 p.m. try your hand at creative crafts—days, prices, and type of craft vary throughout the year, and again, the crafts program is covered in the all-inclusive recreation program.

**Recreation:** The Amelia Links, thirty-six holes of golf designed by Pete Dye and Bobby Weed, offer variety in play, as each course has its own personality. Oak Marsh weaves through groves of oak, palmetto trees, and marshlands, while Ocean Links skirts the Atlantic Ocean, with five holes along the sand dunes and sea oats of the beach. The eighteen-hole Long Point Golf Course, designed by Tom Fazio, is set in primal marshland and sand dunes. Lessons can be arranged through the pro shop, where you will also find equipment and fashions.

Racquet Park is well situated among beautiful live oaks, a lovely setting for twenty-three Har-Tru courts. Three are lighted for evening play. The site of the Bausch and Lomb Women's Championships, this tennis complex offers adult and junior clinics, ball machines for solo practice, and a pro shop for equipment and apparel. Junior players (fifteen and under) play free with an adult.

Also part of Racquet Park is the Health and Fitness Center. Complete with racquetball, indoor heated lap pool, exercise equipment, steam room, sauna and whirlpool facilities, and aerobics classes, it fits the bill for a good workout. For relaxing rejuvenation, visit the spa, with full services and delightful treats like a Watsu massage, performed in thermal mineral water.

Swimmers can choose the ocean or pools for their hours of fun in the sun. In addition to two large pools, a kiddie pool, and a hot tub at the Beach Club, each of the groups of villas (except the Lagoon Villas) has a swimming pool—twenty-three pools in all.

The Nature Center is open daily from 9:00 a.m. to 5:00 p.m. with several naturalists, resident critters, a fun retail shop, and a large classroom for presentations. Explore the natural beauty of the island on several different excursions, geared for all ages and interests. Beach bounty, edible plants and wildflowers, birds of Amelia, and nature photography are just the beginning.

Along the 4-mile beach, you can collect shells, sunbathe, play volleyball, ride horseback (the Seashore Stables are just 2 miles away), and fish in the surf for whiting, sea trout, and bluefish. Surrounding the island in bays and sounds and the Gulf Stream are tarpon, flounder, trout, redfish, red snapper, and king mackerel. The waters in this area give up some beautiful prizes, and for advice, insider's hints, tackle, and information on charters, head to the Amelia Angler.

Bicycle along 7 miles of trails (rental bikes with baby seats and children's bikes are available), jog along the wooded paths and down the beach, or maybe even challenge the kids to a half hour of video games at the Beach Club Game Room.

Always wanted to try one of these new Segway self-balancing, personal transportation devices designed to go anywhere people do? Here's your chance! Satisfy your curiosity or take a tour through the natural surroundings along the bike paths. Junior Segway Experience allows kids to participate with parents in this novel activity. If you really like it, you can buy it on the spot.

For an outing of a different sort, browse through the shops at Amelia Island Plantation, or discover the Victorian district of Fernandina Beach at the north end of the island. The Amelia Island Plantation Resort Guide is worth checking upon your arrival; here you'll learn of classes, movies, hayrides, and cookouts.

Venturing out, visit the Amelia Island Museum of History, Florida's only oral museum, for fascinating stories of the eight flags that have flown over Amelia Island; and Fort Clinch State Park, where on the first weekend of each month, rangers reenact the 1864 occupation. Jacksonville attractions are just a forty-five-minute drive; and farther south (one and a half hours from the resort) history buffs will find St. Augustine, the oldest European settlement in the United States, founded in 1565 by the Spanish. Visit the restored Spanish Quarter, and of course, Ponce de León's Fountain of Youth.

---

**6800 First Coast Highway**
**Amelia Island, Florida 32034**
**(904) 261-6161, (800) 874-6878**
**www.aipfl.com**

# THE BREAKERS

## Palm Beach, Florida

In the 1880s Henry Flagler, a railroad magnate and cofounder of Standard Oil, was advised to spend time in Florida for his health. From this happenstance evolved a world-class luxury resort. Flagler discovered the warm climate of the Atlantic coast, was captivated by the scenery, expanded railroad lines down the eastern seaboard, and set into motion the development of Palm Beach as a winter playground of the wealthy.

The original Palm Beach Inn, built in 1896, was destroyed by fire in 1903. A second hotel, The Breakers, also succumbed to fire in 1925. Efforts to rebuild were begun immediately, and the new facility was opened at the end of 1926. The project was inspired by buildings of the Italian Renaissance; the era's artistic influence is evident in the loggias, courtyards, and handpainted vaulted ceilings that adorn The Breakers. Open year-round, the hotel has completed a $100 million renovation and maintains its status as a Mobil five-star and AAA five-diamond resort. Listed on the National Register of Historic Places, The Breakers is also a member of the Leading Hotels of the World. The grand beauty of this sparkling structure is perhaps met only by its natural setting on 140 acres of lush semitropical landscape bordering the blue-green waters of the Atlantic Ocean.

**Accommodations:** The 560 comfortably elegant and well-appointed guest rooms, including fifty-seven suites, have views of the ocean, the well-tended formal gardens, or the golf course. During the summer (low season), from mid-May to October 31, rates for a single/double room are $375 to $630 per day; there is no charge for children sixteen and under sharing a room with parents.

Cribs and rollaways are provided at no charge but must be requested prior to arrival. You may also request complimentary childproofing for children under three. During the high season, from November to early May, room rates range from $470 to $1,085 per day. Holiday and vacation packages are also available. Suites range from $760 to $4,950.

For those who enjoy more privacy, choose the Flagler Club, The Breakers's concierge level located on the top two floors, with restricted access and additional guest services and amenities. Rates here are $560 to $1,190.

**Dining:** Dining at The Breakers can be as formal or as casual as one desires, with eight restaurants to choose from. An array of hot and cold breakfast items, as well as an a la carte menu, is available in the Circle Dining Room, with splendid ocean views and an intricate handpainted ceiling. Dine indoors or out, with a side order of ocean and pool views, at the Beach Club or the new Ocean Grill, where shoes and bathing suit cover-up are the only dress requirements. Breakfast, lunch, and sometimes dinner are served Wednesday through Sunday, weather permitting. Lunch and dinner are served in The Seafood Bar, an upscale oceanfront raw bar reminiscent of the plantation homes of old Florida; or The Flagler Steakhouse, featuring oversize steaks and chops. For dinner only, experience the AAA five-diamond L'Escalier, with its French ambience; jackets are required and reservations are recommended. To say L'Escalier's wine list is exceptional is an understatement; it has consistently earned *Wine Spectator*'s "Grand Award" every year since 1981. Five minutes from the hotel, in the heart of Palm Beach, Echo offers a culinary adventure with unique and sophisticated Asian cuisine. For cocktails, appetizers, and afternoon tea, the elegant Tapestry Bar is the place to be.

At The Breakers restaurants, the under-elevens have their own menus. Children under two eat free, and everyone gets a special coloring book. A family-friendly dining facility, located in the new Family Entertainment Center and called simply the Italian Restaurant, serves dinner daily.

**Children's World:** With its broad spectrum of amenities, creative recreational programs and activities, and family-friendly mind-set, The Breakers formed a Kids' Advisory Board, composed of young people ages five to twelve, to advise the resort on children's wants and needs. In response to this advice, there is now a year-round children's program called Coconut Crew Camp.

Children ages three through twelve enjoy Coconut Crew Camp's year-round supervised activities, including active sports, contests, pool and beach games, arts and crafts, indoor games, seashell hunts, nature walks, lawn games, swimming, croquet, and more. Offered daily from 9:00 a.m. to 3:00 p.m. as a full-day experience ($100, lunch included) or a half day ($70, morning or afternoon; lunch included).

The agenda for all programs is relaxed and flexible, so your child has the freedom to choose only specific events or to stay with the group for longer periods. Parents are encouraged to participate with their children, or monitored free play for ages five to seven is $15 per hour. Babysitting is available around the clock.

The new Family Entertainment Center houses an arcade, movie, huge TV, computers, crafts, playroom, and pizza available right next door at the Italian Restaurant. Children ten years and older are welcome on their own; younger children may be accompanied by parents, or supervised by on-site staff for a $15 hourly fee.

From March through October families have lots of options for activities. Every week on Friday, the complimentary Family Fun Pak orients families with activities and refreshments. On Saturday, Kids Rule! is another complimentary event where kids "compete" against their parents in a game, and January through March, Friday Beach Bonfires kick off the weekend. Holiday weekends, everyone can take part in Saturday's Family Night Out theme party (Harry Potter, Survivor, Palm Beach Rodeo); $60 per person includes dinner and a souvenir. On other Saturdays, The Breakers Fun Zone ($20 per child, no dinner) provides unlimited tokens for the arcade—a child's dream. Families may also arrange A La Carte Time together; snorkeling, croquet, biking, or a kayaking trip are some ideas.

**Recreation:** Allow yourself to be pampered; a staff of 1,800 people is dedicated to making a stay here memorable. Stroll through the beautiful gardens or the half mile of private beach, linger under the palm trees, find the children's Secret Garden, relax on a patio surrounding a fountain, or indulge at the new Oceanfront Spa and Beach Club.

The award-winning Breakers Palm Beach features a vintage golf experience, resulting from the recent renovation of its historic eighteen-hole Ocean Course and the creation of a golf and tennis clubhouse designed in the grand "Old Florida" style. Another eighteen-hole course, Breakers West, is located 10 miles away.

On par with the revitalized golf facilities are ten newly constructed tennis courts, all of which are surrounded by lush gardens and lighted at night. Tennis fans will enjoy the spaciousness of the easily accessible clubhouse. The Breakers Junior Golf and Tennis Academy has age-appropriate programs during summer and holidays designed to help kids learn skills and appreciate the game.

The Mediterranean-style Beach Club offers four pools, including a lap pool and children's pool, a Jacuzzi, and ten cabanas overlooking one-half mile of private beach. The Spa at The Breakers features seventeen private treatment rooms, steam and sauna rooms, men's and ladies' lounges, a beauty salon, and an ocean-view fitness center.

Sunbathe beside the majestic Atlantic, or sip a tall, cool cocktail on the patio or at the Reef Bar. Bicycle or jog on the paths through the gardens, join a deep-sea fishing or fly-fishing excursion for an offshore adventure, go snorkeling, or sign up for scuba instruction. For periods when you are not feeling so energetic, play a game of shuffleboard, croquet, horseshoes, bocci ball, bridge, or backgammon. Other events throughout the week include exercise classes such as water aerobics, yoga, and Tai Chi; family movies; shopping at any of the resort's twelve boutiques; and historical tours. Add lectures, crafts, garden tours, concerts, shopping on the famous Worth Avenue, and cooking demonstrations, and you'll have to stretch your vacation to fit it all in.

1 South County Road
Palm Beach, Florida 33480
(561) 655-6611, (888) BREAKERS
www.thebreakers.com

# CALLAWAY GARDENS

## Pine Mountain, Georgia

Cason Callaway was a textile industrialist in Georgia. In the 1930s he became so enamored of the countryside around Pine Mountain that his life began to change. He turned from industry, first to farming and then to gardening. He learned that the plumleaf azalea was peculiar to this area of Georgia, and he was determined to nurture it and share its beauty with others. He established the Ida Cason Callaway Foundation, in honor of his mother, and opened his gardens to the public in 1952. While the gardens remain the focal point of the setting, the resort has grown to include gracious lodging, pleasant restaurants, and sports activities such as golf, tennis, swimming, and fishing. This naturally wooded and carefully cultivated land—14,000 acres of lakes, woodlands, and gardens—is located 70 miles south of Atlanta, in the Appalachian Mountain foothills of west Georgia. Callaway's stated purpose is to provide a wholesome family environment where all may find beauty, relaxation, inspiration, and a better understanding of the living world. A public, educational, horticultural, and charitable organization, it is owned and operated by the nonprofit Ida Cason Callaway Foundation. Its wholly owned subsidiary, Callaway Gardens Resort, Inc., a regular business corporation, operates the recreational, lodging, and retail facilities at Callaway. After-tax proceeds go to the foundation to support its efforts. And it shows. Highway 27 bisects Callaway Gardens and makes it seem very spread out; having a car is helpful, if not essential, and it's easier to find your way once you get oriented to the layout.

**Accommodations:** Four types of accommodations provide a choice of floor plans and location. Centrally located, the charming Mountain Creek Inn has 323 accommodations overlooking the pool or the Great Lawn. Also available are large Roof Garden suites with one or two bedrooms and a parlor. The Lodge at Callaway Gardens contains 150 deluxe rooms and suites with exterior balconies that bring forest and gardens right inside your room. The lodge has its own swimming pool with cabana bar—what a gracious way to connect with nature. The Cottages, favorites for families, are one to two bedrooms set in tall pines, and the Villas (one to four bedrooms) at Callaway Gardens are also popular. Both feature full kitchen, screened porches, and fireplace; the villas add washer/dryer and separate baths for each bedroom. Rates vary over five seasons; all rates are based on double occupancy and include admission to the Gardens and Robin Lake Beach and use of the Fitness Center. The Mountain Creek Inn ranges from $119 to $149; the Cottages are $179 to $229 (one bedroom) and $309 to $339 (two bedrooms); the Villas range from $199 to $259 (one bedroom) and $319 to $389 (two bedrooms); weekends are $10 more. Mid-March through early August and mid-November through December have highest rates. High season for Lodge rooms is mid-March through May and November–December holidays; rates are $209 to $269, and weekends are $40 to $60 more.

Summer Family Adventure, a tradition for forty-eight years, includes four-day packages beginning on Tuesday, as well as the weekly Saturday to Saturday packages. Monday through Friday, from 9:00 a.m. to 3:00 p.m., guests participate in "day camp." Mom and Dad can participate in planned activities for adults or have time to enjoy their own activities while the children are at camp. Evening events focus on the entire family. Four-day rates are $1,730 for cottages, $1,946 for villas. Seven-day rates are $2,521 (cottage) and $3,203 (villa); rates are for two-bedroom units, up to five people. Many other packages are offered; inquire about weekend, recreation, or mini-breaks. Cribs are provided at no charge; rollaway beds are $15 per day in the inn only.

**Dining:** At the inn, the Plant Room, open for breakfast, lunch, and dinner, always has Southern charm on the menu. The buffet and soup and salad bar lets everyone choose their favorites—the Friday night Seafood Buffet is not to be missed. Children five and under dine free. The Piedmont Dining Room, in the Conference Center, is open daily for all three meals, and offers both a la carte and buffet service.

With red-checked tablecloths supporting the atmosphere that its name connotes, the Country Kitchen, located in the Country Store on Highway 27, serves breakfast, lunch, and dinner in a friendly, family-style setting. It's famous for its muscadine bread and country bacon. Sandwiches and snacks are available in Champions at the golf pro shop. At the Robin Lake Beach Pavilion, grab a snack and sit at one of the picnic tables overlooking Robin Lake. The Fine Cone is perfect for ice cream on a summer day. A welcome addition to Callaway dining is the Discovery Café, where the view is as enjoyable as the food. It offers indoor/outdoor eating overlooking mountain and lake. The Gardens Restaurant, with a lovely porch overlooking lake and golf course, invites you to tarry.

At the end of the day, stop at the cozy Vineyard Green Lounge in the Mountain Creek Inn for a drink and a light meal, or visit Ironwood Lounge for billiards and a drink by the fireplace.

**Children's World:** Sicne 1960 Florida State University's Flying High Circus has performed at Callaway Gardens. With the big top pitched at Robin Lake Beach, this area becomes the focus of the Summer Family Adventure Program from June through mid-August, and it's summer camp for everyone. If daily (except Wednesday) circus performances are not enough to charm youngsters, the performers also act as counselors, directing kids in games and sports and teaching them a few juggling tricks and circus acts too. In addition, kids go sailing, swimming, waterskiing, roller skating, and biking and grow imaginative in crafts classes. Day camp activities for children ages three to twelve are offered Monday through Friday, from approximately 9:00 a.m. to 3:00 p.m. Children are divided by ages and often have a choice of activities, such as arts and crafts or swimming, or an hour of each. Teens and adults can play as well, with the same schedule and activities, such as waterskiing, ropes course, beach volleyball, tennis, and circus activities.

The Summer Discovery Program provides an informal look at the animals, plants, and ecology at Callaway Gardens. Family events, such as barbecues, square dances, and movies, are also planned.

If you cannot schedule the Summer Family Adventure and are staying a couple of days at the inn, you can enroll your child on a daily basis for $68 a day. Besides the program, there are children's playgrounds at the inn and at the cottage area.

**Recreation:** The Virginia Hand Discovery Center, nestled in the woods on the edge of Mountain Creek Lake, should be your first stop. It's several facilities in one, all devoted to enhancing the harmony between humans and earth. A staffed information desk and interactive kiosks provide guests an overview of all there is to see and do in the Callaway's 14,000 acres. Inside an orientation theater, the film *Time & the Gardens* plays continuously, depicting the evolution of the Gardens at Callaway. The

center also houses an education wing, lecture hall, museum/exhibit hall, the Discovery Gift Shop, and Discovery Café. Outside, a transportation court provides guests with alternate means of getting around.

The gardens are a continuous source of beauty, pleasure, peace, and serenity. This is a place to enjoy, to reflect, and to learn. The colorful, changing displays of begonias, snapdragons, geraniums, zinnias, pansies, tulips, marigolds, chrysanthemums—the list seems endless—are presented in the outdoor garden of the John A. Sibley Horticultural Center. Depending on the season, visitors who explore the walking trails are treated to mountain laurel, hydrangeas, narcissus, magnolias, dogwoods, crabapples, hollies, wildflowers, and 700 varieties of azaleas (the famous plumleaf blooms during the summer). At Mr. Cason's Vegetable Garden, you can wander through row after row of more than 400 different types of fruits and vegetables. Workshops on topics like flower arranging and bonsai techniques are available year-round. The Sibley Horticultural Center, a five-acre, innovative greenhouse design, is an architectural as well as a horticultural feat. The Day Butterfly Center houses up to 1,000 butterflies (representing more than fifty species) in a lush tropical setting. Learn about eagles, hawks, and owls as they swoop over your head in the Birds of Prey show.

The world's largest azalea garden, the Callaway Brothers Azalea Bowl, features more than 5,000 specimens of both hybrid and native azaleas in a forty-acre landscape.

Besides its magnificent gardens, the resort also offers more traditional diversions. Two golf courses unroll past forests and lakes. The names of the courses are descriptive of their surroundings—Mountain View (the most challenging and home to the PGA tour's Buick Challenge for twelve years) and Lake View (the most picturesque). A driving range, two pro shops, the nine-hole Sky View course, and a year-round instructional program complete the golfing facilities.

The Roger Federer in your party has ten lighted tennis courts from which to choose. Eight clay and two Plexipave courts are at the Tennis and Racquetball Club, which also houses two racquetball courts and the pro shop. The instructional program includes private or group lessons, or you can practice on your own with a ball machine. *Tennis* magazine consistently awards the Tennis Club with a "Top 50 Tennis Resorts in the Nation" ranking.

Robin Lake is the center of lots of summer fun, from paddleboat rides and circus performances to swimming and sunbathing along the mile-long sandy beach. Besides the lake, overnight guests can enjoy the pools at the inn, at the Mountain Creek Villas, and at the cottage area.

On the shores of Mountain Creek Lake is a boathouse where you can rent a motorboat and fishing tackle—the lake is stocked with bass and bream—or a Sunfish sailboat, paddleboat, or canoe. You can also discover the lakes from their shores as you bicycle along the trails and paths.

Sportsmen enjoy fly fishing on thirteen lakes or shooting skeet, trap, and sporting clays at the Gun Club. You may want to spend an afternoon at an organ concert (daily during the summer) in the chapel on Falls Creek Lake. For indoor exercise the Fitness Center offers equipment for unwinding. The recently opened Spa Prunifolia prides itself on pampering, surrounded by garden motifs and woodlands. Of course, herbal and nature-based treatments are featured. For an afternoon of history, you can take the 15-mile trip to Warm Springs and Franklin Roosevelt's Little White House.

---

**U.S. Highway 27, P.O. Box 2000**
**Pine Mountain, Georgia 31822**
**(706) 663-2281, (800) 225-5292**
**www.callawaygardens.com**

# CHEECA LODGE AND SPA
## Islamorada, Florida

Stretching more than 150 miles south from Miami, the Florida Keys enjoy a subtropical climate and a friendly, laid-back philosophy. Just getting there is an adventure. As you travel along U.S. Highway 1, you get the feeling that you're the string connecting a necklace of islands. And sometimes there are no islands—just a narrow ribbon of concrete in the middle of a very wide ocean—or two! The Atlantic Ocean and the Gulf of Mexico both border this strip of islands. Islamorada is just 75 miles from Miami, but really it is another world.

Cheeca Lodge and Spa is a twenty-seven-acre luxury oceanfront resort (AAA four diamonds, a RockResort, and member of Small Luxury Hotels of the World), with more than 1,000 feet of palm-lined beach, not often found in the Keys. "Barefoot elegance" is Cheeca's trademark, and it was named one of *Travel + Leisure*'s "500 Greatest Hotels in the World" in 2005. Cheeca is becoming increasingly private, and some areas are for club members only.

**Accommodations:** Set in the main lodge and low-rise villas spread throughout the landscaped grounds, 199 rooms and suites await your pleasure. Generous in size, all guest rooms are air-conditioned and also have ceiling fans, and many have a private balcony. Sixty-four villa suites feature kitchen, screened-in porch, living room, and one or two bedrooms. Mid-December to June rates are the highest, when standard rooms range from $419 to $529; oceanfront rooms begin at $579; and one-bedroom suites average $739. In summer the rates drop to $179 to $465 for rooms, $475 to $825 for one-bedroom suites. Children under sixteen stay free in their parents' room. Specials and packages are offered year-round. A daily resort fee of $39 covers housekeeping gratuities and other amenities and is inclusive for tennis, golf, kayaks/paddleboats, spa exercise classes, beach cabanas, fitness studio, and more.

**Dining:** Savor fine dinners at the Atlantic's Edge, a plantation-style restaurant with lovely panoramic views of the ocean. Dine inside or outside next to the free-form swimming pool at the Ocean Terrace Grill, sampling the local specialty, stone-crab claws, or soups and sandwiches; there is a special children's menu. Another indoor/outdoor dining option is the Curt Gowdy Lounge, great for snacks, cocktails, and piano entertainment in the evenings. Kick back at the beach Tiki Bar for cocktails, wide-screen TV, and the famous Cheeca burger. Nearby dining choices range from casual to fine dining, and nightlife options include sunsets, live music, cigar bar, and billiards or darts.

**Children's World:** Award-winning Camp Cheeca has a mission: learning about the environment while having fun. Children ages five and up are busy Tuesday through Saturday from 9:00 a.m. to 1:00 p.m. year-round. Cost is $40 per child for the morning session, including lunch.

Learning to snorkel and fish, creating nature art or sand sculpture, feeding the fish, or exploring the beach—everything has an ecological approach that kids really respond to. There's a good mix of activities, with field trips, scavenger hunts, arts and crafts, and Saturday Sundae (everyone's favorite). "Kids Night Out," Friday and Saturday from 6:00 to 10:00 p.m., costs $40 and includes entertainment, pizza dinner, movies, crafts, and games. Families with three or more children receive a reduced rate. Babysitting rates vary according to season.

**Recreation:** You can be on the go from dawn to dusk, or make the most strenuous activity of the day deciding between a hammock, chaise longue, or tiki hut on the beach. Consider renting a catamaran or beach cruiser bicycle, or try parasailing. Paddleboats and kayaks are complimentary. Deckboats, sailboats, and Windsurfers are available to rent, with instruction. Maybe just a pool float is more your speed. The three pools are all very different; a free-form swimming pool, a lap pool, and a saltwater lagoon keep boredom at bay. Play tennis on one of the six lighted courts, or try the Jack Nicklaus–designed nine-hole executive golf course. Take a self-guided walk along Cheeca's Nature Trail, or watch the sunrise from the pier—or maybe the sunset.

Indulge yourself at the state-of-the-art health spa and fitness center, offering the latest in massage therapy, facials, aromatherapy, and body wraps.

It's a fisherman's paradise here, with more than 600 species of marine life and a calendar of what's running each month that fills a page. No wonder Islamorada is known as the sportfishing capital of the world. A nice touch is that the chef will, on request, prepare your hard-won catch. If you prefer to swim with the fish, Cheeca has snorkeling at a living coral reef, with equipment and instruction. The *Cheeca View* doubles as a dive boat twice a day and then does sunset and moonlight cruises. The biggest problem is trying to fit in all the options.

Theater of the Sea, the world's second-oldest marine park, is a natural lagoon where humans and marine animals interact (kids love getting kissed by a sea lion!). They've gone beyond a glass-bottom boat—here they have a bottomless boat. Hmm, neat trick. If you want to range farther afield, the concierge can help arrange a swim with the dolphins or a trip to either Key West, the southernmost U.S. city, or Pennekamp State Park, the first underwater state park. Combine a visit to Miccosukee Indian Reservation with an airboat ride through the Everglades.

---

**81801 Overseas Highway, Mile Marker 82 Islamorada, Florida 33036 (305) 664-4651, (800) 327-2888 www.cheeca.com**

# THE CLOISTER
## Sea Island, Georgia

Charming, gracious, and oh, so civilized—The Cloister is in the heart of the "Golden Isles," one of the most historic areas of the old Spanish Main. Family holidays at this fine old resort are fun-filled, and the elegance of a bygone era prevails. The Cloister boasts that here children learn manners as well as golf, tennis, and swimming. The dress-for-dinner standard and the children's weekly dances (seasonally) reinforce this philosophy.

Sea Island's rich history dates back to the antebellum days of the Old South. The Cloister opened its doors in October 1928. It successfully weathered the Depression and over the years has warmly greeted guests from the rich and famous to the mere plebeian with good taste. Ivy-covered walls, gently swaying palm trees, impeccable gardens, and wide verandas set the stage for a memorable vacation.

The Cloister is completing a five-year, $200 million renovation project. The new Main Building opened in April 2006; it is elegant, with many refurbished elements of the original that were custom-designed. The Spa opened in October 2006. In the plans are a new Equestrian Center, Beach Club, Chapel, and Arts Center. Awards from 2006 and 2007 include "World's Best Places to Stay," *Condé Nast Traveler;* "50 Best Family Resorts" and "Best Hotels in the World," *Travel + Leisure;* and *Condé Nast Traveler's* "Gold List of World's Best Places to Stay." The resort is open year-round.

**Accommodations:** The Cloister Main Building feels like a private mansion, set in landscaped grounds and tiled courtyards. River-view rooms are situated along the Black Banks River with glorious views, and all 156 luxurious rooms and suites have full amenities, including twenty-four-hour butler service. Set on the nearby private beach, The Cloister Ocean Houses feature rooms and suites with balconies overlooking the Atlantic or a scenic nature view. Also available are privately owned "cottages" (two to eight bedrooms) ranging from modest to grand. View them at www.seaislandcottages.com.

Room rates (up to four people, not including meals) range from $450 to $875 per night, depending on the type of room and time of year; suites are $875 to $2,500. A service charge of $35 per day, per room applies.

**Dining:** Guests may dine either at The Cloister or at The Lodge at Sea Island, a premier destination on neighboring St. Simons Island. At The Lodge, The Terrace is like dining in a fine old Southern home; collared shirt is required for breakfast and lunch; add long pants for dinner. You know seafood is fresh when you're overlooking the ocean, and the casual Beach Grill with open kitchen is dedicated to just that, with a creative menu for breakfast, lunch, and dinner. Colt & Alison, overlooking the Plantation Course, has Sunday brunch and nightly dinner, complete with tableside preparation and a fireplace. At the Retreat Course, the Davis Love Grill is a more casual dining spot for lunch, dinner, and cocktails, dedicated to Sea Island's pro, Davis Love III. Included in *Esquire*'s "Top New Restaurants of 2006," the Georgian Room is the epitome of elegance and "estate dining," with only the best of everything. It serves dinner only, and coat and tie are required for gentlemen over twelve years of age. While the Main Dining Room is more family-oriented (requiring only a coat and collared shirt for gentlemen), the service is equally excellent; it serves breakfast, lunch, and dinner, with a children's menu, great views of the Black Banks River, and alfresco dining in season. The Oak Room offers an expanded pub menu, leather ceilings, a fireplace, and an outdoor terrace for dinner and, seasonally, breakfast and lunch. The River Bar is the late-afternoon to late-evening place to gather with friends or to meet new ones. You can enjoy light snacks and appetizers, beer on tap, or a traditional Mint Julep or Front Porch Lemonade—here the only dress requirement is a collared shirt. The Loggia Bar at the Beach is ideal for a cold drink or light fare without missing anything going on at the beach.

For light refreshments during spring and summer, there's a snack bar near the swimming pools at the Beach Club. In the Spanish Lounge, afternoon juice and cookies are a treasured tradition. A lovely Sea Island tradition, the Plantation Supper on Rainbow Island is a Friday event. Bluegrass music, Southern gospel, pulled pork barbecue, and pecan pies—it's the best, and a vacation to Georgia is just not complete otherwise.

**Children's World:** The Junior Staff of specially selected college students will charm your child with active days. All year long, energetic, friendly counselors provide daily supervised play for youngsters ages three (no pull-ups or diapers, please) through eleven, from 9:30 a.m. to 1:00 p.m. for $45 per child. Program operates daily except Sunday. From mid-March to mid-April, and again in summer, the hours extend to 3:00 p.m. for ages five and up. Cost becomes $65 for the day. Fee includes lunch. Activities include swimming, fishing, crabbing, art sessions, games, boat rides, dunes discovery, and nature walks, just to mention a few. As part of the renovations, a dedicated children's activity center is planned, and seasonal activities are plentiful. The Cloister's program is very popular and well attended and is constantly being updated, so be sure to see what's planned during your stay. Everyone's favorite is the Saturday cookie extravaganza—$20 to make, bake, and eat cookies for an hour. Club Sea Island is a new program for children ages nine to twelve who want more excitement and adventure, such as kayaking, jeep train shelling, stables and riding, and field trips. Based on a minimum of five participants, cost and hours are the same for adults and kids; some special activities are priced separately. Junior versions of most sports are taught here—golf, tennis, kayaking, sailing, and gun safety introduce the youngest to these activities and perfect skills for others.

Year-round, Friday evening is New Flick Friday for children ages three to eleven, and Saturday's Pajama Party is also a favorite. The fun goes from 6:30 to 10:00 p.m. and includes dinner, movies, and a craft project for $45 per child. The Saturday afternoon Children's Dance Party, in Sunday dress, is a long-standing tradition.

During the summer months children can join their counselors for dinner from 6:30 to 10:00 p.m., Monday through Saturday, allowing parents to dine at their leisure. For younger children, babysitters are available.

Juniors and teens also have access to excursions and activities, including shopping trips to the Village of St. Simons Island, "dive-in" movies in the pool, and socials. Some excursions do require small fees, such as Friday night bowling or Saturday at the Island Cinema. It's essential to check the weekly calendar for additional events, because the Junior Staff also plans various activities for different age groups. Teen dances and pool parties, table tennis tournaments, swimming and hamburger parties, and crabbing parties frequently appear on the agenda. A Family Activity Hour features fun for all ages.

**Recreation:** Whether you choose a leisurely stroll along the 5 miles of private beach, a rigorous game of tennis, a round of golf, or a refreshing dip in the pool, your vacation stay can be as relaxing or active as you wish.

The Cloister offers twenty-five well-maintained Har-Tru clay courts, an automated practice court, and instruction by a professional teaching staff. Even a little criticism of your backhand is easy to take in a setting graced by oak trees and azal-

eas. Junior Tennis Clinics begin at age four and continue to age sixteen.

The Sea Island Golf Club, located on neighboring St. Simons Island, is just a short drive over the small bridge spanning the Black Banks River. Once you arrive, you'll be charmed by the Avenue of Oaks—majestic moss-draped oak trees leading up to the Lodge at Sea Island Golf Club. There are thirty-six championship holes. The Seaside Course, redesigned in 1999 by Tom Fazio and listed on numerous top courses lists, is a par 70 links course. The Plantation Course, redesigned by Rees Jones in 1998, is a par 72 parkland-style course. A third course, Retreat, was redesigned by Davis Love III and reopened in 2001. The Golf Learning Center, a joint venture of Sea Island and *Golf Digest,* offers state-of-the-art practice and learning facilities with a video analysis system. There's a driving range at each club, and back on Sea Island you'll find a putting green and a chip 'n' putt area for some extra practice time. And if you're a real devotee, rest assured that golfing interests do not fade with the setting sun; join the discussions with the pros at golf seminars two evenings a week.

The Beach Club overlooks the Atlantic, so you can choose an ocean swim or a few laps in one of the two pools. Besides a dining room and a snack bar, the Beach Club offers table tennis, volleyball, shuffleboard, and a terrific soak-up-the-sun atmosphere. Other water sports include sailboarding and sailing in the ocean, snorkeling and scuba diving, and boating and fishing in the river, all with instruction. After excursions through the waterways, you might try exploring the grounds as you jog, bike, or ride horseback. Many folks enjoy a horseback ride along the beach or through the marshes, or you may contact the stables about moonlight supper rides. At the Shooting School you'll find instruction in sporting clays, trap, and skeet shooting as well as all the equipment necessary to learn these sports. And after golf, tennis, swimming, sailing, and skeet-shooting lessons, if you're still dying to try something new or to brush up on dusty skills, sign up for dance instruction. After a couple of sessions, you'll no doubt be a hit dancing nightly to the hotel's Sea Island Orchestra.

The Sea Island Spa offers a full range of services. You can join an exercise class, develop an individualized program, consult a nutritionist, have a massage, relax with a facial, or walk a labyrinth and study mindfulness.

Special programs are planned throughout the year; they may be just the thing to schedule a family vacation around. Food and wine seminars, bridge festivals, and a personal financial-planning seminar are standard events at The Cloister.

At any time of the year, be sure to check the weekly calendar. You might want to see a movie, play bingo, listen to a classical piano concert, head to an exercise workout, join a nature walk, or take in a lecture on the local wildlife. But don't crowd your schedule too much, for one of the nicest pleasures at The Cloister is simply strolling through the gardens and discovering the camellias, gardenias, wisteria, geraniums, petunias, and time.

**100 First Street**
**Sea Island, Georgia 31561**
**(912) 638-3611, (800) SEA-ISLAND**
**www.seaisland.com**

# CLUB MED/SANDPIPER
## Port St. Lucie, Florida

Club Med is practically synonymous with a carefree, fun-in-the-sun holiday, a tradition going back to 1957. In fact, they opened the first Mini-Club for children in 1967. The only village that Club Med operates in the United States is Sandpiper, and it has not only a Mini-Club but a Baby Club as well. Located in Port St. Lucie, Florida, about an hour's drive north of Palm Beach, the Club Med village covers more than 400 beautifully landscaped acres along the St. Lucie River. The verdant green landscape and the clear blue waters make an attractive setting for a fun-filled, sun-filled vacation.

**Accommodations:** Sandpiper is one of the most luxurious Club Med properties, termed the "finest." It seems more like a deluxe hotel, boasting brick-colored tile floors covered with kilim carpet, original artwork by local artists, and a separate dressing area, with large closets. Unlike most Club Med villages, the rooms here have telephone, TV, and minifridge. Each room has a private balcony or terrace and is located in one of seven two-story buildings near the river. Club Med, which has a Florida country club look, now offers limited special accommodations: family marina suites, two connecting rooms with DVD player, turn-down service, and fully stocked refrigerator; and one family suite, two bedrooms with kitchen and Florida room.

Club Med pioneered the concept of all-inclusive vacations—rates here include everything except scuba, ATP tennis, the Baby Club, and some golf. And that's everything! Accommodations, all meals, children's programs, sports and instruction—even all-day snacks, drinks, and an open bar. Rates are complex and changing—it's best to inquire for your specific dates. Club Med has three seasons: winter, summer, and holiday. Winter and summer weekly rates are similar, beginning at $1,030 per adult, $555 for children ages four to fifteen years, and $625 for toddlers two to three years. Infants under two stay free, but pay $50 per day for the Baby Club. Prices are based on availability, where you live, and when you book—early reservations can result in substantial savings. During certain weeks in spring and fall, kids under twelve (one per adult) stay free. Club Med rates may include air flights—ask for specifics. Three-night packages and day passes are also available. A Club Med annual membership is required; $55 per adult and $25 per child.

**Dining:** The Magnolia dining room is informal, serving breakfast, lunch, and dinner buffets. Dining at Club Med is a bountiful experience, with selections of American, French, and continental delicacies. It's also a good chance to meet people and socialize. The Club has its own baker and pastry maker—yum. No fewer than twelve different fresh-baked breads are served at every meal. But not to worry; there are enough activities daily to work off any calories from over-indulging. A special kid-friendly menu is served to children early at lunch and dinner. Parents may join their children while they eat, and the G.O.s (*gentils organisateurs* —French for "gracious organizers") supervise as well. High chairs and booster seats make life easier for the little ones. After their early dinner, kids return to the Mini-Club. Mom and Dad, meanwhile, savor a superb and blissfully quiet dinner, perhaps in the Riverside specialty restaurant, which is beautifully decorated, smaller, and more

intimate; table service is the order of the day here. Complimentary wine is served with lunch and dinner, thanks to the French heritage of the Club. A new policy at Club Med is a completely open bar, so drinks and snacks are now available all day long, whenever you desire. No more pop beads!

An all-day casual grill is available between meals to assuage any hunger attacks. Need juice or milk in the middle of the night? No problem; just go to the twenty-four-hour convenience room.

**Children's World:** Kids are thoroughly entertained at Club Med. The Baby Club is available six days out of seven for infants ages four to twenty-three months from 9:00 a.m. to 5:30 p.m. Baby Club is a paid service with an additional charge of $50 per day. Babies are welcome at Sandpiper, so sign up for the Baby Welcome when you reserve. Included in the Club Med package are child-care equipment in the rooms (cribs, bottle warmers, changing tables, monitors, baby bath, high chair), a special Baby Zone equipped with food and meal preparation equipment, and simple strollers. A nurse is on-site, and local pediatricians are available. Each baby gets her own crib, and there's even a special Baby Chef, who prepares food using only natural ingredients. Lunch is handled by the G.O.s, but parents are on duty for dinner. Depending on their ages, babies are changed, fed, napped, and played with in the garden, with swings and toys. The more mobile go on walks or play on the beach.

Little ones, four months to seven years, may be brought to the Siesta Club in the evening, in their pajamas, and can sleep there while parents take in a show or stroll along the river. The Siesta Club is provided from 7:30 p.m. to midnight six days out of seven at a cost of $20 per child per night.

The Petit Club is for two- to three-year-olds and can be included in the package rate. Open six days a week, it runs from 9:00 a.m. to 5:30 p.m. and again from 7:30 to 9:00 p.m. Generally toddlers are divided into two age groups. Children are so busy and engaged that you may have to make an appointment to even see them. The Mini-Club (further divided into ages four to five, six to seven, and eight to ten) and the Junior Club (ages eleven to thirteen and fourteen to seventeen) are an integral part of the Club Med experience. The Junior Club operates during school holidays and peak holiday times only. Each has its own area with clubhouse, its own G.O.s, and an unbelievable number of age-appropriate activities.

In addition to all the usual activities of children's programs, Club Med also offers circus workshops, with real trampolines, trapeze and low-wire work, juggling, trick bikes, and clowns. At the end of the week, the entire group puts on a show under the Big Top for adoring parents. It's really terrific, and the kids are so proud of themselves. There's intensive tennis for kids eight and older, and soccer, softball, in-line skating, sailing, waterskiing, and much more—all included in the one price. A program called Mini-Scientist makes science fun and engaging (and educational, although no one notices). Hip Hop Kids brings out musical talents, as does the Musical Discovery Adventure. Evening fun continues with "disco," pajama parties, and games.

**Recreation:** The sun is warm, the water inviting. You have five swimming pools (one exclusively for adults and one for Mini-Club) to choose from and a little sandy beach where you can splash in the river. It's a twenty-minute ride to the Atlantic for ocean swimming. In the calm water of the river, you can glide along on a sailboat and later have a go at waterskiing or wakeboarding (summer only). Tennis clinics are held daily on the nineteen courts; after intensive sessions, you will surely find improvement in your game. Nine courts are lit for evening play. Aerobics classes, calisthenics, and volleyball games always pop up on the agenda. Perhaps you prefer a routine in the fitness center or biking and jogging along the paths through the property. Group lessons are to be had in just about every sport; catamaran sailing and archery are only at beginning levels, but golf, tennis, waterskiing, wakeboarding, circus school, and in-line skating are taught at all levels. A real thrill is the flying trapeze—with the greatest of ease, of course. Free play with just about any kind of ball you can think of: volleyball, mini-soccer, table tennis, pitch 'n' putt minigolf, water polo, basketball, softball, and bocci ball. Did we miss any?

Unique to Sandpiper is a concentrated golf program with free group lessons at all levels. On-site golf includes an eighteen-hole championship golf course, Sinners (greens fee), designed by Mark Mahannah, as well as a driving range, a free nine-hole par 3, two putting greens, a chipping green, and a practice sand trap. For serious golfers, individual lessons and optional clinics are available. You may want to bring your own golf balls (or purchase them there); clubs may be rented. Greens fees are $83 for two days or $118 for three days and include a golf cart.

The Mini-Clubs run from 9:00 a.m. to 9:00 p.m. Afterward the whole family can enjoy the evening entertainment, usually a show or participatory fun. After the kids finally fall into bed, the nightclub continues into the night.

If you have time, which we doubt, Club Med offers a mind-boggling array of excursions. You may not want to mention it to the kids, but Disney World is only two hours away. Also nearby are the Kennedy Space Center, hot-air ballooning, and deep-sea fishing. Palm Beach shopping is also within close striking distance.

3500 SE Morningside Boulevard
Port St. Lucie, Florida 34952
(772) 398-5100, (800) CLUB-MED
www.clubmed.com

# HAWK'S CAY RESORT
## Duck Key, Florida

Located in the heart of the Florida Keys is Hawk's Cay Resort, on a tropical sixty-acre island. The resort, built in the late 1950s, has hosted numerous presidents and film stars. The rambling Caribbean-style hotel sets the tone for the relaxed, indulgent atmosphere that you'll find here. Ceiling fans, indoor plants, wicker furniture, and French doors in the lobbies and lounges echo the easygoing pace. The temperatures are mild, averaging in the low eighties in summer and the low seventies in winter, and the water stays warm and comfortable year-round. Water sports, from deep-sea fishing, fly fishing, sailing, diving, and snorkeling to swimming, sunset sails, ecotours, and water-skiing, are, naturally, the main focus of this island resort. The only living coral reef in the continental United States is just offshore, and Hawk's Cay has six resident dolphins.

**Accommodations:** This comfortable inn has the ambience and style of a Caribbean resort. Most of the 161 rooms and 16 suites are wrapped around a saltwater lagoon and several freshwater pools, with views of the Atlantic Ocean or the Gulf of Mexico. Each spacious room has a private balcony, separate dressing area, and a small refrigerator. During the high season, January through April, room rates range from $329 to $539; suite rates, including the presidential suite, range from $549 to $1,300. Low-season rates, May through mid-December, are

$279 to $459 and $479 to $900, respectively. Children sixteen and under stay free with existing bedding. The resort also has 295 two- and three-bedroom villas, modeled after Key West conch houses, which offer water settings and a full kitchen. They are the perfect home away from home for families and range from $449 to $1,000 in low season; $519 to $1,400 in high season. A daily resort activities fee of $10 per unit for the inn and $20 per villa covers parking, unlimited tennis, daily access to Indies Club and fitness center, chaise longues, towels, and more. For two adults and two children under twelve, the Family Island Explorer offers three nights' lodging, daily breakfast for all, one-day kid's club, and a kayak ride for the kids; kids also eat free from the children's menu when accompanied by an adult. Rates begin at $915 to $1,035 in a guest room.

**Dining:** If you like fresh seafood, you'll find dining here a treat. There are four tempting restaurants to choose from, each with its own distinctive style and menu selections.

Start the day with a fabulous breakfast buffet presented in the Palm Terrace. Breakfast hours begin as early as 7:00 a.m. and continue until 11:00 a.m. For casual lunches and dinners, the Cantina at poolside offers a variety of Mexican or Caribbean fare, as well as rum concoctions that recall the island's history as a stopover for Prohibition rumrunners. Also enjoy casual outdoor dining at the Indies Grille, featuring sandwiches, snacks, and a kids' menu.

WatersEdge, dockside at the marina, is open for dinner, specializing in steak and fresh-off-the-boat seafood. Porto Cayo features a blend of Mediterranean and Floridian specialties in an elegant indoor setting or outdoor cafe ambience. Truman's Bar brings back the nostalgia of when President Harry Truman vacationed here.

**Children's World:** Hawk's Cay is going all out to please the kids, and the program is growing and changing as their returning families change. Operating daily year-round, the schedules are flexible and geared to the needs of guests. The Indies Club is the new area dedicated to kids. Here you'll find two pools, one with pirate ship/water cannon playground in the center, and a new tree house that presents the opportunity for hours of climbing fun with slides, a bridge, tire swings, and lots more. Dolphin Dayz is the area for kids eleven and under, while teens have the Cove, their own recreation room filled with all that's dear to teenage hearts: music, dance floor, Internet, karaoke, games, and beverages. Cover charge is $5. Open 4:00 to 7:00 p.m. for ages nine through twelve years; teens only (thirteen to seventeen) between 8:00 p.m. and midnight. There's a teen spa (ages eight to fifteen) with mini-treatments and a fitness center.

Hawk's Cay is experimenting with some new concepts. When the resort is filled, the more traditional program will be in effect. Daily full- and half-day Kids Club programs will keep children happily occupied with swimming, tiki-boat races, scavenger hunts, fishing, and ecology tours. Little Pirates is for children ages four to five years, while the Island Adventure Club entertains ages six to eleven years with sports and nature-oriented games. Cost for either program is $55 for the full day (9:00 a.m. to 4:30 p.m.), including lunch; $28 for half days. Lunch is $7 for half-day sessions, and hours vary according to whether or not lunch is served.

A more flexible plan designates a supervised area where kids can come and go on a sign-in/sign-out basis, participating only in activities that interest them. Charges will vary. Additionally, every day there are at least two free planned activities—volleyball, limbo contest, face painting, and the like.

Kids Night Out, for ages four to eleven, includes dinner, a movie, and a make-and-take craft. It's available on Friday and Saturday evenings from 7:00 to 10:00 p.m. for $30 per child. Individual babysitting can also be arranged.

**Recreation:** Hawk's Cay guests have playing privileges at the eighteen-hole Sombrero Country Club championship course, approximately 10 miles away. For tennis buffs, two Har-Tru courts (lit for night play) and six Laykold courts beckon. Get instructions from on-site pros, participate in a variety of scheduled clinics, tournaments, and round-robins, or sharpen your skills with a ball machine.

But truly, the water tempts, entices, and captures the heart of visitors. It establishes the mood and is the setting for most of the recreation. Swim in one of the many pools or the saltwater lagoon, or stretch out beneath the tropical sun, but don't forget the sunscreen!

Discover the mysteries and wonder of undersea life. The coral reef offshore is home to a colorful array of tropical fish and is one of the best spots in the country for snorkeling and scuba diving. The Scuba Center has everything you need to immerse yourself in the scuba and snorkeling experience. Sailing clinics from two hours to ten days can make you an expert, while water-skiing, wakeboarding, kayaking, and parasailing allow you a familiarity with the water from all angles. Wrap it all up with champagne and a sunset on a catamaran—does it get any better?

Fishing here puts you in the big league, and it's exciting. Just offshore you'll find red snapper and mackerel; farther out in Gulf Stream waters are marlin, dolphin, and tuna; and tarpon ply the waters in Florida Bay. Charter a vessel at the marina for an excursion. The Marina at Hawk's Cay offers eighty-five slips and can dock yachts more than 100 feet long.

Explore the five islands of Duck Key by bicycle—child-, teen-, and adult-size bikes are available for $6 per hour, with helmet. Or take a self-guided walking tour to learn about the indigenous vegetation and tropical birds such as the brown pelican and the blue heron. Family, kids', and adult activities are scheduled just about

every hour or two; some are complimentary, and some have a nominal fee. After all that activity, a trip to the Indies Spa may be in order for massage, facials, a Vichy shower, and a complete fitness room to care for your entire body. Teens even have a special spa experience to revel in.

Unique to Hawk's Cay is the Dolphin Connection, a program designed to study, protect, and increase public interest in dolphin biology and ecosystems. Training sessions and interactive programs are offered daily. Sign up for a once-in-a-lifetime memory-making swim with the dolphins.

**61 Hawk's Cay Boulevard**
**Mile Marker 61**
**Duck Key, Florida 33050**
**(305) 743-7000, (800) 432-2242**
**www.hawkscay.com**

# JEKYLL ISLAND CLUB HOTEL
## Jekyll Island, Georgia

Jekyll Island, midway between Savannah, Georgia, and Jacksonville, Florida, and just 6 miles off the Georgia coast, is truly a gem. A barrier island, it's only 1½ miles wide and 9 miles long. Part of the state park system, a state law limits development on Jekyll to 35 percent of land above mean high water. Therefore, only one-third of the island can be developed, leaving wonderful beaches, ancient oaks, and dense maritime forests untouched and in their natural state. Of the approximately 5,000 acres, 65 percent will remain a nature preserve for future generations to enjoy.

Jekyll has an illustrious history that began in 1886 when it became a huge pri-

vate club for some of America's wealthiest tycoons. The Rockefellers, Vanderbilts, and Morgans were the first families to vacation here, so you're keeping good company when you vacation on Jekyll Island. Their "cottages" (only 8,000 square feet or so, not the size of the Newport mansions) are now part of the Historic District, with museum, tram, and carriage tours.

The club has been restored to its original splendor, has been completely modernized, and is now enjoying a new life as the Jekyll Island Club Hotel. The hotel complex is the focal point of the historic district, and their goal is much the same as a century ago—to provide relaxation and recreation in an exclusive setting. The four-diamond, four-star resort is part of the National Trust for Historic Preservation and is a registered National Historic Landmark. *Travel + Leisure* ranks the club one of the 500 best hotels in the world, and its elegant architecture, proud heritage, and excellent service explain why.

**Accommodations:** One hundred and fifty-seven guest rooms and suites tastefully blend century-old mahogany furnishings and Victorian fireplaces with marble bathrooms with whirlpools and telephones with dataports. The Queen Anne–style Clubhouse, opened in 1888, sits like a dowager aunt, with turrets, bay windows, porches, and high, high ceilings, and is altogether charming and elegant. Sans Souci was originally built in 1896 as a six-unit apartment building for visitors—perhaps the first condominium? The annex (don't be alarmed by the name; it was added in 1901) was the first to have indoor plumbing—now that conjures up some visions of vacations prior to its addition! High season is early March to mid-August; rates range from $229 for a deluxe double-king room to $399 for the Presidential Suite; from December 1 to early March, rates range from $199 to $369 for the same accommodations; children eighteen and under stay free in their parents' room. Another option is one of the beautifully restored historic "cottages": Crane Cottage, offering thirteen rooms and suites within a grand Italian-style villa, or Cherokee Cottage, a stately villa with ten rooms, named for the Cherokee roses growing at the entrance. Crane and Cherokee Cottages have comparable rates—talk with the resort for the best selection for your family. The Summer Family Getaway package offers a traditional room with two double beds, breakfast for the kids, and the children's program for $639 for three nights,

or $839 for five nights. Meal plans, per person, are $86 for Full American Plan, and $68 for Modified American Plan (breakfast and dinner); children twelve and under pay half.

All rooms are subject to a $10 per night resort fee, which provides housekeeping gratuity, beach chairs and umbrellas, pool towels, phones, newspapers, bottled water, and coffee in the Boars Head lobby.

**Dining:** The Grand Dining Room is open daily for breakfast, lunch, and dinner and boasts a scrumptious Sunday brunch. Emphasis is on seafood and gourmet continental cuisine. It is all you would imagine Victorian dining to be—with soaring Ionic columns, three fireplaces, and wide windows to draw your eye to the lawns and river. Soft piano music and candlelight accompany dinner, so eye, ear, and palate are well pleased. The new Courtyard at Crane, open for lunch daily and dinner Sunday through Thursday, offers alfresco dining with Northern California cuisine. Crane Cottage was designed in 1917 to resemble an Italian Renaissance villa. The courtyard and loggia are a wonderful setting for casual dining; indoor seating is also available. Café Solterra bakes its own yummy pastries and breads, along with New York deli offerings, and will pack a picnic lunch for you to take on your travels. Sit on the sunshine-filled porch and enjoy your food, but watch out for the crows—they are bold enough and big enough to steal half of your croissant while you read the paper! Grab a light snack at the Beach Pavilion or the Poolside Bar and Grill and never have to leave your lounge chair, or get "fancy" with the daily Victorian Tea in the Riverview Lounge. At the end of the day, Vincent's Pub serves up big-screen TV, cocktails, and snacks. The Lobby Bar is the place for evening cocktails and conversation—it's an exact replica of the bar in *The Legend* of *Bagger Vance* and a splendid place to tarry.

**Children's World:** Memorial Day to mid-August, Club Juniors is available for ages five to twelve years, Monday through Saturday from 9:00 a.m. to 4:00 p.m. Cost is only $20 per day per child, with lunch included. Half days are $10. There may be additional fees for some activities. Days are filled with bicycle safaris, sand casting, treasure hunts, a dolphin cruise, tennis, canoeing, crafts, and crabbing at Clam Creek. And, of course, swimming, including trips to the nearby water park, is high on the favorites list. Kids will be delighted and should certainly sleep well after all of this activity. That's Entertainment! livens up Friday mornings in summer with a series of performances and workshops showcasing Jekyll Island. Kids learn pizza baking, how to be a clown, all about sea turtles, how to make shadow puppets, archaeology, and storytelling.

**Recreation:** Choose between the outdoor swimming pool or the Beach Pavilion, 1 mile away on the Atlantic Ocean. Of course, the club has a regulation-size croquet lawn, so do bring the proper white clothing—you know, long flowing dresses for women, white duck for the men, short pants for boys, and hair ribbons for the girls. Rent a bicycle or try the putting green and in August and October enjoy a hands-on cooking school at Crane Cottage. Just strolling around the grounds is a trip back in time to another century, as the hotel is the centerpiece of the island's Historic District. Visit the shops for unique souvenirs, stop by the museum to see the telephone from which the first transcontinental phone call was made, see where the Federal Reserve Banking System originated, or enjoy the sights from the motor-tram or horse-drawn carriage. Art galleries, sculpture at Mistletoe Cottage, and restaurants will beckon. Don't miss the Faith Chapel with its fabulous Tiffany stained-glass window, one of only two remaining.

Complimentary transportation is provided for guests to points throughout the island.

**Jekyll Island Recreation:** Families have the entire island as their playground. The island is actually a state park, so much of the recreation is leased or run by the state. When entering the island, there is a $3 entry fee per car. In fact, Jekyll Island has Georgia's largest public golf resort. Sixty-three holes (three eighteen-hole and one nine-hole course), with professional instruction and a clubhouse with pro shop, rental clubs, restaurant, and lounge, meet your every golfing need. Picturesque but demanding, Dick Wilson's Oleander is consistently ranked among the best courses in the state. A driving range, putting greens, and practice bunker complete the golf scene. And for the budding Tiger Woods in your family, start at the two miniature golf courses or try some junior instruction. A first-class tennis center with thirteen courts (one indoors); Summer Waves Water Park; and boating, from paddleboats on the lake to sea kayaking, are all here. Fishermen can choose from surf fishing, off the pier, or two freshwater lakes. Crabbing and seining for shrimp are options, but be aware that wading birds and porpoises may follow you.

There's a wonderful new playground for children, with areas for both toddlers and older children. A relaxed sunset horseback ride along the beach promotes mind and body relaxation. And the beach stretches the length of the island, calling for nice long walks, jogging, or collecting shells. Twenty miles of bicycle trails and jogging paths provide the perfect way to enjoy this island. Treat all your senses as you watch for deer, marsh hares, and beautiful shorebirds; smell the wonderful pinewoods and salt air; listen to the sound of the ocean and feel the wind on your skin. For GPS fans, geocaching is a new "sport"—those of us without can rent a unit at the airport for the day. Find all twelve caches, take something, leave something, write it up in the logbook, and see the prettiest parts of the island, all at the same time! It's a big hit with kids and adults alike. The Tidelands Nature Center educates and explains about barrier islands and encourages kids to "please touch" the flora and fauna. Loggerhead sea turtles have found a safe haven on Jekyll Island, and nightly turtle walks on the starlit beach allow

guests to share that magic. The hotel is adding a special research/educational exhibit about these fascinating creatures. Jekyll Island is also part of Georgia's Coastal Birding Trail, with three sites and an October festival. Many restaurants and shops will beckon. For a change of view, take a water taxi to nearby St. Simons Island. It's definitely easy to adjust to this lifestyle.

---

**371 Riverview Drive**
**Jekyll Island, Georgia 31527**
**(912) 635-2600, (800) 535-9547**
**www.jekyllclub.com**

# MARCO ISLAND MARRIOTT RESORT
## Marco Island, Florida

---

Close to 2,000 years ago, native peoples discovered the beauty of Southwest Florida's Gulf Coast and Marco Island, and people have been coming here ever since. The Calusa tribe lived off the abundant shellfish and used the discarded shells to raise their dwellings above water level. Many of these ancient mounds remain today. Perched on the northernmost point of the Ten Thousand Islands of the Everglades and just south of Naples, the island is graced with miles of white-sand beaches and is noted for its gorgeous sunsets. The resort's guests get lost in the intriguing contrasts: Waves of sun-drenched beaches, always-warm Gulf waters, and passionate sunsets present a tame, pampered complement to the tangled wildness and sweeping sawgrass prairies of Florida's famous nearby Everglades.

Not just your typical high-rise-on-a-Florida-beach, the three-star, four-diamond Marco Island Marriott recently completed the final phase of a $187 million renovation. All deluxe guest rooms have been redesigned and renovated, plus there are new restaurants, a Fantasy Tiki pool with water slides and cool features, and the Balinese-style spa.

**Accommodations:** All of Marco Island Marriott Resort's 669 guest rooms and 63 suites have private balconies. Daily rates, depending on size, day, and location, are $250 to $600 in the low season (May through September) and $350 to $700 in the high season (December through April). Suites range from $500 to $1,800. Ask about the Family Escape package—two nights' lodging in two connecting rooms, a $25 recreation credit, pizza and an in-room movie, four drinks at the Tiki Bar, and—ta-da!—unlimited ice cream for up to two children under twelve!

**Dining:** Shimmering turquoise-flecked waters, sweeping white sands, and lush gardens create a tropical backdrop for four distinct restaurants at the resort. Tropiks provides great family dining for breakfast lunch, and dinner, while Kurrents has an upscale and trendy ambience for fine seafood and steak dinners with an open Exhibition Kitchen. The recently opened beachfront cafe, 400 Pazzis, is a large indoor/outdoor brick oven pizzeria overlooking the Gulf of Mexico that will set the bar for fun. Most restaurants have children's menus. Quinn's on the Beach cooks up a treasure trove of savory sandwiches and Caribbean appetizers from almost dawn until after dusk, served with sunsets and entertainment. Have a light lunch and drinks poolside at the Tiki Bar and Grill; for coffee and pastries, try San Marco Café. For a change of pace, just 7 miles away in Naples, you may have breakfast or lunch at the Rookery Clubhouse on the golf course.

**Children's World:** The Tiki Tribe at Marco Island Marriott Resort—the first resort in North America to be awarded the National Parenting Center Seal of Approval—is a lot of pint-size fun, occupying youngsters ages five to twelve with sand-castle creations, coconut bowling, arts and crafts, and zany relay races. The program operates daily year-round, from 10:00 a.m. to 3:00 p.m. The cost is $70 for a full day, including lunch and an ice-cream snack. A second child is $60. A unique Rainy Day program offers hours of indoor entertainment for the whole family on those rare days without sunshine.

**Recreation:** Choreographed by a team of fun-in-the-sun experts ten to fifteen years old, daily activities are scheduled and include silly sandy beach games, live crab races, family waterside bingo, sailing and shelling tours, ceramics and coconuts, hair braiding, yoga and fitness classes, pool games, and kids' edible creations. Some activities are complimentary, and some have fees. Sun worshippers and soul searchers relax under thatch-topped tiki huts, play beach volleyball, or scour the shore for seashells. Endless Gulf activities include sailing, kayaking, windsurfing, waterskiing, bumper tubing, Wave Runners, and parasailing. Two swimming pools offer refreshing plunges; the Tiki Pool begins at zero depth, good for splashing with toddlers. Older kids and even adults enjoy the water slide and other special water features found here. Quinn's Pool is brand new and very impressive, blending fire and water elements. Again with zero-depth entry, it is totally magnificent.

Golfers can enjoy the off-site, Robert Cupp Jr.–designed eighteen-hole championship golf course called the Rookery. The clubhouse facility includes an elaborate pro shop, complete locker room facilities, the Clubhouse Grill for breakfast or lunch, and Nick Faldo's Golf School. For tennis enthusiasts there are eight red clay courts (four lighted for night play), a tennis shop, daily clinics, private lessons, and round-robins. Fabulous fishing is accessible, or you can work out with Florida-style aerobics and fitness programs.

Treat yourself to a session at the Balinese-style spa for a massage and perhaps a milk-and-honey or lavender-and-rose-petal Bali Bath. Be sure, though, to save time for ecotour adventures. Briggs Nature Center is only 8 miles away, or you can visit Everglades National Park (30 miles). Unlike many tropical places, Marco Island and the surrounding area have an abundance of art galleries, museums, concerts, cultural heritage centers, and even a film festival. The Big Cypress Gallery, located in the heart of the Everglades, showcases Clyde Butcher's nature photography, described by some as the Ansel Adams of the new millennium.

**400 South Collier Boulevard**
**Marco Island, Florida 34145**
**(239) 394-2511, (800) 438-4373**
**www.marcoislandmarriott.com**

# MARRIOTT'S GRAND HOTEL RESORT, GOLF CLUB & SPA
## Point Clear, Alabama

The charm and graciousness of the Old South has not faded in southern Alabama. Marriott's Grand Hotel has preserved its rich tradition of elegant service as a premier resort for more than 160 years. Known as the Queen of Southern Resorts, the four-diamond hotel is set on 550 acres in Point Clear, on a peninsula in Mobile Bay and 23 miles from downtown Mobile. In this secluded location the quiet lagoons, majestic oak trees draped in Spanish moss, and beautiful gardens can make you forget the worries and concerns of the workaday world. Leave your troubles and anxieties on the doorstep and enter this vacation retreat, where your biggest dilemma will be how best to enjoy yourself.

The fascinating legacy of the Grand Hotel captures the heart of many a history buff. First discovered as an ideal location for a resort retreat in 1847, the hotel was the site of lively antebellum social events in its early years. Then, during the days of the Civil War (or as some folks down here still call it, the War of Northern Aggression), it served as a hospital for Confederate soldiers. After the war the hotel resumed its original function and once again became the center for leisure activities. A fire in 1869 and a hurricane in 1893 destroyed some of the old facilities, but rebuilding efforts and expansion were frequently

undertaken in order to maintain accommodations for guests. That still holds true today, and the hotel completed a $50 million renovation in 2006.

**Accommodations:** The main building has been described as rustic, but don't be deceived; this is rustic in a grand old manner. The lobby here is a charming octagonal structure that focuses on a massive fireplace. From its wide planks of pine flooring to its cypress-beamed ceiling, visitors immediately sense a warm, hospitable atmosphere. There are a total of 405 guest rooms in the different buildings and the cottages. Many rooms are decorated with white cypress paneling and ceiling fans (maintained primarily for ambience, but also to capture the bay breezes; air-conditioning relieves the sultriness of summer days); most rooms offer private balconies with bay/marina or pool/garden views. Open year-round, the hotel has two rate structures. In the winter season (November through February), daily room-only rates range from $184 to $244 midweek. Special rates that include breakfast for two are just $10 more, and children under five can dine from the special children's buffet. Summer rates (March through October) are higher: $199 to $259 weekdays or $299 to $359 weekends. There is no charge for cribs and rollaways. Inquire about the many specials and packages available.

**Dining:** While dining is grand here, don't get confused by all the Grands. Start your day at the Grand Coffee Shoppe with latte and pastries. Move on to the Dining Room for a casual breakfast or lunch and an award-winning Sunday brunch. Dinner at the Grand Dining Room is an event—eclectic menus, bold new wines, the freshest ingredients, and hand-grown herbs prepared by an all-star staff of chefs. Serving dinner since 1847, with piano accompaniment, the dining room raises Southern hospitality to an art form. Resort attire and reservations are required. Kids and parents alike are entertained during dinner at the Saltwater Grill, where the emphasis is on fresh food, fun, and efficient service, and the atmosphere is upbeat and casual.

The Lakewood Golf Club, set in a wooded landscape, serves lunch and dinner. While soaking up the sunshine, you may choose snacks, sandwiches, and grilled favorites poolside at either the Pelican's Nest or the Blue Marlin Bar. Bucky's Birdcage Lounge also serves light snacks and delightful cocktails with spectacular views, and live entertainment nightly.

**Children's World:** The Grand Fun Camp is in operation daily year-round. Every day a group of friendly counselors coordinates fun-filled activities. Four- to twelve-year-olds frolic from 10:00 a.m. to 2:00 p.m. and from 6:00 to 10:00 p.m. The cost is $40 per session, including lunch or dinner. The second sibling is $20, and the third is only $10. Shuffleboard, putt-putt golf, arts and crafts, video games, fishing, and sand-castle building entertain children, who will no doubt entertain their parents as they recount a day's adventures. Special events include movies and puppet shows. A swimming pool on Mobile Bay with waterfalls and slides also has a children's area with

playground and tree house that kids love. Individual babysitters are also available on an hourly basis.

**Recreation:** In the old days of the resort, two favorite spots were the wharves—one for men and one for women, because sunbathing and swimming in mixed company were unacceptable. Having come a long way since then, the Grand now offers innumerable popular activities for its guests. Given this prime location and mild climate, water sports attract many visitors. After a little warm-up fishing in the bay, you might take on the challenges of deep-sea fishing. Your catch may be your evening's dinner, prepared especially for you by the hotel chefs. Reserve a kayak, sailboat, or paddleboat for an afternoon's outing, or bring your own boat to the thirty-seven-slip marina. Splash in the waters of the bay along the sandy beach, or take a dip in the beautiful pool, the largest on the Gulf Coast, with waterfall and slide. There's also a family pool, a child-entry pool, as well as an indoor pool and two whirlpools.

If you're more of a landlubber, the championship thirty-six holes of golf on Dogwood and Azalea courses are a suitable diversion. Regardless of their level of play, all golfers appreciate the rolling, wooded setting of the Golf Trail Courses designed by Robert Trent Jones. The facilities of the club include instructors, carts, putting greens, and locker room. The eight rubico tennis courts (four lighted) lure many ace players, and novices can enroll for lessons with one of the pros. Head to the stables at Ocala Farms for horseback riding around the picturesque lakes and lagoons, or jog or bicycle (rentals available) through the gardens and along the boardwalk.

Slower-paced activities include croquet, a putting green, and video games. You may want to wind up the day in the hot tub or with a treat from the full-service spa, where treatments are luxuriously relaxing in a serenely beautiful setting. In the 1930s the Grand Hotel advertised itself as the place of "Every Creature Comfort." Many visitors today feel that reputation has withstood the test of time.

If you feel like venturing off-property, visit the nearby Bellingrath Home and Garden, where something is in bloom year-round. The Gulf Coast Exploreum and Science Museum in Mobile has wonderful interactive exhibits, an IMAX theater, and special shows. The battleship USS *Alabama* and the National Museum of Naval Aviation may appeal to the military-minded.

**1 Grand Boulevard**
**Point Clear, Alabama 36564**
**(251) 928-9201, (800) 544-9933**
**www.marriottgrand.com**

# THE RESORT AT LONGBOAT KEY CLUB
## Longboat Key, Florida

An island retreat, the Resort at Longboat Key Club specializes in relaxation and recreation for golfers and tennis players. Located on a barrier island in the Gulf of Mexico just west of Sarasota, it doesn't shortchange swimmers and sun worshippers either. It was ranked as one of *Travel + Leisure* magazine's "Top 500 Resorts in the World," so consider it your private oceanfront country club. The resort enjoys a lush, tropical setting between the Gulf and Sarasota Bay that seems worlds away from regular routine, yet it is only fifteen minutes away from the Sarasota Airport.

**Accommodations:** Seven modern buildings, four to ten stories high, are arranged throughout the property to afford guests magnificent views of the Gulf, the bay, and the golf course fairways. Of the 232 accommodations, each with its own balcony, the majority are suites, each with a king-size bed, a sleeper sofa, and a fully equipped kitchen. Summer (June through September) is the low season, when guest rooms range from $215 to $295 a night and club suites start at $250 a night; the deluxe two-bedroom suites command $550 to $580 a night. During the high season (February through April), a guest room is $340 to $355 a night, while suites cost $410 to $600 a night. During the rest of the year, prices fall between these parameters; holidays are more expensive. Up to two children (seventeen and younger) can stay in a suite with their parents at no additional charge. A resort fee of $15 per room or $25 per suite applies.

**Dining:** Dining can be as elegant or as casual as you choose. On the sophisticated side is Sands Pointe, the signature restaurant. Tempting fresh seafood dishes are frequently featured on its menus; it is open for breakfast, lunch, and dinner. Next to the restaurant, try the Pointe Lounge for a light menu, specialty drinks, homemade desserts such as raspberry-key-lime pie, and live entertainment in the evenings. For more casual dining, drop by Spike 'n' Tees for breakfast or lunch overlooking the fairways; and for truly relaxed mealtimes, saunter over to Barefoots, at poolside; no shoes required, with live music on weekends.

Enjoy lunch and dinner at the nearby Grille at Harborside, 11:30 a.m. to 4:30 p.m. on weekends, set among gigantic oak trees on the Harborside Course. Traditional country club lunches and steak and seafood dinners are a welcome option. Overlooking the marina, the Dining Room, with its view of the marina waterways lined with mangrove trees, serves seasonal evening buffets and Sunday brunch as well. Or simply enjoy room service served on your own private balcony.

**Children's World:** The Kids Klub operates year-round, Tuesday through Saturday. Experienced counselors direct youngsters ages five to twelve in a full 9:30 a.m. to 3:00 p.m. program. Swimming, beach fun, volleyball, basketball, field trips, and arts and crafts are all part of the schedule. The program is $35 per child per day and includes lunch and admission to attractions. Regularly visited attractions and things to do include the Mote Marine Laboratory, Sarasota Jungle Gardens, Gulf Coast World of Science, Planet Fun, movies, bowling, skating, and miniature golf at Pirate's Cove. The average cost of individual babysitting is $15 an hour, with a three-hour minimum.

**Recreation:** The Islandside Golf Course has eighteen holes, and the Harborside Course offers three nine-hole layouts. The courses are the recipient of *Golf Magazine*'s Silver Medal. With palm trees and quiet lagoons throughout these courses, who can have a bad game? Two complete pro shops, a golf school, and professionals to guide players in private lessons and tournaments round out the picture for golfers.

Thirty-eight Har-Tru tennis courts await your ace serves and graceful lobs. Six of these are lighted for night play. Two tennis shops, ball machines, a videotaped game analysis, and a professional staff will urge you on to better play. The Resort at Longboat Key has been recognized as a "Top 50 Tennis Resort" by *Tennis* magazine, and tennis play is complimentary here.

Swimming in the outdoor pool or the gentle waters of the Gulf may top off your day. Bicycle along the nature trails, stroll on the snow-white beach, spend an afternoon with rafts, kayaks, and boogie boards, or go snorkeling or sailing. You can even organize a deep-sea fishing expedition through the concierge.

The resort's newest recreational amenity is a 4,000-square-foot fitness center, which features weight-training and cardiovascular equipment as well as instructor-led aerobics classes. Fitness-center equipment is available to guests on a complimentary basis. For soothing life's daily stress and the ultimate in personal pampering, indulge yourself at the Island House Spa, where you can have a massage or luxuriate in a body piña colada or a Couples Double Chocolate Body Sundae.

---

**301 Gulf of Mexico Drive**
**Longboat Key, Florida 34228**
**(941) 383-8821, (800) 237-8821**
**www.longboatkeyclub.com**

# SOUTH SEAS RESORT

## Captiva Island, Florida

Located at the northern tip of Captiva Island on the Gulf of Mexico, 3 miles off Florida's southwest coast, Captiva Island is connected to the mainland via Sanibel Island and the Sanibel Causeway. It has a fascinating history going back at least 5,000 years and involving Calusa Indians, pirates, homesteaders, and a prosperous key-lime plantation. South Seas Resort is approximately 30 miles from the Southwest Florida International Airport in Fort Myers.

Dubbed "Florida's Tahiti" for its subtropical climate and lush foliage indigenous to the Southern Hemisphere, Captiva Island—famous for its shell-covered beaches—has been rated one of America's most romantic beaches. South Seas Resort is a 330-acre island resort with 2½ miles of beach, a full-service yacht harbor and marina, and a complimentary open-air trolley transportation system.

South Seas Resort suffered extensive damage in 2004 from Hurricane Charley. The positive effect of this is that the resort has now had a $140 million rebirth, and most everything is new and even better. This entry is as accurate as it can be under the circumstances, but we encourage you to check directly with the resort to ensure up-to-the-minute information.

**Accommodations:** The South Seas Resort boasts more than 600 luxurious units, ranging from deluxe hotel rooms and villa suites to three-bedroom beach homes and cottages. South Seas rates are based not only on time of year and location but also, more importantly, on occupancy levels. Therefore, it's almost impossible to state even a range with any accuracy, but the resort promises to always offer the best rate available. As an example, on request, a one-bedroom tennis villa was between $199 in summer and $369 in winter; the five-night summer family package (including kids' club) ranged from $171 to $180 per night in those same accommodations; children sixteen and under stay free. Booking directly with South Seas Resort is the only way to ensure that you have access to all the resort facilities.

**Dining:** Start your day with a latte at the Starbucks Café in Chadwick's Square, at the entrance to the resort, where you may wake up leisurely, read the paper, or take your laptop for the free wireless Internet access; the cafe is open until 8:00 p.m. Also planned in this area is the Captiva Provision Company, a general store and grocery/deli. Currently, you may call the resort to stock your refrigerator before your arrival. The new "in place" on Captiva is The Pointe, in Harborside Village on the north end of the island. Between the sound and the new pool/cabana complex, water views abound. You'll enjoy an innovative Caribbean Grill lunch menu, umbrella drinks until 6:00 p.m., and spectacular sunsets. Coming in 2007, the Sunset Beach Chalet will feature sun, sand, outdoor seating, and classic beach fare, such as grouper sandwiches and cheeseburgers; and for nostalgic Americana you can't beat a light snack on the beach at the 1950s Airstream trailer. The Tiki Bar by the pool keeps you nourished without leaving the sun, while Scoops and Slices offers, you guessed it, ice cream and pizza.

The new signature restaurant at South Seas is Harbourside Bar & Grill, casually elegant with indoor/outdoor seating and fresh, fresh local seafood. Chef Jeffrey Lunak creates some amazing dishes;

Drunken Shrimp is only the start. Find evening entertainment at The Pointe or Harbourside Bar.

**Children's World:** Activities for children are available year-round. With the Gulf, the beach, and a huge wildlife sanctuary as a playground, children are entertained as well as enlightened. Monday through Friday, from 9:00 a.m. to 1:00 p.m., children ages four to twelve exercise their imaginations, as well as their bodies, with active play and themed activities such as pirates, beach day and shelling, or wacky Olympics. Kids Night Out, a dinner party from 6:00 to 9:00 p.m. on Tuesday (Hawaiian Luau) and Saturday (Carnival), gives parents a chance to also play a little, have a quiet dinner, or stroll along the sea under the stars. Cost is $35 per session and includes lunch or dinner. Saturday is Carnival Day, from 11:00 a.m. to 3:00 p.m. For $15 per person, everyone, all ages, can participate in the fun and games.

Captiva Teens Club has a wide variety of structured and semistructured activities to entice this group to play. Kayaking tours, message in a bottle, teen cinema, jewelry making, or coconut crafts are popular pastimes. The Game Room, open from 11:00 a.m. to 9:00 p.m. daily, is always a favorite gathering place; all the virtual-reality games are here. All-day access is $10; children under twelve need to be accompanied by an adult.

**Recreation:** Dozens of recreational activities are available to guests of South Seas Resort. Golf includes a par 27 regulation nine-hole seaside course or an eighteen-hole course at Dunes Golf and Tennis Club on Sanibel Island. You can pleasurably fill your days with tennis on eighteen courts; biking; and water sports, including game fishing, sailboarding, snorkeling, sailing, and excursion cruises to nearby islands. Paddle a kayak into a mangrove forest, zoom around on a WaveRunner, keep your eyes peeled for dolphins, or just watch the manatees play around the marina.

Workshops feature yoga, professional fitness training, aerobic exercise classes, canoe excursions, sailing clinics, guided shelling excursions, family fishing, shell art, and more. Family activities include log-rolling contests, bingo, alligator races, or perhaps hydrocycles. A variety of nature activities for the whole family include Dolphin and Manatee Awareness, Shells of Captiva, Wildlife Refuge Trips, and Birds of Captiva. The Nature Center celebrates the biodiversity of these barrier islands with a "please touch" approach. All of these activities are somewhat in flux and subject to change, so do pick up the resort's bulletin, *South Seas Today,* upon your arrival. Many activities are complimentary, others may have small fees, and there are probably some that we haven't even heard of! Neighboring Sanibel Island is also a rich resource for recreation. The two islands together are ranked among the top three shelling beaches of the world, so don't miss the delights of low tide.

---

**P.O. Box 194**
**5400 Plantation Road**
**Captiva Island, Florida 33924**
**(239) 472-5111, (800) 965-7772**
**www.southseas.com**

# SUNDIAL BEACH RESORT

## Sanibel Island, Florida

Sanibel is a barrier island off the southwest coast of Florida that has some of the best shelling in the world. Two-thirds of the island remains a nature preserve—it also preserves a taste of Florida as it once was. No neon and high-rises here; in fact, locals call it Nature's Theme Park. The Sundial is the island's only full-service resort, set on thirty-three lush, tropical acres along the Gulf of Mexico. Completely renovated in 2005 as an aftermath of Hurricane Charley, it's back and in fine shape.

**Accommodations:** Two hundred seventy condominium units provide a home-away-from-home atmosphere; choose a one- or two-bedroom unit and revel in full kitchens, comfortable and roomy bedrooms, and living areas, most with screened balconies. Select a garden view, partial Gulf view, or Gulf-front unit. The Sundial is under the same management as South Seas Resort, so rates here are based not only on season and location but also principally on occupancy. Therefore, it is almost impossible to give even a range of rates with any accuracy. As an example, a one-bedroom unit might be $169 to $189 in July and $259 to $279 in January. May through October, family packages with a five-night minimum stay provide an excellent value; sample rates of $153 to $171 include lodging, kids' club, water sports, a family portrait on the beach, and more.

**Dining:** At Sundial, Crocodial's Poolside Bar & Grill tempts you with Croc Dogs for the kids and fresh tropical-fruit salads and frozen drinks for grown-ups. At Beaches Bar & Grill, sample the happy-hour specials and enjoy live entertainment. Stop by The Shoppe for grocery and deli items. Nearby, visit Ellington's Jazz Bar & Restaurant,

where award-winning chefs serve seafood, steak, and pasta; it is open for breakfast and dinner daily.

A five-minute drive brings you to Rassa, at the Dunes Golf and Tennis Club. Creative seafood and traditional steakhouse favorites are served up in this intimate setting. Named after Punta Rassa, the old port used to ship cattle to Cuba, meats are positively works of art here. Dine indoors or on the patio. Lunches of salad, homemade soups, and sandwiches are offered Monday through Saturday; Rassa is open for dinner Tuesday through Saturday. You have an entire island of dining choices as well. In fact, two islands, as a bridge connects Sanibel to nearby Captiva Island and its associated property, South Seas Resort. Stock your larder or buy goodies to take home at local grocery stores and shopping centers.

**Children's World:** The concept behind Explorer Kid's Club is that if kids don't have a good time on vacation, you won't either. They're dedicated to helping you achieve that goal. Every day of the year from 9:00 a.m. to 1:00 p.m., children ages four to twelve gather at the Kid's Club next to the pool, prepared for a morning of fun. Arts and crafts, beach games, and pool activities work up an appetite for the lunch that's included. Cost is $40 per child. To receive recreation and Kid's Club discounts, make sure to sign up as a member of Explorer when you check in at the front desk. In addition, activities are planned daily between 10:00 a.m. and 4:00 p.m.; some are age specific (four and up or seven and up), and some are for all ages; everyone may participate as they like. Some are complimentary, while others may have a small fee for materials. Afternoons are for family time, and for most kids, more water play. Make sure to find out the time for low tide—that's when the shelling is the best. Find a Junonia shell, and have your name printed in the *Island Reporter* newspaper.

Kid's Night Out from 5:30 to 8:30 p.m. on Friday and Saturday ($40) has a weekly theme, such as Luau, and gives parents a chance to kick up their heels.

**Recreation:** A professional recreation staff plans myriad daily activities for all ages. In addition to the Explorer Kid's Club Camp, teens and tweens are enticed into participation with beach volleyball, bicycles, or boogie boards. Family activities bring everyone together.

Close by, the Dunes Golf and Tennis Club offers a championship course, an aqua driving range, and two practice greens. Better practice your swing before hitting the course, as the back nine is part of a wildlife preserve and plenty of critters are watching. It's equal parts sports and nature experience. Are you a tennis family? Sundial has tennis clinics for all ages. The resort has twelve courts for practice and play. Some courts are complimentary for guests, and two of the hard courts are lighted for night play. Golf and tennis pro shops have all the latest gear and game advice.

Fish from beach, pier, bridge, or boat—Gulf waters have more than 1,000 species of marine life. Snorkeling and scuba dives are popular, or stay on top of the water with kayaks, Windsurfers, and catamarans. Swim in one of the five heated pools—kids love to slide down the huge Nautilus Shell.

Work out in the fitness room, or rent a bicycle to explore the island—it's pretty flat, easy terrain.

Sanibel has an exciting selection of cruises: Cruise the bay with a marine biologist to watch dolphins and visit a deserted island; take an out-island luncheon cruise to Cabbage Key and Useppa, a shelling cruise, a sail, or a beautiful sunset cruise. Environmental Discovery Programs schedule both lectures and hands-on experiences. The ECO (Environmental Coastal Observatory) Center was the first to be situated in a resort. Spend fascinating hours with a simulated mangrove forest, the aquarium, the touch tank, and a hermit crab petting zoo learning about all that surrounds you on this beautiful island. May through October is sea turtle nesting season.

Sanibel is an active place, with theater groups, Tanger outlet shopping center, shops, and art galleries. Since Sanibel is one of the three best shelling areas in the world, it's only natural to have a Shell Museum. Nearby attractions include the "Ding" Darling National Wildlife Refuge, Corkscrew Swamp Sanctuary, Calusa Nature Center and Planetarium, and the Edison-Ford Estates.

---

**1451 Middle Gulf Drive
Sanibel Island, Florida 33957
(800) 965-7772, (239) 472-4151
www.sundialresort.com**

# TRADEWINDS ISLAND RESORTS/ISLAND GRAND

## St. Pete Beach, Florida

Hugging the sugary white sands of the Gulf of Mexico, two stellar beach resorts, the Island Grand and Sandpiper, comprise TradeWinds Island Resorts. These properties occupy twenty-five of the most desirable acres on St. Pete Beach. With limitless beachfront recreation, sumptuous dining, and exclusive golf privileges at the area's private country clubs, the TradeWinds Island Resorts offer guests access to two resorts in one.

The Island Grand is a classic yet casual beach resort. The first thing that strikes you is the number of children on the grounds—happy children and relaxed parents having fun. The AAA four-diamond rating doesn't interfere with their motto, "Just Let Go." And it's easy to do that here. Canals with white swans meander through the property, awaiting your visit via paddleboat. The Grand Palm Colonnade, a garden atrium lined with two-story palm trees, provides a shady welcome. The children's program is headquartered here, so it's most convenient for families. An eighteen-acre island hideaway, TradeWinds Island Grand offers endless diversions, award-winning service, and classic Florida charm.

**Accommodations:** The 378 guest rooms and 207 suites all sport bright, colorful tropical furnishings and clean white accents. Every room features a microwave, refrigerator, coffeemaker, toaster, and dishware. Suites have separate bedrooms, kitchenette, and living area, most with balconies. February, March, and April are high season, when hotel rooms range from $229 to $369 and one-bedroom suites are $325 to $459. May through mid-December rates are lower:

$188 to $270 for rooms and $267 to $377 for one-bedroom suites. No charge for children eighteen and under sharing the room. A daily resort amenity fee of $25 is required; this covers parking, telephone, tennis courts, fitness center, beach cabanas, paddleboats, wireless Internet access, and much more. Family packages are well priced and offer many extras; ask about "Beach Blanket Bingo," with a 1950s theme, or "Swashbuckling by the Sea," with pirates and a yo-heave-ho, or "It's Easy Being Green," in keeping with the resort's emphasis on being environmentally aware and energy conscious. TradeWinds has earned Florida's Green Lodging Certification for its efforts. Recognizing that 65 percent of remarriages involve children, the resort began "Familymoon" packages, designed for fun-filled family bonding. A two-bedroom suite, sunset sail, dinner for two, and one $50 TAZ pass per child plus lots of special things (like a "Yours, Mine, and Ours" DVD) smooth the way to a new lifestyle. Contact the resort for information on the many packages offered with a price range that is sure to fit your family quite nicely.

**Dining:** Enjoy breakfast buffets, poolside lunches, and elegant sunset dinners. Indulge in room service or set the kids loose for deli specialties, an ice-cream shop, and even a Pizza Hut. Unwind at the waterside piano bar or enjoy evening entertainment in the lounge. A dozen on-site dining and entertainment venues keep everyone well fed and happy. Bermuda's is open all day, with hearty breakfasts, seafood, steaks, and a children's menu. The Palm Court is an intimate, elegant bistro with excellent fare;

dine indoors or on the patio under the stars. To experience a Florida "cracker cottage," stop by the Flying Bridge, docked over the main canal—probably one of the only restaurants you can boat under! Food and dress are casual. It's B.R. Cuda's to catch the big game, or you can seek seasonal live entertainment at several venues. Cap'n Redbeard's Sharktooth Tavern is the place to meet a pirate, have an exotic drink or pub fare, race crabs, or make a shark's-tooth necklace. At the Sandpiper, Piper's Patio is a full-service restaurant with casual, outdoor beachfront dining for breakfast, lunch, and dinner; the Sand Bar provides a front-row seat for sunsets. Add to that at least two dozen restaurants within 1 mile of the resort, and you'll need all the exercise facilities of the resort.

**Children's World:** Tuesday through Saturday, the enthusiastic recreation counselors (known as TAZ Team members) of TradeWinds Action Zone offer activities from A to Z, with recreational options for every member of the family. TAZ Team members supervise tons of planned fun stuff, from aerobics to zany, wacky wordies, family swim meets, suncatcher creations, or a hunt for treasures.

The KONK Club (short for "Kids Only, No Kidding!") is specially designed for children four to eleven years old. Each day's program is themed a little differently, lasts from 9:00 a.m. to 1:00 p.m., and includes lunch ($25). KONK kids even have their own special nighttime programs from 6:00 to 9:00 p.m. (Tuesday through Saturday; cost is $25 with dinner), providing a great way to make friends with other kids, and giving Mom and Dad a little time alone. The evening can be extended to 11:00 p.m. for an additional $10. On Wednesday and Saturday, when Captain Redbeard comes to Pirate Island, all the kids get dressed up, and tall tales and swashbuckling songs

break out. After a search for shark's teeth, everyone heads for the pool for a "dive-in" pirate movie—great fun for all.

Be sure to look for Beaker, the TradeWinds huggable purple toucan mascot. You're likely to spot Beaker at KONK Club activities or having breakfast. Or call Activities to schedule a bedtime tuck-in: Beaker will come to your room to make sure all kids are tucked in toucan-style ($14).

Teens will enjoy the variety of activities and attractions at the resort and in the surrounding area. With tennis, golf, swimming, snorkeling, WaveRunners, Shell Island and Dolphin Watch Cruises, minigolf, parasailing, and numerous other activities, teens can be as active as they choose. If there's enough interest, the TAZ Team will schedule excursions or special events, a great opportunity for young people to meet casually. Preregistration is required for off-site trips.

**Recreation:** Escape to the magic of the TradeWinds Island Resorts and discover a place where you can do "everything under the sun"—or absolutely nothing at all. The Golf Concierge Desk will arrange tee times at any of the public courses in the Tampa Bay area; guests also enjoy privileges at the private Pasadena Yacht and Country Club, just ten minutes away. Two Har-Tru clay courts serve all resort guests, so reserve early. The Action Zone Activities Center coordinates all the recreation activity for every member of the family—and it's extensive. Whether it's aqua aerobics, tie-dye towels, glow-in-the-dark volleyball, or Hunt for Redbeard's Buried Treasure, the TAZ staff has you covered. So many activities are scheduled that you need a foldout brochure to list them; pick one up from the concierge on your arrival. Minigolf, life-size chess, or sunset yoga may tempt you; the water beckons with parasailing, snorkeling, WaveRunners, water-skiing, boat rental, and deep-sea fishing charters; take a dolphin or manatee encounter cruise; walk along acres of soft, white-sand beaches; or try your hand at beach volleyball.

The swirl of whirlpools, the heat of sauna, the refreshing depths of five pools entice. Dip into the shimmering surface of the sea. Comb the sandy beach for shells. See how fast you can descend the three-story High Tide Slide. Curl up with a book in a tropical courtyard or a beach cabana. Toast the sunset. Explore the resort's meandering waterway by paddleboat, but don't run over the swans, ducks, and egrets. Pamper yourself at Body Works salon with massage, aromatherapy, and body wraps. Relax. You're a million miles away . . . from everything. You're now on island time, so "Just Let Go."

---

**5500 Gulf Boulevard**
**St. Pete Beach, Florida 33706**
**(727) 363-2212, (800) 360-4016**
**www.tradewindsresort.com**

# MIDWEST

Arkansas
Illinois
Kansas
Michigan
Minnesota
Missouri
Wisconsin

# BIG CEDAR LODGE RESORT

Ridgedale, Missouri

Deep in the heart of the Ozark Mountains—once the frontier, when the West was new—is a restful retreat, a playground for today's explorers. Big Cedar, only a ten-minute drive from Branson but a true escape from the outside world, awaits your family. In the 1920s, just after the railroad had opened this wilderness area, two wealthy Missourians decided to build country homes on their 300 acres. One chose a log mansion, the other a Tudor style. Time passed, and in 1947 a lodge, pool, and stable became the Devil's Pool Ranch guest resort; later the White River was dammed to form Table Rock Lake. In 1987 Bass Pro Shops acquired the land, restored the original mansions to their former glory, and began Big Cedar. Hospitality and attention to detail are key values here. Big Cedar has been voted "Connoisseur's Choice" by *Great Resorts and Hotels,* "Best of the Best" by the *Wall Street Journal,* and "One of the Top 10 Resorts in the Country" by *Southern Living* magazine and has won awards for landscaping, Audubon's top 200 best environmental golf courses, and National Arbor Day Foundation's Good Steward Award. Table Rock Lake's 745 miles of shoreline provide endless recreation to visitors. Atop the hillsides, Big Cedar's grand lodges overlook the lake, while log cottages nestle among the trees. This much rustic wilderness takes a lot of planning! Each of the four seasons brings its own beauty and delights.

**Accommodations:** Rooms in three unique lodges, cottages of knotty pine, and log cabins provide a choice for guests to be near the action or nicely secluded. Spring View Lodge is near the restaurant and pool, and each room has a view of the lake. Val-

ley View Lodge accommodations offer standard rooms or two-bedroom suites, with kitchenette. Falls Lodge is the newest, with balconies, whirlpool baths, and gas fireplaces. Knotty Pine cottages are conveniently located, with earth-toned decor and native woods. Private log cabins are tucked into the woods or on the lake. With full kitchen, deck, fireplace, and whirlpool bath, the cabins are a real escape. For even more privacy and unspoiled nature, try the Dogwood Canyon cabins, about 16 miles from Big Cedar and bordering on the nature park. Winter and spring rates are the lowest; summer, fall, weekend, and holiday rates are the highest. Winter/spring per-night room rates for two adults in the lodges range from $79 to $167; one-bedroom suites are $178 to $239. Rooms in summer/fall are $119 to $206; one-bedroom suites are $229 to $345. Falls Lodge is more expensive. Knotty Pine cottages are $89 to $251 in winter and $189 to $296 in summer; a one-room cabin with loft is $179 to $347, going to $419 to $526 in summer. Depending on the rating, children up to twelve stay free; children over twelve pay $15 per day. Packages usually provide a saving, and a variety of them can be arranged.

**Dining:** Set in a century-old Adirondack-style log structure, the Devil's Pool Restaurant serves history along with your meal. A huge stone fireplace and wrought-iron chandeliers shed a soft light; the mahogany bar gleams; and antique furnishings, native materials, mounted heads, and bark-covered logs add to the sporty atmosphere. Start with Ozark smoked trout and Cedar Chips; try hickory-smoked prime rib, catfish, or one of the many steaks. Outdoor seating is seasonal. Devil's Pool is open for breakfast, lunch, and dinner, with children's menus. Downstairs at the Buzzard Bar, the menu is similar, with the addition of sandwiches and salads; it's open daily until midnight for lunch and dinner. Dine indoors or out, surrounded by the usual collection of furred and feathered "friends"—but no live buzzards. The singing cowboy or the barmaid may share the legend with you, though. The Truman Smokehouse is situated in a charming little 1920s Tudor-style building, once a garage. Meats and fish are actually smoked here, so just follow your nose. Open seasonally, with indoor or patio seating, it's a good place for breakfast. Top of the Rock reopened with signature grilled steaks, seafood, and pasta, plus some new items. On Friday and Saturday evenings, enjoy an elegant dinner with lakeside views at the Worman Steakhouse; the Sunday Champagne Brunch here is famous. You will find all your traditional favorites plus special treats. Bent Hook Market at the Marina has grocery supplies and will stock your cabin before arrival, if requested. If you have a grill, call room service to bring a Backyard Basket with everything you need for a meal.

**Children's World:** With Little Cedar Kids Club, for children ages four to twelve years, the focus is on fun and environmental awareness. The great outdoors beckons, and all eagerly respond. Memorial Day through Labor Day, on Monday, Wednesday, and Friday, choose from morning or evening sessions (or both!); on Tuesday, Thursday, and Sunday, sessions are in the afternoon. Worm races, bubblegum-blowing contests (who do you think cleans it out of their hair?), pool games, hula hoops, and scavenger hunts are just a small sample of what happens daily. Each session is three hours, action-packed, and usually with a theme; cost is $25 per child. Kids can also join the Activities Team for fun and games ($15 per hour). Evening sessions are four hours, including dinner, for $40. Complimentary kids' activities are also offered seasonally. Since this is a Bass Pro resort, the young angler's fishing program is very popular. Kids must be accompanied by an adult—who knows, parents may learn too!

**Recreation:** Golfers look forward to the Top of the Rock Golf Course, a short drive from the entrance and the first par 3 Jack Nicklaus signature course. Designed to challenge, it's also an Audubon Cooperative Sanctuary, with forests, panoramic views, and wildlife habitat sharing the water challenges and fairways. Bent Hook Marina opens up the lake for your pleasure. A section is cut out of the floor for viewing and feeding—but no fishing! Bring your own boat, or rent bass, ski, or pontoon boats as well as canoes. Table Lake is nationally ranked for bass and crappie, and guides can show you the secret spots. And of course Bass Pro Shops have everything you need; there's even a fish-cleaning shack. Take a one-hour Champagne Cruise on board the *Goin' Jesse,* a replica of a 1934 Chris Craft, with walnut and teak polished wood, V-8 engine, and all. Back on land, pony rides for the under-ten set can include a sheriff's badge, cowboy hat, and photo for Mom; trail rides for ages six and up create fun family time. For tenderfoots, carriage rides or a campfire wagon trip with roasted marshmallows may be just the thing. Complimentary recreation is bountiful here—borrow the horse's shoes to play horseshoes; try volleyball, badminton, basketball, animal croquet, or miniature golf; or sign up for one of the two lighted tennis courts. Explore the nature trails; jog, hike, and walk to your heart's content; or use the fitness center.

Take a garden tour, get a movie, play board games, or turn the kids loose on the playground. And we haven't even gotten to the swimming possibilities! Two outdoor heated pools (one open year-round), an indoor pool, two kiddie pools, three hot tubs, and a Lazy River keep everyone happy. Evening bonfires in summer bring it all together and create new friendships. Plus, the Carriage House Spa is waiting to pamper you—even the younger crowd has special services available. Dogwood

Canyon Nature Park is a short drive away, offering 10,000 acres of wilderness preserve. If you like spelunking, many caves are to be found and explored. And if it's your style, did we mention that Branson is only ten minutes away?

---

**612 Devil's Pool Road**
**Ridgedale, Missouri 65739**
**800-BCLODGE**
**www.big-cedar.com**

# EAGLE RIDGE RESORT AND SPA
## Galena, Illinois

With 6,800 acres of rolling, wooded terrain and sixty-three challenging holes of golf, Eagle Ridge is a major Midwest golf resort, awarded *Golf Magazine's* "Silver Medal" for excellence eight times. When you're not on the links, you'll find that 220-acre Lake Galena is a focus of resort activity. Located in northwest Illinois, just minutes from historic Galena with its well-preserved nineteenth-century architecture, Eagle Ridge is only 150 miles from Chicago, great for weekend escapes.

**Accommodations:** The Eagle Ridge Resort, with its eighty rooms, sits in the center of the property on a bluff overlooking the lake. Enjoy relaxing and share good conversations around the fireplace in the spacious common room. In addition, resort homes and villas are scattered throughout the hills and consist of one- to eight-bedroom accommodations; choose from views of the fairway, the lake, or secluded woods. During peak season, from late May to late October, inn rooms are $199 to $289 a night (children under

eighteen sharing a room with parents are free); a one- to three-bedroom villa is $249 to $429; the resort homes are $399 to $1,129 a night. January to mid-May and late October to mid-December, inn rooms are $149 to $309; villas run $169 to $329, and homes are $309 to $989. The resort homes are also available for weekly rental, and many different packages are offered.

**Dining:** An elegant dining spot in the inn is Woodlands, where you'll enjoy steaks, pastas, and seafood along with beautiful views of the lake. Next door is the Woodlands Lounge, for cocktails and more casual dining at breakfast and lunch. A children's menu is available. Each golf course has its own snack bar and nineteenth hole. Spike's Bar and Grill offers great views of Eagle Ridge's newest golf course, the General, and a casual lunch menu of appetizers, soups, salads, sandwiches, and barbecue favorites. At dinner, the specialty is only the finest-cut steaks. Paisano's, offering a casual cafe and take-out, satisfies your (or your child's) passion for pizza, and they deliver. When stocking up on provisions, stop by the General Store for deli selections, fresh produce, and freshly baked pastries.

**Children's World:** The Camp Eagle Youth Program is in operation from Memorial Day through Labor Day as well as Saturday and holiday times throughout the year; it is designed for four- to twelve-year-olds. Monday through Saturday the 9:00 a.m. to 4:00 p.m. day is filled with swimming, hiking, boating, games, and arts and crafts; the fee of $50 a day includes lunch. A half day with lunch is $35 (9:00 a.m. to 1:00 p.m. or noon to 4:00 p.m.). The second child in a family pays $35/$25. An all-ages playground adjacent to the tennis courts requires parental supervision and can entertain children for hours with the tot tree for toddlers and more challenging slides and climbing for older kids. On Saturday nights, dinner, movies, and games entertain children from 7:00 to 10:00 p.m. ($35 an evening). In summer, Kids Night Out is offered on Friday. June through August and major holidays, teens are able to meet their peers around canoe trips, paddleboat races, volleyball, and other games. If enough interest exists (sometimes unpredictable with teens), the resort will arrange activities. Individual babysitting is available at $10 an hour.

**Recreation:** The North and South Courses each provide eighteen holes of championship golf set in rolling hills and wooded countryside. The nine-hole East Course, characterized by elevated tees, is an excellent test of accuracy. The General is a challenging layout rated best in the state and ranked one of the "Best Golf Resorts in America" by *Golf Digest.* The Eagle Ridge Golf Academy has designed a program that lets you decide what you need. You can improve your game and lower your score with the latest techniques and technologies, analyze your swing, and even take home your lessons on DVD. In summer, budding golfers under seventeen may attend forty-five-minute junior golf clinics every Saturday for $5 or all-day camps once monthly ($199).

On Lake Galena, fishermen go in search of bass, walleye, and crappie, and fly-fishing school improves their catches. Boaters head out in paddleboats, canoes, and pontoons. Swimmers can take a dip at the indoor pool adjacent to the fitness center in the inn; or pamper yourself at the Stonedrift Spa. Horseback riding along 40 miles of trails begins at the Shenandoah Riding Center. Rent a mountain bike or hike the trails to seek out native plants and wildlife. For a solitary excursion, the fitness trail has twenty-one exercise stations, or round up the whole family for a volleyball game (two courts) or a tennis match (four courts). Family Time activities feature Movies in Tubies in the pool, junk-food bingo, and Pictionary. Special events happen all the time at Eagle Ridge. In June the Great Galena Balloon Race fills the sky with more than twenty hot-air balloons. All season you can discover the thrill of ballooning with a daily dawn or dusk flight ($165 per person). Fourth of July brings a rodeo and carnival; and in August the Civil War returns with battle reenactments, Lincoln's Gettysburg Address, and a Victory Ball. In October the annual Galena Country Fair, in nearby Galena, of course, showcases artists and their work, with games, raffles, and prizes. From the end of July to mid-August, you can combine an Eagle Ridge holiday with watching the Chicago Bears in summer practice at nearby Platteville. You'll keep busy with Ghost tours, Tea and Tarts with the General's Lady, night sky viewing, scads of demonstrations—cooking, stained glass, beads, pottery—

history lessons, and costumed presentations; check the Web site or the concierge for all the happenings during your visit.

In the winter, sports lovers turn to tobogganing, sledding, and ice-skating. Forty miles of cross-country ski trails are carefully groomed. Nearby Chestnut Mountain offers downhill skiing on seventeen runs.

Other area attractions centering around Galena are art galleries and shops; a vineyard; The Belvedere, an Italianate mansion dating from 1857; the museum of Architecture and Design; and the home of Ulysses S. Grant. The *Celebration Belle* is a deluxe riverboat plying the waters of the upper Mississippi River on a daylong cruise. And cross the state line into Dubuque, Iowa, to find casinos, botanical gardens, Crystal Lake Cave, and the National Mississippi River Museum. A little farther afield, you can visit the *Field of Dreams* movie site and sit in the bleachers with dreams of your own.

---

**444 Eagle Ridge Drive**
**Box 777**
**Galena, Illinois 61036**
**(815) 777-5000, (800) 892-2269**
**www.eagleridge.com**

# GRAND GENEVA RESORT
## Lake Geneva, Wisconsin

Tucked into the southeastern corner of Wisconsin, between Milwaukee and Chicago, are Lake Geneva and the Grand Geneva Resort. Less than a day's drive from nine states and sixty million people, the resort sits in the midst of 1,300 acres of pristine Wisconsin countryside and has as its stated goal "to be a destination for relaxation and pleasure." Built in the 1960s as a Playboy Club, it has undergone extensive renovations, overcome its past, reopened in 1994 with a brand-new image, and currently enjoys AAA four-diamond status. The town of Lake Geneva has been called "the Newport of the Midwest," and that flavor is cultivated here.

**Accommodations:** A total of 355 guest rooms, including forty-one suites, overlook the rolling green hills and private clear blue lake (some also overlook a courtyard parking area, so specify view desired when you book). Decor is that of an elegant and comfortable vacation home. In summer, rooms are $249 to $319 and in winter $149 to $239. Junior suites range from $229 to $249 in winter and from $359 to $440 in summer. Timber Ridge Lodge provides 225 one- and two-bedroom all-suite accommodations. Located near the water park, it's spacious and convenient for families. Rates begin at $129 to $299 and include admission to the water park. Children stay free in the room with parents; a daily resort fee of $12 per day covers transportation within the resort, telephone, Spa and Sports Center, newspaper, and in-room coffee. Rollaways are $15. A one-night water park package offers accommodations, four admissions to the water park, and resort fees; cost is $179 weekdays, $239 weekends.

**Dining:** Almost everyone likes Italian food, so the bistro-style Ristorante Brissago is sure to please. Open for dinner only, the restaurant features wood-roasted pizza and homemade pastas; the atmosphere is special without being stuffy. Another restaurant choice, the Geneva Chophouse, puts the kitchen right on display, so you get the full effect of sight and aroma as well as the taste of typical Midwestern dishes such as grilled steak, chops, and fresh seafood. The Chophouse is open for dinner only but serves a bountiful Sunday brunch. The Grand Cafe offers American cuisine and buffets; it's open for breakfast, lunch, dinner, and a special Sunday brunch. From 6:00 a.m. till dusk, snacks and sandwiches are available in the Links Bar and Grill at the golf pro shop. At Timber Ridge Lodge, Smokey's Barbecue House serves dinner (and lunches in summer season), or grab a bite at the Hungry Moose Food Court throughout the day. All of these restaurants have a children's menu. For evening cocktails or live entertainment, stop by Evolve or the Lobby Lounge.

**Children's World:** Located in the Spa and Sports Center, Kids Are Grand provides children ages four to twelve years with fun, age-appropriate activities year-round. Scheduled on demand, morning sessions from 10:00 a.m. to 1:00 p.m. and afternoon sessions from 1:00 to 4:00 p.m. are $40 per child per session. Each week is themed, and activities are central to that theme: Carnival; Wild, Wild West; Art of Culinary; the Great Outdoors; and more. Swimming, pony rides, paddleboating, and hiking are regular activities. Evening sessions from 6:00 to 10:00 p.m. also follow a theme, such as a slumber party, Mexican fiesta, or Hawaiian luau, and are available on Friday, Saturday, and Sunday for $50 per child. Sessions are daily from June through August.

On winter weekends, kids can join Mountain Mites (ages six to fourteen) or Snow Cubs, designed to introduce youngsters from four to six years old to skiing. Two-hour morning or afternoon lessons with learner area lift ticket are $30 each.

In-room babysitting services are available for children under four years of age. Cost is $18 per hour for up to two children ($5 for each additional child); a two-hour minimum is required.

**Recreation:** All the amenities for a resort vacation are here. Two championship golf courses lure golfers. The Highlands, one of the first Scottish-design courses in the United States, was designed by Jack Nicklaus and Pete Dye. The other course, the Brute, designed by Robert Bruce Harris, is one of the longest courses in the Midwest, measuring over 7,000 yards. Putting greens, driving ranges, and scrupulous attention to grooming keep golfers coming back. *Golf for Women* recently placed Grand Geneva on its list of "Top 100 Women-Friendly Fairways." So much for "the Brute"! Other awards include *Golf Magazine*'s Silver Medal for seven consecutive years, and its reader survey for being one of the top three courses in value and in the top four for speed of play. Pick up a tennis game on one of the two indoor or five outdoor courts, or work out at the Sport Center, which features a variety of cardio and weight-resistance equipment and indoor volleyball, basketball, and a climbing wall. The Spa and Sport Center is an adult facility, and an adult must accompany children and teens at all times. Age restrictions also apply; ages sixteen and up may use the basketball court; ages ten and up may use the climbing wall by appointment ($20 per half hour for up to four people); and ages vary for spa treatments. Facials, massages, and herbal body wraps are guaranteed to make you feel like a new person. A private lake provides paddleboating or hydrobiking opportunities. Exercise your arms with a rowboat or your legs with a paddleboat, or just relax and cruise beautiful Lake Geneva on one of the excursion boats, like the *Lady of the Lake,* a modern reproduction of a Mississippi paddle-wheel steamer. More water opportunities present themselves at the indoor and outdoor 50,000-square-foot water park, Moose Mountain Falls, at Timber Ridge Lodge. Slides, pools, a Lazy River, and two activity pools make this a very popular spot. Admission is $21 per person per day; admission is included if you are staying at Timber Ridge Lodge. For serious swimming, try the lap pool. Jogging, biking, and hiking trails wind through the property, taking advantage of the natural beauty. For something other than your own two feet, rent a mountain bike or even a horse. Finish the day with a quiet carriage ride under the stars.

In the wintertime Grand Geneva has its own skiing. Even if there is no snow elsewhere in Wisconsin, with snowmaking there will be snow at the resort. Eighteen slopes descend from the top elevation of 1,086 feet, with a 211-foot vertical drop. Night skiing, 10 kilometers of cross-country skiing, and a special area for snowboards ensure winter fun for everyone. The Ski

School uses Station Teaching to allow individuals to progress at their own rate, mastering each "station" and then moving on. Enjoy sleigh rides, hot chocolate, and ice-skating when the pond freezes over.

Lake Geneva is the city, the body of water is Geneva Lake, and of course the resort is Grand Geneva! However you say it, there are lots of activities and events nearby. We always talk about what to do *on* lakes; in this case, the interesting fun facts are *under* the lake—an elephant was buried in Delavan Lake when the city was a winter home for circus troops; and at the bottom of Geneva Lake you can find, among other things, a Nash, a Volkswagen, and a cabin cruiser from the 1950s. Go to www.lake genevawi.com for a complete listing of mansions, mazes, festivals, cruises, hot-air balloon and parasailing rides, museums, parks—more than we can list.

---

**Highway 50 East at Route 12**
**7036 Grand Geneva Way**
**Lake Geneva, Wisconsin 53147**
**(262) 248-8811, (800) 558-3417**
**www.grandgeneva.com**

# GRAND HOTEL
## Mackinac Island, Michigan

The world's largest summer hotel since 1887 is also the grande dame of Mackinac Island. Afternoon tea, croquet on the green lawn, seemingly endless white columns stretching to the blue sky, and flowers everywhere reflect the best of the Gilded Age. Relax on the front porch, the longest in the world, and visible even from Lake Michigan.

Offering gracious hospitality, the serenity of age and privilege permeates the AAA four-diamond Grand Hotel, open from May through October. A note about Mackinac Island, which has been a favorite summer resort since the Victorian era: The only access is by boat or plane. No cars are allowed on the island. In fact, only 600 people live on the island year-round—and in summer there are more than 500 horses!

Regarding a visit, the Grand once listed 129 "Reasons Grand and Small": #11, it's listed by *Travel + Leisure* magazine as one of the top-ten kid-friendly hotels in the United States and Canada; #112, Mark Twain lectured here; #12, room keys are actually keys; #1, no tipping please; #21, a self-serve snow-cone machine by the pool; #20, a giant caterpillar in the pool; #53, having fun in a tie; #28, dancing with your six-year-old to Big Band sounds at dinner; #41, the barbecued salmon with peppermint ratatouille; #55, the way the waiters pour milk; #42, the stuffed animal in every baby's crib; and #56, taxis with four hooves. The list is history now, but we're sure the other 117 reasons were just as compelling.

**Accommodations:** Past the red-carpeted entry and beyond the impressive Victorian Parlor and public rooms lie 385 guest rooms and suites, no two of which are alike. Each has its own unique character, and the suites are filled with antiques and furnishings from around the world. They are also named: after presidents, first ladies, and famous people and places. Take some time choosing, as a wide variety of room sizes, locations, and rates are available. When the hotel opened in 1887, the rates were $3 to $5. Today's rates in the peak Social Season (mid-June to late August) are per person, MAP (breakfast and dinner), and range from $220 for a small inside room to $300 for a deluxe lake-view. Weekends are $20 to $30 more; shoulder season rates are approximately $20 lower. Children to age eleven are complimentary, twelve to seventeen are $49, and eighteen and older are $109. A $6.50 per person baggage transfer fee is automatic. Internet and special packages are available for special dates.

**Dining:** In all public areas of the hotel, the dress code is casual resort wear during the day and formal attire after 6:00 p.m.; jackets and ties for men, ladies in their finest. Start the day with breakfast in the Main Dining Room with a wide selection of choices. Dinner at the Grand is everything you'd expect, right up to demitasse in the Parlor and nightly orchestra music. And here's an obscure fact about the hotel's most popular dessert, Grand Pecan Balls—more than 50,000 are served each season! Guests receive a $20 per adult credit toward the food portion of their bill when dining at one of the following restaurants: The Jockey Club at the Grand Stand, Woods, The Gate House, or Fort Mackinac Tea Room. Lunch choices include The Jockey Club at the Grand Stand, Pool Grill, Carleton's Tea Store, Fort Mackinac Tea Room, and Woods. The Main Dining Room tables groan under the weight of the Grand Luncheon Buffet, a tradition here ($30 adults; $20 to $25 for children). Full breakfast and five-course dinner are included; children under eleven eat free. Four bars provide quite different atmospheres: The Terrace Room features Big Band sounds and dancing; the Audubon Wine Bar is the spot for viewing sporting events; the Cupola Bar, at the very top of the hotel, offers panoramic views and nightly entertainment; and the Geranium Bar, just off the Front Porch, specializes in pre-dinner cocktails.

**Children's World:** From Memorial Day to Labor Day, children ages five years and up are welcome to join the complimentary daily activities from 11:30 a.m. to 2:30 p.m. and again from 6:00 to 9:00 p.m. Different things are planned each day; for example, a hike, picnic lunch, and duckpin bowling; a trip to Fort Mackinac; or dinner and a movie. Older children (twelve to teens) are welcome if the program interests them; they often come with friends or younger siblings. Babysitting is available at $15 per hour.

**Recreation:** The Jewel is the Grand's golf course, comprised of Grand nine and Woods nine. Although you arrive at the course by horse-drawn carriage, there are gas-powered carts on the course. The tennis pro will help you with your game on the clay courts, and you can stay in shape on the jogging trail or the ½-mile Vita exercise course. Exercise machines and masseuse are in the cedar grove by the swimming pool, and bicycles are available to rent. Riding stables are near the hotel, with more than 40 miles of bridle paths. The serpentine-shaped Esther Williams swimming pool is a popular gathering spot—*This Time for Keeps* with Esther Williams and Jimmy Durante was filmed here in 1949. Another movie involving time was filmed here in 1979: *Somewhere in Time,* with Jane Seymour and Christopher Reeve. If you wish, sit on that famous porch in one of the hundred rocking chairs, and watch the gardens, the ferries, and activity on the ever-changing lake, largest body of fresh water in the world; play croquet or bocci ball in the tea garden; enjoy the art and antiques that surround you; tour the butterfly conservatory; visit Rebecca's or Carleton's Tea Store for delightful treats; or treat yourself at the Grand Spa. Delight-filled days are what it's all about. The hotel is happy to arrange any off-site excursions you desire, such as a carriage or bicycle tour of the island. Explore history at Fort Mackinac National Historic Landmark, in fourteen original buildings filled with period artifacts and guides dressed in costume, complete with cannon and rifle firings.

Mackinac Island, Michigan 49757
(906) 847-3331, (800) 33-GRAND
www.grandhotel.com

# GRAND TRAVERSE RESORT AND SPA

## Acme, Michigan

Long known as the Cherry Capital, this area of northwest lower Michigan has a lot more to offer visitors than just its beautiful orchards and fine fruit. Besides providing memories of Ernest Hemingway, who spent many summers here and used this area as the setting for several short stories, Grand Traverse Resort and Spa offers guests golf, swimming, sailing, cross-country skiing, and a complete sports complex and spa. Set on 900 acres of forests and orchards with ½ mile of shoreline on East Grand Traverse Bay, the year-round resort boasts fine golf courses designed by Jack Nicklaus and Gary Player.

Now owned by the Grand Traverse Band of the Ottawa-Chippewa Nation, the resort was extensively renovated in 2004–2005.

**Accommodations:** The six-story resort hotel and seventeen-story Tower, which together house 424 rooms, are adjacent to the Plaza, the site of summertime barbecues and wintertime ice-skating. With four distinct seasons, daily hotel room rates range from $125 in winter to $235 in summer, midweek; weekends are generally $20 more. The deluxe Tower encompasses 186 suites, 2 lounges, a restaurant, and boutiques. Rates range from $165 to $299 for luxury with a view and your own private whirlpool. The 190 condominium units are spread throughout the grounds. Some overlook the bay, and some skirt the golf courses; a shuttle service connects the condominiums with the other resort facilities. Rates for a one-bedroom unit range from $135 to $295; about $30 more with valley view. Studios, two-, and three-bedrooms are also available. Children under eighteen sleep free when sharing a room with their parents. Be sure to inquire about the many package plans. Cribs are available at no charge; rollaway beds are provided at a daily charge of $15.

**Dining:** Sweetwater American Bistro offers casual family dining with a children's menu and local in-season specialties such as cedar-planked whitefish and cherry cobbler. It is open seven days a week for breakfast, lunch, and dinner. The Trillium Restaurant, located on the sixteenth and seventeenth floors of the Tower, serves panoramic views of the bay and golf greens along with a fine dining experience of northern Michigan regional specialties. It is open for dinner daily, and an a la carte Sunday brunch is also served; reservations are recommended. A children's menu is available in most restaurants. The Grille, in the resort's Clubhouse, also provides an informal setting for dining and cocktails. Marketplace is where you'll find sandwiches, pizza, ice cream—even the daily newspaper. Other choices include Jack's Sports Bar, the Trillium Lounge, and the Shores Beach Club, on the bay. For a serious cocktail, try the Grand Lobby Bar.

**Children's World:** Grand Traverse provides grand care for children ages three months to eight years, Monday through Saturday, year-round at a state-licensed 2,000-square-foot day-care facility called the Cub House. Rates are hourly; $7.75 per hour for children under two and a half, and $6.75 for older children; snacks are included. The ratio is one caregiver for up to four infants and toddlers. Hours are Monday through Thursday from 7:00 a.m. to 8:00 p.m.; to 10:00 p.m. on Friday and Saturday. In summer, hours are extended to 10:00 p.m., and 11:00 p.m. on weekends. Diapers are provided for a small fee, or you may bring your own. Each event through the day is geared to a specific age group; you must register in advance.

Camp Traverse operates mid-June to August for ages six to twelve, and offers a full- or half-day program with a weekly theme and field trip, plus sports, crafts, cookouts, swimming, and hiking. Generally the camp is divided into two groups for more age-appropriate activities. Full-day (9:00 a.m. to 4:00 p.m.) cost is $40; 9:00 a.m. to noon is $25; and noon to 4:00 p.m. is $30. Lunch is $3 extra. A full-week camp is $145 plus lunches. Kids may arrive early (7:00 to 9:00 a.m.) or stay late (4:00 to 6:00 p.m.), having a pre- or post-camp adventure, for $8 per child. Kids Night Out, on Friday and Saturday from 6:00 to 10:00 p.m., is when kids gather for dinner, games, crafts, tennis, or a swim and maybe a bonfire while parents enjoy a little time alone. Cost is $28, or $33 until 11:00 p.m.

An adventure playground near the Spa Complex also keeps youngsters well entertained, and the electronic-game room may mesmerize them. Also somewhat mesmerizing is Bogey Bear, an amiable 6-foot-tall teddy bear, who makes surprise appearances, usually dressed as a golfer or a surfer. Individual nannies can be scheduled with the assistance of the spa staff.

**Recreation:** The pride of Grand Traverse Resort and Spa is the Bear. Designed by Jack Nicklaus, this golf course meanders through cherry and apple orchards, with plenty of hardwood forest areas for contrast; it is quite scenic as well as challenging. The older course, Spruce Run, also offers championship play. The resort's third course is the Wolverine, a championship course designed by Gary Player in 1999, complete with a state-of-the-art clubhouse. Located within walking distance of the main resort, the clubhouse serves all three courses. The Jim McLean Golf School program provides sessions from May through September. For your comfort and refreshment, beverage carts tour the greens, and there's a halfway house, the After Nine, on the Bear.

Year-round, tennis plays a major role here. Instruction, leagues, tournaments, and junior clinics keep the staff busy and guests happy. Four outdoor and five indoor courts are available for play. The Spa Complex is a championship setup too. With indoor and outdoor swimming pools and an exercise/weight room, you'll get quite a workout. Afterward you'll probably head straight to the saunas. A full-service spa provides all the pampering you need, with signature services such as hydrotherapy, body wraps, massage, and exfoliation featuring the area's famous cherries.

If water sports capture your interest, Grand Traverse has just about every type of boat imaginable: powerboats, ski boats, sailboats, sailboards, Jet Skis, parasailing, catamarans with special breakfast cruises for children, sunset cruises, canoes, kayaks, fishing boats, and even tall ships. River floating is an adventure for the whole family, from knee-deep streams to more challenging rivers. Swim or sun at the private Beach Club, with its own pool and poolside bar, where lazing away the afternoon is a worthwhile activity in itself. Fishermen seek out the many lakes and streams for trout and salmon; farm fishing or a charter trip on the bay are also options. Hike or jog through the hills and past the orchards; the scenery is so good for the soul that you may not notice you're also helping your body. Or rent horses from a nearby stable and let them do the work! Croquet and volleyball are complimentary, so challenge the kids, if you dare. Picking fruit at one of the nearby orchards allows you to truly savor the results of your work—cherries, apricots, peaches, apples, or blueberries, depending on the season. And speaking of savoring something, at Moomer's you can sit on the porch eating homemade cherry ice cream while watching the cows in the pasture. Yum.

But don't be deceived; Grand Traverse is not just a summertime resort. In the fall trees burst into autumn colors and make a beautiful backdrop for horse-drawn hayrides and trips to nearby wineries for sampling and festivals. In the winter cross-country skiing takes over; on-site, the golf course transforms into a ski trail (up to 2 kilometers) with woods and gently rolling hills, covered only with natural snow. More dedicated skiers can do cross-country at the Vasa Pathway, less than 1 mile away; and three downhill ski/snowboard areas are less than an hour away. Take a sleigh ride through the woods; or try the complimentary sleds, tubing, or ice-skating in the Plaza. And remember, while working out at the Spa Complex, you'll never know how low the temperature dips outside.

In the spring, when the weather is warm enough for you to want to pick up a golf club, the cherry orchards come to life. The white blossoms of the trees blanket the hillsides for more than half the month of May.

---

**100 Grand Traverse Village Boulevard
Acme, Michigan 49610
(231) 534-6000, (800) 748-0303,
(800) 236-1577
www.grandtraverseresort.com**

# GRAND VIEW LODGE

## Nisswa, Minnesota

Nestled among the Norway pines on the north shore of Gull Lake is Grand View Lodge, the focal point of this 900-acre resort. Built in 1918 of native cedar logs and now a National Historic Site, the lodge welcomes guests year-round. If charm and friendly service, style, and attention to detail are important to you, this is your place, as the tradition of hospitality goes back almost ninety years. Located 142 miles northwest of Minneapolis, the lodge is within a fifteen-minute drive of the Paul Bunyan Center. Dive right into the "North Woods" feel of the area with a plethora of local attractions, such as A&J's Up North Buffalo Ranch, lumberjack shows, Paul Bunyan Land, and This Old Farm theme park.

**Accommodations:** In addition to the lodge, sixty-five cabins border the lake. Deluxe suites and townhomes are also nearby. The twelve rooms in the lodge are comfortable for couples, while a cabin is the right choice for a family. Since these range in size from one to eight bedrooms, owner Fred Boos explains that they "try to fit the cabin to the family." Some cabins feature a kitchenette and living room; all have decks as well as large picture windows and views of the lake. Daily maid service is provided for both the lodge and the cabins. Reservations are accepted on a daily as well as weekly basis. Based on two adults, daily summer rates are $305 to $397 in a one-bedroom cabin and include two meals a day; golf at the Garden Course; discounted golf rates at the Pines, the Preserve, and Deacon's Lodge championship courses; unlimited tennis with clinics; nonmotorized boats; and the children's program. For children ages three to eleven, the charge is $45 to $60.

**Dining:** There are several restaurants: the Grand Dining Room in the historic lodge, Freddy's Tavern in the Pines Clubhouse, the Preserve Steak House in the Preserve Clubhouse, Palmer's Grill, Sherwood Forest (also a historic building, nestled in the woods), and the Italian Gardens Trattoria, a magical little cottage really in a garden. Dress is casual. From Memorial Day to Labor Day, enjoy a burger or a cold drink from the Beach Pavilion while sunning yourself, and sample yummy cappuccino, cookies, and pastries at Julia's, a charming French country cottage/gift shop. Barbecues on the beach are often planned. Children may dine with their parents or their counselors when on the kids' program. A special menu for children features fresh fish, steaks, chicken, and ribs. Cocktails are served on the large, three-level redwood deck or in the North Woods Lounge, where you'll hear live music nightly. The smorgasbord is a traditional Sunday event—great fun and all you can eat.

**Children's World:** From Memorial Day weekend to Labor Day weekend, Grand View has two well-organized programs: Kids Club for children ages three to six and Adventure Club for ages seven to twelve. There is a wonderful wooden playhouse in the woods with slides and climbing equipment, a well-stocked play area, the beach along Gull Lake, and a swimming pool that your kids probably won't want to leave—ever. This pool has jets, geysers, waves, and slides, oh, my! The programs run from 9:00 a.m. to 3:00 p.m. and from 6:00 to 8:00 p.m., Monday through Saturday. The schedule includes arts, games, storytime, movement activities, exercise, and swimming.

The staff is college age and generally has past experience with children. The program is included in many of the packages; otherwise the cost is $25 for a full day, $15 for half-day sessions. For those under age three, the front desk can arrange babysitting with either an off-duty staff member or selected local persons.

**Recreation:** The lake, with a fine 1,500-foot natural-sand beach, attracts swimmers, fishermen, sailors, and sunbathers. Here you can also venture out in a pontoon or kayak or practice some waterskiing. Gull Lake is home to walleye, trout, and bass—pontoon fishing is a great outing. The eighteen-hole championship golf course is aptly named, given its setting: The Pines. The nine-hole Garden Course is perfect for the entire family. The Preserve, an eighteen-hole championship course, is located just 10 miles north of Grand View Lodge. Arnold Palmer's Deacon's Lodge, rated one of the "Top 10 New Public Courses in the Nation" by *Golf Magazine,* is the newest addition to area golf.

A tennis complex with seven Laykold courts is set among tall trees. Court time is free. The tennis pro teaches private lessons, organizes tournaments, and conducts free group lessons for children eight to nineteen years old. Two hitting walls and an auto-matic ball machine allow for extra practice before a good match. For a change of pace, take a yoga or cooking class, visit the fitness center and hot tubs, or enjoy the new indoor pool and water slide. Rent a bike, or go for a horseback ride through the wooded trails. Walking trails on the grounds, the nearby paved Paul Bunyan Trail, or Pillsbury State Forest provide hours of diversion, or you can delight in the thousands of flowers in the Grand View gardens. Then relax, spend some time in the game room, and see if you can beat the kids at table tennis or billiards. Celebrate the new Glacial Waters Spa, an Aveda Concept Resort Spa with full services. In winter the North Woods become a wonderland of snow. Enjoy ice-skating, build a snowman or snowwoman (or snowchild!), or go for walks in the snow. Then jump in the Jacuzzi, cozy up to the fireplace, and just enjoy.

**23521 Nokomis Avenue**
**Nisswa, Minnesota 56468**
**(218) 963-2234, (800) 432-3788**
**www.grandviewlodge.com**

# GREAT WOLF LODGE
## Kansas City, Kansas

Great Wolf Lodge is a first-class, full-service, year-round family destination resort designed to capture the atmosphere and adventure of the North Woods.

Great Wolf Lodge began in 1997, with the concept of providing drive-to locations specifically for families to enjoy, with the things kids love the most—water and game arcades. Apparently, it was a great idea. Ten years later, the original Wisconsin Dells, Wisconsin, location has now expanded to include nine more resorts. So really, this entry is a bonus, giving you ten possible vacation spots, since the basic premise of each lodge is identical. Other locations include Mason, Ohio; Sandusky, Ohio; Traverse City, Michigan; Williamsburg, Virginia; the Pocono Mountains, Pennsylvania; and

Niagara Falls, Ontario, Canada. Great Wolf Lodge properties are currently under construction in Grand Mound, Washington (early 2008), and Grapevine, Texas (late 2007). While it's slightly different from our other resorts, in that there is no supervised children's program, it seems to be an increasingly popular concept and a definite change of pace.

This Great Wolf Lodge is located in Village West, Kansas City's new tourism district. While it's hardly the North Woods, a 49,000-square-foot indoor entertainment area offers lots of fun year-round. The Grand Lobby soars three stories and contains the Grand Clock Tower. Four times daily, this animated clock demonstrates the "Rhythm of Nature," and there's usually a group gathered to sing along.

**Accommodations:** Rooms are functional and simply decorated; the 281 family-size suites offer innovative, themed sleeping arrangements. KidKamp allows kids to sleep in "tents," while KidCabin is just that—a little cabin set in the room; Wolf Den has an enclosed cavelike "den," and family suites have a semiprivate living area. Suite layouts vary but usually have a queen bed, a sleeper sofa, and the separate kid's area with bunk beds and 20-inch television. Rates are based on number of people (four to six), and additional persons are $15 each, up to maximum occupancy. Water-park-level rooms are $15 additional per night. All rooms have free wireless Internet access, refrigerator, wet bar with microwave, and coffeemaker; most rooms feature a private patio or balcony. Admission to the water park is included in the rates. Weekend rates are always higher; summer and holiday rates are the highest. Family suites usually have lower rates, from $149 to $229; Wolf Den suites are $169 to $324; KidKabin rooms range from $209 to $329. KidKamp is only on the water park level; summer rates begin at $204. Packages and specials are frequently offered.

**Dining:** Camp Critter Bar and Grille is open daily from 7:00 a.m. to 10:00 p.m. It feels more like a camping trip than a restaurant, with maple and oak trees surrounding you, a life-size tree house, and private dining tents and cabins. The menu is filled with fun items, like Getchurgooey Nachos or FungusAmungus (mushroom appetizers), sandwiches, pasta, and also some entrees for Mom and Dad. Of course there's a kid's menu with all their favorites. The Bear Claw Café keeps even longer hours and is the place to find that Starbucks coffee or Krispy Kreme donut, ice cream, candy, and other goodies. Can't get the kids out of the water park? No problem. The Spirit Island Snack Shop has drinks and snacks to keep them going. There's even a Pizza Hut Express just inside the water park; both are open from 10:00 a.m. to 10:00 p.m.

**Children's World:** Although there's no supervised children's program at Great Wolf, just about the whole place is a children's world. Kids ages four to twelve can join Cub Club and visit the Cub's Cabin for daily arts and crafts; Biko the Bear and Wiley the Wolf often join in. Make a T-shirt, magnets, shrinky dinks, simple projects, and art to take home. Every morning brings a Wolf Walk, to learn about animals. For $5 (and up), choose to wear a waterproof tattoo; don't worry, Mom, it lasts only a few days. Lodge Life will keep you up-to-date on all the available activities; pick one up when you check in. After a full day of action, everyone enjoys a traditional bedtime story in the Grand Lobby, every evening at 8:00 p.m. Kids wear their pajamas, the fire crackles, sleepy eyes close—a nice way to end the day.

**Recreation:** The main attractions here are the Northern Lights Arcade and the

Waterpark. Forget the weather, and don't even think about the season, because all the action's inside. The arcade is 6,000 feet of black-light glowing carpet and more than a hundred video games—a child's dream, a parent's nightmare. But it's all in good fun, and time limits can be set. The Eagle Peak Rock Wall (three climbs for $10) challenges up to four climbers at once and ensures that time in the hot tub will be appreciated. At Bear Park Landing it's always 84 degrees. This 38,000-square-foot centerpiece of the lodge holds five pools, eight water slides, and a four-story tree house/water fort. Water takes every form imaginable here—splash, spray, wave, fall, plunge, rocket, and roll. Don't miss the Howling Wolf, a three-person toboggan that goes forever, it seems. Fort Mackenzie defies description: suspension bridges, nets, and web crawls with twelve levels of water activity, some activated by you, and about 1,000 gallons dumped everywhere, every three to five minutes, by someone else! And for those good-weather times between Memorial Day and Labor Day, Thunder Bay outdoor pool area will keep everyone just as wet. Zero-entry, with geysers and sprays, and the Oasis Bar & Grill and live music on Saturdays soothe it all over. Three family cabanas provide shade, refrigerator with drinks, and even TV.

If you're wrinkled like a prune and all watered out, relax into the Elements Family Spa for a quiet retreat and some yummy body services to restore your balance. Various massages, facials, and body wraps will restore you in no time, using Aveda products. And, since it's all about the kids, Scooops Kid Spa services offers chocolate-covered strawberry, coconut cream pie, caramel apple, or gummy worm pedicures and manicures. Who could even imagine?!

**10401 Cabela Drive**
**Kansas City, Kansas 66111**
**(913) 299-7001, (800) 608-WOLF**

# THE HOMESTEAD
## Glen Arbor, Michigan

The Great Lakes are truly great—and not just in size. While Lake Michigan's 22,400-square-mile area is indeed impressive, imagine the possibilities it affords in recreation and relaxation: swimming, boating, and fishing in the water, and on land, hiking and biking the wooded trails beyond the lake's sandy beach. At The Homestead all this great potential is realized, and that may be why it's called America's "freshwater resort."

Voted "The #1 Nature Escape in the Midwest" by readers of *FamilyFun* magazine, The Homestead is a waterfront resort community located on the northwest shore of lower Lake Michigan. Its 500 acres embrace gently rolling land covered with pine trees, aspens, and oaks; 1 mile of sandy beach on Lake Michigan; and 6 miles of shoreline along the banks of Crystal River. Surrounding the resort is the Sleeping Bear Dunes National Lakeshore; besides ensuring The Homestead's secluded position, this national preserve opens up additional opportunities for nature explorers. The resort is closed in April and November; only the hotel is open.

**Accommodations:** Choose from two small hotels, a lodge, an inn, resort condominiums, or private homes. The Village is the center of most activities; accommodations, restaurants, shops, and a heated swimming pool are located here. Fiddler's Pond and Little Belle in the Village offer guest rooms and suites overlooking the pond. Fiddler's Pond underwent a $1.2 million upgrade and renovation in 2002, harking back to the traditional decor of decades of wooded lakeshore summer cottages—the kind one remembers from childhood. One- to four-bedroom condominiums, each with a full kitchen, are located on the beach, along Crystal River, on a ridge overlooking the shoreline, and in the Village. Crystal River cuts through the hills and runs more or less parallel to the lakeshore a short way before emptying into the lake. Where the river and the lake merge is another center of activity, the Beach Club. The Inn, a historic bed-and-breakfast, is located here.

Fiddler's Pond rooms are $90 to $239 a night; Little Belle's rates are $123 to $287 a night. In Stony Brook Lodge a one-bedroom condominium unit ranges between $175 and $403 a night, depending on the location you choose; lakefront and lake-view units are the most expensive. High season is mid-June to mid-August. Rates vary with season, location, and view; from May through October, an "Unlimited Family Fun" package offers two nights' accommodation and is all-inclusive for meals and activities at the resort and at the National Seashore. Based on two adults and two children, rates begin at $95 per person per night, and you even get to take your picnic basket home with you! Ask about other weekend packages. Cribs are provided at no charge; children are free when staying in their parents' room. An on-property shuttle service is available to guests.

**Dining:** At the Beach Club the Cafe Manitou draws diners to its ideal location on the beach; it is open daily in the summer only, its setting and attire are casual, and you can dine indoors or out.

Around the bend in the Village, Nonna's boasts a bountiful breakfast and northern Italian dinners, and Beppi's attracts pizza and burger fans. Also in the Village, at Cavanaugh's you can pick up groceries, deli sandwiches, a ready-to-serve meal, or snacks all day long. In the winter skiers gather in CQ's Cabin for its cozy atmosphere and friendly conversation.

**Children's World:** Camp Tam-A-Rack was built especially for children and is the center of the summer program. Indoors, there's space for art, cooking, music, stories, film, and napping. Extensive outside play areas include a tepee, a multilevel fort, water cannons, woods, creeks, lawns, and two gyms. Care is available for ages eighteen months to three years; cost is $12 per hour with a three-hour minimum. Scouts is geared toward three- to ten-year-olds. Sessions are from 9:00 a.m. to noon, 1:00 to 4:00 p.m., and 5:00 to 8:00 p.m. Cost is $27 for half-day or evening sessions and $50 for the full day; a $10 discount is given for the second child. It's available from June through late August and on select weekends throughout the year.

Teenagers enjoy meeting other teens at the game room or during canoe races, volleyball games, tennis matches, and pizza parties. Like the events for the younger group, some are free, while others require a fee. Private swimming lessons can be arranged; junior tennis and golf clinics are offered for young adults ages twelve to seventeen and juniors ages six to eleven.

In the winter the children's program teaches three- to ten-year-olds fun-in-the-snow activities with ski lessons. It is offered for two and a half hours twice a day, Friday through Sunday, and on holidays from late December through March. Costs are comparable to the summer program.

Any time of year, individual babysitters can be hired, at approximately $8 per hour. The resort staff assists in making the arrangements.

**Recreation:** The clear waters of Lake Michigan are fine for sailing, boating (rentals available), fishing, and swimming. Maybe still a little nippy in June, the lake's temperature averages 65–70 degrees by July and August, and its sandy bottom is particularly attractive to young swimmers. The Crystal River waters tend to be warmer, and both the Beach Club and the Village have a heated pool and a hot tub, so guests have their pick of swimming conditions. Fishing is good sport in the river as well as in the lake, and canoeing up the river allows you to investigate the local wildlife. Sailing and windsurfing in the river can be a challenge, but tubing, kayaking, and canoeing are very manageable. And Lake Michigan is always an option. The mile-long beach along the shore is a real luxury.

Hike, jog, and bicycle (children's bikes and bikes with children's seats are available for rent) on the 24 miles of wooded trails; a self-guided nature tour can introduce you to the area's flora and fauna.

For tennis players, the Beach Club, with its five clay courts, is the site of many exciting matches. Here you can join a clinic, take private lessons, and watch real talent during professional exhibitions. If you're still looking for things to do, drop by the aerobics exercise class; work out on the fitness trail, with twenty exercise stations; head to the playground at River Park; or throw your hat into a volleyball tournament. Now here's ingenuity in utilizing space: A nine-hole par

3 golf course is built in part on the downhill ski slopes! Four nearby golf courses will suit your mood on any given day.

Many fun family activities are scheduled; most involve a small fee. Participate in family-friendly golf, Mishe-Mokwa's cookout, songs and s'mores, a bonfire, a tubing flotilla downstream, a fishing derby, and a great white-water duck race just for a sampling.

Being surrounded by the Sleeping Bear Dunes National Park is a real treat. The largest freshwater sand dunes in the world, some reach up to 450 feet and 40 degrees of steepness. The Dune Climb is a thrill for everyone; you may climb and play on the land-side of the dune or sit at the picnic tables and laugh at others. It's a memorable experience either way. Take a ferryboat ride to the islands in Lake Michigan, sample the wines of local vineyards, or just take a relaxing stroll along the beach at sunset.

When the weather cools, the swimmers give way to skiers and snowboarders, who discover nature's wintertime beauty. Take a brisk hike on the beach or boardwalks. Try cross-country skiing, snowshoe the wooded hills, or ride a sled down. The frozen ponds are ideal for ice-skating. Downhill skiing is modest, with fifteen runs and 350 vertical feet, but the view down a snowy slope to whitecaps on the lake is an uncommon juxtaposition you'll long remember. All runs benefit from artificial snowmaking, and those lighted for nighttime skiing add another dimension to a winter holiday.

---

**Wood Ridge Road**
**Glen Arbor, Michigan 49636**
**(231) 334-5100**
**www.thehomesteadresort.com**

# HORSESHOE CANYON RANCH

## Jasper, Arkansas

Want a dude ranch experience, but can't make it all the way out west? How about a "Western Experience with Southern Hospitality"? Sounds like a great combination, and Horseshoe Ranch in northwestern Arkansas is the place to find it. The Ozarks are a totally different mountain experience from the Rockies, but the horses and cowboys are the same. Green and rolling, the vistas have been described by almost every superlative adjective—magnificent, spectacular, breathtaking, memorable. The "music" here is amazing: birds during the day and crickets, frogs, and whip-poor-wills at night. And having the silence to appreciate it is wonderful. Jasper, the nearest town, has a population of 550. As for the hospitality part, many guests praise the staff, who make it "feel like family." Four generations of the Johnson family are involved with running the ranch, so it really is a family affair; the youngest member is four years old, and the oldest won't say. Every morning, very early, the horses are rounded up for the day, and what a sight it is to hear and see them galloping to the corral! You'll travel back in time, to an earlier, simpler place, where folks have time to talk, where "work" is fun and rewarding, where serenity lurks, just waiting to be discovered. The ranch is no stranger to accolades: *Midwest Living* called it one of the "Top 40 Resorts"; ESPN focused on the rock climbing/bouldering in a *Destination Outdoors* episode; and *FamilyFun* voted it one of the "Top Three Family Resorts" in the country.

**Accommodations:** "Down in the valley, valley so low . . ." Horseshoe Canyon Ranch sits in a lovely valley, surrounded by trees, bluffs, and meadows. Warm wood and leather are everywhere, and less is more in the simple furnishings of the cabins and Lodge. The Lodge is the center of meals and activities, and the cabins are your private little place to be. For you "city slickers" who can't live without your laptop, Internet access is available, but plan to take a real vacation—there are no TVs or telephones in the cabin. Rates are all-inclusive, with nothing extra except babysitting. Included is the cabin, three meals daily, maid service, the children's program, canoeing, rock climbing, and lots of horseback riding plus all other ranch activities. Sunday is generally arrival day and a holiday for horses and staff, so only continental breakfast is provided. There's a 5 percent family discount for four or more persons in a cabin; nonriders also receive a special rate. During summer the minimum stay is three days, although most people find six to seven days preferable, just to get into the spirit of ranch life and partake of everything there is to do. A two-night minimum applies in spring and fall. March to early November is the regular season; call if you're interested in Christmas. Rates are per person: daily/weekly rates during summer for adults are $185/$990; children eight through sixteen are $145/$780; children three through seven are $95/$510; and kids two and under stay free. Rates for nonriders are $150/$810. Spring and fall rates are $15 to $25 less per person.

**Dining:** The smell of coffee in the early morning, even if you don't drink it, is special. Add bacon and homemade biscuits and gravy, and you have to smile. Hearty breakfasts or fruit and yogurt—it's your call. Once a week, ride out to a daybreak breakfast on the trail, and earn the right to call yourself a cowboy or cowgirl. Lunch is the time to share your morning adventures and fill up on more down-home cooking. Dinner offers delicious options, and even though you may want to totter off to bed, some good ole Southern socializing is in order. Moonlight rides (if you have the stamina) or maybe eating ice cream and singing karaoke or watching a little local entertainment will tempt you to stretch your day out a little longer. Meals are buffet style, and seating is casual. The ranch is located in a dry county, so if you like an evening cocktail or wine with dinner, you're invited to BYOB (bring your own bottle).

**Children's World:** Children ages three to six are welcome in the youth program, and there's plenty to do. Learn new skills and crafts, discover what nature's all about with plant and animal study, keep a goat company, and practice being cowhands on the Little Buckaroo Ranch. Fishing, the petting zoo, playing in the tepee, or scavenger hunts occupy the time pleasantly. The program operates morning and afternoon, basically during trail rides. Children ages six and older can go on trail rides with the adults. Prepare for the Friday night L'il Britches Ranch Rodeo. Yee-haw! Younger children get to ride in the arena, so everyone has a horse to call their own, to talk to and brush. The whole ranch is a playground, and very safe. Activities are really family-oriented.

**Recreation:** Well, it's a ranch, right? So horses are a big part of everything. The Head Wrangler will assign a horse based on your level of riding expertise, so be honest. Lessons are available for all ages and stages. Morning and afternoon rides last about one to one and a half hours; the terrain is tricky, so trotting is probably the highest gear. Small groups of eight to ten

people of similar skill ride together. Arena rides for games, barrels, or just loping come later in the week.

A four-hour wilderness ride to Busby Hollow for experienced riders stops for lunch along the way. Special rides include a breakfast ride, a moonlight ride, and a steak-fry ride. When you're on two legs instead of four, lots of nature walks and hikes pass by sheer bluffs, springs, and streams and quiet pools where you can take a dip or cool off. Locals call these "cowboy Jacuzzis." Caves and Indian shelters invite exploring, and the possibility of finding arrowheads is quite real. The Buffalo National River flows between incredible bluffs and is so clear that you can see the fish swimming beside your canoe; it's hard to know whether to look up or down. Other shared family activities are fishing, rock climbing, and riding the zip-line, the largest and tallest in Arkansas. Many outdoor magazines have called Horseshoe Canyon one of the best climbing areas east of the Rockies. It's great for beginner or expert climbers, so don't miss it.

Want more options? Well, we haven't yet gotten to skeet and target shooting, archery, disc golf, bonfires, wagon rides, and live music with dancing. Did we mention caving or swimming in the river? Or the swimming pool and hot tub, which is so welcome after a couple of trail rides? And so the days go, and one thing everyone takes away is great memories and an even greater appreciation that places like this exist.

---

**Office: 3900 Lochridge Road**
**North Little Rock, Arkansas 72116**
**(501) 791-2679, (800) 480-9635**
**www.gohcr.com**

# THE LODGE OF FOUR SEASONS

## Lake Ozark, Missouri

Lake of the Ozarks, a man-made lake developed in the 1930s, has provided scenic and recreational diversions for the residents of central Missouri for more than sixty years. Overlooking the lake, in the wooded gentle hills of the Ozarks, is the Lodge of Four Seasons. Opened in 1964, the family-owned lodge has grown over the years into a major year-round resort. Today it is a convenient escape from city cares for St. Louis and Kansas City residents and is a vacation spot for visitors from farther afield as well. Native limestone decorates the entrance, and the warmth of a Midwest welcome is balanced by the beauty and serenity of the Japanese gardens.

**Accommodations:** Guests select from 350 spacious guest rooms or two- and three-bedroom condominiums—lodging is spread throughout the 3,500-acre resort community. Connecting rooms are available, and most feature balconies. Choose from standard, deluxe, or premier rooms or VIP suites in the main lodge, Lanai, or Atrium. Two-bedroom Lodge Condos (starting at $290) are located in a landscaped, semi-secluded community; Charleston Condos are set on a cove overlooking the Lake of the Ozarks and are three-bedroom only. Room rates for fall, winter, and spring range from $89 to $169 weekdays; summer rates are $159 to $219; weekends are $20 to $40 more year-round. Children under eighteen share their parents' room at no extra charge; complimentary cribs are available.

**Dining:** HK's, in the lodge, has atrium windows that encompass views of the lake and the Japanese garden. Order Angus beef from a custom grill or try the signature favorite, turkey steak. Have breakfast or lunch inside or outdoors at Breezes; and be sure to be there Friday evenings for the Pasta Bar. Breakfast with warm, freshly baked bread and pastries or light lunches may be consumed while enjoying the "sidewalk waterfall" at Soleil. It only feels like it's outside. Seasons Ridge Sports Bar & Grill is found on the nineteenth hole; in summer, the poolside Parrot Bar is great for a sandwich and drink and sunning. Start the evening with cocktails and friends at the Lobby Bar, and wrap it up with dancing and easy listening music at the Blue Moon. The Blue Moon also has the requisite large-screen TV to catch your favorite game.

**Children's World:** The Adventure Club provides a fun-filled day of activities for children ages four to twelve. The Adventure Club is open every day Memorial Day to Labor Day, from 10:00 a.m. to 6:00 p.m. The cost is $7 per hour for the first child, $5 per hour for each additional sibling. And everyone gets a free Club T-shirt. Kids enjoy swimming, nature walks, fishing, games, movies, arts and crafts, theme days, and cookouts. Kids Night Out operates from 7:00 to 10:00 p.m. on Friday and Saturday during the summer and includes dinner, games, movies, and time well spent with peers. The cost is the same. Many resort activities encourage quality time for families to enjoy together, such as ice-cream socials, crafts, and demonstrations. The Adventure Club's staff is certified in Red Cross first aid and water safety training.

**Recreation:** The sports enthusiast will be well satisfied at the Lodge of Four Seasons, named one of the "Top 50 Golf Resorts" by *Condé Nast Traveler* and "Best in the Midwest 2006" by *Travel + Leisure*

*Golf.* Witch's Cove, a championship eighteen-hole golf course designed by Robert Trent Jones Sr., interests players with its narrow, undulating fairways and glimpses of the lake's blue waters. A second eighteen-hole championship golf course, Seasons Ridge, is carved into the rolling Ozark terrain, where multiple tee boxes accommodate golfers of all skill levels. Golf instruction is offered at both of these courses. In addition, golfers may cross the bridge to the Club at Porto Cima, a private Jack Nicklaus signature course. Equipment and attire can be purchased at the pro shop, if you've forgotten anything. If water sports are your life's love, you certainly won't feel slighted, with both indoor and outdoor pools to enjoy. Swimmers can also venture out into the lake or sunbathe on the private beach. The lake is a favorite of boaters; the full-service marina can handle more than 200 boats and is the base for lake activities, from boat rentals, WaveRunners, and waterskiing to fishing guide services and parasailing. The Lodge of Four Seasons also offers a scenic excursion boat that takes guests on a smooth journey around the lake.

Guests can truly unwind at Spa Shiki. Try a massage or other signature treatments at the full-service spa. Browse through on-site shops, catch a movie in the lodge's cinema, or simply take a stroll through beautifully landscaped Japanese gardens. If you have any energy left, hike along wooded paths or try your hand at trapshooting. Volleyball, basketball, and tennis are even more options to fit into a busy schedule. At the end of a very full day, you may choose to stop and have a drink at the Lobby Bar, dance at Blue Moon, or retire early for a well-deserved repose.

---

**Horseshoe Bend Parkway**
**Lake Ozark, Missouri 65049**
**(573) 365-3000, (800) THE-LAKE**
**www.4seasonsresort.com**

# LUDLOW'S ISLAND RESORT
## Cook, Minnesota

---

Minnesota has a reputation as the land of 10,000 lakes (ever wonder who counted them all?), and Ludlow's Island Resort is well situated on one of these—picturesque Lake Vermilion. The resort facilities are located on Ludlow's Island and on the north and south shores of the lake. And there's nothing on the island except the resort—talk about private! A boat shuttle connects the three areas. Water-related activities are the primary recreation at this three-star, three-diamond wooded resort "where luxury and wilderness meet." Fishing, swimming, sailing, and exploring any of the 365 islands provide wonderful experiences. The seclusion among the pines and birches, with the lake practically at your front door, makes this retreat a real back-to-nature experience. The resort is open May through September and is a member of the "Distinctive Lodges of America." The resort is run by the Ludlow family—for families—and has been for sixty-eight years.

**Accommodations:** Twenty cabins with enchanting names like Stardust, Evergreen, and Wakemeup are located on the island and the shores; Dream Catcher was featured on the Travel Channel in February 2004. Designed with knotty pine or cedar interiors, all have a fireplace and outdoor deck; most have a screened porch. They range from one to five bedrooms, with a fully equipped kitchen (yes, even a dishwasher and microwave). Spring (May) and fall (September), daily rates start at $250 for two adults and $30 for each child under seventeen. Early June through September, rentals are generally weekly. Rates for two adults range from $2,400 to $3,650. Dream Catcher, a four-story "tree house," is $3,400. Ages eighteen and over are $175 per week; ages six to seventeen are $100; and ages five and under are $40. Daily summer rates are calculated at one-sixth the weekly rate, and packages are available. Ludlow's rates include just about everything except meals—the newspaper delivered to your cabin, daily towel exchange, firewood at your door, all the facilities of the lodge, tennis, boating, camping (with gear!), and recreation. Blissfully, television is limited to off-island cabins and the lounge. Maid service is available daily; cost is $200 to $230 per week.

**Dining:** You may dine in your cabin, and do your own cooking. The Gourmet Pantry is open twenty-four hours—here you can find groceries, tackle, or personal toiletries, and woks, waffle irons, and ice-cream makers can be borrowed at no charge. More grocery stores can be found 8 miles away, in Cook. Or you may dine in your cabin and have meals delivered by The Harvest Moon Cooking Co., owned by the Ludlow's son and daughter-in-law. Full menu choices are posted in the cabins; entrees range from $14 to $28, and burgers and pizzas are also available. Place your order by 5:00 p.m. and dine by 7:00 p.m. Or, if you're getting cabin fever, try one of the several local restaurants, where dining is casual and family-oriented and someone else does the dishes!

**Children's World:** At least one planned activity (from one to three hours) just for children is scheduled every day Monday through Friday. Boat rides, nature hikes, and fishing derbies introduce kids to the surrounding woods and waters. Pontoon tours give an opportunity for viewing beaver lodges and eagles' nests; and planting a white pine with your name on it is a great introduction to ecology. Waterskiing, tubing, basketball, and picnics keep kids active, and seaplane and Friday afternoon amphibious car rides in the lake are exciting for the whole family. Unique is the only word for a 1954 Chris-Craft Constellation converted to a "playhouse," and kids love it for picnics and fantasy voyages to faraway places.

The island is not open to the public, and no cars or traffic are allowed, so children have the security and freedom to roam—with an entire island to explore, Ludlow's keeps structured activity to a minimum. Movies are shown in the afternoons, and one lodge has a goodly supply of books and games. Teens like to gather at the video-game room or in the evening for more "grown-up" movies. The two-story tree house and a small camping island for overnight trips are among the biggest attractions for the younger set, but the swings, the lake (with a section roped off for children's safety), and the sandy beach are good play areas, too. Kids are fascinated with the "Iceberg," an 8-foot climbing wall—but in the water! Kids also enjoy exploring the trails in the forest, just like Paul Bunyan of Minnesota lore. The recreation complex on the south shore has a children's play area. The management will arrange babysitters; cost is $6 per hour.

**Recreation:** Fishing buffs relish this bit of paradise on the south shores of Lake Vermilion. Walleye, bass, and crappie lure fishermen to these waters. There's no excuse for not landing the big one; a fishing clinic is held every week, and a guide is available for private excursions. The staff at the lodge will fillet and freeze your catch. Besides fishing boats, the lodge has canoes, kayaks, paddleboats, old-fashioned rowboats, and a sailboat for guests' use. Waterskiing and hydrobikes add a new dimension of fun to water sports. There is a rental fee for motorboats.

The South Shore Sports Complex houses an indoor racquetball court, two Tru-Flex tennis courts, and a fitness center. After a good workout there, you may enjoy a leisurely swim or a relaxing sauna. Along the north shore you can take a stroll down the 1½-mile hiking trail. There are many additional miles of hiking and biking trails in the area. Half a dozen or more golf courses are within an hour of Ludlow's, including the Legends, *Golf Digest's* pick for the number-one public golf course in the country. Exciting adventures within an hour of Ludlow's Island include the Soudan Underground Mine State Park; Iron World, dedicated to Minnesota's mining history; the U.S. Hockey Hall of Fame; International Wolf Center; and Bear Center.

---

**P.O. Box 1146**
**Cook, Minnesota 55723**
**(218) 666-5407, (877) LUDLOWS**
**www.ludlowsresort.com**

# MISSION POINT RESORT
### Mackinac Island, Michigan

---

Northern Michigan is known for its glorious outdoors; add to this the quaintness of a historical island, subtract automobiles, and you have the perfect equation for a family resort. Mission Point nestles gracefully on its eighteen acres overlooking Lake Huron, just minutes from the village. Its style is summer Victorian, but substantial, and quite pleasing to the eye.

Taking advantage of existing architecture, Mission Point has renovated the Observation Tower, offering island visitors extraordinary views of Lake Huron and the Straits of Mackinac. This all-glass structure on the resort's property serves as the perfect spot to watch sailboats approach the southeast coast during the island's annual yacht races.

**Accommodations:** In the renovated 242 guest rooms (including ninety-two suites), casual and comfortable elegance is reflected in three styles: Nautical, Lodge, and North-ern Michigan. Views of the island are superb, some rooms offer fireplaces and Jacuzzis, and all have goose-down comforters and feather beds. Shoulder season rates range from $119 (Carriage room) to $309 (Lodge Suite); weekends cost more. Peak season (June through August) rates are $194 to $449, respectively. Rates are based on double occupancy, and children eighteen and under stay free with parents. Family packages are available starting from $325 to $375 per night and include lodging, some meals, ferry transportation, and activities. Teens (thirteen to eighteen) pay $45 per night; under twelve stay free. Regular season is May through October. A $4.50 per adult luggage transfer fee gets your bags from ferry to room.

**Dining:** Here's the great thing about dining at Mission Point: Not only is it delicious, but it's free for ages twelve and under when ordering from the children's menu and accompanied by parents. Well, a $1.50 service charge is added for each child, but really! Who could complain? And most restaurants have children's menus. Dinner at the Epicurean offers a culinary palette of fresh fish and steaks. For the casual side of island dining, try the Round Island Bar and Grill, where guests can watch passing freighters while enjoying appetizers, sandwiches, and spirits in an alfresco setting. It's also the place for "late nighters" and live entertainment. Lakeside Marketplace offers sandwiches and salads for guests on the go as well as indoor and outdoor dining with spectacular views of Lake Huron and the Straits of Mackinac. Bistro on the Greens, an open-air dining experience, serves a tempting array of European dishes from the chef's own personal recipes. It's worth noting that the resort has gourmet picnic baskets to go, a great addition to a day of island exploration.

**Children's World:** The Kids Club is Mission Point's answer to that age-old question, "What can I do now, Mom?" Near the Activity Center, the Kids Club offers 3,000 square feet of indoor space plus activities throughout the resort and field trips for older children. Little Ones, ages two to four years, have circle time, balloons and bubbles, or a teddy bear picnic. Ages four to ten enjoy themed days, such as Wild Kingdom or Space Day, with outdoor games, arts and crafts, storytelling, and nature hikes. Tweens, from eleven to fifteen, are not too cool to enjoy pool and pizza parties and back-to-the-'60s tie-dye sessions. Age groups under four years and over ten years may operate based on participation. Kids Club sessions for ages four to ten run regularly from 9:00 a.m. to 10:00 p.m. throughout the week from Memorial Day to Labor Day, and on weekends only to the end of the season. The program is flexible, and activi-

ties vary depending on the average age of the group. Each counselor accepts only six children, so it's a good idea to sign up early. The cost is $18 per half-day session, *but*— a half-day session is either 9:00 a.m. to 4:00 p.m. or 4:00 to 10:00 p.m.! And it's $25 for a full day (both sessions). Meals are extra.

With a 3,000-square-foot area, kids spark their imagination with a variety of interesting activities. Kids Club includes a Parent and Toddler Room, Gross Motor Skills Rooms, and a Kreative Korner Room, as well as some of the kids' traditional favorites like the 12-foot tepee. The active atmosphere of the resort is complemented by Mackinac Island itself, a natural adventure park offering outdoor explorations and historic sites.

At Kids Club kids enjoy a variety of supervised opportunities, including arts and crafts, learning ancient Indian lore, plus field trips to the island's Butterfly House, the 150-year-old British Fort, or along the island's bluff for bald-eagle spotting. Parents are encouraged to sign children up one day in advance, allowing the counselors to plan appropriate activities and guarantee its one-to-six counselor/child ratio. As an added convenience, pagers are available for parents of young guests.

Activities for the entire family embrace poolside bingo, build your own sundae, lawn games, a video arcade and billiards room, and old-fashioned picnic games. Mac the Moose is a favorite, making surprise appearances at the Kids Club or around the hotel. For a small fee he'll do a bedtime story and tuck-in—always a thrill!

**Recreation:** The Greens, an executive eighteen-hole putting green, is identified as "a short course in relaxation." With picturesque views and restaurants within walking distance, it's a fun course. Several championship courses are nearby; guests receive a discount. If you're a tennis buff, register early for the one court. The Activity Center is the heart of the resort's recreation, sheltering the Health Club and Spa, with Kids Club adjacent. Tennis, mountain cruisers and tandem bikes, in-line skate rentals, and the indoor game room are here, along with exercise equipment and massages—marvelous at the end of an active day. Relax by the outdoor heated pool or hot tub with a cool drink or take a leisurely stroll drinking in the view. Enjoy a hayride, lawn bowling, or croquet.

Step back in time at the early-twentieth-century theater, which presents the latest movie releases Monday evenings in summer. The waterfront gazebo, with glorious views, is a great place to relax.

---

**1 Lakeshore Drive**
**Mackinac Island, Michigan 49757**
**(906) 847-3312, (800) 833-7711**
**www.missionpoint.com**

# RUTTGER'S BAY LAKE LODGE
## Deerwood, Minnesota

If you have ever entertained thoughts of owning your own lakefront cottage in the land of 10,000 lakes, Ruttger's Bay Lake Lodge may satisfy your yearning. Set on 400 acres directly on Bay Lake, in north-central Minnesota, the Lodge emphasizes relaxed outdoor recreation in surroundings of clear lake waters, tall trees, and pine-scented air. Open May through September, it is family run and family oriented. With its old-fashioned hospitality, a family tradition since 1898, the lodge allows you a well-deserved escape to the peace and serenity of the North Woods.

**Accommodations:** When the lodge first opened, $5 would get you bed, board, and boat. Prices may have changed over the last hundred years, but the ambience hasn't. For years the lakefront cottages and the lodge rooms have been favorites among vacationers. To these have been added condominiums and villas. Many have kitchens, porches, and views of the lake, and all include a refrigerator, cable television, and air-conditioning. Ruttger's has both EP and

MAP rates. The Modified American Plan includes not only breakfast and dinner daily but also complimentary golf on Alec's Nine and Kids Kamp, plus many other resort activities; the same rate applies to a variety of accommodations and is mandatory for the Lakeside Cottages. Children under three years old stay at no charge; ages four to eight are $65; ages nine to fifteen are $85 in high season; rates drop to $45 to $55 per child over three at other times. On the European Plan, rates vary according to season, weekends, and size and location of accommodations; children under the age of eighteen are free. Mid-June to mid-August is the high season, and weekend rates are the most expensive. As an example, the Lakeside Cottage MAP plan ranges from $105 to $199 per adult. On the EP plan (lodging only, use of pools, tennis, and beach), per-room rates vary from $98 to $199 in the lodge or west villas; $120 to $310 in a one-bedroom, and $165 to $398 in a two-bedroom golf course condo. Located 1 mile from the main lodge and secluded in the woods overlooking the lake, the newly reno-vated Battle Point condominiums offer studio to three-bedroom units. Rates range from $98 (low season, studio) to $398 (high summer, two-bedroom) per night. On all lodging, MAP is always an option; rates vary. Inquire about weekend and family fun packages. Cribs and rollaways are $10 each.

**Dining:** The Modified American Plan is mandatory for cottage guests, and the homemade pastries are practically a requirement. Ruby's Dining Room, built in the 1920s, is an inviting setting, with natural logs, an open-beamed ceiling, and a stone fireplace. Service is a la carte or buffet, and for more than twenty years, Chef Dot has maintained Ruttger's tradition of excellent food. For casual dining and drinks, lunch and dinner are also served at Zig's, which overlooks Bass Lake and the eighteenth hole of the Lakes golf course. Auntie M's Kaffeehaus offers specialty coffees, panini sandwiches, pastry, and ice cream. The main lodge and Zig's both have picture windows that are great for viewing the North Woods while sipping a cool drink. Enjoy casual dining at Zig's between 11:00 a.m. and 9:00 p.m. The Bear Pine Bar is a full-service bar with appetizers and sandwiches, which can be enjoyed on the deck or around the pool with a spectacular view of Bay Lake.

**Children's World:** Kids Kamp is a supervised program for ages four to twelve that runs Monday through Friday, from mid-June to Labor Day. Planned by a certified teacher and kept in motion by energetic young counselors, from 9:00 a.m. to 3:00 p.m. (9:00 a.m. to 1:00 p.m. on Wednesday) kids are occupied with swimming, boating, fishing, and nature hikes. Indoors the fun continues with music, crafts, and games or time at the playground near the cottage. Teens are neither ignored nor overstructured; golf mixers, or waterskiing and wave-boarding clinics suit them just fine. Kids Kamp is compli-mentary on the MAP program; for EP guests, the charge is $25 for the day session, $20 on Wednesday. Babysitting can be arranged by the staff.

**Recreation:** With such a beautiful lake, you might find yourself drawn to the water almost continuously through the day—for sunning, swimming, waterskiing, water tubing, teen wakeboarding, fishing, and boating, and for building sand castles along the beach. Take a morning coffee cruise or an evening pontoon cruise and relax on the lake. Swimmers also enjoy the indoor and outdoor pools, and tennis fans turn to the two Omni-turf and three Laykold courts. Round up a game of volleyball, basketball, or horseshoes; play table tennis and shuffleboard; or go walking through the woods. Practice on the putting green, and plan a round of golf on the Lakes, the eighteen-hole championship course, or Alec's Nine. Ruttger's was *Golf Minnesota* magazine's "Golf Resort of the Year" in 2004. And treat yourself to pure relaxation in the lounge or TV lobby, the whirlpool or sauna, or just pull up a lawn chair and kick back.

The Day Spa follows Ruttger's tradition of using existing buildings, renovating and updating while keeping the original flavor. Set in a house in the woods, guests can take pleasure in massage, body wraps, facials, and all the beautifying rituals. Other old places to explore are the Country Store, now offering upscale clothing and home furnishings, but set in a building that over the years has been a general store, a feed store, the post office, and an antiques shop. Next door is The Garage—just that, it's an old filling station from the 1920s, now rejuvenated with toys, books, and casual clothing.

The staff naturalist directs programs introducing visitors to the loon, osprey, and bald eagle, along with garden tours and nature trails. Waterskiing, sailboats, motorboats, pontoon boats, and fishing boats are available. Families can partake of bonfires and cookouts, pontoon cruises, stargazing, talent shows, and family movie nights. Evenings come alive with adult pleasures such as wine tasting, bridge socials, or karaoke.

**25039 Tame Fish Lake Road**
**Box 400**
**Deerwood, Minnesota 56444**
**(218) 678-2885, (800) 450-4545**
**www.ruttgers.com**

# SHANTY CREEK
Bellaire, Michigan

Shanty Creek, a four-season resort located in northern Michigan, is actually three resorts in one, which translates into a bit of variety for guests. Summit Village is comfortable and contemporary, with stunning 360-degree views encompassing Lake Bellaire; Schuss Village has the European charm of an Alpine village; and Cedar River Village sits amid the gentle hills and hardwoods and is home to the Lodge, a collection of eighty-five modern luxury suite condominiums. Together they encompass 4,500 acres of rolling woodlands on the shores of Lake Bellaire. In the summertime golfing is the favorite activity; in winter skiing is the preferred sport.

**Accommodations:** Lodging choices are innumerable: guest rooms, studios, condominiums, and chalets. Some are equipped with a fireplace or whirlpool; others have a deck. You might have a view of the lake, the forests, a fairway, or the Alpine village. High-season rates start at $120 to $157 a night for a guest room and rise to $340 to $414 a night for a deluxe two-bedroom condominium. Children ages seventeen and under stay free when occupying a room with their parents. Cribs can be added to your accommodation for a fee of $10 a day. The many package plans available offer good savings.

**Dining:** The Lakeview Dining Room is an elegant restaurant at Summit Village. Open for breakfast, lunch, and dinner, it's hard to decide which is better, the food or the view. Lakeview draws its menu from the fields, forest, orchards, and lakes of northern Michigan and has a children's menu. La Vigna Italian Bistro at Cedar Ridge Village serves dinner nightly overlooking the eighteenth green at Cedar River Village. Other dining choices are Arnie's, in the Clubhouse at the Summit, serving sandwiches and soups at lunch and dinner; light fare and hearty breakfasts at the Weiskopf Grill in the Lodge at Cedar River; or Ivan's at Schuss Village. On weekends, choose your preferred style of evening entertainment: dueling pianos at Arnie's, cool jazz at Cedar River, or American favorites at the Lakeview.

**Children's World:** We may have become accustomed to purple dinosaurs, but a purple goose? That would be Gandy, Shanty Creek's mascot, with his own Web site fun page so kids can meet him before they actually meet him! Shanty Creek programs serve children from two months to twelve years old during most of the year. The programs are planned and supervised by a recreation specialist and an experienced childhood educator, so there's expertise combined with enthusiasm.

The Shanty Creek Children's Center is open every day from 9:00 a.m. to 5:00 p.m. for children ages two months through six years, mid-June through Labor Day, and late November through mid-March. It's a nurturing, playful, and safe environment, with a separate area for naps. Full-day rates are $48 with snacks; lunch is $7. If you prefer, hourly rates are $10.

Camp Gandy, operating daily from mid-June to Labor Day, has hiking, swimming, fishing, disc golf, music, and arts and crafts and is specially designed to meet the needs of school-age children (five to twelve years). Camp is open from 8:00 a.m. to 6:00 p.m. in Schuss Village. Full-day sessions are $35; half-day sessions from 9:00 a.m. to 1:00 p.m. or 1:00 to 5:00 p.m. are $25. Lunch is $7. Reservations by 4:00 p.m. the day prior are critical—if no children are registered, camp will not operate.

Sessions for children ages eight to twelve have the same hours, rates, and location, but the activities are more challenging and age-appropriate and include sports, disc golf, field trips, and longer hikes.

When the ski season starts, the daily Children's Center program combines stories and indoor play with the excitement of outdoor play in a winter wonderland. The same fees as above are charged for this program.

Young skiers-to-be, ages three to five, combine indoor play with sledding and ski instruction in their 10:00 a.m. to 4:00 p.m. schedule. Snow Stars, for ages three to five years, helps kids learn to ski and have fun doing it. Cost is $57 for a full day, $45 for a half-day session, and includes lunch, lift tickets, and snacks; equipment rentals are $10 to $14 additional. Snow Angels is a similar program for the same age group but is more individualized, with smaller groups. It's the "fast track" and is generally available on weekends. Cost is $97 for the full day and covers everything, even a pager for parents.

Kid's Academy, for older children (ages six to twelve), runs from 10:00 a.m. to 4:00 p.m. daily. This is more serious instruction but still doesn't lose sight of the fun of skiing. The fee is $57 full day, $45 half day with lunch. Ski rentals are not included in these fees. Smart Riders is for budding snowboarders, ages six to twelve years. Sessions are at 10:00 a.m. and 1:30 p.m. and the cost is the same.

Just for You is a babysitting service that matches caregivers with your child's age and needs. Cost is $9 per hour, with a two-hour minimum. A second sibling is $1 per hour. With parents' permission, children may use the resort facilities under this individual supervision. Shanty Creek also will do their best to accommodate children with special needs—call them. In February the resort hosts the Special Olympics.

**Recreation:** Golfers experience a bit of a dream come true here. The resort's original course is the eighteen-hole Summit Golf Course. Another championship eighteen holes make up the beautiful Schuss Mountain Course. And the crowning gem is the Legend, an exciting eighteen-hole course designed by Arnold Palmer. The new Cedar River Golf Club, designed by Tom Weiskopf, is another winner. With the carefully maintained courses complemented by an experienced teaching staff, all golfers will surely improve their games here. Awards are numerous: *Golf Magazine* rates Cedar River among the "Top Ten in the U.S. You Can Play"; the Legend as one of the top four courses; and Shanty Creek in the "Top 5 in Quality of Main Course." *Golf for Women* calls Shanty Creek "one of the most women-friendly." PGA professionals at the Golf Academy can give you all you need to really enjoy the game.

Other summertime activities include tennis, with eight courts; biking on the mountain trails; and boating. At the Fitness Center work out on the Nautilus equipment, hit the steam room or sauna, and wind up the day with a massage. Schedule time at the Wellness Spa for a real treat. Water urges may be satisfied at one of the five swimming pools or sandy beaches at Torch Lake, Lake Bellaire, or Elk Lake. With indoor swimming pools and a heated pool outdoors, swimmers are satisfied whatever the season.

On-site diversions are too numerous to list, but start with basketball, croquet, disc golf, volleyball, board games, and shopping. The state's only solar-lighted disc golf is here at Shanty Creek, and evening family clinics are fun for all. Add evening entertainment and nightly family activities such as bardic storytelling at the campfire, and you may not have time for a sunset sail on board a tall ship, or a visit to the Turtle Creek Casino or nearby Traverse City.

The ski season starts in November and continues through late March or early April, depending on how generous Mother Nature has been. On the two mountains, Summit and Schuss, there are forty-nine runs for downhill skiers, almost 20 kilometers of groomed trails for cross-country skiers, two terrain parks for snowboarders, and a Tubing Park. When you're not on the snow, pile the whole family into a horse-drawn sleigh for an old-fashioned ride in the woods. Or if you're brave enough, take a dip in the heated outdoor pool. Après-ski at any of the three villages is easy with the free resort shuttle service that operates year-round.

**1 Shanty Creek Road**
**Bellaire, Michigan 49615**
**(231) 533-8621, (800) 678-4111**
**www.shantycreek.com**

# TAN-TAR-A RESORT

## Osage Beach, Missouri

Located in central Missouri, the Tan-Tar-A Resort rests comfortably in the foothills of the Ozark Mountains. The resort complex covers 420 lush acres and stretches along the shores of the scenic Lake of the Ozarks. Once the largest man-made lake in the world, it was created in 1931 with the construction of Bagnell Dam, a project of the Union Electric Company. This 54,000-acre lake with 1,150 miles of shoreline (more than the state of California, they boast) is now the centerpiece of Missouri recreation. As their publicity says, "Lake of the Ozarks offers visitors gallons (about 617 billion) of fun and adventure." The hilly terrain and lakeside exposure provide a lovely backdrop for many recreational activities. Tan-Tar-A is a AAA three-diamond resort and was rated by *Midwestern Living* magazine as one of the top three resorts "families would love most." Tan-Tar-A is only a three-hour drive from either St. Louis or Kansas City.

**Accommodations:** The 989 guest rooms and suites are in the main resort buildings and in smaller two-story accommodations bordering the lake. Some have a fireplace and a deck or patio. This is the resort complex, within walking distance of dining and most activities. A variety of room plans exist: two-double-bed rooms and one-bedroom units with kitchenettes, and two bedrooms with full kitchen. The Estates complex surrounds the nine-hole golf course and is a seven- to ten-minute drive from the restaurants and activities. With the ambience of a neighborhood, units of two to four guest rooms appear to be houses from the outside; floor plans are different and contain rooms or suites, each with its own private entrance. Winter rates for a standard lake-view room are $96 to $139; suites are $116 to $241. The Estates units are $10 to $20 more. In peak summer, daily rates average $175 for rooms, $245 for suites, and $380 for a two-bedroom unit in the Estates. Packages are available for five to seven nights and provide considerable savings.

**Dining:** If you like to start your day with a latte, Java Lakes is the spot for you. For casual family meals, the Black Bear Lounge serves breakfast, lunch, and dinner in a rustic hunting lodge setting and has a deck for summer dining. Children three years and younger have complimentary breakfast and Sunday brunch. For a fancier evening, try Windrose on the Water, where you'll enjoy luscious steaks and fresh seafood. If all you want is a quick bite, the Food Court has Burger King, Sbarro, and Eskimo Pie ice-cream shop. At the golf course, the Oaks serves lunch overlooking the course or while you watch a game on the big-screen TV. For liquid refreshment and snacks, the Jetty Bar is adjacent to the Arrowhead Pool (seasonal). Mr. D's Lounge serves cocktails and entertainment at days' end.

**Children's World:** Camp Tan-Tar-A, for children ages four to eleven years, is in session Monday through Saturday, from mid-June through mid-August. The fee for the 10:00 a.m. to 4:00 p.m. schedule is $50 for the first day and $35 for each additional day and includes lunch and a T-shirt. Half-day sessions are $35. Activities include swimming, beach games, races, treasure hunts, and crafts.

A less structured routine is found at the Kids Cabin—filled with games, toys, dress-up, Legos, and more. In summer the Cabin is open in the evenings only, Monday through Saturday, from 5:00 to 10:00 p.m. Fall, winter, and spring, the program operates on Saturday only, from 5:00 to 10:00 p.m. The cost is $50 and includes dinner at Burger King in the summer. Children under age four are welcome to the Cabin on Friday and Saturday evenings but must be supervised by a parent. In-room babysitting, available on a limited basis, with a three-hour minimum, is $9 per hour ($1 for each additional child).

**Recreation:** The lake is the venue for boating fun for everyone. You can rent ski boats (waterskiing instruction available), sailboats, paddleboats, kayaks, fishing boats, and WaveRunners. You can even try parasailing. Though there's a small sandy beach that's nice for sunbathing, the lake is primarily the domain of boaters and fishermen. Swimmers usually opt for time at one of the three pools (two outdoor, one indoor). The Arrowhead Pool complex beckons with waterfalls, the Jetty Bar, a 125-foot water slide, and a toddler splash pool.

You may lose the children forever in the Timber Falls Indoor Waterpark. Set in a three-story wilderness tree house topped with a 6-foot-wide wooden bucket, it's filled with interactive fun, water blasters, suspension bridges, and web crawls; plus four water slides, an activity pool, and a lazy river area for tubing. And what about that bucket, you may ask? Oh, it tips over every two minutes or so, drenching everyone below with 700 gallons of water! The water park is open daily in summer, on weekends year-round; passes are $17 per person per day.

Golfers can take on the challenges of the Oaks (an eighteen-hole course) or Hidden Lakes (nine holes). Liquid refreshments from the on-course "jigger joggers" may or may not improve your game. The Racquet Club houses indoor tennis and racquetball courts as well as billiards. Outdoors and adjacent to the club are basketball and volleyball courts. Tennis buffs can also try the complimentary outdoor tennis courts near the Racquet Club.

At the fitness center you can use the exercise room and whirlpool, or indulge in programs at the Windjammer Spa. Facials, massages, aromatherapy, and detoxification treatments are just some of the pleasures from which to choose.

If it's to do with video or electronics, the Bear's Den Arcade probably has it. It's fun for all ages, and tickets won can be exchanged for prizes.

Back in the great outdoors, find a good horse at the stables for a nice trail ride, jog along the paths around the property, or challenge the kids to a round of miniature golf. If you still have time and energy, try bowling, billiards, shuffleboard, or table tennis. Be sure to take an afternoon cruise on the lake; the *Ozark Princess* sails four times a week during the summer season.

Lots of activities and attractions in the area may pique your interest. Budding spelunkers take note: More than 5,000 recognized caves exist in Missouri, and 300 of them surround the lake. "Show" caves have been tamed with paved walkways and lights—four of the twenty-two are within 30 miles of one another. For shoppers in your party, Factory Outlet Village may satisfy; if you want to rummage through history rather than read about it, several antiques shops will oblige. Country Western music shows are great for family entertainment, and more outdoors can be celebrated at two nearby state parks. Ha Ha Tonka is the newest park in Missouri, with lots of wildlife, natural bridges, and spectacular scenery. Lake of the Ozarks State Park is the largest park and has not only foot trails but also the unique Aquatic Trail, designed for boaters to explore the lakeshore.

---

**State Road KK**
**Osage Beach, Missouri 65065**
**(573) 348-3131, (800) 826-8272**
**www.tan-tar-a.com**

# SOUTHWEST

Arizona
New Mexico
Texas

# THE BISHOP'S LODGE RESORT AND SPA

Santa Fe, New Mexico

Just a ten-minute drive north of Old Santa Fe, 1,000 acres of the foothills of the Sangre de Cristo Mountains comprise the range of the Bishop's Lodge. At an elevation of 7,200 feet, this area of north-central New Mexico shares its warm sunny days with cool crisp nights. The clean mountain air, the setting, and the atmosphere of the lodge combine to enhance the flavor and traditions of the old Southwest. The adobe architecture, a reminder of the area's Spanish and Native American heritage, and the friendly spirit of the staff give the Bishop's Lodge its true Western flair.

In the nineteenth century the ranch was the home of Archbishop Jean Baptiste Lamy, a pioneering French cleric who became the Southwest's first Catholic bishop. His life was the inspiration for Willa Cather's novel *Death Comes for the Archbishop* (good background reading for an introduction to the history and topography of the region). The private chapel built by the archbishop still stands, a sentinel to the lodge's history. The property was purchased by the newspaper publisher Joseph Pulitzer and then acquired in 1918 by James Thorpe. A National Historic Hotel, the lodge has undergone expansion and renovation, with a strong emphasis placed on customer service and satisfaction. The lodge is open year-round, and many families return year after year; three generations of family visitors are not uncommon.

**Accommodations:** Chips and salsa and that special Santa Fe light welcome you to your room. The lodge's one hundred–plus rooms and suites are grouped in several adobe buildings nestled among fruit trees

and flower beds. The North and South lodges are the oldest, both having been grand summer homes before World War I. All of the rooms are decorated in warm earth colors with a Southwestern flair; deluxe rooms include fireplaces, and many have outdoor sitting areas. The beds are simply delicious, firm mattresses with soft, feathery inserts. Rates are based on double occupancy; children under age four stay at no charge, and others pay $15 per day. Cribs and rollaways are available on request at no charge. Historic rooms range from $189 to $489; summer is high season. Deluxe rooms are generally $50 to $75 more. Holidays and weekends are more expensive, as are suites.

A resort fee of $14.50 per day per person (thirteen and older) allows use of the facilities (pool, tennis, fitness center); any complimentary family programs; activities such as yoga, Tai Chi, aerobics, and hiking; fishing, with all the equipment; and shuttles to Santa Fe and the nearby ski area in winter. Also included is in-room high-speed Internet access, coffee and tea, daily newspaper, parking, and local telephone access.

**Dining:** Las Fuentes (The Fountains) reflects a new concept in cuisine, Nuevo Latino, bringing together the color, taste, and music of Puerto Rico, Cuba, Argentina, Salvador, Colombia, the Caribbean, and other Central and South American countries, for your dining pleasure. It's open for breakfast, lunch, and dinner, with a children's menu in summer. The decor is classic Santa Fe: beamed ceilings, Navajo rugs, Spanish chandeliers, and four life-size murals done in the 1920s by W. E. Rollins. For cocktails and lighter fare, stop by Las Fuentes Bar, a cozy corner bar opening onto the Terrace, with alfresco dining for all meals. Relax and enjoy poolside drinks and snacks from 10:00 a.m. to 8:00 p.m. at the Oasis Bar and Grille, by Santa Fe's largest outdoor pool. Sunsets, stars, and soft summer breezes accompany the nightly entertainment. Santa Fe, with its myriad dining possibilities, is ten minutes away.

**Children's World:** During the summer months, Memorial Day to Labor Day, kids five to eleven years old gather down by the corral, at Camp Apaloosa. Children under five are welcome when accompanied by an adult. Different activities every day and a ratio of one counselor to seven children keep it interesting and interactive. From 8:30 a.m. to 1:30 p.m. (includes lunch), there's a mix of activities: nature hikes, pony rides, archery, tennis, a "Kid's Rodeo," and Frisbee golf on the active side; sand art, plaster sculpture, murals, and animal masks for artistic expression. In addition a pond stocked with trout and an outdoor play area with swings, a slide, jungle gym, and a sandbox translate into active fun for kids. Labor Day through Memorial Day, Camp Apaloosa is offered the same hours, but on Saturday only. Summer afternoons between 2:00 and 4:00 p.m. are open to all and are dedicated to family activities; nature hikes, water games, hula hoops, scavenger hunts, potato-sack races, and multiple crafts are just the beginning.

Evening Round Up offers parents a night or two out on the town or just relaxing at the resort. Take advantage of this program Monday through Saturday from 5:00 to 9:00 p.m. Kids enjoy dinner, games, movies, and skits. Every Saturday night in summer brings a Dive-In Movie at the pool for families. From September through May,

Evening Round Up is available Friday and Saturday evenings only. Morning programs including lunch are $60; Evening Round Up including dinner is $45.

Children may have meals with their counselors in their own dining room or at picnics, pool parties, and cookouts.

While Bishop's Lodge doesn't have a winter program for kids, Chipmunk Corner Children's Center at Ski Santa Fe, fifteen minutes from the lodge, offers day care from 8:30 a.m. to 4:30 p.m. for ages three months to three years. Snacks and lunch are provided, and children are divided by age. Snowplay, which has the same hours, is a fun introduction to the skiing environment for ages three and four, with indoor and outdoor play, games, and activities.

The Little Chips Ski Program for four-year-olds provides a full day that includes a two-hour lesson in the morning, with lunch and snacks provided. The afternoon continues with Snowplay (outdoor and indoor ski play), activities, and games. The half-day session is a two-hour lesson only, with snacks and lunch included. Chipmunk Corner, for ages five to nine, places children into classes according to their age (five to six and seven to nine) and abilities. All children are tested to determine accurate levels. Rates are $66 to $70; equipment rental is $14 for either program. Call (505) 988-9636 for reservations.

**Recreation:** Except on Tuesday, the horses' day of rest, recreation at the Bishop's Lodge begins with horseback riding on scenic mountain trails. Experienced wranglers match you and your ability with the appropriate steed from a stable of thirty horses. Children must be over eight years old and 4 feet tall (free pony rides are offered for the little ones), and the maximum weight is 225 pounds. Choose from a group ride (more sedate), or schedule private rides if you want to canter and gallop through the mesa. A memorable experience is a sunrise or sunset ride through the canyons and foothills of the Sangre de Cristo Mountains; once a week in summer you can enjoy a hearty "cooked on the range" breakfast or an evening barbecue. The Santa Fe National Forest is adjacent to the grounds of the lodge and provides more opportunities to explore the gorgeous scenery on horseback. If you're a little skittish about mounting a horse, there are many hiking trails both on the resort grounds and nearby, ranging from moderate to strenuous, with the same great views.

Lots of other recreational fun can easily fill your days. Fish the mountain streams for trout, swim in the pool, improve your skill at the Skeet and Trap Range, or just bask in the glorious New Mexico sunshine. The nearby country clubs of Santa Fe, Cochiti Lake, and Towa Golf Resort grant lodge guests golfing privileges on their eighteen-hole courses. At the Tennis Center, you can play on one of the two courts, have a lesson with the resident pro, and purchase some new accessories at the pro shop. At 7,000 feet, you'll need stamina, lots of water, and perhaps special tennis balls. On the skeet and trap-shooting ranges, experts offer instruction, and rental equipment is provided. Play a game of table tennis or treat your sore muscles to a relaxing hour in the whirlpool.

*ShaNah* is a Native word meaning vitality and wisdom, and the highly acclaimed ShaNah Spa & Wellness Center is more than a place to be pampered; it's also about healing, nurturing, and ancient Native wisdom. You can experience a facial, massage, body polish, Native hot stone massage, or Ayurvedic treatment. All sessions begin with an optional (but highly recommended) Native American Blessing Ceremony to open the heart and set the intention—it may change your whole outlook on life. A real treat is having an outdoor massage under that very special New Mexico sky.

Be sure to reserve at least a day to discover the narrow streets, interesting adobe architecture, quaint shops, and art galleries of Old Santa Fe. Open-air performances of the Santa Fe Summer Opera Festival are a special attraction, and dance and music performances abound. Pueblo Indians show their jewelry and pottery on blankets around the Palace of the Governors or at the famous Tesuque Indian Market, and visitors are often welcome to attend the colorful ceremonies at nearby pueblos.

Fall brings crisp days with dazzling colors. The horses are energized, and the ski lift opens for spectacular views from the top of the mountains. In winter Santa Fe's cultural events are still in full swing, entertainers are showcased at the reservation casinos, and the big fireplace at the lodge is a welcome gathering spot. The lodge offers a "Ski and Spa" package in winter: Monday through Thursday two adults ski free at the nearby Ski Santa Fe slopes and then return to enjoy a rejuvenating spa visit. The 12,053-foot summit at Ski Santa Fe boasts 1,703 vertical feet of skiing and sixty-seven trails winding through stunning terrain with the perfect powder typical of New Mexico.

---

**P.O. Box 2367**
**1297 Bishop's Lodge Road**
**Santa Fe, New Mexico 87501**
**(505) 983-6377, (800) 732-2240**
**www.bishopslodge.com**

# ENCHANTMENT RESORT

### Sedona, Arizona

Nature was about 350 million years creating the incredible landscape surrounding this area, but it was well worth the wait. Reputed to have special magnetic energies, Sedona has become a focal point for metaphysical healing and "New Age" spirituality, as well as an international art scene. Whatever it is, there is indeed something magical in the air, in spite of encroaching commercialism. Enchantment Resort is very well named. Nestled within the walls of Boynton Canyon, 5 miles northwest of town, it is surrounded by the Coconino National Forest and is a welcome escape from touring and town. The land surrounding the resort is sacred to the Yavapai-Apache as the birthplace of their tribe; in fact, the resort has a Native American ambassador on staff to explain the land and share tribal stories and tradition. This four-star, four-diamond resort has been named one of the "Top Hotels in America" by *Condé Nast Traveler*, 2007 Gold List, and *Zagat Survey 2007;* has been recognized as a "Top Family Resort" by Familytravel.com, *Parents Magazine,* and *Family Tree Magazine;* has been named as one of the "Top 20 Hotels in the World" by *Fodor's Choice;* and has won *Travel + Leisure*'s "World's Best Awards, Top 100."

**Accommodations:** Pueblo-style architecture blends in with the landscape, and the 220 rooms can be arranged in various combinations of guest rooms, studios, and junior suites; when connected, these create one- or two-bedroom casitas or haciendas. This also creates many rates. Based on double occupancy, daily rates for guest rooms and studios begin at $350; junior suites start at $450; one-bedroom suites are $750 to $1,050; and two-bedroom suites are $1,125 to $1,625 (with a private pool).

Children twelve and under stay free. To create a lasting memory, a three-night family package ($2,508 to $4,638) provides full breakfast for everyone, including Sunday brunch, one sixty-minute spa treatment daily per adult (sixteen and older), daily Camp Coyote, and the daily resort fee and gratuities. Suites feature Southwestern decor with beehive fireplaces, high ceilings, Native crafts, and patios with dramatic views. High season is mid-February to mid-June, and the end of August through December. A daily $22 per room resort fee covers use of the spa, mountain bikes, courts, and most activities, with the exception of tennis lessons, Camp Coyote, and spa treatments.

**Dining:** People drive up from Phoenix and down from Flagstaff just to experience the AAA four-diamond-rated Yavapai Restaurant. With menu items such as cold smoked buffalo tenderloin; Anaheim chile relleno, stuffed with duck and rolled in blue corn; and Southwest spiced salmon with lobster potato cake, it's no wonder! Huge windows reveal a 180-degree vista of the stunning red rocks of Boynton Canyon; dinner, lunch, and a breakfast brunch are served daily, while a Sunday Jazz Brunch is very popular. Collared shirts and no jeans or athletic shoes are requested in the evening. Tii Gavo, a more casual restaurant serving lunch and dinner, has a children's menu and entertainment on weekends. Mii amo Cafe is part of the self-contained spa, offering eclectic and healthy cuisine. In summer, guests may dine on their terraces or poolside as well.

**Children's World:** Daily year-round, trained counselors at Camp Coyote keep children ages four to twelve active and engaged at the colorful Camp Center. Kids enjoy treasure hunts, swimming, tennis and golf, outdoor crafts, and games, all with a daily theme: Desert Dweller, Canyon Fun, Wild West, Southwestern, or Native American days. Often, a park ranger or a Native American storyteller will drop in for a surprise visit. A full day, including lunch, is from 9:00 a.m. to 3:30 p.m. and costs $70; half-day morning ($35) or afternoon with lunch ($40) is another option. On Friday and Saturday, the dinner and evening program operates from 5:00 to 9:00 p.m. ($45). The Resort Concierge can arrange babysitting for $15 per hour, with a three-hour minimum, for one child. Additional children in the same family are $2 extra per hour per child. Payment in cash is requested directly to the party providing the sitting services; there is no charge from the resort.

**Recreation:** If you can tear yourself away from just staring at the landscape, lots of activities await. At the resort, activities are nonstop from 7:00 a.m. to evening: Tai Chi, cooking demonstrations, yoga, basket making, power Pilates, aqua aerobics, Quigong, a vortex walk, tennis drills, photography—the list goes on and on. Walk leisurely along the trails with your sketchbook or take a more strenuous hike. Mountain bikes are here for the adventurous, or championship croquet, bocci ball, and table tennis for a slower pace; swimming, of course, under an unimaginably blue sky; or combine the two with a rousing water volleyball game. A Cayman-style pitch-and-putt golf course and a putting green will whet the golfer's appetite for the two championship courses nearby in Sedona. Tennis players are well served by a variety of clinics and mixers on the seven courts. U.S. Park Rangers are stationed at the resort and give lectures and guided walks three times weekly. Enchantment Resort and the U.S. Forest Service have jointly established the Boynton Canyon Preservation Fund, a privately funded effort to create programs to improve and preserve the tranquil beauty of the canyon. It's a stellar spot for stargazing through the resort's telescope, especially with an expert to explain what you're seeing. Curious about what a vortex really is? Come to the lobby on Tuesday at 5:00 p.m. and understand the mystery. Enchantment Marketplace is not the usual resort retail shop; here you'll find local art, photography, music, and jewelry.

Mii amo is a full-service destination spa located within the resort—the name is a Yuman word for "journey, or moving forward; a passage." Actually a boutique hotel within the resort, it offers seventeen rooms and suites, with three- to seven-day packages. It has its own fitness room, indoor and outdoor pools, and a restaurant, along with twenty-four treatment areas where magic is created with blue-corn body polish or Sedona-clay wraps. Mii amo blends spa services with Native American healing and spirituality and takes full advantage of an exquisite natural setting. Enchantment guests over age sixteen have access to spa facilities and treatments.

In other venues, music and nature blend at the 5,000-seat amphitheater in the Sedona Culture Park, Oak Creek Canyon beckons you with gorgeous winding drives and picnic areas along the creek, and Slide Rock is a natural combination of smooth rocks and splashing water that kids love. The Grand Canyon is only two hours away. You can even get there by steam locomotive. Tour this spectacular Sedona area by four-wheel-drive vehicle or helicopter or on horseback. It's awesome any way you approach it.

---

**525 Boynton Canyon Road**
**Sedona, Arizona 86336**
**(928) 282-2900, (800) 826-4180**
**www.enchantmentresort.com**

# FLYING L GUEST RANCH

## Bandera, Texas

Bandera, 40 miles northwest of San Antonio, claims to have invented dude ranching during the Depression when an enterprising rancher decided to take in "dudes" for extra money. So now, in true Texan style, they have laid claim to being the "Cowboy Capital of the World." Seven rodeo world champions have hailed from here, however, so there may be something to it. Set in the midst of the beautiful Texas Hill Country, this is not the dry, barren Texas of the movies. Here there are verdant hills, oak and maple trees, wildflowers, and flowing rivers, not sagebrush and sand.

The Flying L Ranch was first settled in 1874. It became a dude ranch in 1946 when Jack Lapham, a retired Air Corps colonel, started to realize his dream of a place where "a modern person can go and find himself in the midst of yesterday." (OK, who can figure out the name of the ranch based on this story? You already did? Good!) The ranch became a favorite "watering hole" for celebrities, including John Wayne, Tex Ritter, Buck Owens, Chill Wills, Slim Pickens, and Willie Nelson; the television program *The Cisco Kid* was filmed here. Recognitions include *Family Vacation Magazine*'s "Top 100 Family Vacations"; one of the best spring break family vacations from *Southern Living* magazine; *Golf for Women* rated it one of the top 100 places for women; and *Smart Money* magazine put it in the top 5 vacation spots in the country. The motto of this award-winning ranch is "Whoever says you can't have it all has never been to the Flying L."

**Accommodations:** You can bunk in style here—all forty-four suites offer real Texas-style lodging with room to spread out. The villas are geared toward comfort; all include a refrigerator, microwave, coffeepot, cable TV, daily maid service, and a real wood-burning fireplace. Daily room rates in high season (March to October) are $159 for a one-bedroom villa (maximum four guests), $259 for a two-bedroom villa (maximum six guests), and $259 to $299 for golf and ranch villas. Holiday rates are higher. Rates include use of amenities, nightly entertainment, and the new water park. Low-season room rates range from $119 to $199. Family packages include villa accommodations, breakfast and dinner buffets daily, horseback riding and use of the ranch amenities, nightly Western entertainment, and the supervised children's program. Discount rates are given for five nights or more.

**Dining:** The "Cowboy Capital" meal package is an additional $30.90 per adult per day ($18.90 for children twelve and under) and includes breakfast, dinner, entertainment, and s'mores. A la carte meals are also possible: $12 ($8 for kids) for breakfast and $19 ($11 for kids) for dinner and the Sunday buffet. Meals are hearty examples of fine Texas Hill Country cuisine. Seven days a week, from 7:30 to 9:30 a.m., start your day with a delicious breakfast buffet in the Main House dining room. Breakfast here was rated "#1 in Texas" by the tourism council. Lunch is on your own, with burgers and fries at the pro shop or an afternoon picnic from your refrigerator. Buffet dinner is from 5:30 to 7:30 p.m., either in the Main House dining room or creekside. During summer and holidays, the "Buckaroo Buffet" is loaded with favorites that "kids hanker for." Always popular are the Tuesday and Saturday cookouts by the creek, under the open sky and old live oaks. Especially when you arrive by hay wagon and horseback.

At 5:00 p.m. the Branding Iron Saloon opens, and there's family entertainment every night—cowboy music, dancing, gun slinging, or a rodeo, usually topped off with a marshmallow roast and making s'mores. Do the kids love that!

**Children's World:** Children are divided into two groups, ages three to six and seven to twelve. Programs run from 8:30 a.m. to noon, when children lunch with their parents, and from 1:00 to 3:00 p.m. Activities include feeding animals, nature walks, scavenger hunts, sports, fishing, and crafts, such as making leather bracelets and vests. Older kids can learn archery or BB gun and slingshot skills, while the little ones can take pony rides at the Kids Korral every day. Afternoons usually feature an activity for the entire family, such as roping lessons or a family greased-pig chase. The program runs Monday through Saturday year-round. The supervised children's activities program is $25 for a full day or $20 for a half day.

**Recreation:** Since this is a ranch, and it is Texas, of course horseback riding is a major focus. The winding San Julian Creek and huge old oaks amid the rolling hills are great for riding, and you're likely to encounter all types of critters like rabbits and even deer. With approximately forty horses to choose from, you'll soon have a new best friend. Rates are $35 to $70, based on time and terrain; lessons are $40. Children must be at least six years old and ride with parents.

Just added in 2007 is everyone's next favorite sport, the Lone Star Lagoon. This water area is a dream come true for kids, with wave pool, slides, and wading area. A lazy river runs through it, and a sandy beach or deck area with umbrella shade suits parents just fine, thank you!

Drive, chip, and putt on the popular par 72, fully irrigated course. Greens fees, cart, and tax are $31 to $42 regular; $24 to $29 for juniors. A driving range lets you perfect your skills if you don't get distracted by the beautiful view; private lessons are also available from two PGA professionals. Try the outdoor heated swimming pool or venture off the ranch to the Medina River for a little inner tubing or canoeing. Tennis, sand volleyball, horseshoes, hayrides, rodeo events, a playground, and a seasonal petting corral add to the fun. And after all that exercise, a good soak in the outdoor Jacuzzi may be just what the old bones need.

In the Bandera area, fish in the crystal waters of Medina Lake, tour a working longhorn ranch, visit the Cowboy Artists Museum in Kerrville, tour the World War II Nimitz Museum, or enjoy antiquing in the German town of Fredericksburg. On Bandera's Main Street there's a working blacksmith shop. Nearby excursions include San Antonio (the Alamo, Market Square, and the River Walk) and various theme parks such as SeaWorld, Fiesta Texas, and Splashtown. Visit natural wonders such as the caverns. All in all, the ranch promises "a rootin', tootin' time."

---

**566 Flying L Drive**
**Bandera, Texas 78003**
**(830) 460-3001, (800) 292-5134**
**www.flyingl.com**

# HYATT REGENCY
# HILL COUNTRY RESORT

San Antonio, Texas

The Texas Hill Country is as much a state of mind as it is a region. It certainly doesn't look like Texas—its green rolling hills, abundance of water, wildflowers, and variety of trees surprise the first-time visitor. San Antonio calls itself "a big city with small-town charm," and, as the number one tourist destination in Texas, has a multitude of attractions for families to enjoy—including the famous Alamo, centerpiece of Texas history, and the River Walk, lined with shops and restaurants along the tree-shaded banks of the San Antonio River.

Twenty minutes from downtown, a scenic drive meanders through the landscape, culminating at the Hill Country Hyatt lobby entrance, reminiscent of a Texas ranch house and complete with fireplaces, antler chandeliers, and overstuffed furniture—even a shady back porch. In fact, the resort's 200 acres are a part of the Rogers–Wiseman Ranch, honored for being in continuous agricultural production at the hands of one family for a century or more. Hyatt has successfully adapted a full-scale destination resort into this casual, laid-back lifestyle; the results are downright pleasurable. Especially the Ramblin' River—the centerpiece of the property and the greatest place to get into an inner tube, kick back, and just relax. Accolades include being one of *Travel + Leisure's* "Top 25 Family-Friendly Resorts" and on *Condé Nast's* 2004 Gold List of the world's best places to stay.

**Accommodations:** Of traditional German-style Hill Country architecture with native limestone and decorative wood exterior, the two- and four-story hotel has nine guest-room wings, housing 500 rooms. A stand-alone two-story luxurious guesthouse styled after a ranch house is in the courtyard—there's even an authentic windmill! As usual with Hyatt, the rooms are large and well decorated, ranging from standard to Regency Club level, with no-smoking rooms and suites available. In summer, room rates range from $279 to $369 daily; suites are from $715 to $1,250. Regency Club level ($350 to $490) includes breakfast, snacks during the day, and evening cocktails and hors d'oeuvres plus other amenities. Children under eighteen stay free in the same room as parents. Packages are a good value and may include golf, the children's program, or other family excursions. Sunshine on Sale, for example, gives you the third or fourth night free. At most Hyatt Resorts, Family Plans allow an opportunity to reserve a second room for children at half price, based on availability—be sure to ask.

**Dining:** The flavor is definitely Tex-Mex, so expect tortillas even for breakfast, but you have lots of options here. The Springhouse Cafe features regional specialties, a large buffet and salad bar, and Sunday brunch. A wood-burning oven makes great pizzas. In the clubhouse, the Antlers Lodge has the ambience of a country lodge and puts the accent on regional Southwestern cuisine of steak, chicken, and seafood. Many entrees are mesquite-grilled and accompanied by a spicy Tex-Mex sauce. Golfers will find sandwiches and light snacks in the Cactus Oak Tavern at the halfway point on the golf course. It's a strange phenomenon that in this part of Texas, cacti that normally like sand have decided to grow in oak trees, hence the name. The General Store offers hamburgers, deli sandwiches, and home-baked cookies as well as licorice sticks, wine, sodas, fresh coffee, and muffins. The Windflower Café at the spa has healthy salads, wraps, and smoothies, while Papa Ed's Pool House serves up sandwiches and grilled food by the pool. In the evening relax at Aunt Mary's Porch, an open-air bar just off the lobby, or kick up your heels at Charlie's Long Bar, an old-fashioned Texas saloon complete with tin ceiling and a 56-foot copper-top bar. Yes, they have the tequila with the worm. Pool, shuffleboard, backgammon, and chess enhance the bar area.

**Children's World:** Camp Hyatt, only at select Hyatt resorts, offers not only supervised programs but also children's menus and an opportunity to buy a second room for the kids at half price. Custom tailored for ages three to twelve, Rowdy's Camp Hyatt operates daily year-round. The program runs from 8:00 a.m. to 5:00 p.m. and keeps the kids busy with games and activities. Activities have a decidedly Western flavor, with a cowboys-and-Indians theme predominating: searching for arrowheads, watching for coyotes on the golf course at sunset (yes, they are sometimes there), totem poles, Wild West collages, and rodeo round-up games join the nature hikes and sand-castle building. A special Camp Hyatt room serves as a meeting place and for indoor activities; a different schedule is posted for every day of the week. Full- and half-day sessions may be arranged; cost for half-day sessions is $35; lunch is $10 extra. If you want to have an evening for grown-up pursuits, the evening session runs from 6:00 to 10:00 p.m. daily in summer, on Friday and Saturday year-round, and costs $40 with dinner.

The perfect "spot" for youth may be the new *SPAhhht,* a first-class spa experience for today's youth—bright and colorful, with the accent on vibrant energy, not serene calm. Air-brushed nail art, hair weaving and up-do's, henna tattoos, and massage are what's happening here. The Underground is the newest attraction for teens, who helped with the concept and design. Totally fluid, it may change venues or activities but will remain a teen hangout space, with dance, "mock-tails," snacks, and arcade games. The concierge will always have the skinny on "whassup" here. For twelve- to sixteen-year-olds, the Underground is open daily from 7:00 to 11:00 p.m. Parents can do their "inspection" at 6:00 p.m.

**Recreation:** Golfers enjoy the Arthur Hills–designed course, with its 170 acres of rolling, scenic terrain. It truly blends into the countryside and has been recognized as one of the premier courses in the United States. Tennis is available on three courts, with a pro on hand. Walking, jogging, and biking paths crisscross the property, and the health club features aerobics classes and all the latest equipment—and, of course, a massage to help you recover from your workout. Windflower, the Hill Country Spa, has twenty-one treatment rooms to pamper you. Using all-natural, mostly local ingredients in the services, treatments include such indulgences as a peach pecan body scrub and what else? Yellow rose facials, of course.

By far the most popular spot, though, is the Ramblin' River, modeled after all those Hill Country river experiences. Pick up an inner tube, drop your cares, and let the lazy current carry you away. The journey varies from brisk to slow and allows riders to swim, walk, float, or take detours into two swimming pools, a cascading waterfall, or even a little sand beach.

Day excursions to SeaWorld, Six Flags, Fiesta Texas, Splashtown water park, or many of the nearby Hill towns, each with its own personality and charm, can pleasurably fill your days or evenings. Visit the Natural Bridge Caverns, with active formations more than 140 million years old, or stroll through Bandera, the self-proclaimed "Cowboy Capital." The Alamo is a must, and missions, museums, and Market Square, which feels like shopping in Mexico, are all nearby.

**9800 Hyatt Resort Drive**
**San Antonio, Texas 78251**
**(210) 647-1234, (800) 233-1234**
**www.hillcountry.hyatt.com**

# HYATT REGENCY SCOTTSDALE RESORT AND SPA AT GAINEY RANCH
## Scottsdale, Arizona

Entering the private road that leads to this resort does not prepare you for the beauty of this lush and luxurious oasis in the midst of the Arizona desert. Water surrounds, cascades, falls, bubbles, flows, even sprays from the air; water and flowers are everywhere. You feel as though you are part of the landscape, not separated from it. Twenty-eight fountains, forty-seven waterfalls, and hundreds of palms, fir trees, and flowers create a twenty-seven-acre garden, part of the 560-acre Gainey Ranch, a planned residential complex that includes golf, parks and lakes, private homes, and businesses. Ecologically, this is a fragile area; fortunately the Hyatt has an admirable environmental program that focuses on reducing energy consumption and landfill; a waste-water reclamation plant irrigates the golf course.

**Accommodations:** The double "H" shape of the four-story resort provides five courtyards and four glass-enclosed atriums, with a movable 820-square-foot glass wall at the center of the lobby that allows a panoramic view of the McDowell Mountains and Sonoran Desert. The main building, inspired by the desert work of Frank Lloyd Wright, houses 493 rooms and suites; on either side are seven two- and four-bedroom freestand-

ing casitas with fireplaces and terraced balconies overlooking the lake. The decor blends with the desert setting, using natural textures and artifacts. Children under eighteen stay free in existing bed space of parents' rooms, and every room has the Disney Channel. Rates vary according to season and range from $359 to $635. Rates are higher in the Regency Club, which offers VIP service, complimentary breakfast, beverages, and evening hors d'oeuvres. Casitas are adjacent to the lake, with a residential feel; rates range from $690 to $3,000 per night. Subject to availability, parents receive 50 percent off a second room. It may be a good idea to take Grandma and Grandpa—seniors over sixty-two also receive a 50 percent discount based on availability! Or ask about the Sunshine on Sale package, offering one free night at certain times.

**Dining:** Vu, the innovative and award-winning restaurant open for dinner only, has a two-story design. Sophisticated is the key word, with 10-foot floor-to-ceiling windows to showcase the lagoon and resort gardens, and outdoor dining in the gazebo. On the second level, Pre-Vu invites you into the comfort of Southwest colors amid suede and velvet to enjoy designer martinis and "pre-apps." The

Squash Blossom restaurant is open for breakfast, lunch, and dinner, with a warm Southwestern ambience and regional specialties (try the Arizona toast or a wide variety of salads and sandwiches or fajitas). Ristorante Sandolo is a casual Italian bistro, overlooking the pool, where the servers serenade you. After you dine, enjoy a Venice-style gondola ride on the resort's waterways. Again, a *sandolier* will sing to you. (You can enjoy the gondola ride for $8 even if you don't eat.) Both restaurants have a children's menu and indoor/outdoor seating with very clever "air-conditioning." A very fine, invisible mist cools and moisturizes the air above you, making it comfortable year-round. Poolside, the Waterfall Juice Bar and the Water Garden Grill serve snacks, lunch, yogurt, and fruit drinks. The Coffee Bar features gourmet blends complemented by homemade Italian biscotti. In the evening watch the cascading fountains and listen to classical flamenco guitar or perhaps a marimba band as you relax in the Lobby Bar.

**Children's World:** Camp Hyatt Kachina, designed in 1989, is the prototype children's program for all Hyatt resorts. It operates daily year-round and offers three- to twelve-year-olds a well-balanced program of activities focusing on the flora, fauna, culture, and geography of the area. A specially appointed Camp room has all the crafts and games children like best. And don't forget the ten swimming pools, one complete with a white-sand beach and a three-story water slide. Each day has a different theme, related to the geographic area. Making tribal clay beads or arrowhead necklaces, designing sand pictures in the Salt River, listening to a Hopi storyteller, or planting a cactus garden puts children firmly in their environment while having fun. Campers enjoy a desert scavenger hunt, puppet theater, close encounters with desert critters, Mexican bark painting, Native American dancing, and much more.

Age groups are three to five and six to twelve. The morning session, from 9:00 a.m. to noon, is $30, and the afternoon session, from 1:00 to 5:00 p.m., is $40. Lunch, from noon to 1:00 p.m., can be added to either session for $10. The full day costs $80, including lunch. Friday and Saturday only, Camp Kachina continues with an evening session from 5:00 to 9:00 p.m. The cost is $50, including dinner. During holidays the resort offers activities designed for the entire family, from cowboy roping, cowboy guitarists, and Native American dancing to family fun sing-alongs round the campfire and "dive-in" movies. Another pursuit that families enjoy is the Lost Dutchman Mine, a hands-on "dig" for jewels. A poster helps identify your find, and you get to take your treasures home.

**Recreation:** Where do we start? With the twenty-seven-hole championship golf course at Gainey Ranch Golf Club? Actually, it's composed of three separate, individually designed courses—the Dunes; the Lakes, with five lakes and lots of water hazards; and the Arroyo, the most difficult. Ranked one of the "Top 75 Golf Courses in the United States" by *Golf Digest* and one of the "Top 100 Resort Golf Courses in the World" by *Golf Magazine,* this innovative course has "junior tees," designed to allow children twelve and under to play with Mom or Dad. With a paid adult, children fifteen and under can play the course for $25 per round. You can also work out on the eight tennis courts or 3 miles of jogging and cycling trails. The Spa Avania, a personal, holistic spa experience, is choreographed to your body's daily rhythms.

The two-and-a-half-acre water playground is most impressive in this dry, desert area. The design is a combination of Roman, Greek, and Art Deco and is truly spectacular. Zip down the three-story water slide; stroll over an aqueduct connecting six of the ten pools; swim around (or through!) the "Big Gun," a 5-foot-wide waterfall, or "thunderfall" as the hotel terms it, at the end of the aqueduct. Relax in the Grecian temple with 16-foot hot tub and four "cold plunges" in each corner. Water comes from all directions—from fountains, trailing down tall glass columns, and from waterspouts along the roof. Build sand castles on the beach at one end or play volleyball at the other. Kids may never want to leave this watery fantasyland.

Hyatt at Gainey Ranch's goal is to combine luxury with learning and light adventure. Toward this end, guests may enjoy presentations on Hopi silver overlay, Native American and Gypsy dancing, a docent-led tour of the hotel's extensive art collection, or Southwest flora and fauna. During holiday periods, lots of complimentary activities introduce the entire family to history, reptiles, birds of prey, the Anasazi, singing cowboy songs, sampling Native American food, and the tale of El Conquistador, a first-person narrative.

As part of the Native American and Environmental Learning Center, the Native American Sculpture Garden features the bronze and marble works of Apache artist Craig Dan Goseyun. The award-winning Native Heritage Seed Garden, with more than thirty indigenous plants, has been carefully researched and developed and represents early agricultural practices of the Natives of the area. And it's practical as well—plans are to eventually use the produce in the resort's signature cuisines.

Phoenix attractions include a zoo, a desert botanical garden, and stately old homes; in Scottsdale, find an IMAX theater, the world's highest fountain, and shopping on Fifth Avenue. View large cats in the wild at Out of Africa; experience a re-creation of the Old West at WestWorld or Rawhide, Arizona's largest Western-themed attraction. Pick up a copy of *GUEST* for lots more ideas. If you have time to venture farther, the concierge will help you plan excursions to the Grand Canyon (five hours away) or Montezuma Castle, a 600-year-old Pueblo Indian cliff dwelling only ninety minutes away. Who knew the desert could be like this?

---

**7500 East Doubletree Ranch Road**
**Scottsdale, Arizona 85258**
**(480) 444-1234, (800) 233-1234**
**www.scottsdale.hyatt.com**

# HYATT REGENCY TAMAYA RESORT AND SPA
## Santa Ana Pueblo, New Mexico

Not many families can boast a vacation on a Native American reservation. Set on more than 500 acres of protected land along the Rio Grande between Albuquerque and Santa Fe, in an area steeped in history that goes back over 1,000 years, the Hyatt Tamaya is unique. Owned by the Santa Ana Pueblo tribe, it is actually on the reservation. The architecture is reminiscent of a Southwestern pueblo, and artwork and cultural treasures are displayed throughout. Every effort has been made to honor the culture, history, and people of the area, and the natural beauty of the Sandia Mountains and the Bosque surrounds you with tranquillity. Feel the magic of the land and people and the warm welcome as you enter through the courtyard reminiscent of a traditional dance plaza. You're invited to experience this very special place and step into the traditions and sanctity of another culture.

**Accommodations:** Open-air courtyards and patios or balconies overlooking the scenic mountains abound throughout the resort's 350 pueblo-style guest rooms and suites. Traditional designs used in Santa Ana pottery and blankets decorate the rooms, along with textures of natural stone, wood, and adobe and the colors of maize, pumpkin, and turquoise. Coffeemakers and refrigerators add convenience, and suites offer a small separate parlor. Rates during the low season (November through March) are $235 to $350; $295 to $400 during the April to October high season. Children seventeen and under stay for free in the room with parents, or a second room for children may be reserved at a 50 percent discount. There is also a $14 per room daily resort fee. The resort-fee amenities include tennis; fitness room; trail bikes; cultural events such as tribal dances, storytellers, and nature walks; shuttles to the golf courses and casino; parking; and organized recreation.

**Dining:** The Corn Maiden, the signature restaurant, serves dinner only, Tuesday through Saturday. Tapas, grilled specialties, an exhibition kitchen, and perfect sunsets are the order of the day. The Santa Ana Café has unusual regional cuisine, such as wild-mushroom and duck enchiladas, in an indoor or outdoor setting for breakfast, lunch, and dinner casual dining, with a children's menu. Expect red and green chilies—they're found in most dishes, even breakfast eggs, but are generally mild. The Atush Bar and Grill on the Twin Warriors

Golf Course attracts nongolfers as well as golfers for lunch and cocktails, while the Plaza Pool Bar and Grill satisfies your hunger without having to leave the pool. The Trading Post Deli and General Store can supply morning coffee and pastries along with sandwiches and snacks—and the requisite jars of salsa and chilies to take home. Turquoise margaritas and live entertainment are enjoyed from the porch of the Rio Grande Lounge—the sunset and view of the Bosque are on the house.

**Children's World:** Camp Hyatt activities for ages three to twelve are steeped in the history and lore of the Santa Ana people, the Tamaya; but it's so much fun the kids barely realize they're learning. Tribal storytellers and traditional dances both entertain and educate; learning about the Rio Grande, the local vegetation, and native wildlife such as reptiles and coyotes occupy the nature hikes; and learning to weave or baking bread in traditional ovens gives a tangible reward for effort. Camp Hyatt operates year-round, daily from 9:00 a.m. to 9:00 p.m., with an option for lunch ($10 extra) with the morning or afternoon sessions ($45). A full-day session is $80. Evening sessions (5:00 to 9:00 p.m.) include dinner; cost is $55.

**Recreation:** Golf fans will like the eighteen-hole, par 72 Twin Warriors Golf Course designed by Gary Panks, with cascading waterfalls, arroyos, and juniper and piñon trees. At the stables you'll find horses to suit every taste. Complimentary pony rides are available on weekends for the younger set, and guests from eight to eighty can enjoy a calm trail ride through the back country of the Santa Ana reservation's cottonwood forests, ancient ruins, and 1,200-year-old Indian petroglyphs. Special twice-weekly half-hour trail rides are scheduled for children ages five to eight. A wonderful (and comfortable) way to enjoy the sunset is on a carriage ride.

A huge circular swimming pool dominates the courtyard, looking very much like a kiva (the sacred place in the pueblo, generally underground). Two other pools and a two-story water slide provide plenty of water time. Two tennis courts, bike riding, and nature trails along the Rio Grande, plus a fitness center, keep you active. More sedate pleasures might include a tour of the art collection or a visit to the on-site Tamaya Cultural Museum and Learning Center. Ashtanga yoga and meditation areas contribute to a feeling of relaxed yet energized well-being. The Tamaya Mist Spa, a full-service luxury spa, uses distinctive treatments with native herbs and natural ingredients of the earth to soothe your inner self. Shop at the Galleria Tamaya, take a hot-air balloon flight—the sky's the limit here. Branching out from the resort, you'll find Harley-Davidson rentals, mountain biking and hiking, rafting, and fly fishing. In the wintertime, enjoy downhill and cross-country skiing. And of course, the pleasures of Albuquerque and Santa Fe are quite close by.

Srai-Wi is the new family program with unique and unforgettable shared experiences—in fact, the word means "to gather children together and share with them" in the Tamayan language. The program features cooking, baking bread in traditional huruno ovens, stargazing, nature hikes, storytelling, adobe-making lessons, lassos and horse care, making a traditional Pueblo drum to take home, and much, much, more—all with the distinctive Native American perspective and tradition. The program operates April through October.

---

**1300 Tuyuna Trail**
**Santa Ana Pueblo, New Mexico 87004**
**(505) 867-1234, (800) 233-1234**
**www.tamaya.hyatt.com**

# LOS ABRIGADOS
# RESORT AND SPA
## Sedona, Arizona

Close to the Grand Canyon and just two hours from Phoenix, Sedona is noted for its spectacular red rock formations and scenic canyons. For centuries it has been a sacred place to the People, the earliest inhabitants, and legend holds that the Grandmother Spirit of the World still lives here. There is a magic quality in the air that many attribute to the energy points that converge here. At the least, the light, color, and awe-inspiring red rocks combine with the many artisans living here to create something special.

**Accommodations:** Los Abrigados, Portuguese for "the shelters," is in the heart of the small town of Sedona but stands in the midst of twenty-two acres of private ranchland/park and feels more secluded. The resort is a time-share property, part of ILX Resorts. All 175 guest suites have oversize living rooms and separate bedrooms plus a balcony or private patio. Many feature a private whirlpool and fireplace. Plazas, walkways, and bridges connect the suites and main hotel area. Suites range from $225 to $285 (one bedroom); $240 reserves one with views of the red rocks. Two-bedroom suites range from $375 to $395, but can be confirmed only ten days prior to arrival.

Children fifteen and under stay free in the same room with parents. Cribs are available at no charge. The Los Abrigados Lodge, a sister property located a short mile away, provides optional lodging. A two-story motel-like structure in the heart of "uptowne," it's literally in the middle of the action. Steps away are restaurants, galleries, shops, and tours; the rooms are pleasant, with balconies, gas fireplaces, and limited views (the back side is the nicest). A concierge in the well-appointed lobby is helpful in planning your stay, and guests here enjoy privileges at the Los Abrigados Resort. Rates range from $139 to $189 nightly.

**Dining:** Stakes and Sticks Sports Bar has "staked its claim" as the best in Sedona. A creative menu, twenty flat-screen TVs, billiards, and backgammon support this claim. The clincher, however, just may be the live horse races, simulcast from tracks across the country. Plus, sports fans have access to a betting booth inside the restaurant! For those who wish a quieter dining experience, the patio provides great views of the red rocks. More intimate dining is found in the Celebrity Room, lined with caricatures of famous guests and serving breakfast, lunch, and dinner. Imaginative dishes with an accent on indigenous ingredients make dining an adventure. The restaurant offers a children's menu and also features a "spa cuisine menu," lighter versions of many favorites. On the Rocks Bar & Grill serves lunch, snacks, and dinner in a casual atmosphere. You'll always know the score, as the television with the area's largest screen is here. Frequently kids eat free when accompanied by an adult diner—be sure to ask. Forty "Joes" from literature, sports, and entertainment line the walls of Joey Bistro. Think you know Italian food? The imaginative dishes here may challenge you. Imagine marsala sauce mozzarella, roasted eggplant pesto, or Gorgonzola and mascarpone cheeses in crisp pasta shells— it's not just spaghetti and meatballs! A variety of restaurants can be found right next door at Tlaquepaque Village, a re-created Mexican village/plaza with tiled courtyards, fountains, and many craft shops.

**Children's World:** Leapin' Lizards! No, you won't find Little Orphan Annie here, for kids are far too well looked-after. But that is the name of the children's program at Los Abrigados. Children entering kindergarten (age five) through age twelve can spend the day (9:00 a.m. to 4:00 p.m.) or pick and choose from a different list of a la carte activities each day. Monday through Saturday, from early June until mid-August, kids are entertained by such things as wacky water relays; sand castles and sculptures; tie-dye shirts; wet-and-wild super soakers, beach-ball bash, play in the pool, and the mushroom waterfall; and games galore. There are plenty of things to do: tennis, miniature golf, volleyball, giant beach ball, and other ball games; swimming, playing at the creek, or a water rodeo Wet Wild West. Kids can even bead their own leapin' lizard. Twice weekly, from 5:00 to 8:00 p.m., Kids' Kamp Out features campfires, flashlight tag, burgers, hot dogs, and s'mores ($20). A la carte activities last from one to three hours, and prices range from $10 to $20 when purchased individually. Cost for the full day with lunch is $35; supervised free play occupies the time between organized activities. Preregistration is not required. Babysitting can be arranged.

Teens may select from activities that interest them and participate within their own peer group. Movie nights, bingo, and "Wet and Wild" at the pool are popular and enable them to socialize with their peers, but casually, with a lot of space, and in a cool way, dude.

**Recreation:** Roll over Beethoven, Tchaikovsky is playing through! Next to Oak Creek, among tall sycamore trees and color-

ful flowers, the eighteen-hole family miniature golf course not only offers fun for
golfers of all ages and skills, but it's done to
classical music!

After a game of tennis, basketball, or
volleyball, relax at the heated outdoor pool
and chat with other guests. Enjoy the jogging and walking trails or just sit by the
creek or in the sculpture garden and dream.
The World Peace Labyrinth is a lovely medi-
tative space, with signs of peace in many
languages; another great place to reflect
and learn is Mia's Place, a bird sanctuary
with a gazebo and recorded bird sounds. It
may be difficult to choose between the family pool with water features and the adult
pool with Jacuzzi, but you can do both. The
Sedona Spa—10,000 square feet of state-
of-the-art equipment and professional services—provides a combination of fitness and
relaxation. Hot stone massage, full body
treatments and masks, facials, and fitness
classes/personal training contribute to
physical and mental well-being. Take a
class in herbs, yoga, jewelry, pain management, or other topics that may be of interest. Complimentary weekly lectures at the
Institute of EcoTourism may be on the natural history of Sedona, the scientific and
spiritual aspects of its famous vortexes, how
to be your own psychic, the Indian perspective, or the unique geology of the area.

For golf fans, nearby are two championship golf courses, designed by Robert
Trent Jones and Gary Panks. Hiking, fishing
streams, horseback riding, and four-wheel-
drive tours can also be arranged. The Grand
Canyon is a two-hour drive away; and closer
is Oak Creek Canyon, with Slide Rock State
Park, aptly named for the stretch of slip-
pery creek bottom that forms a natural
slide. For Southwestern art at its best,
Tlaquepaque Village, next door to the
resort, demands a visit.

Red Rock Fantasy is the West's largest
holiday light display, with more than one
million lights. From late November until
mid-January, it transforms Los Abrigados
into a spectacular holiday light show.

**160 Portal Lane**
**Sedona, Arizona 86336**
**(928) 282-1777, (800) 521-3131**
**www.ilxresorts.com**

# POINTE SOUTH
# MOUNTAIN RESORT
## Phoenix, Arizona

Phoenix is synonymous with golf, sophisticated shopping, museums, and cultural
activities. Noted for a nearly perfect climate, it has more than 325 days of sunshine per year and an average high
temperature of 85 degrees. Phoenix is the
fifth-largest city in the country and has
almost 1.5 million residents, but it's quite
laid-back and friendly. It's also a tourist
destination, with more than three dozen
luxurious resorts and 200 golf courses.

Pointe South is a four-diamond property,
set on 220 acres at the base of South Mountain Preserve. It has garnered many awards
for golf, tennis, and meetings, along with
"Best Guest Relations" and an odd, but

important category: It is listed as one of the "Top Ten Theme Parks" by the Travel Channel. The Oasis Water Park is a big draw for families. Kids are always attracted to water, and there's plenty of it here—a wave pool, river float, kiddie pool, twenty-five-person Jacuzzi, and three giant water slides. All this, in the middle of the desert, is truly an oasis.

**Accommodations:** The resort has 640 spacious suites, so making your selection is easy—just choose your view. Well, almost. Different styles may complicate matters; the majority are resort suites, plus 205 deluxe, 27 executive boardroom, and 10 presidential suites. Suites all have private balcony/patio and separate living rooms with sofa bed and large work area; the layout and number of bedrooms vary, and all are smoke-free. All have Internet access, in-suite movies, and coffeemaker. A pre-arrival concierge will assist you in planning your stay and will suggest activities. Estimated rates for a resort suite are $129 to $179 in summer, $199 to $399 in winter. A $16 resort pass per day, per suite includes Internet access, phone calls, coffee, newspaper, tennis, volleyball and croquet, the Athletic Club, the shuttle to Arizona Mills Mall, and entrance to The Oasis. The Splashdown is a good package for families since it includes a $50 food-and-beverage credit per night and a complimentary entree from the children's menu for each adult meal purchased. May through Labor Day, rates are from $179 per night; September through December 31, rates start at $239 per night. The Customer Choice package allows a choice of golf, tennis lesson, Swedish massage, or food credit for each day of your stay; rates begin at $289 in summer, $349 in fall, and $479 in winter.

**Dining:** Six restaurants offer a variety of menus. Latitude 30° is new and blends California cuisine with Asian influences. A distinctive style and the freshest of ingredients create a celebration of flavors, such as Macadamia Nut and Avocado Stuffed Mahi-mahi. Latitude 30° for centuries has been the primary sea route from Asia to the Pacific coast. The restaurant is open Tuesday through Saturday for dinner; a children's menu is available. Aunt Chilada's is casita-style dining with Mexican specialties, homemade chips, award-winning salsa, and a children's menu. On Friday, mariachis keep it lively. It is open daily for lunch and dinner. The Phantom Horse Grill serves breakfast, lunch, and dinner with a Southwestern flair and an open, airy ambience; a children's menu is available. Next door is the Sports Bar, the place to watch the game with a cold drink and bar fare. If you just can't leave the sun and water, La Cabana at East Pointe or the Oasis Bar & Grill provides poolside sustenance. You can even swim up to the bar at La Cabana. To call Rustler's Rooste a steakhouse is an understatement. It's more like a Wild West experience. Climb the mountain; say hello to "Horney," the live steer who lives by the mineshaft; and then enter the dining room by sliding down a tin slide—or let the kids tell you about it. Western fare is accompanied by a cowboy poet, country-and-western music, and dancing. Ya-hoo! It's open for dinner nightly.

**Children's World:** Buckaroo Roundup is a year-round program and will accept children ages one to twelve, although it's primarily for younger children. It is available Monday through Friday from 8:00 a.m. to 7:00 p.m. and from 8:00 a.m. to noon on Saturday and Sunday. Toys, coloring, story time, and lots of play are just right for younger toddlers; activities are planned by age as needed. Rates are $7 per hour, $10 for two or more siblings, and there is a three-hour per day maximum. Parents must remain on-site. Cactus Kids Club is open daily from early March to Labor Day and Saturday and Sunday year-round. Kids ages five to twelve can spend a more active day discovering secrets of the desert, making crafts, and playing energy-filled games. Each day is themed: Monster Monday, Terrific Tuesday, Wild West Wednesday, and so on. Activities may change based on season or weather but tend to feature crafts in the morning and a movie and pool time in the afternoon. Camp runs from 9:00 a.m. to 4:00 p.m., but that's also seasonal. Call (602) 438-9000 to check. Cost is $60 for a full day and $35 for a half day; both include lunch and snacks. A 20 percent discount applies for additional children.

**Recreation:** The Phantom Horse is a challenging par 71, eighteen-hole championship golf course blending traditional links with desert target golf. One of the features is a 7,000-square-foot practice green with sand bunker and chipping area. Golf pros here use the innovative Skill Tec 3D golf trainer to improve skills. Five lighted tennis courts are complimentary. *Tennis Magazine* voted Pointe South one of the "50 Greatest U.S. Tennis Resorts," and Tennis Resorts Online ranked it twenty-eighth best in the world. Try the popular Cardio Tennis; lessons and drills are also available. Hourly children's tennis clinics for ages six to thirteen are designed to introduce them to the sport; cost is $20 per child. The Phantom Horse Athletic Club is included in your resort pass but is restricted to ages sixteen and older. This 65,000-square-foot facility has just about everything athletic you could want. Racquetball, cardio machines, fitness classes, free weights, yoga, outdoor basketball court, and heated lap pool share space with the tennis courts and spa. The resort has six leisure and lap pools. Horseback riding is provided by Koli at Pima Crossing stables. The South Mountain Preserve, the country's largest municipal park, is the perfect place for jogging, hiking, or mountain biking. Slightly tamer (or maybe not) and also for your pleasure are pool tables, table tennis, horseshoes, shuffleboard, and sand or water volleyball. At this point, you could probably really use the services of the spa for massage, body treatments, and relaxing.

Now we arrive at the pièce de résistance. The center of the resort, the Oasis Water Park, is also included in your resort fee. We're talking almost six acres of splish, splash, and splatter. And it's heated, for year-round use. But it's not just water—tiers and terraces, fountains, and lush landscaping allow plenty of spots for sunning, reading, or lounging the day away. You can visit the gift shop if you get bored or need something, or the Bar & Grill if you're hungry or thirsty. And best of all, with so many lifeguards around, you can relax just a little and let older kids romp and play. Kids under twelve must be accompanied by an adult, and 48 inches is the required height for slides and the river; aqua socks or flip-flops can protect little (and big) feet from the hot decks. The water park features three slides in the eight-story-high Slide Canyon Tower; a wave pool (movies are shown here at night) with 2-foot waves and a lagoon waterfall; and the Zuni Active River, the only side-by-side river for double inner tubing in the Valley (parents like this one). Wildcat Springs is perfect for the littlest ones, who can wade or play on a water spray deck while dodging water jets. And Mom and Dad aren't forgotten either—the Caliente Springs hot tub helps remind one how wonderful vacations can be.

---

**7777 South Pointe Parkway**
**Phoenix, Arizona 85044**
**(602) 438-9000, (877) 800-4888**
**www.pointesouthmtn.com**

# TANQUE VERDE RANCH

Tucson, Arizona

In the Arizona desert, 2,800 feet high in the foothills of three mountain ranges, Tanque Verde Ranch has been serving travelers since 1868. Once merely a stagecoach stop, today it is a year-round resort, voted one of the "Top Ten Family Fun Resorts of North America" by the Travel Channel. The owners live on the property, adding to the feeling of a "family place." Because the rates are all-inclusive and the staff so welcoming, you even begin to feel like family. The area is rich in the history of Native Americans and Spanish settlers, who dubbed the area Tanque Verde—immortalizing the deep pools of artesian water found here. Located 12 miles outside Tucson, it borders Saguaro National Park. The saguaro cacti are immediately recognizable to anyone who has seen a Western movie or a picture of the desert. They stand quite tall, with "arms" curving up toward the sky.

**Accommodations:** The seventy-four guest rooms and suites are scattered throughout the grounds in individual cottages called "casitas"; most of the casitas have patios, corner fireplaces, and a feeling of privacy. The decorative motif is Native American/ Western, and antiques and original art are carefully arranged to lend warmth. Cribs are available, and there are refrigerators in the rooms. From May through September is low season, when daily room rates are $330 to $400, based on double occupancy. October through mid-December rates are $370 to $470, and in high season rates are $420 to $570. Suites are slightly more. Children under four pay $15 per day; for ages four and up, it's an additional $100 to $110 daily. These rates are all-inclusive and cover just about everything except spa services and alcohol. Included are lodging, three meals daily, all ranch activities, and the very extensive children's program.

**Dining:** Most meals are served in the Main Dining Room, with beautiful views of the pool and the Rincon Mountains. A variety of tables, seating from two to ten people, make shared dining easy and encourage an informal, friendly atmosphere. Dress is casual, and appetites are generally big due to the desert air and the exercise. American and continental dishes are standard fare, and, as expected, Spanish and Mexican specialties also appear on the menu. A separate children's dining room is reserved for youngsters and their counselors, who can take breakfast and lunch together. Children are also welcome to dine with their parents. The food is delicious and plentiful. Breakfast combines a buffet and a la carte ordering; lunch is a lavish buffet with the famous "sweet talk" table. Gourmet dinners from award-winning Chef Mark Shelton always include a choice of five specialty dishes; they can also accommodate special dietary requests. Early-morning rides with a cowboy breakfast on the trail and a twice-weekly outdoor barbecue around the campfire in the cottonwood grove with foot-tapping live Western entertainment are popular meal options.

**Children's World:** The ranch offers a year-round, seven-day-per-week, fully supervised program for four- to eleven-year-olds; twelve-year-olds may participate if they like. This is an active program that provides a fantastic ranch experience. Horseback riding forms the core of the program and is adjusted to fit the abilities and interests of the youngsters. Buckaroos (ages four to six) generally ride in the corral, starting at 7:00 a.m. in the summer (8:00 a.m. in winter). Riding lessons, swimming, hikes, tennis, nature lessons, playtime, and Western crafts are nonstop until 3:00 p.m. If that's too strenuous for your child, pick up a weekly schedule at the front desk and pick and choose. Kids are excited with the playground featuring slides and a fort. The Wrangler Kids (ages six to twelve) have the same hours, but a more active, individualized riding program geared to their skills. Again, it's go, go, go all day, but the kids love it. Parents may ride with their children if they wish. In the winter months the fun continues with an evening program from 6:00 to 8:00 p.m., including supervised dinner, games, and crafts. The children's programs are included in the rate. Babysitting can be arranged for infants and toddlers at an additional cost.

During the summer, Tanque Verde also runs a totally separate Kids Camp—ten-day sessions for children ages nine to fourteen years. Kids get their own horse, they bunk in a separate building riverside, and all activities are separate from daily guests at the ranch. In 2005, the ranch added a teen camp for girls ages fourteen to sixteen. This camp involves more advanced riding and a few days' excursion to Bellota Ranch, another smaller ranch on the east side of Tucson in the valley between the Rincon and Santa Catalina Mountains. Cost is approximately $1,500—call the ranch for details.

**Recreation:** Active relaxation is the byword at Tanque Verde. The clear desert air and low humidity, coupled with abundant sunshine, make all the activities pleasant. Horseback riding is the major part of the program. Whether you're interested in a slow-moving trail ride or a spirited sprint, the right mount can be found from a string of 150 horses. Three scheduled trail rides daily may send you directly to the spa!

Early morning and late afternoon are perfect times for strenuous outdoor activities such as tennis on one of the five courts. In the middle of the day, seek out one of the two swimming pools or the children's wading pool for a cool dip. Numerous guided nature walks introducing visitors to the Sonoran Desert ecology are conducted along trails throughout the 25,000 acres. Some 200 species of birds have been identified in the area, making the ranch very popular with avid bird-watchers. It's not uncommon to see wildlife such as rabbits, coyotes, and snakes on trail rides. Catch-and-release fishing is also a popular pastime. If you prefer wheels to hooves, take a mountain bike for a spin. The final touch to the active relaxation concept is the El Sonora Spa, well equipped with a swimming pool, sauna, whirlpool, exercise room (although who would really need it?!), and lounge. The Nature Center allows a fascinating close-up view of desert life. Weekly classes encourage you to capture the essence of the desert in watercolors, charcoal, pottery, and mixed media. In nearby Tucson six championship golf courses grant playing privileges to ranch guests. From here visitors can take side trips to Tucson, to old Spanish missions, and even to Mexico, about a ninety-minute drive away.

**14301 East Speedway Boulevard
Tucson, Arizona 85748
(520) 296-6275, (800) 234-3833
www.tanqueverderanch.com**

# TAOS SKI VALLEY

## Taos Ski Valley, New Mexico

In the early 1950s Ernie Blake searched carefully for just the right spot for a ski resort and rediscovered this bit of northern New Mexico. Since then, skiers have been coming to Taos Ski Valley for the incredible powder snow and the glorious sunshine. Several ski magazines are calling Taos one of the hottest places to ski, citing the steep, challenging terrain and trails for all abilities so that all levels may ski together. Taos is consistently among the top ski schools in North America, featuring the Ski-Better-Week. Grouped according to ability, each group remains with the same instructor, developing new, close friendships and improving skills at all levels.

Two hours from Santa Fe, or a three-hour drive from Albuquerque, Taos Ski Valley combines lodging, restaurants, shops, and a beautiful mountain. The town of Taos is only 18 miles away and, with its Native American and Spanish heritage, is an interesting alternative for dining, shopping, and entertainment. The Taos Valley ski season generally runs from Thanksgiving through mid-April and provides good value for families. Summer/fall (June through October) is becoming more of a "season" in Taos Valley, although still a low-key one. Some properties remain open, and offerings include music, dance contests or chili cook-offs, lift excursions and hikes, barn dances, mountain bike contests, fall foliage, and Oktoberfest. Check before you make plans.

**Accommodations:** Every skier's dream is to be on the mountain. The Taos Valley Resort Association (800-776-1111) represents more than 95 percent of all lodging in and around Taos. Taos Valley has an amazing variety of lodging: bed-and-breakfasts,

hotels, ski lodges, condominiums, and private houses/cabins snuggled in the trees—it's all here. We've selected just a sample of what's available; you'll find complete details on all lodging options at www.ski taos.org, or you can call the Resort Association.

At the base of the mountain, for almost fifty years the Hotel St. Bernard has honored the European Alpine skiing tradition. They are most welcoming to families, with their own evening program for children, and are located just across Strawberry Hill from the Taos Children's Center. Kids participate in Junior Elite programs on the mountain and then enjoy supervised dinner and evening activities at the hotel, such as sledding, treasure hunts, or roasting marshmallows. The Ski Week package includes seven nights' lodging, six days' lifts and lessons, and three meals daily. During regular ski season adults pay $1,966 each; children ages three to twelve sharing a unit pay $1,250. Add a hot tub, massage, evening entertainment, and an extensive wine cellar, and all you need to do is smile.

Built in 1946, the Inn at Snakedance claims the honor of being Taos Ski Valley's oldest structure, there even before the first ski slope. Originally a hunting lodge, with ten rooms and an outhouse, Snakedance is definitely not living in the past. Located slopeside and less than 10 yards from the lift, it was extensively remodeled in 2006 and now offers condominium suites with full kitchen. The newest amenities include a restaurant, spa and fitness area, and grocery store; you can also take advantage of a concierge and ski valet, complimentary shuttles to Taos and Albuquerque airports, and free continental breakfast. Daily room rates in a one-bedroom unit begin at $95 in summer, $375 in regular ski season, and $475 at holidays. In ski season, packages are a good value. Three-day packages begin at $329 per person and seven-day packages begin at $890; children under fifteen pay $30 per day extra.

Opened in 2005, the Edelweiss Lodge and Spa is a ski-in ski-out, hand your skis to a valet and hit the riverside hot tubs kind of place. Upgraded from an existing property, there's now a spa, fitness room, game room, a heated outdoor plaza, and entertainment. A one-bedroom unit with kitchen ranges from $275 to $550 per night based on season. Another favorite property is the Bavarian, an alpine-style ski-in ski-out lodge on the back side of the mountain. Already considered one of the most luxurious accommodations in Taos Valley, the Bavarian began a five-star expansion in early 2007, creating condominium chalets and the centerpiece of a planned Kachina Village. The Schulze family came from Bavaria, bringing a true European flavor to New Mexico. The main hotel is a log cabin, but on a grand scale—perhaps a log mansion? Antiques sit comfortably among marble baths, mountain views, and vaulted ceilings. Full breakfast is included in the rates. All units are suites, and daily rates range from $275 to $600.

**Dining:** On the mountain there are quick and easy stops like the Phoenix Grill at Kachina Bowl, where you can sit on the outdoor deck and watch others ski, or the Whistlestop Cafe, serving soup, sandwiches, and pizza. Tenderfoot Katie's Cafeteria, with big windows facing the slope, is the breakfast spot and serves a quick, economical lunch of burgers, tacos, and pasta, with a fresh salad bar. Upstairs at the Martini Tree Bar is the après-ski action. Meet your friends, play pool, eat, drink, and watch Monday Night Football. Rhoda's Restaurant, slopeside in the Resort Center,

is open from 11:00 a.m. to 9:00 p.m. Savor an overstuffed sandwich or some dish with those famous New Mexico chilis; be prepared, as the most frequent question you'll be asked is "Red or green?" If you don't know, say "Christmas," and you'll get both! Dinner offers steaks, chicken, and seafood at affordable prices, and a kids' menu. The outside deck is the place to watch what's happening at the base of Al's Run. Tim's Stray Dog Cantina is a bar and restaurant with a wide variety of satisfying food. Many of the hotels and lodgings in Taos Valley have restaurants. On the way to Taos, you'll find the Old Blinking Light, a fun Mexican restaurant; or try the Steak Out, with beautiful views overlooking the Rio Grande Gorge. In the town of Taos, a wide selection of restaurants awaits you. And, of course, there's always your own fine cooking in your condominium!

**Children's World:** The Kinderkäfig is Taos Ski Valley's children's center and site of the ski school and day-care facility. It's the hub of activities for children ages six weeks to twelve years and is a safe and creative learning environment, with its own pint-size lifts, terrain, and qualified instructors. It's totally for the kids, and there are areas where the NO PARENTS ALLOWED sign is up. You'll find kids-only bathrooms, snacks, and shops. BebeKare is for infants six weeks to one year old. Operating from late November until the end of March, the nursery staff keeps your "bebe" comfortable and happy. Full day is $70, half day is $50, or $20 per hour. Early- and late-season prices are $45 per day.

The Kinderkare (one to three years old) full-day program includes two snacks, lunch, creative activities, and nap time. The half-day program includes snack and either snow play or nap time. Reservations are required. Walk-ins are accepted on a space-available basis only; the cost for this program is the same as for BebeKare. The Junior Elite program for three- to twelve-year-olds is also divided by age groups and includes all-day lesson, lift ticket, lunch, and rentals. Junior Elite I is for children ages three through first grade, while Junior Elite II covers second grade up to twelve years, with further breakdown of ages. Junior Elite I kids learn the basics of skiing and have fun with indoor and outdoor play. The programs run from 8:00 a.m. to 4:00 p.m.; older children are on the slopes from 9:45 a.m. to 2:30 p.m. Full-day cost in regular season is $99. Five- and six-day packages are $470 and $564. The Junior Elite programs are all-inclusive: lift tickets, rental equipment including helmets, morning and afternoon lessons, and lunch. The last lesson finishes at 2:30 p.m., so you may ski with your children, or they are welcome to remain in the center until 4:00 p.m. Children should be checked in between 8:15 and 9:00 a.m.

Also for kids, there's tubing on the bunny hill, Wednesday through Saturday between 5:00 and 7:00 p.m. The cost is $7, and parents need to supervise (or participate!). There is no snowboarding at Taos Ski Valley. When not on the program, kids under six years old ski free with a ticketed adult.

The new Teen Center has comfortable couches, TV, games, pizza, and the latest extreme skiing movies to inspire them and put mother's heart in her throat! Snacks and drinks, and open from 11:00 a.m. to 8:00 p.m.—what more could teens ask? Activities at the Out-to-Launch Terrain Park are for all ages, but teens find a lot to do with their friends there.

**Recreation:** Partially located in the Carson National Forest, the Taos ski area is in the Sangre de Cristo Mountains, the southernmost part of the Rockies. The base village sits at 9,207 feet, and the peak towers above at 12,481 feet, affording skiers more than 2,600 feet of vertical drop. This is a challenging mountain with more than 1,200 acres of skiable terrain down 110 different runs; just over 50 percent of its runs are classified as expert. However, even the novice can feel that classic mountaintop high, since some beginners' runs descend directly from the highest lift at 11,819 feet. In a ski season that lasts from about Thanksgiving to Easter, there are 300-plus days of sunshine, and the average annual snowfall is over 305 inches, plus there's snowmaking on more than 98 percent of beginner and intermediate terrain. Be aware of the high altitude here, and take precautions.

When you can pull yourself away from the open bowls, dramatic chutes, and lazy meandering-down trails lined with spruce and aspen, you might consider an evening skier's seminar on such topics as avalanches and adjusting to the altitude. Take a snowmobile tour with Big Al to the peaks above the valley for some amazing views. Taos is too steep for cross-country skiing, but if you're a real fan, it's available about forty-five minutes away. This is a family-owned and family-enjoyed resort, and Alpine skiing is really the focus. One of the best-kept secrets? Taos seldom has a lift line.

Skiers in January experience the added pleasures of Taos's jazz festival. Also in January is the two-week Winter Wine Festival, when the grape takes over the Ski Valley. Scores of vintners come from faraway places bringing their wares; seminars and wine tastings warm the winter cold. Several restaurants in Taos build special menus around a particular vineyard, and your dinner is accompanied by a lesson in wines and food.

Taos Pueblo has been inhabited for more than 1,000 years, and residents are willing to share their past and the traditions of the Tiwa tribe. Check www.taospueblo.com to see when they are open to the public. Another adventure is a hot-air balloon ride over the Rio Grande Gorge; sunrise is incredible, but if that's too early, other times are also beautiful.

**P.O. Box 90**
**Taos Ski Valley, New Mexico 87525**
**(505) 776-2291, (800) 776-1111,**
**(800) 347-7414**
**www.skitaos.org**

# ROCKIES

Colorado
Montana
Utah

# ASPEN/SNOWMASS VILLAGE

## Aspen, Colorado

Say "a small mountain town in Colorado with a very cosmopolitan feel" to anyone, and the response likely will be "Aspen." Aspen is synonymous with chic, the playground of the rich and famous; Snowmass is devoted to its motto "A Mountain of Family Fun." Each has its niche, and who splits hairs when the best of both worlds is all within a 10-mile radius in one resort area? When talking Aspen skiing, you've actually got four mountains to consider: Aspen Mountain (sometimes called Ajax), Snowmass, and Aspen Highlands, with Buttermilk in between. A combined skiable terrain that totals more than 4,000 acres on one lift ticket provides more runs and variety than you could possibly test in a two-week ski vacation. Both resort areas are open year-round.

Aspen's origins are rooted in the silver boom of the early 1880s. Many of the charming Victorian structures have been preserved and renovated; today they house boutiques, art galleries, hotels, and restaurants just waiting to tempt you. Folks here boast that 75 percent of their visitors return every year and more than 90 percecnt come back sooner or later. So if you give it a shot, you may just have to plan on being hooked.

**Accommodations:** Whatever your preference in lodging, you should have no problem finding the perfect place to hang your hat in the Aspen and Snowmass area. From moderate to expensive, from quaint to modern, all the possibilities seem to be here. For the most part, lodgings in Aspen are in the village; at Snowmass they're slopeside with immediate access to trails. This is not, however, a hard-and-fast rule, and because shuttle buses always cruise the roads, there's no problem getting to the lifts and from one mountain to another.

With close to one hundred hotels, lodges, inns, and condominiums in the Aspen area, it is indeed fortunate that the resort associations publish descriptive lists to help you sort through the possibilities. You'll discover everything from a cozy cabin to a five-star deluxe hotel. Just have your priorities straight and decide what's important to you—space, location, a hot tub, spa shower, or fireplace and bear rug? Contrary to the image, costs begin at $79 for a room; in keeping with the image, the cost is up to $5,000 for a presidential suite. If you're adventurous and a last-minute type, you may find great deals at the Virtual Hostel, which features last-minute specials on lodging and lifts within the upcoming two-week period, winter and summer. Central Reservations (www.stayaspensnowmass .com or 888-649-5982) has all the details and can help you plan what's exactly right for your family, as far in advance as you want.

**Dining:** As with lodging arrangements, the dining possibilities seem almost limitless. Whether you've got a hankering for pizza, quiche, fresh veggies and salads, a juicy steak, spicy Szechuan, or northern Italian cuisine, you'll find the right spot among the more than one hundred restaurants in and around Aspen. Seventy-five are listed under "family-oriented atmosphere." Particularly family-friendly restaurants are Boogie's Diner, Brothers' Grill, Little Annie's Eating House, and S'no Beach Café and Bar. And, of course, restaurants and refreshment stops are at the mountain bases and on the mountains. For sweets, stop by the Paradise Bakery.

**Children's World:** For the 2007–2008 season, Snowmass has plans for a brand-new, state-of-the-art children's center, to be located at the base of Fanny Hill for easy snow access from slopeside lodging. Children two months to eighteen years will have 25,000 square feet of fun with an interactive design that incorporates reading caves, sound systems, climbing structures, mobiles, and aquariums just for starters. A private on-snow learning area and nighttime offerings for both kids and teens will provide excitement for all ages.

At Snowmass, even the youngest traveling companion will not keep you from days on the slopes. From 8:30 a.m. to 4:00 p.m., Snow Cubs caters to infants and toddlers, eight weeks to three and a half years old, in a play program filled with puppet shows, stories, arts and crafts, snowman building, and sledding.

Children are grouped by age, with dedicated rooms for each group; lunch is included. Three-year-old Cubs can learn to ski on a contoured slope with magic carpet. The Bear Den is the indoor center for Big Burn Bears, kids three and a half to four years old; preschoolers learn to ski in their own area; ski time varies by individual child. Grizzlies, for ages five to six, spend their day on the mountain with their own beginner area and direct lift; classes range from beginners to accomplished. A full day is $115; half day is $74 for all programs; equipment is not included.

Powder Pandas is Buttermilk Mountain's ski school for three- to six-year-olds, with the same hours and rates; it's convenient for parents skiing Aspen Mountain. For Aspen Highlands, Bighorns provides ages five and six, levels five and up the ski experience at the same times and rates. The listed rates are for pre-booking; "at the window" is more expensive. Call (970) 923-0570 for reservations and information.

Bears and Pandas on Boards are the popular snowboard programs for ages five to six.

Groups of three children learn safety and skills; the full-day cost of $179 includes equipment, five-hour lesson, and lunch. Bears are at Snowmass, while Pandas gather at Buttermilk.

Older kids and teens are also well treated at Aspen/Snowmass. Kids First Turn introduces seven- to twelve-year-olds to skiing and snowboarding; Kid's Group Lessons divides into small groups by ability. From 9:30 a.m. to 3:15 p.m., both programs provide instruction and lunch for $86 and are offered at Buttermilk and Snowmass. The teens "Too Cool for School" skiing and snowboarding program operates every day of the season at Snowmass ($82 for instruction only, 9:30 a.m. to 3:15 p.m.). Optional evening activities with other teens include ice-skating and pizza parties.

Snowmass is looking forward to completion of the new Children's Center to gather all activities into one area. Evening camps, and probably summer activities as well, are planned. Programs will change, so be sure to contact them for up-to-date information.

Operating a summer program (June through August), Camp Aspen/Snowmass emphasizes a healthy, active outdoor schedule of fishing, hiking, swimming, nature walks, visits to the nature preserve, and picnics. The camp is located slopeside at the end of the Snowmass Mall and is divided into Junior Base Camp for ages three and four, Finally Five Base Camp for five-year-olds, and Base Camp for ages six to ten. Age-appropriate nature play groups, short field trips to Hallom Lake and the gondola, and walk-around horseback rides entertain the youngest. Base Camp and Ultimate Base Camp add paintball, mountainboarding, rafting, horseback riding, and minigolf. For a day's events from 8:00 a.m. to 4:00 p.m. Monday through Friday, the cost for ages three to ten is $85 for a full day, $65 for a half day. All-day sessions for older children are $121; multiple days receive a discount, as does early booking. Kids can bring their own lunch, or it's provided for $10. Adventure Series, for ages seven to teens, allows children to create their own adventures. That way they can't complain at the end of the day! They may choose their own excitement for $142 per day. Winter into Summer lets kids practice ski and snowboard skills on "imported" snow. Skateboarding and paintball are also options. Friday is generally special-activities day, with such events as rafting, go-karts, climbing wall, miniature golf, swimming, and the fairy caves. Rocket Days, where budding scientists build their own rockets, and Nights on the Mountain (overnight camping) are also planned at special times, for an extra fee.

Fun for Kids, on Aspen Mountain, has free activities and entertainment for kids of all ages and families from mid-June to Labor Day. A different two- to three-hour activity every day might include arts and crafts, cooking classes, storytelling, digging for silver nuggets, or scavenger hunts. ARC, the Aspen Recreation Center, is 83,000 square feet of fun, with an NHL-size ice rink, climbing wall, and Aquatic Center with pools, beach, river currents—the works. And Aspen boasts one of the top five skateboard parks in the country. Whew, almost too much fun!

**Recreation:** From the end of November to mid-April, skiing is on everyone's mind, and regardless of your skiing ability, you'll have plenty of runs to schuss down. Aspen's reputation as a mecca for advanced skiers is well earned, with 26 percent of the runs down Ajax ranked as expert, 26 percent most difficult, and the remaining 48 percent more difficult. But beginners and intermediates should not grow faint in the face of overwhelming ventures, for the other mountains accommodate those not quite so adept.

Aspen Highlands is 30 percent intermediate and 18 percent each in advanced and beginner categories; the total vertical drop is 3,635 feet. The vertical rise at Snowmass is almost 4,400 feet, and 55 percent of the runs are intermediate. Buttermilk, with 2,000 vertical feet, is known as the best place to learn, with almost half of its runs designated for beginners. A teaching staff that totals more than 1,000 ski professionals can introduce a beginner to the slopes (except at Aspen Mountain) as well as help an expert perfect techniques in mogul skiing, snowboarding, and telemarking. But each mountain has its secrets: Parks and pipes are popping up at Buttermilk, and it was home to the 2003 X Games, the world's largest alternative sports championships; although Aspen Highlands is famous for black and double black runs, there's actually more green and blue; Snowmass is a haven for snowboarders and offers everyone easy, uncrowded access to the mountains; and who knew that Aspen Mountain has groomed, intermediate cruising runs?

On-mountain family adventures are waiting everywhere. The Family Zone at Snowmass has adventurous kids' trails, a children's race arena, Trenchtown terrain park, and interactive tree trails. On Buttermilk, Max the Moose hosts Fort Frog, an adventure center with a Western fort and Native American village. Twilight snowcat rides to dine in a rustic cabin, magic shows in Snowmass, sledding, tubing—no wonder *Child Magazine* calls this the number one family resort.

Wintertime fun continues with ice-skating, dogsled rides, snowshoe tours, cross-country skiing, sleigh rides, snowmobiling, and hot-air ballooning (yes, even in winter!). A real treat is to ride with the trail groomers in the big rigs. It's free, but space is limited, so call early (970-925-5756). Many of the lodging complexes have swimming pools and exercise equipment. The tennis and athletic clubs also provide opportunities for indoor workouts. Evening entertainment includes films, concerts, plays at the Wheeler Opera House, and classical music at Harris Hall.

Though skiing is practically synonymous with Aspen, this place does not turn into a ghost town when the snow melts. During the summer, the hills are alive with cultural events. The Aspen Music Festival runs from the end of June to the end of August and is complemented by the Aspen Community Theater and the Jazz Aspen Snowmass Music Festivals. The Anderson Ranch Arts Center in Snowmass has a summer program of classes in photography, ceramics, painting, and printmaking.

You can just about have your pick of outdoor activities: horseback riding, hiking, jogging, rafting, kayaking, fishing, and four-wheel-drive tours. Snowmass Mountain Outfitters offers all sorts of adventures: hot-air balloon rides, run and gun paintball,

bungee trampoline, and especially for the children, trout fishing and panning for gold. There is also lift-served mountain biking at Snowmass Ski Area, and it's free! At the top, test your agility on the climbing wall. All ages are welcome. An eighteen-hole golf course is located on the west perimeter of Aspen; another is in Snowmass. Tennis courts at condominiums and racquet clubs dot the valley. Free naturalist programs include daily guided nature walks on both Aspen and Snowmass Mountains. In short, all the things to do here are simply too many to list! Even in summer you have to take at least one gondola ride—to the top of Aspen Mountain for a spectacular view of this bit of the Rockies.

425 Rio Grande Plaza
Aspen, Colorado 81611
(800) 598-2004, (888) 649-5985
www.aspensnowmass.com

# BIG SKY OF MONTANA
## Big Sky, Montana

The sky isn't really bigger in Montana—not by scientific measurements, that is. But don't tell the folks around here that. These die-hard Westerners believe they've got the market cornered on the best, biggest, bluest sky ever; and if you don't watch out, by the end of a visit here, you'll be a believer too.

In the wintertime, skiing Lone Mountain (summit elevation 11,166 feet) can make you feel that it's almost possible to touch that beautiful, clear sky. Lone Mountain and adjacent Andesite and Flat Iron Mountains are carved with more than 150 named

runs covering 85 miles on three mountains; a terrain park and a half-pipe add up to fine skiing at Big Sky.

During the summer, these mountains and their evergreens, the sunshine, and clean mountain air make the perfect setting for hiking, horseback riding, mountain biking, scenic gondola rides, white-water rafting, and fishing, as well as golf and tennis.

Open late November through mid-April and early June through early October, Big Sky is located in southwestern Montana just north of Yellowstone and is surrounded by rivers and national forests.

**Accommodations:** Two tall structures, the Shoshone/Huntley/Yellowstone Center and the luxurious new Summit at Big Sky, mark the Mountain Village at the foot of Lone Peak. Combined, they total nearly 500 hotel rooms, suites, and condominiums. Many more accommodations are in the vicinity, including cabins. Big Sky Resort was the vision of the late NBC newscaster Chet Huntley, who built it in 1973 and owned it until 1976.

The Huntley Lodge is at the base of Lone Mountain; the Explorer chairlift is right out the back door. The lodge has 200 rooms, some with views straight up the mountain, and an outdoor heated swimming pool, sauna, and Jacuzzi. In the complex you'll find a dining room, lounge, shops, and ski storage.

Attached to the Huntley is the Shoshone Condominium Hotel, with ninety-five suites; it's also ski-in, ski-out. The newest property, the ten-story Summit, combines the best of a hotel and condominium stay. Ski-in, ski-out convenience, dining, lounge, and fitness center, and flexible lock-offs allow a variety of accommodations.

Children ten years and under stay free with existing bedding; $15 for cribs and rollaways. Hotel rates are based on season and number of people in the room; winter has four seasons. At the Huntley, based on four people, rates range from $163 to $308 nightly. The Summit begins at $199 and goes to $421 during the prime season; holidays are higher.

At the area's condominiums, the studios and one- to four-bedroom units have kitchens and fireplaces. While all the complexes are in close proximity to the slopes, Snowcrest is closest to the lifts. Some complexes feature heated swimming pools, saunas, and Jacuzzis. Winter condominium

rates have a wide range: from $235 for a one-bedroom in budget season to $1,445 at the Summit for a three-bedroom sleeping ten.

Summer rates begin at $160 for a deluxe room at the Huntley Lodge and go up to $872 for a three-bedroom unit at the Summit. With dozens of choices for accommodations and several seasons from which to choose, you are sure to find amenities that meet both your expectations and your budget.

**Dining:** If you are staying in the Huntley Lodge or just cannot face cooking after a busy day, you can dine at the Huntley Dining Room. A breakfast buffet is included in room rates at the Huntley Lodge. Chet's Bar and Grill is popular for its warm atmosphere, nightly entertainment, and regular poker games. The Summit features the Peaks Restaurant and the Carabiner Lounge. In winter take the sleigh ride up into the mountains for dinner, and in summer join an outdoor Western barbecue. Next door to the Huntley Lodge is a collection of shops, restaurants, and bars in the Mountain Mall. Here you'll find casual spots for pizzas, deli sandwiches, and burgers; in winter, the Lone Peak Cafeteria offers hearty meals at breakfast, lunch, and dinner. On-mountain dining during ski season includes M. R. Hummers, Whiskey Jack's, The Pinnacle, and, of course, pizza and coffee carts. Timbers Restaurant is in the new area, Moonlight Basin. In summer the Bunker Bar and Grill is a good stop for lunch or dinner after a round of golf. Expanding out to the Big Sky area, restaurants and nightspots offer live music, dancing, and family fun nights.

**Children's World:** During the ski season, Lone Peak Playhouse, located at the base of the slopes, is open daily from 8:30 a.m. to 4:30 p.m. for children six months to eight years old. Lunch and two snacks are served daily, and nap rooms provide a spot to rest. Little ones enjoy a combination of indoor and outdoor play: sledding, snow play, stories, songs, and arts and crafts. It's open daily from Thanksgiving to mid-April; reservations and immunization records are required. Rates vary by age and activities and do not include ski equipment and lessons. Infants six months to two years are $90 for a full day, $65 for a half day; two to eight years are $80 full day, $55 half day (lunch included in morning session). Primarily for younger children, the center does offer skiing options (additional cost) for those children four and over who may not wish to ski all day. Lessons last two hours for ages four to eight. Ski equipment is not included. Day-care rates, including skiing, are $122 for a full day, $87 for half-day sessions.

The Snowsports School programs are for children ages three to fourteen. The Small Fry Try for ages three and four is a forty-five-minute private lesson and the perfect introduction to skiing—of course, it takes almost that long to get them ready! The cost is $72, not including day care and equipment. Ski and snowboard camps are divided by age and skill level. Mini-Ski (ages four to six) and Mini-Rider (ages seven to nine) Camps have a smaller child-to-instructor ratio, and times are more flexible. Schedules allow for early drop-offs and afternoon activities ($12). Morning or afternoon sessions are $57/$67; all day is $143/$139. Lunch may be added for $15. Ski (ages seven to twelve) and Snowboard (ages ten to fourteen) Camps have a longer lesson; cost is $57 for morning or afternoon session, $119 for a full day. Prices do not include equipment and lift tickets for children eleven and over. Kids ten and under always ski free.

The Teen Mountain Experience is in operation during Christmas week and Presidents' week in February. Teens explore the mountain with a similar-age-and-skill group while refining techniques. Full day is $124, with lunch; half-day cost is $62, no lunch.

Daily from 3:30 to 6:00 p.m. in winter, the Kids Only Clubhouse in the Huntley Lodge lobby hosts fun after-hours sessions, free to guests of Big Sky Central Reservations. Original artwork, short hikes combined with crafts, face-painting, tie-dye bandanas, rescue dog demonstrations, and indoor/outdoor games keep kids happy and busy. Free family movies almost nightly round out the fun. The game rooms at Mountain Mall and in the Huntley Lodge, open from 10:00 a.m. to 10:00 p.m., are the gathering spots for video games and television. In summer, the Kids Only Clubhouse offers supervised activities from 3:00 to 5:00 p.m. for ages four and up; the program is free for guests.

Babysitting arrangements can be made any time of the year through the activities desk at the lodge.

**Recreation:** The 4,350-foot vertical drop takes you through open bowls and tree-lined trails. The average annual snowfall is an amazing 400-plus inches. Skiing starts mid-November (an opening guaranteed by snowmaking if Mother Nature is skimpy with her supply) and continues into April. Whatever your level of skiing, you can join lessons at the ski school. Cross-country skiers enjoy treks over broad meadows and through stands of pine trees. Just 5 miles from the resort, the Lone Mountain Guest Ranch maintains 65 kilometers of cross-country trails. When you're not on skis, swim in one of the heated pools or take a trip to Yellowstone for snowshoeing and sightseeing with free ranger-guided wildlife tours. Dogsledding is fun, and evening tubing gets the entire family laughing. For the hardy, backcountry skiing gets updated avalanche forecasts with maps and rental equipment. Or take a sleigh ride combined with hearty food, live entertainment, and songs and stories. On Saturday night fireworks over the village thrill young and old.

When the weather warms up, the mountains are terrific for hiking, biking, and backpacking. For horseback riding, you can find a mount through the resort concierge. You may prefer adventures in white-water rafting or the quiet solitude of fishing for prize-winning trout in the mountain streams.

The eighteen-hole golf course was designed by Arnold Palmer and is well situated in the mountain meadows. Try your hand at disc golf, a cross between golf and Frisbee that's anything but traditional. A nine-hole course at Andesite Mountain gives you a good workout. The game is free, and you can rent discs. Play tennis (six courts, two of which are at the resort) and volleyball, or relax with a Swedish massage at the Solace Spa. Take a leisurely guided nature walk, learning about the wildflowers, animals, and birds of Big Sky. Spend the day at Yellowstone National Park—it's in your backyard.

---

**P.O. Box 160001**
**1 Lone Mountain Trail**
**Big Sky, Montana 59716**
**(406) 995-5000, (800) 548-4486**
**www.bigskyresort.com**

# BRECKENRIDGE SKI RESORT
## Breckenridge, Colorado

The town of Breckenridge likes to say it was born in the rowdy gold rush of the 1860s, spent its childhood in Prohibition and its teen years in the 1960s, and reached maturity at the turn of this last century. It's a town where there's action-plus, all the time. An old gold- and silver-mining camp proud of its history, Breckenridge is charming, with carefully restored buildings that attest to its Victorian-era heyday. And the years of skiing have resulted in the development of 2,208 acres of skiing territory on four beautiful mountain peaks. All this skiing in a historic setting is a one-and-a-half-hour drive west of Denver—not so close that it is inundated by Denverites, yet close enough that once you land at Denver International Airport, your ski holiday begins immediately with a scenic tour through the Arapahoe National Forest on your way to Breckenridge.

Best known as a winter recreation area, Breckenridge is in fact open year-round. A new gondola (2006) connects the town and mountain and starts two new base villages at Peaks 7 and 8. Not only does it save fuel, but sixty-five acres are dedicated to open space and conservation.

**Accommodations:** Like every other Western mining town turned ski resort, Breckenridge has numerous hotels, vacation homes, and condominiums that can be explored through Breckenridge Central Reservations (800-221-1091).

Beaver Run Resort (800-265-3560; www.beaverrun.com) and the Village at Breckenridge (877-428-7829; www.villageatbreckenridge.com) warrant special attention because of their locations and amenities. With lifts just steps away from either one, these self-contained resorts make life just a little bit easier for families. Besides their own restaurants and shops, the resorts both have independently operated child-care centers.

Beaver Run is an attractive complex of granite and wood buildings just skirted by the Country Boy trail and home to the Beaver Run Superchair. The 500 hotel rooms are spacious, and condominiums vary from suites with in-room spas to four-bedroom units. Fireplaces and private balconies are features of the condominium units; they also have fully equipped kitchens. Children stay for free when staying with their parents, and cribs for infants and toddlers are provided without charge.

During the regular ski season, a double hotel room is $189 to $305 and a one-bedroom/one-bath condominium that sleeps four is $250 to $545 a night. Summer rates are $159 for a hotel room and $195 for a one-bedroom suite. Two-, three-, and even four-bedroom suites are available. Packages and special offers include third night free, 30 percent discount for early booking, and ski, golf, and spa packages.

Newly remodeled, the Village at Breckenridge is a Western-style resort with 240 guest accommodations, ranging from hotel rooms to condos; the Liftside Inn building features studio apartments; and Plazas I, II, and III house one- to three-bedroom condominium units. Most of the condo accommodations have kitchens, fireplaces, and balconies with views of the mountains or Maggie Pond, the ice-skating center. A great riverside location, and just steps to a pedestrian plaza and Main Street, it's also ski-in, ski-out. Children twelve and younger sharing a room with their parents stay for free; crib rental is available on request.

The ski season is early November through late April; during this time a double hotel room averages $225, studios are $300, and a one-bedroom/one-bath condominium is $320. Rates are lower during early and late weeks of the season and higher at holiday time. During the summer a double room is $89 to $150 a night, and a one-bedroom/one-bath condominium is $129 to $179 a night.

**Dining:** Elegant dining at Beaver Run takes place at Spencer's Restaurant in a warm setting enhanced by oak and cane furnishings. Menu offerings include inexpensive family dining as well as fine dining. Serves breakfast, lunch, and dinner. The Copper Top Bar and Food Court is open winters only for skiers, but G.B. Watson's Deli is good for snacks year-round, and Tiff's Nightclub provides evening and nighttime amusement.

The Village at Breckenridge has lots of dining options, including Breck's Burger Bar, open for all meals and après-ski. Dining choices at Peak 8 include Bergenhof, serving breakfast, lunch, and après-ski in a tropical setting with Tiki Bar; Bergy Beach; and Vista Haus, a food court with great views. Peak 9 boasts The Maggie, open early and known for après-ski; Ten Mile Station, a mining-themed barbecue place and food court; Peak 9 Restaurant; and Beaver Run at the base.

In town almost four dozen restaurants and saloons (out West bars are called saloons—don't forget that!) offer atmospheres from quiet to lively and cuisines that run all over the globe—Mexican, Italian, Greek, German, even Jamaican. Families enjoy Downstairs at Eric's, which is casual, with an arcade next door; Horseshoe II, serving hearty American food in a Victorian setting and voted "Best Family Restaurant in Summit County" by *Skiing* magazine; the Whale's Tail, for seafood; and Fatty's, the oldest pizzeria in Breckenridge for a reason (and they deliver). One of the most interesting spots is the Dredge Boathouse, a floating restaurant in the Blue River, modeled on the huge dredges used in the early 1900s. Find all listings at www.breckenridgedining guide.com.

**Children's World:** Children of all ages have a plethora of riches in Breckenridge. Two child-care programs are located near the village at the Base of Peak 8 and Peak 9 at the Village at Breckenridge, near the children's ski schools; a third, Kinderhut (www.khut.net), is slopeside at Beaver Run resort. For the wee ones, Breckenridge's child-care programs accommodate ages eight weeks to five years with age-appropriate activities, including outdoor time when weather and nap schedules permit. Healthy snacks and lunches are included for one year old and up, and parents provide bottles and baby food for infants. Both centers meet Colorado licensing standards. The full-day program runs from 8:00 a.m. to 4:30 p.m., for $105; the half-day program runs until 12:30 p.m. and is $90. Rates are $10 less when booked in advance (800-789-SNOW). Kinderhut is a state-licensed facility for ages six weeks and up and provides child care and child care combined with its own Professional Ski Instructors of America–affiliated introduction to skiing for children ages two to six years. Full-day care from 8:15 a.m. to 4:15 p.m. is $96; half-day care (mornings only for toddlers) is $78. For ski school, the rate is $118 for a full day, $78 for a half day, and includes lunch, snacks, two-hour ski lessons in the morning and afternoon, and chairlift for older kids. Equipment for rent is available at the center. Each child is evaluated individually and can switch between day care and skiing as desired, or have lunch and rest period with siblings.

Breckenridge's Ski & Ride School helps skiers and boarders of all ages improve their skills while having fun. Ski School is from 8:30 a.m. to 3:30 p.m. for the under-seven crowd, and reservations are required; value-season and regular-season pricing applies and includes lunch and snacks. Rates for all age groups are $105/$119; lift tickets are $11 more. Ages three and four have a half day of ski and a half day of play, while seven- to thirteen-year-olds ski from 9:45 a.m. to 3:45 p.m. Breckenridge advises that all children under twelve use helmets. Snowboarding for ages seven to thirteen has the same cost and hours. A new program allows five- and six-year-olds to learn to ride—inquire for details.

In winter and summer, the Kids Day Off program at Beaver Run Resort is loaded with activities for kids ages five to twelve. From 9:00 a.m. to 5:00 p.m., youngsters can swim, enjoy the Alpine Super Slide, visit museums, and go on hikes, treasure hunts, and gold-mine tours. Cost is $80 for a full day with lunch; $40 for each sibling. Half days are available, also with lunch. Cost is $60 for one child, $30 for each sibling. The program operates daily in summer, mid-June through mid-August; it can be scheduled on other dates and in the winter with prior arrangements. Kids Night Out, from 6:00 to 9:00 p.m., offers dinner, indoor miniature golf, arts and crafts, and more fun activities for $40; $20 for each sibling. The program is flexible, generally on Saturday in the summer and three times weekly in the winter, and will run for three or more children. Mid-June through Labor Day, you can drop off your children, ages two months to five years, at the Peak 8 Children's Center for fun activities, snacks, and lunch. It's open Monday through Friday from 8:00 a.m. to 4:30 p.m.; call (970) 453-3258.

Summertime is busy and fun-filled. Limited but convenient, the Breckenridge Recreation Center offers "Bearly Big," a great space where professionals care for ages two months to six years while you work out or play racquetball.

Kinderhut offers child care for ages one (and walking) to three years. Lots of action, even for the toddlers, includes visits to the children's museum, Gym & Jam, library visits, and free play time at local parks. The Adventure Camp entices three- to seven-year-olds to play. Kinderhut's goal is to provide children with the opportunity to explore new activities in a safe, nurturing environment and to build confidence through successful interactions with the world. Horseback riding, yoga, swimming, rock climbing, ice-skating (yes, even in the summer), story time at the library, or a trip to the fire station are just a taste of the fun in store. Kinderhut's summer schedule is Monday, Wednesday, and Friday in May and September; Monday through Friday during June, July, and August. Cost is $60 for the full day (8:30 a.m. to 5:00 p.m.) and $45 for the half-day morning (to 1:00 p.m.).

The Mountain Top Children's Museum encourages interaction and imagination with hourly workshops on Tuesday and Wednesday to entertain ages two to five. From June to August, each of twelve magical weeks is filled with themed summer camps for five- to ten-year-olds. Operating from 9:00 a.m. to 4:00 p.m., for one day or one week your child will experience hands-on fun and field trips centered around Creature Feature, Spy Agency, Medieval Madness, Take One, or Walk Like an Egyptian, just to mention a few. Cost is $70 per day with snacks and drinks; children provide a bag lunch. Call (970) 453-7878 for more information. Wow! How much can one kid do?

**Recreation:** If you said to some skiers that you'd found 152 trails, an average annual snowfall of 300 inches, a ski season from early November to late April, and a vertical drop of more than 3,398 feet, they might think you'd died and gone to heaven.

Breckenridge gives you all this on its four interconnected mountains—Peak 7 is the latest addition in skiable terrain, while Peak 10 boasts the highest elevation, at nearly 13,000 feet. It also gives outstanding views over Summit County, with 55 percent expert runs, 32 percent intermediate runs, 13 percent beginner runs, bowl skiing, above-the-timberline skiing, and lots of famous Rocky Mountain powder. You can line up a free guided tour of the mountains or plunge right away into group or private instruction.

Cross-country enthusiasts head to the Breckenridge Nordic Center for more than 40 kilometers of groomed trails. Try snow-mobiling or dogsledding; ice-skating on Maggie Pond or the indoor, year-round ice rink; and a horse-drawn sleigh ride to a steak-and-baked-potato supper on the mountain.

At both the Village at Breckenridge and Beaver Run, you can jump into the indoor/outdoor pools, relax in one of the many outdoor hot tubs, or, if your muscles weren't tested enough on the slopes, finish up in the exercise rooms. An additional Beaver Run attraction is an indoor miniature golf course, where you can count on a fun family evening in a huge indoor area for video games and active play.

During warm-weather months venture out from the resorts and go biking through town, hiking in the woods, fishing in mountain streams, sailing on Lake Dillon, horseback riding on trails bordered by wildflowers, and white-water rafting on the Arkansas and Blue Rivers. Play a round on Breckenridge's twenty-seven holes of championship golf, a course designed by Jack Nicklaus; four other courses are nearby, two of them at Keystone. During July and August the mountains ring with classical and jazz music from the Breckenridge Music Institute. You can tour a gold mine or take a ride on Mount Express, the highest charilift in North America.

The Riverwalk Center, an award-winning performing-arts facility, is the focal point for summer cultural activities, including a kids concert series.

The Breckenridge Recreation Center is a state-of-the-art facility with both indoor and outdoor pursuits. Inside you'll find tennis, racquetball, and wallyball courts, a gym with running track, two pools (lap and leisure), dance/aerobics, and rock climbing. Outdoors there are more tennis courts, a basketball court, two softball fields, rugby and soccer fields, a skateboard park, a sundeck, and a playground.

Peak 8 Fun Park has a little bit of everything: a mountain bike park with 35 miles of trails; SuperChair rides for easy access to hiking trails; a SuperPutt miniature golf course; and a climbing wall. Six zip lines enable you to fly across the mountains. And check out the Bounce House and Spin Cycle. Most popular is the SuperSlide, which gives downhill thrills while sitting down. It's a ½-mile, three-track slalom course on a small sled. Add to this a Power Jump (a modified trampoline where you go so high you have to wear a harness) and Colorado's largest human maze, two levels of labyrinth twists and turns; the price tag for all this unlimited fun is $50 for a half day and $60/$65 for a full day for ages seven and up. Tickets for each attraction range from $5 to $15. You just may need a longer vacation!

**Box 1058**
**Breckenridge, Colorado 80424**
**(970) 453-5000, (800) 789-SNOW**
**www.breckenridge.snow.com**

# THE BROADMOOR
## Colorado Springs, Colorado

As majestic as the neighboring Rocky Mountains, The Broadmoor reigns over Cheyenne Lake and 3,000 surrounding acres. The original hotel, known today as Broadmoor Main, was built in 1918 by Spencer Penrose, an enterprising man who made his fortune in gold mining in Cripple Creek (less than 20 miles from Colorado Springs) and copper mining in Utah. He dreamed of fashioning a Colorado resort along the lines of the grand European hotels that he had seen. The Mediterranean-style structure, with its pink-stucco facade, almost glimmers in the sunshine. Inside, the Italian Renaissance trappings include wood-beamed ceilings, crystal chandeliers, gilt-framed mirrors, and handpainted wall and ceiling decoration. Penrose's dream was realized—The Broadmoor fared well indeed when compared with its European counterparts. And the guests who followed were as impressive as the hotel, from royalty and presidents to movie stars and millionaires.

Over the years, facilities and buildings were added to the original complex. Broadmoor South stands next to Broadmoor Main and is architecturally compatible with the original, because its design utilizes light-colored stucco for the exterior walls. Across the lake is Broadmoor West. A modern structure, it nonetheless blends well within the context of the resort as a whole. In

1995 an additional 150 guest rooms were completed, and Lakeside Suites was completed in 2001. This newer twenty-one-room building hosts the most luxurious accommodations on the property. The architecture of this wing is reminiscent of Broadmoor Main. The newer structures reveal precise attention to architectural design, aesthetic decoration, and fine art. In 2003 The Broadmoor completed a $75 million refurbishing, bringing new grandeur and elegance. The resort is open year-round and is the longest-running consecutive winner of both the Mobile five-star and the AAA five-diamond awards.

**Accommodations:** Some 700 rooms and suites are divided among the five main buildings of The Broadmoor. All are handsomely decorated and look out at either the clear blue Cheyenne Lake, the gardens, or the dramatic Colorado mountains; it's a tough task to find a view that's less than terrific. Broadmoor West features rooms with private balconies. During the high season, from the first of May through October, superior rooms are $510 to $550 per night. Winter room rates are $260 to $370; suites begin at $400. Rates are for one to four people. An "incidental services" fee of $14.00 per room and $2.50 per person (more than two guests) is added daily. Holiday family packages include extras such as complimentary meals for twelve and under, bikes and paddleboats, movies, and passes to the Cheyenne Mountain Zoo. Cribs are provided at no additional charge. For an extra $15 a night, a rollaway bed can be added to your room.

**Dining:** In the eighty-nine-year history of the hotel, there have only been four executive chefs, so it's clear The Broadmoor's fifteen restaurants have a tradition of excellence. On the top floor of Broadmoor South, the four-star, four-diamond Penrose Room is an elegantly formal restaurant, with traditional French menu, superb views, dinner music, dancing, and an Edwardian decor, with emphasis on elaborate styling. Jackets are required for men. Charles Court, another award-winning restaurant in the West building, offers fine dining without the formalities, yet still with wonderful lake views. One of the world's most extensive wine lists (more than 600 choices and 3,000 bottles, with prices ranging from $25 to $1,300 a bottle!) complement such entrees as Colorado rack of lamb and Copper River salmon. Summit is the resort's newest restaurant, a sleek and contemporary-styled American brasserie with eclectic menu and wines; it was voted one of *Esquire* magazine's "Best New Restaurants 2006" and "Best Design."

Also at Broadmoor Main are the Tavern, open for lunch and dinner, and exquisitely adorned with Toulouse-Lautrec lithographs; and the Lake Terrace Dining Room, opening onto the Sun Lounge, with palms, ficus trees, and a tiered Italian fountain. Sunday brunches here are an extravaganza featuring more than seventy items. Café Julie, a sidewalk cafe in Broadmoor West, offers a relaxed shirtsleeves-and-shorts atmosphere for sandwiches, salads, and burgers. Espresso News is a favorite stopping place for cappuccino, pastries, quiche, sandwiches, and eclairs in Broadmoor Main. One of the merriest dining spots is the Golden Bee, an authentic nineteenth-century English pub located behind and below the International Center; it is open for lunch and dinner and until the wee hours, with live ragtime and sing-alongs. The Golf Club Dining Room is open for breakfast, lunch, and dinner with traditional American fare during the day and a focus on families. The Grille at the Golf Club has all-day dining with a big-screen television, as well as take-out for sports enthusiasts. The Pool Café has two locations: seasonally outdoors with salads and grilled meats and fish plus summer drinks, and year-round at the spa with light snacks and smoothies.

Relax in the West Lobby Bar, with dark oak and overstuffed chairs, or on the outside terrace overlooking Cheyenne Lake; for the atmosphere of a fine English library, sip port in the Penrose Lounge.

**Children's World:** Memorial Day to Labor Day, daily from 9:00 a.m. to 4:00 p.m., things are buzzing with the Bee Bunch. Scheduled for ages three to twelve years, activities vary daily and include trips to the Cheyenne Mountain Zoo, arts and crafts, cooking classes, paddleboating on Cheyenne Lake, picnics in the park, and scavenger hunts. Kids can also enjoy golf clinics and tennis lessons. Separate day and evening programs are also offered to give parents maximum scheduling flexibility. A one-week advance reservation is requested, and a twenty-four-hour cancellation policy applies.

The brand-new Bee Bunch Room in the West Building is the gathering center, and the staffing ratio is one counselor to five campers. Groups are divided into Explorer Bees (three to six years old) and Adventure Bees (seven to twelve years). Morning sessions meet from 9:00 a.m. to noon; afternoons from 1:00 to 4:00 p.m.; cost is $40 per session. Lunch can be added to either session for $15 and is served from noon to 1:00 p.m. The full-day program includes lunch and is priced at $75; family rates are available for additional children on the full-day program and evening camp. The youngsters meet again for dinner and games or a movie from 6:00 to 10:00 p.m., granting their parents opportunities to sample the gourmet creations of the Broadmoor chefs. The children's meals are planned to ensure cleaned-up plates; the pizza, fried chicken, and hamburger dinners are favorites among the younger set and are included in the program cost of $55. Babysitting is available

($12 per hour), again with one-week advance registration. Contact the Children's Concierge (ext. 5160), who also has information on family activities at the hotel and nearby. With at least two weeks' notice, the Bee Bunch may be arranged throughout the year for a minimum of three children. Programs are scheduled at Christmas and Easter as well.

**Recreation:** Golfing at The Broadmoor began when the original hotel opened in 1918. The East Course, ranked five-star by *Golf Digest,* was originally designed by Donald Ross and is slightly more forgiving than the West Course. In 1959 Jack Nicklaus won his first national title at The Broadmoor, and nearly half a century later, he designed the nine-hole Mountain Course, which reopened in 2006. Once golfers discover the challenging variety of these forty-five holes, the incredibly scenic setting, the top-quality equipment and accessories of the golf shops, and instruction with the resident pro, they may never explore the rest of The Broadmoor—and that would be a pity.

*Tennis* magazine named The Broadmoor the third greatest tennis resort in America and has ranked the year-round tennis program under Dennis Ralston number one for three years. Seven landscaped Plexi-cushioned courts, all with Rocky Mountain views, are located at the Tennis Club. The club includes one stadium court, and two courts are covered with a heated, illuminated bubble for play during winter months. Play a set or sign up for classes and clinics.

An afternoon can be spent swimming at one of two heated swimming pools at Broadmoor Main and the Golf Club. A spectacular new infinity edge pool at the north end of Cheyenne Lake boasts two water slides built into Slide Mountain, a connecting swim-under bridge, a children's wading pool, two fourteen-person hot tubs, thirteen cabanas, and the Main Pool Cafe. Rent a paddleboat for a spin on the lake or a bicycle for a tour around the lake. Twenty minutes away, the Stables at Broadmoor give you a chance to experience wilderness beauty close-up; along your trail ride, you may glimpse elk or buffalo. The many biking, walking, and running trails are another way to spend rewarding time in the great outdoors. Or stroll along One Lake Avenue to enjoy a variety of specialty shops and an art gallery.

The Broadmoor Spa, Golf and Tennis Club is more than 90,000 square feet of luxury: state-of-the-art fitness facility, full-service spa, full-service salon, and private locker rooms with all amenities, including fireplaces!

A nonstop itinerary of off-property activities includes white-water rafting, hot-air ballooning, fly fishing, mountain biking, and hunting expeditions. Or perhaps you'll opt to take the famous cogwheel up to Pikes Peak. The quaint town of Cripple Creek, Garden of the Gods, the new Olympic Training Center, the Cheyenne Mountain Zoo, Manitou, and Seven Falls all make wonderful family excursions.

**1 Lake Avenue**
**Colorado Springs, Colorado 80906**
**(719) 577-5775, (800) 634-7711**
**www.broadmoor.com**

# C LAZY U RANCH
## Granby, Colorado

Ride 'em, cowboy! With a little time at C Lazy U Ranch, you could live up to this label. Experienced wranglers match you with just the right horse to call your own during a vacation stay, and guide you on trail rides through the gorgeous Colorado high country. Beautiful vistas stretch in every direction, with mountains everywhere. Expect to meet some locals on the trail rides—moose, coyotes, owls, and even mountain lions share the area. Situated two hours west of Denver, at an elevation of 8,300 feet, the ranch sprawls across more than 8,000 acres of Peaceful Valley. A lot of territory to roam combines with warm sunny days that give way to cool nights—a spectacular setting for learning Western ways. Since 1946 C Lazy U has operated as a guest ranch. That adds up to a lot of experience, not only in riding and roping, but also in welcoming and entertaining visitors. For

thirty consecutive years, C Lazy U earned the Mobile five-star and AAA five-diamond ratings. Open from early June through mid-October, September is reserved for adults only. The ranch opens again from mid-December to mid-February for the winter holidays. The owners' philosophy is that C Lazy U is not just a hotel, nor is it a resort. Rather, it is a unique vacation spot, your home for the duration of your stay.

**Accommodations:** Forty comfortable rooms and suites are in the main lodge and the guest cottages that surround it. About 75 percent of these have a fireplace, stocked with wood and ready to take the chill off the evening. With no televisions or telephones in the rooms, it's a real vacation. But don't be nervous; at the Executive Corral you'll find two dataports, telephones, and a fax machine; and two public areas have televisions. Enjoy the little touches of luxury here—a plush bathrobe, fresh fruit basket, snacks, and nightly turndown.

Minimum stays vary by season: Summer requires a seven-night stay (Sunday to Sunday); holiday season (December 20 to January 3) has a five-night minimum; Winter Playtime has a two-night requirement; and September, which is reserved for adults only, requires a three-night stay. Rates are per person and vary based on season, number of people, and size of accommodation. Kids stay free the first week of June, and grandparents stay free the last week of June. What a deal! Rates per adult, based on double occupancy, average $2,350 per week in early June; mid-June to mid-August averages $2,975. Daily rates during winter and holiday season are $245 to $315 per person per day. Children from three to five years old receive a $200 discount. During the winter season, children seventeen and under receive a 20 percent discount. These rates cover virtually everything you'll want or need during your visit: upscale lodging, three meals a day, afternoon and bedtime ice cream, all-day tea and lemonade, your own horse with five hours of daily trail rides or instruction, use of the recreational facilities, and the supervised children's program. The only extras are trap and skeet shooting, bar drinks, and a massage, if you choose.

**Dining:** At C Lazy U you'll get the hearty meals that you need to maintain an energy level consistent with the fresh air and outdoor fun. And note that hearty does not mean plain. The warm, rustic dining room is located in the lodge, the main building of the ranch. Here guests sit at tables set for ten, a good way to make friends and enjoy relaxed dining. But don't expect baked beans and coffee in a tin pot. C Lazy U's outstanding menus include Black Angus prime rib, rack of lamb, and jalapeño-stuffed mountain trout. Breakfast is the family meal, with just about anything you want to order; or try the

special of the day—breakfast burritos, raspberry pancakes, or chocolate chip waffles for starters. Lunch is generally buffet-style, by the pool at the Patio House. Children and teens eat lunch and dinner with their counselors; families regroup at about 4:30 p.m. for ice cream and cool drinks and again after dinner for the evening activities. Evening cookouts are planned frequently.

The lodge also houses a comfortable living room, well stocked with books, and a cozy bar, where drinks and hors d'oeuvres are served nightly at 6:30 p.m. Another bar is located in the Patio House, adjacent to the swimming pool, with both a television and fireplace; enjoy an evening cocktail and swap tall tales with other guests about the day's adventures. Then cap the day off at 9:00 p.m. at the Ice Cream Bar with something special for your sweet tooth.

**Children's World:** With C Lazy U's special attention to youngsters, the kids may turn into wranglers before you do. Starting at age three (the ranch does not provide care for younger children), kids get a good introduction to life out west. Three-year-olds are instructed in how to ride, and a little of how to feed and care for their horse, and they get the thrill of pony rides in the corral; at age six they can go out on trail rides. Everyone is assigned a horse for the entire week, based on individual ability, and children are divided into three groups: three- to five-year-olds, six- to twelve-year-olds, and teenagers. Some boots are available if children (or even adults) do not have their own, and helmets are recommended but not required.

The day begins at 9:00 a.m. with horseback lessons or a ride, and maybe lunch on the trail or a swim in the reservoir along the way. Lunch with the counselors, then "cabin time" during the heat of the day, or a nap and movie in the Children's Center, a comfortable indoor place for reading, art projects, and resting. Afternoon brings another trail ride or swimming, tennis, or games—the program is very individualized. Ice cream at 4:00 p.m., with a little "parent time," and then kids gather at 5:45 p.m. for dinner and evening activities until about 8:30 p.m., when families regroup for a hayride, games, or dancing. Teens, as they much prefer, have their own separate program of riding, hayrides, and cookouts. C Lazy U is well arranged and safe for children to roam a bit; there's little or no traffic, and everything is within easy walking distance.

The ranch opens again in mid-December and remains open through Presidents' Week. During this time, the children's program is in full swing.

**Recreation:** The main attraction of a ranch is horseback riding, and this is one of the most comprehensive programs we've seen. From a string of more than 160 horses, you'll be assigned a mount that suits your ability. Guided by experienced wranglers, you'll ride the high country across mountain meadows or sage-covered hills, and through tall evergreens along Willow Creek. For three hours in the morning and another two in the afternoon, the focus is on horses. The programs are flexible, and participants may decide which they wish to join—it might be instruction (basic or advanced) in the outdoor or indoor arenas, or a choice of trail rides (slow and scenic, medium, or fast). On Friday mornings, family rides are scheduled. Everyone looks forward to the "shodeo" at the end of each week, especially kids as they "show off" what they've learned.

But there's more to this ranch than just horses. Enjoy a group walk before breakfast. Between trail rides, sneak in a little fishing in the pond near the lodge or at a secluded spot along Willow Creek, and then have the trout for breakfast! Ranch hands are glad to instruct you in the art of fly fishing. Adults

have a catch-and-release policy, while kids can catch up to two fish. Take a pedal boat on the lake, go hiking, spend an afternoon on the skeet range (trap and skeet shooting are the only activities not covered in the package rates), play tennis on one of the two Laykold courts, or swim in the heated pool. Try volleyball, basketball, shuffleboard, or horseshoes, or take the ranch's name to heart, and simply laze about in the sunshine or the shade of a tree with a cool drink.

For more activities, seek out the Patio House, a favorite "watering hole," with a well-equipped fitness room, locker rooms, and showers. When you fear that saddle sores or tennis elbow may set in, retire to the whirlpool or sauna. A game room features foosball, table tennis, and billiards; a television room and a large all-purpose activity room with fireplace invite relaxing or socializing, as you desire. Complimentary laundry facilities are also found in this complex.

In the evenings the entire family joins in on campfire sing-alongs, hayrides, square dancing, and rodeos—just so you don't forget you're "out west." Nearby excursions might include Rocky Mountain National Park, with stunning scenic vistas, or the glacial snow fields and the Alpine terrain and tundra of the Continental Divide. Or visit the little town of Hot Sulfur Springs, with more than twenty naturally heated therapeutic pools. Off-site, white-water rafting and golf can be arranged.

During the winter season guests take to skiing—cross-country on the 25 kilometers of trails maintained by the ranch and downhill at Winter Park (25 miles) and Sol Vista (10 miles) ski resorts, accessible via the ranch's complimentary shuttle service. Enjoy horseback riding in the snow or in the indoor 12,000-square-foot heated riding arena, or take a sleigh ride on an old-fashioned cutter.

Ride an inner tube down the tubing hill or across a meadow behind a snowmobile, and ice-skate or play hockey or broomball on the groomed skating pond. Then snuggle in for hot drinks, the fireplace, Western dancing, and cowboy songs. Yippee-yi-ay!

**3640 Colorado Highway 125**
**P.O. Box 379**
**Granby, Colorado 80446**
**(970) 887-3344**
**www.clazyu.com**

# DEER VALLEY RESORT
## Park City, Utah

Skiing for most folks means a little bit of the rugged outdoors—windburned cheeks, the raw natural beauty of mountain vistas, fresh tracks through pristine powder. Deer Valley has redefined skiing somewhat. It's all of the above but with an added twist. Instead of the Western flair you'd expect in Utah, there's a more sophisticated atmosphere at Deer Valley. This is warm hospitality with a heavy dose of pampering—from the guest-service attendants who help you unload your skis to the quite comfortable chairlifts to the signature food items in Snow Park Lodge.

Deer Valley, less than 40 miles east of Salt Lake City, is actually four mountains: Bald Eagle Mountain, whose summit is 8,500 feet; Bald Mountain, which rises to 9,400 feet; Flagstaff Mountain, with the summit at 9,100 feet; and Empire Canyon, with a summit of 9,570 feet. The hubs of activity are Snow Park Lodge at the base of Bald Eagle Mountain and Silver Lake Lodge at midmountain. Silver Lake Village is in effect the midmountain point, for it is from here that lifts ascend to Bald Mountain's summit. With the feel of a European village, the area has three restaurants and a small ski shop. Snow Park Lodge houses a restaurant and lounge, the ski school, the ski rental shop, the children's center, and a well-stocked ski shop. Free buses connect all areas with Park City (1–3 miles away).

Both lodges are very tastefully designed; inside the columns are natural tree trunks at least 2 feet in diameter, and wood accouterments abound—from the handrails to the ceiling beams, from the facial tissue dispensers to the trash cans. You'll find no plastic chairs or Formica-topped tables in the dining areas here—no indeed! Understated elegance and tasteful attention to detail are hallmarks of Deer Valley, home of the first country club for skiers. Deer Valley has been rated by *Ski* magazine as one of the three top resorts in North America for the past nine years.

**Accommodations:** At 8,200 feet amid the aspens and pines, the midmountain Stein Eriksen Lodge (www.steinlodge.com) is a Norwegian-style hotel built of stone and wood. Stein Eriksen's name has been synonymous with elegant skiing since his gold-medal victory in the 1952 Olympics. It's fitting that the 2002 Winter Olympics were on his home mountain. Today, Eriksen serves as both host of the lodge and director of skiing for Deer Valley Resort. The ski-in, ski-out lodge consistently garners awards and is a four-star, five-diamond property. Daily rates during regular season start at $735 for a deluxe room and $1,030 for a luxury room; suites start at $1,350 to $1,970. A four-night minimum is required on weekends. In the summer season (mid-

April to mid-November), bedrooms start at $175 to $260; suites begin at $255 to $575. Shops, two restaurants, a swimming pool, a health club, and a full-service spa complement the lodge.

Deer Valley Central Reservations (800-558-DEER) has a wide range of lodging and economical packages with individualized service—they even give you a one-year subscription to *Ski* magazine when you book with them. There are more than 500 units at the base of the mountain, along the trails, and near Silver Lake Lodge. The condominiums range from one- to five-bedroom units with fully equipped kitchens and living areas with fireplaces. Most have private Jacuzzis and individual decks or balconies; some include saunas, and some feature ski-in, ski-out access. In winter, one-bedroom condos begin at $325 (towels and trash service only) to $555 (full maid service and lots of amenities) at the Lodges. A two-bedroom unit here begins at $800. Value season, typically early December and April, has substantial savings, while rates increase during holidays. Summer rates begin at $175 and include two chairlift ride vouchers.

**Dining:** Dining at Deer Valley is a gourmet experience. The award-winning Glitretind at the Stein Eriksen Lodge heads the list in elegance. Also here, the Troll Hallen Lounge serves lighter fare and libations. Wintertime on the mountain equals good eating. The Snow Park Restaurant and the Silver Lake Restaurant in the lodges are "cafeterias." What misnomers! Though they're self-service, the lavish breakfast and lunchtime displays (homemade breads and pastries, salads, quiches, deli sandwiches) are hardly typical of the standard quick bite between ski runs. The newest day lodge in Empire Canyon offers deck dining with scenic views of the Daly Bowl and Chutes. Start with morning espresso, have lunch from the gourmet grill,

and snacks are available until 3:30 p.m. For evening dining in the winter season, the seafood buffet at the Snow Park Lodge is known for fresh seafood and lots of it; *Zagat Guide* even lists it in "America's Top Restaurants." The Mariposa at Silver Lake Lodge offers classic and current cuisine and candle-lit dinners. Every Wednesday, Thursday, and Friday evening in winter, try the unique fireside dining at Empire Canyon Lodge, featuring four courses served from the grand fireplaces. Each one is different; they are all mouth-watering. Want to take a little break between courses? Just step outside for a moonlit ride on a horse-drawn sleigh. The Royal Street Café, at Silver Lake Lodge, is open daily in winter for lunch, après-ski, and dinner; it's the only midmountain restaurant open in summer, for lunch only. Want to grab a quick bite and just keep skiing? Stop by Snowshoe Tommy's atop Bald Mountain or Cushing's Cabin on Flagstaff Mountain, winter days only. If desserts are your favorite part of the meal, the Snow Park Bakery is the place for you—fortunately, it's also year-round! Another summer dining treat is to order a Deer Valley Gourmet Picnic Basket; $60 for two. Stelvio at the Goldener Hirsch Inn serves Italian/Austrian cuisine; and the Olive Barrel is always popular for northern Italian hearty dishes from the brick oven.

**Children's World:** Deer Valley's Children's Center is a state-licensed facility providing indoor activities for nonskiing children ages two months to twelve years. Located on the main level of the Snow Park Lodge, the center is open daily from 8:30 a.m. to 4:30 p.m. during the ski season; cost for all children is $94 for a full day with lunch; reservations are essential, especially in peak winter months. Children are divided by age into groups for two to eight months, nine to twenty-four months, and two to twelve years old. Activities include storytelling, art, singing, toys, and lots of play time, and quiet time for the littlest ones.

The Ski School instructors are trained specifically in techniques that teach children not only how to ski, but to love skiing. A safe, fun, nurturing environment prevails; programs end at 3:45 p.m., so you may take a run with your child, and you'll get daily progress reports. Children may be dropped off early at the Children's Center. Fawns (three to three and a half years) meet from 9:00 a.m. to 4:30 p.m. and alternate Children's Center activities with snow play and a one-hour private ski lesson. Children must be four to participate in Bambi Club and will have morning and afternoon lessons, along with indoor activities. Children must be willing to ski. The daily program cost is $150; ski rental is $18. Reindeer Club meets from 10:00 a.m. to 3:45 p.m. for ages five to six years and costs $150 for lesson, lift ticket, and lunch. Average class size is four to six students of similar ability; Children's Center activities are available when needed. Adventure Club ($150), for the seven- to twelve-year-olds, has an average size of seven to ten students, and all levels will have the opportunity to improve their skiing. Classes begin at 10:00 a.m. Adventure and Reindeer programs feature theme-oriented activities with coloring books, fun races, special mountain scavenger hunts, and friendly animals who share secrets of safety and fun. And finally, the Teen Escape (ages thirteen to eighteen, $150) lets teens enjoy a mountain experience with their peers while being coached on the dynamics of skiing. They'll need pocket money for lunch, and the program is only offered during holiday and peak periods. During other time periods younger teens may join the Adventure Club, and older teens participate in Max 4 lessons, grouped by ability.

Deer Valley's Summer Adventure Camp is one of Park City's longest-running summer camps. Beginning mid-June, it operates from 9:30 a.m. to 4:00 p.m. Monday through Friday until mid-August. Drop-in hours are 8:00 a.m. to 5:30 p.m. at the Children's Center. Campers bring their own sack lunch and water. Programs are split into three groups, with excellent counselor-to-camper ratios: Adventure Camp Mountaineers for first graders through twelve years (1:8, $51); Adventure Camp Explorers for ages five through kindergarten (1:5, $51); Trekkers for ages three to four; and Jamboree for the wee ones, ages one to two years (1:4, $56). Half days at Trekkers and Jamboree are $35, and based on availability; reservations are required. Jamboree activities include little-red-wagon rides, a walk to the duck pond, wading pool water games, and art, music, and movement.

All ages get to enjoy usual summer camp activities plus leisurely time to simply enjoy and appreciate the great outdoors and play with friends. Each week's activities revolve around a different theme and include nature studies, swimming, mountain biking and hiking, team sports, along with mini–film festivals (kids produce their own videos), karaoke, and talent shows. Weekly field trips incur an extra cost ($15 to $20).

**Recreation:** Combine ninety-one downhill runs, twenty-one lifts, and a vertical drop of 3,000 feet with well-groomed trails and a restricted number of skiers on a daily basis— what more could a skier ask for? Beginners are able to ski each of the four mountains. The mountains are beautiful, and the attention to them and to the skiers is high quality. Full- and half-day private and group lessons are available. Cross-country ski lessons are also offered nearby; trails roll over broad, open expanses and through aspens and evergreens. No snowboards are allowed at Deer Valley. Other winter pleasures include snowmobiling, snowshoeing, sleigh-ride dinners, heli-skiing, and even hot-air ballooning. Park City is alive with shopping, art galleries, theater, bars, and clubs. And of course, the Utah Olympic Park provides ski jumping, bobsledding, and luge rides.

If you don't have a sufficient workout on the slopes, maybe the exercise rooms will test your limits. Then relax your weary muscles in one of the saunas or Jacuzzis.

Though primarily a winter wonderland, Deer Valley operates year-round. In warmer weather, June to Labor Day, guests enjoy 50 miles of lift-served mountain biking/hiking and scenic chairlift rides. The Utah Symphony stages outdoor concerts, and all the

summer mountain pleasures are here: golf, tennis, swimming, horseback riding, fishing, boating, rafting and kayaking, and hot-air ballooning. Stroll along Park City's Historic Main Street, which offers shops and dining options. Refer to the Park City Mountain Resort entry for more ideas.

**P.O. Box 1525**
**Park City, Utah 84060**
**(435) 645-6528, (800) 558-3337**
**www.deervalley.com**

# FLATHEAD LAKE LODGE
## Bigfork, Montana

Mix some city slickers with a few expert wranglers out in Montana horse country, toss in beautiful scenery and clear blue skies, and come up with quite a different vacation experience at Flathead Lake Lodge. On 2,000 acres in northwest Montana, just forty-five minutes south of Glacier National Park, this dude ranch specializes in water sports and just about anything that has to do with horses, from riding them to shoeing them. The lodge is situated in a private bay on Flathead Lake; at 15 miles wide by 30 miles long, it's the largest freshwater lake in the West. The surrounding timberland stretches up into the Rocky Mountains. The ranch is open from May to October, and one- or two-week visits are standard. July and August are popular with families.

Flathead Lake Lodge has been a working dude ranch in the Averill family since 1945; son Doug took over in 1971, and he and his family now live at the ranch. Hospitality is a way of life here, and families

return again and again for a memorable vacation. The lodge has been rated in the top 2 percent of best vacation spots, and acclaimed by *Better Homes and Gardens, Bon Appetit, Sunset Magazine, Travel + Leisure,* and *Good Morning America.*

**Accommodations:** The main lodge is the focus of activities and dining; in a warm and rustic setting, the old stone fireplace lures many guests to gather for cozy chats. There are guest rooms here and in the south lodge; family rooms in the log lodges accommodate four people with a small sitting area. Many families find the two- and three-bedroom log cottages particularly attractive; some of the lodge rooms and the guest cottages have views of the lake. The weekly rate for an adult is $2,989; for a teenager, $2,233; for six- to twelve-year-olds, $1,995; for three- to five-year-olds, $1,246; and for infants and toddlers, $161. A one-week stay runs Sunday to Sunday; rates include lodging, three meals a day, and all recreation, including horseback riding, tennis, use of the boats and sports equipment, and the Kids Camp. Cribs are available at no additional charge.

**Dining:** Dining is a family affair, with good home cooking, and breads and desserts made fresh every day. Guests gather at the long tables in the lodge dining room or at the picnic tables out on the patio overlooking the lake. Children eat together before their parents, allowing grown-ups time to get acquainted and plan the next day's events. Kids eat at 8:00 a.m., noon, and 6:00 p.m.; adults eat half an hour later. A daily happy hour in the Saddle Sore Saloon allows tall tales to be swapped as you wet your whistle. With three hearty meals a day, you better work and play hard, although appetites are always good. An evening barbecue ride gives everyone a chance to sample buffalo, grown on the ranch.

**Children's World:** The children's program is for any child old enough to participate in organized group activities, and divides roughly at age six. The friendly staff—mostly energetic college students who can keep up with excited youngsters—guide children through the day's activities. They can swim, lend a hand with the daily chores, and learn to ride horses. Children six years and older join cowboys on the horseback-riding trails in the mountains. After the trail riders depart, children under six are given special supervised pony rides. All kids can become "junior wranglers" and learn about grooming, barn duties, and caring for the horses. On Saturday mornings kids show off at the Children's Rodeo, much to the delight of parents. Arts and crafts are scheduled in the morning and afternoon, and projects get pretty creative. All the other pursuits dear to kids' hearts are here as well—swimming, boating, tennis, volleyball—all the ranch activities are available to them. Youngsters ages six to twelve get to spend an overnight in authentic tepees,

telling ghost stories around the campfire, and a fire truck ride to the ice-cream store is a real treat. Teens are encouraged to participate in all the ranch activities; some activities such as trail rides, team penning, games, and boat cruises are planned just for them. Child care for children too young for the camp is available but not included in the weekly rates.

**Recreation:** The great outdoors awaits you. Horses are a way of life here; ride 'em, rope 'em, or test your nerve and verve in competition. Take an early-morning breakfast ride to work up a good appetite, then enjoy a breakfast cookout amid the tall pines. Old-fashioned Western rodeos are part of the evening activities.

Take a dip in the large swimming pool or the crystal clear waters of the lake. Sailing, canoe races, and waterskiing may fill your afternoons. Cruises on the lake are organized several times a week. The sailing staff can take you on one of the two 51-foot Q-class racing sloops, prototypes for the America's Cup built in 1928 and 1929—it's quite a treat to sail on these beauties. Fish in the lake or the nearby streams, and add a trout to a cookout dinner or spin a good story about the one that got away.

It's easy to find partners for a game of tennis (four courts) and to organize table tennis, basketball, or volleyball. Eagle Bend Golf Course (twenty-seven holes) is just minutes away. Pick up a game of, what else? Horseshoes! You might take a stroll along the wooded trails and pick berries.

The whole family can enjoy an evening bonfire with roasted marshmallows and sing-along country music. You can schedule full- or half-day excursions for whitewater rafting, river tubing, and wilderness fishing. The National Bison Range, only an hour away, attracts many visitors; seeing real live buffalo is a highlight for kids and parents. Courtesy cars are available for trips to Glacier National Park and Kalispell, "The Best Mountain Town in Montana."

**Box 248**
**Bigfork, Montana 59911**
**(406) 837-4391**
**www.averills.com**

# KEYSTONE RESORT
## Keystone, Colorado

Like many fine Western ski resorts, Keystone first attracted settlers in search of the rich minerals in its mountains. Today visitors flock here seeking light powdery snow and the mountain high for which the Rockies are known. At the base of Loveland Pass, 70 miles west of Denver, Keystone has 121 runs on three interconnecting ski mountains and a vertical drop of 3,128 feet. The resort remains open year-round, so when summer rolls around, many folks hang up their skis and head for Keystone's other mountain delights.

Winter and summer there are more activities for families than you could possibly do in one vacation. There's even a special line, (800) 354-4-FUN, to help you plan it all. And at Keystone, you get more than a room. Summer and winter the Adventure Passport gives you access to lots of discounts and free activities. Be sure to inquire.

**Accommodations:** Keystone stretches out 7 miles along the Snake River, with over 1,500 lodging units in seven neighborhoods; the Web site has an excellent interactive map with all the details of each area's lodging. If you want to walk or short shuttle to the slopes, Mountain House base area and River Run Village are within 200 yards of the lifts. Both areas have ski schools, dining, and après-ski. Mountain House is the original base area. The Inn at Keystone Hotel is an economical choice with a cozy lobby, restaurant, and nightlife—the hot tubs are on the roof, with great views! Rates begin at $149 in winter, $109 in summer. A variety of condominiums offer more space, many only steps from the slopes or golf courses.

River Run Village is the heart of Keystone. Lone Eagle and the Timbers are ski-in, ski-out, upscale condos on the eastern slopes of Keystone Mountain and are the closest lodging to the slopes; for a one-bedroom condo, rates average $699 in winter; $329 in summer. Cross over the Snake River to the pedestrian-style River Run Village for shopping, dining, and nightlife. In East Keystone, deluxe and premium condos are on the outskirts of River Run Village, in the White National Forest along the Snake River, and appeal to those who want to be close to nature and get away from it all. North Keystone, on Tenderfoot Mountain Ridge close to the conference center and Lakeside Village, offers good value condominiums and town houses and is a shuttle ride to lifts and River Run Village. West Keystone and Keystone Ranch shelter a variety of lodgings, the golf courses, and Keystone's best restaurant, the Keystone Ranch. And last, but certainly not least, is Keystone Lakeside Village, center of the conference area. The Keystone Lodge

Hotel, a rustic yet elegant four-diamond property, is in the heart of Lakeside Village, a festive place of shops, galleries, and restaurants spread along the lakeside. It's the center of the action, with a playground, ice rink, and the lake. Free shuttles run throughout Keystone and connect the mountain bases.

**Dining:** From romantic gourmet dinners in a mountaintop restaurant more than 2 miles high to family picnic lunches, unique and award-winning dining choices delight guests. The resort features dining options that range from gourmet six-course meals to sandwiches or a Western family-style cook-out and include Summit County's only AAA four-diamond-rated restaurants—the Alpenglow Stube and Keystone Ranch. The Ski Tip Lodge is where it all began at Keystone. A stagecoach stop in the 1800s, today it is a charmingly rustic bed-and-breakfast with what is claimed to be the best comfort food on the Divide.

At the Keystone Lodge, Champeaux features fine cuisine and a Sunday brunch; the Edgewater is a casual restaurant open for breakfast and lunch. At Lakeside Village, you'll find Pizza on the Plaza and Bighorn Steakhouse. At River Run, Kickapoo Tavern, Paisano's, Pizza on the Run, and Fritz's Alpine Bistro all satisfy families. Several restaurants will provide takeout if you prefer eating in your condo. Two markets, a deli in Lakeside Village, SubFusion (subway sandwiches with a twist, in three areas), and four food courts on the mountain provide quick eating when you have other things to do. In the summertime you can hop a hayride to Soda Creek Homestead—in winter a sleigh ride takes you there—for a multicourse dinner. Take the gondola to Der Fondue Cheese for a fun evening of dipping and Bavarian music.

**Children's World:** Keystone's Children Center, located in Silvermill plaza at River Run Village, makes sure that children ages two months to six years have a great experience, whatever the season. River Run is modeled after a children's museum, with bright colors, a central play area surrounded by breakout areas for different ages, and lots of hands-on, interactive play. Age-appropriate activities and individualized attention keep children happy all day, from 8:00 a.m. to 4:00 p.m. ($95) or mornings only ($80), including lunch. In winter Snowplay is designed to introduce three- to six-year-olds to the joy of snow. The cost is $100 for mornings only; $115 with afternoon day care. For the ultimate in individual attention, the Nanny 1-on-1 provides a qualified caregiver solely for your child.

The Children's Camps have been rated a "Best Bet" by *Ski* magazine. Learn-to-ski/snowboard programs begin at age three with small group lessons and snow play.

At Mountain House and River Run, Ski/Board Camps for ages three to six use children's on-mountain adventure areas and trails. Children are grouped according to ability, and scheduled at the end of the day are a parent-teacher conference, progress report, and a level pin for each child. All packages include lesson, lift ticket, and lunch. Ski and Ride Camps for seven- to twelve-year-olds are divided by age into beginner, intermediate, and advanced sessions so that kids have fun and learn as well. They also receive a progress report. The cost for both camps is $109/$119.

Registration is from 8:00 to 9:00 a.m. and pickup is between 3:00 and 3:30 p.m. Equipment rental is $19. Helmets are recommended and may be rented for $15. Mom, Dad, and Me is a one-hour private lesson for two adults and one child every day at 3:45 p.m.; cost is $90, and it's a great way to spend family time on the slopes.

Keystone's summer program for ages two months to twelve years is set at River Run and runs from mid-June to late August, Monday through Friday, from 8:00 a.m. to 4:00 p.m. The cost is $80, and reservations are required. Half days are $65. For the wee ones, beginning at two months, the state-of-the-art day-care center is their kingdom. Keystone Mountain entertains children from three to six years old with a full calendar of events: pony riding, games, relay races, paddleboats, swimming, gold panning, hikes, and scavenger hunts. Some activities may have an age requirement. Summer X-Camps for ages seven to twelve follow the same format but with more challenging fun: a resort field trip, hiking to back ranch for fishing, scavenger hunts, Frisbee golf, and silly human challenges. Afternoons are generally devoted to something wet—swimming or a wet-and-wild gauntlet. Keystone schedules family activities almost daily. Babysitting is available through the Children's Center.

**Recreation:** With three interconnected mountains—Dercum Mountain, North Peak, and the Outback—Keystone offers terrain for skiers and snowboarders of all levels. Dercum Mountain offers mainly beginner and intermediate terrain. North Peak challenges guests with more intermediate slopes and runs that plunge down mogul-filled terrain. The Outback features only intermediate and expert runs. Some of Summit County's best tree skiing is found on the Outback. Skiers can find deep powder in open bowls adjacent to the Outback. The A51 Terrain Park sports rails, more rails, wall rides, pipes and super pipes, funboxes, and lots more in this exciting area. The park has tripled in size and is one of the "Top 10 Snowboarding Parks." Nighttime lighting makes Keystone's terrain garden and ski slopes the largest night-park operation in Colorado.

The ski season at Keystone is early November to mid-April. Whether you're trying to figure out what a snowplow is or you're looking for perfection in powder skiing, the more than 350 ski and snowboarding instructors can guide you through the 3,148 acres of terrain.

Other outdoor winter sports at Keystone include ice-skating at the Skating Center in Lakeside Village, cross-country skiing from the Keystone Cross-Country Center into White River National Forest (cross-country and telemark lessons are offered), snowmobile tours into the backcountry, sleigh rides, tubing, winter fly fishing, and snowshoeing. There's something new at Keystone—Slopecycles or Snowbikes. Become certified (thirteen or older), then rent one for $25 a day, and watch people stare! Indoors, enjoy tennis, yoga, wellness clinics, and weekly wine tastings. Some of these activities are included in your Adventure Passport.

Summertime at Keystone means golfing on the masterfully designed Robert Trent Jones Jr. course; eighteen holes with a Scottish flair respect the woodlands, meadows, and a nine-acre lake. The River Course, designed by Hurdzan-Fry, follows the path of the Snake River for the front nine. The back nine threads through a pine forest, bringing beauty and stunning views to the game. Courses are open from June to mid-October; golf pros offer private lessons and clinics.

Keystone is a haven, or perhaps heaven, for mountain-bike enthusiasts. The resort offers a mountain-bike clinic for ages fifteen and older that provides intense riding for "mud studs" and "wannabes." One-hour beginning clinics are free with the Adventure Passport. In addition, Keystone is the center of literally hundreds of miles of world-class single track. These tracks, combined with branches from the Colorado Trail, make it as good as it gets for mountain bikers. Ditto for downhill biking—aficionados probably recognize terms like burly trail, berms, table tops, and teeter totters, but Keystone's got a trail for you even if you're still riding the hard tail or beginning the sport. Mountain Bike Headquarters has everything you need. And for those of us who think biking means maybe shifting gears now and then along a smooth easy path—we're covered as well. Miles of paths run along the Snake River and hundreds of miles of road wait.

Fishermen take to the local haunts for rainbow trout; boaters sail on Lake Dillon (5 miles west of Keystone) or skim across Keystone Lake in a paddleboat or kayak, while hikers walk along the trails through wildflowers and aspens into the national forest. Horseback ride from the Keystone Stables through the Snake River Valley (breakfast rides are specialties), tour the high country of the White River National Forest by four-wheel drive, go white-water rafting down the Colorado and Arkansas Rivers, be treated to a lunch of rattlesnake meat and buffalo, or enjoy the great outdoors and mountain scenery on a gondola ride to Dercum Mountain's summit.

Learn the basics of rock climbing and mountaineering, play minigolf, or take a tour. Didn't we say there was a lot to do here? Energy Alley in River Run Village encourages extreme games and challenging activities such as a quad bungee, life-size Playstation 2, inflatables, and a dance revolution game—just for starters.

Weekly activities (usually for two to three hours) for kids and families happen almost daily. Many are free: Tuesday is Kid's Discovery Day, a celebration of imagination; Wednesday brings evening S'more Stories at the firepit; Thursday's fare is hilarious comedy ($15); on Friday, sample children's theater ($4); and close the week on Saturday with a Frontier Fair and elegant Open-Air Market, culminating in spectacular fireworks over Keystone Lake. This is the current schedule; of course it changes, so check when you go. Whatever is planned, it's all fun.

Pony rides, guided hikes, and free mountain-bike clinics augment the playground in Lakeside Village and the family fun park in River Run. Miniature golf, strolling around the lake, and feeding the ducks—families don't lack for activities here. The summer-long Music Festival celebrates sounds from classical to pop.

Reservations and more information on these activities (including dining at Keystone's award-winning restaurants) can be arranged by the Mountain Concierge well before a guest arrives, so that everything is already in place at vacation's start. The number to call is (800) 354-4-FUN. You can't help but have fun here.

---

**P.O. Box 38**
**Keystone, Colorado 80435**
**(970) 496-2316, (877) 625-1556**
**www.keystoneresort.com**

# MOUNTAIN SKY GUEST RANCH

### Emigrant, Montana

"Just turn me loose, let me straddle my own saddle underneath the Western sky. Don't fence me in!" At Mountain Sky all guests (age seven and older) are assigned their own special horse. Careful matching of horse and rider according to the latter's age and skills ensures a compatible duo during a vacation stay. Under the guidance of experienced wranglers, you'll be swaggering like a Montana cowboy before the week is out.

Mountain Sky Guest Ranch has a rich history dating back to the mid-nineteenth century. This is no modern mock-up of Old West ranching. It was an active operation during the days of cattle empires and witnessed the excitement of the gold-mining era. With its genuine Western flavor, Mountain Sky offers visitors a combination of "wide open spaces" and upscale comforts. Located just 30 miles north of Yellowstone National Park, Mountain Sky sits in Paradise Valley, in southwestern Montana. Surrounded by national forest and wilderness areas, the wooded mountainous landscape of Montana's high country is a beautiful vacation setting. The ranch is open May 1 through October 15.

**Accommodations:** Guests are lodged in thirty rustic but modern cabins; each one has a refrigerator, and fresh fruit is delivered daily. Cabin units are one to three bedrooms, all with porches and spectacular views. Some have picture windows, while others have a fireplace to warm the cool mountain evenings. A few date back to 1929, when guests first began arriving, but never fear: Everything has been totally renovated within the past five years, so it's now the best of both worlds.

All rates include lodging, all meals, a horse for each guest over six years old, all ranch facilities, and participation in all activities. Spring and fall have no minimum-stay requirements and are for adults only; rates are $355 per person, per night. June, July, and August are for families, and weekly rates are $3,045 to $3,745 for adults; children seven to twelve years old are $2,520 to $3,045; and children six and under are $1,960 to $2,310. Children eighteen months and younger are $630, or $10 per hour for child care. Bring your own nanny and pay half of the adult rate.

During the summer the vacation week runs from Sunday to Sunday; within a couple of days, you'll make friends not only with your horse but also with the other guests. If you really have a hankerin' to get away from it all, stay in one of Mountain Sky's two remote cabins, hidden in the wilderness. Your cabin will be stocked with snacks and meals to prepare, and if you miss civilization, you can hike or ride into the guest ranch. Vehicle transportation is also available, but that defeats the purpose, doesn't it? If this appeals to you, you might also make reservations for a day or two in the middle of your week. Call the ranch for details and rates.

**Dining:** Meals are served in the dining room of the main lodge and at barbecue cookouts. Understanding that the atmosphere of the great outdoors can generate healthy appetites, the chefs prepare hearty as well as gourmet meals. Buffet-style breakfasts with made-to-order omelets and huckleberry pancakes start the day off right. Lunches are generally served outdoors, in a casual buffet style, with homemade soups, salads, fruit and cheese, and "world cuisine" of Mexican enchiladas,

Chinese stir-fry, or Italian pizza and pasta. And evening brings hors d'oeuvres at the Mountain View Lodge and a choice of poolside barbecue hot off the grill or gourmet dinners with wine. Expect the unexpected, like lobster thermidor or spring lamb with saffron root vegetables and baby greens in Gorgonzola sauce, and superb presentation. Desserts are famous here; chocolate decadence with an Irish cream anglaise or warm Valrhona cake with huckleberry ice cream and fresh huckleberries are just the beginning. Yum. Rugged attire (jeans, boots) is standard most of the time; Tuesday- and Saturday-night dinners are a bit more formal, with clean jeans and a denim skirt. For good conversation and evening cocktails, drop by the Mountain View Lounge.

**Children's World:** In summer trained counselors guide children of all ages in a program of activities. The youth schedule includes arts and crafts, nature walks, fishing, and swimming. Children ages seven and older learn horseback-riding skills with the Children's Wrangler. Six years and under have an hour of arena instruction and spend time getting comfortable around horses. Three program sessions each day allow breakfast and lunch together. From 8:45 to 11:30 a.m. and 1:45 to 4:30 p.m., everyone is engaged in what interests them most. Evening session begins at 5:45 p.m. with dinner and ends at about 8:30 p.m. Each age group has its own eating spot and counselors. With the exception of family cookouts twice a week, children can stay with their friends and counselors for evening meals. The Kids' Rec Room is a popular place for all ages, with table tennis, pool table, and lots more. Games are found in other areas of the ranch as well, minimizing "clumping." There is no additional charge for these activities; the supervised children's program is part of the weekly rate.

Mountain Sky promises everything from "cuddling your infant to adventurous outings for your teenager," so parents are free to enjoy some time on their own. The younger children, even infants and toddlers, are included in those activities that are appropriate, always with close supervision and care. All age groups meet on Sunday evening to plan their week, so they can choose their own activities and interests.

**Recreation:** Horseback riding is the primary sport at the ranch. Mounting your own horse and exploring hundreds of miles of trails can be as invigorating or relaxing as you want to make it. Besides morning and afternoon excursions, guests enjoy evening dinner rides, morning rides with breakfast and cowboy coffee, and all-day treks through Paradise Valley with scrumptious picnics.

New in 2007 is the Absaroka Lodge complex, with newly redone swimming pool, kiddie pool, hot tub, and fitness room with space for yoga. In between rides, take a dip in the heated swimming pool, play a game of tennis, or hike in the woods. Go on your own, or join one of the twice-daily hikes or adventures to historic sites, flower-filled meadows, or the wonders of Yellowstone. You might glimpse moose, elk, or even a bear. Big Creek, right in front of your cabin door, beckons anglers; a fly-fishing instructor is ready to teach you the basics, and the trout are waiting. Fortunately for the trout, there's a catch-and-release policy. Table tennis, volleyball, softball, and horseshoes are popular games at the ranch. After active adventures, unwind in the hot tub or sauna, often under a clear, starlit sky. Capping off a fun-filled day, evening Western dances, hayrides, and campfire sing-alongs are frequently planned.

If you have the time or energy, for an additional fee you can hike, ride horseback, or take a van into Yellowstone Park or immerse yourself (pun intended) in a white-water rafting excursion.

P.O. Box 1219
Emigrant, Montana 59027
(406) 333-4911, (800) 548-3392
www.mtnsky.com

# PARK CITY MOUNTAIN RESORT
## Park City, Utah

Park City Mountain Resort has been consistently ranked in the top ten of *Ski Magazine*'s reader's poll for the last nineteen years and is one of Utah's most sophisticated resort communities. Three separate ski areas; a wide variety of lodgings from budget to luxury; a historic Victorian Main Street lined with shops, galleries, and restaurants; a superb setting in the gorgeous Wasatch Mountain Range of the Rockies; and all of this within a 7-mile radius and only 36 miles from the Salt Lake City airport. No wonder the 2002 Winter Olympic Games were held here. It's also very family friendly, and has garnered accolades from *Snowboard Magazine, Snowboarding, Money* magazine, *Fine Living, Freeskier,* and more.

**Accommodations:** Park City offers hotels, bed-and-breakfasts, lodges, and condominiums, with more than 3,000 units available at the mountain base, a couple of blocks from the runs, and throughout town. A free bus connects all three areas. Prices vary depending on the proximity to the slopes and the amenities offered. Value season is usually early December, April, fall, and sometimes summer; regular ski season and holiday season fill in the blanks. Park City Visitor's Bureau brings together complete listings of accommodations, plus lots of other information about the area at two sites: www.parkcity.com and www.parkcity info.com. As an example, a two-night package at a preferred property with a $50 voucher for dinner can be $199 in nonpeak season and $249 in peak ski season.

The Town Lift condominiums, with spacious two-bedroom units in the heart of the historic district, are next door to the Town Chair Lift and Ski Bridge (with access to the mountain) and only five minutes from Deer Valley's Snow Park Base Lodge (888-976-2732). Per-night rates during value season range from $415 to $435; regular is $530 to $665; and summer rates are $155 to $175.

The four-star Park City Marriott is just 1 mile from downtown by complimentary shuttle. An atrium-style pool, hot tub, fitness facility, on-site restaurant, and covered parking make life easy, and the beautiful views are just icing on the cake. Winter rates begin at $209; in summer those rates drop to $69 to $119, with breakfast (800-234-9003).

If you prefer even more peace and quiet, then the Grand Summit Resort in the Canyons might suit you. A four-diamond property with outdoor heated pool and slope-side location, it also has its own children's program (details under Children's World). Also on the slopes is the Sundial Lodge; both properties offer family-friendly options from studios to multi-bedroom condominiums, underground parking, and a Mountain Concierge at the ticket windows to answer all your questions. If the Canyons is your choice, call Central Reservations at (866) 604-4171 to help you plan. Deer Valley is the third area—see that entry for details.

**Dining:** On the mountain, try Legacy Lodge or the heated deck at Summit House for breakfast and lunch; stop by Kristi's Coffee Café for all-day goodies, including fresh-baked cookies in the afternoon. Relax by the fire at Pay Day Pizza or sit outdoors at the cafeteria-style Snow Hut; enjoy casual food and amazing views at the Five Way Café, a European-style coffeehouse inside a rustic yurt.

With one hundred–plus restaurants and bars, it's impossible to list them all. Be aware that in summertime, dining is more limited, so be sure to check before you bounce out to eat as disappointment can ruin your disposition. Your taste buds can really get a workout in the Village. Try the continental cuisine at Adolf's or the River-horse on Main Café, with live entertainment; both are local favorites. Chimayo is imaginative Southwestern with a French technique, and Wahso offers Asian grill, with that same French influence, in a setting reminiscent of 1930s Shanghai. Shabu for sushi, Grappa for the feel of a Tuscan farmhouse, and Zoom, Robert Redford's restaurant in the train depot station, are all delightful diversions. Kids like Main Street Pizza & Noodle, and often the Corner Café & Yarrow Social Club has specials. The Eating Establishment, Baja Cantina, Wasatch Brew Pub, Bandits Grill, and Loco Lizard are good mid-priced restaurants for families. Kristi's Café is open daily year-round for smoothies, coffee, pastry, and gourmet picnic baskets. More summer dining options (and winter too) are listed in the Deer Valley entry or at www.parkcityinfo.com. At the Canyons, lunch at Lookout Cabin, a sit-down venue with great views; Dreamscape Grill; or Doc's at the Gondola, all in winter. Have an elegant meal at the Cabin Restaurant or breakfast year-round at First Tracks Café, both in the lobby of the Grand Summit Hotel. Also year-round, the Island Café features Caribbean-style cuisine; it's located in Canyons Village. You probably need at least one trip to Park City to figure out all your favorite places!

**Children's World:** As with lodging and dining, a wide variety of options exists with programs for children. Comprehensive, in-one-spot winter and summer programs are found at Deer Valley; see the previous entry for details. Park City Mountain has a new Signature Ski/Board Program (800-227-2754), a unique small-group experience limited to three to five children. Divided by age and ability, your child will receive maximum attention from 9:00 a.m. to 3:00 p.m. daily, with lunch and lifts. Signature 3 (ages three to five) has a maximum of three children per instructor and includes two seventy-five minute sessions of ski instruction plus indoor activities ($130 to $145). Signature 5 takes ages six to fourteen exploring the mountain and developing skills in ski or snowboard classes of five students ($150 to $189).

At the Canyons, the Perfect Kids ski school (435-615-3449) uses a proven method to teach children either the rudiments or the fine points of skiing. Programs run from 9:15 a.m. to 3:15 p.m. but can be extended (8:00 a.m. to 4:30 p.m.) at the Day Care Center. Canyon Cubs for two- and three-year-olds combines day care with beginning skiing and snow play; $190 per day includes everything. Canyon Cats allows children ages four to six to enjoy an entire day of mostly skiing; depending on weather and each individual child, indoor games and care are also provided. Cost is $124 for lessons and lunch only, and $135 adds equipment and lift. Ages seven to fourteen, the Canyon Carvers, tackle the mountain on skis or snowboards; cost is $124 for lessons and lunch; $153 with equipment/lift. For ages six weeks to six years, the Little Adventures Children's Center (866-604-4170, 435-615-8036), a state-licensed Day Care Center in the Grand Summit Resort, has toys, books, and various age-appropriate activities. The center operates daily from 8:30 a.m. to 4:30 p.m.; rates are $95 for a full day with lunch, $75 for a half day.

Wachusett Summer Camp runs from mid-June to mid-August for ages six weeks to twelve years, Monday through Friday. Camps Hopi and Nova (up to age three) are $62 for a full day, $38 for a half day. Camps Jicarilla and Tiponi are $58 for a full day, $36 for a half day. Lunch and two snacks are included. Activities vary by age groups and might include hiking, gondola rides, arts and crafts, and swimming or water play.

Parents love for their children to have fun, and sometimes to share that fun. Park City offers lots of activities tailored specifically for kids. Depending on the time and length of your visit, Arts-Kids, Inc. (435-615-7878) offers four one-week art-in-nature camps for ages eight to twelve, sampling photography, mask making, poetry, break dancing—even field trips and the Alpine Slide. The Black Diamond Gymnastics & Sports Center (435-615-1800) has Monday through Saturday classes in gymnastics, trampoline, and tumbling for all ages, one year to adults. With more than twenty-five years of experience, the Norwegian Outdoor Exploration Center (800-649-5322) offers summer youth camps for ages six to seventeen years. Their credo, "Simply stated, we take people outdoors and have fun." Park City (www.parkcity-info.com) has multiple listings for hourly drop-in care, au pair and babysitting services, and special things for kids.

**Recreation:** The Visitor's Bureau boasts that "Nobody does winter like Park City." That could be so. Especially now, with the addition of Olympic Park, activities seem almost unlimited. With an average of 355 inches of snow annually, a ski season from mid-November to late April, and 3,300 acres of skiable terrain, including 104 runs and bowls, fourteen chairlifts, and 3,100 vertical feet, Park City is one of the largest Rocky Mountain ski resorts. Whether you ramble down gentle slopes past old mining buildings, take on the moguls between groves of aspen, or get knee-deep in powder, plenty of variety will keep you happy. There's even night skiing and riding, if you just can't get enough of the slopes. Wolf Mountain is another whole mountain just down the road. Skiing of all types—downhill, cross-country, helicopter, and snowcat; snowboarding, the jumps, luge, and bobsled run at Olympic Park; snowmobiling, hot-air ballooning, tubing, snowshoeing, ice-skating, sleigh rides—is anything missing? Indoors, there are day spas, fitness and health clubs, and massage. Year-round, a ride on the Heber Valley historic railroad along lakes and canyons, following the Provo River, is an exciting trip.

In summertime the clean mountain air, the plentiful wildflowers, and the great outdoors beckon you. Hiking, horseback riding, mountain biking, tennis, racquetball, golf, and bicycling are favorite warm-weather activities. Park City Mountain Resort has a mile-long listing of adventures for all ages, from the Little Miners Park with rides for the wee ones to Alpine slides, the legacy launcher (four—count them—four trampolines to bounce among), diggler scooters, a climbing wall, and the ZipRider, designed to strike fear into the hearts of all but the most extreme. Covering a distance of 2,300 feet with a vertical drop of 550 feet, 110 feet above the ski runs at speeds of up to 60 mph, it's the longest in the world. Tamer, but also fun, is the diversion of a stroll along Main Street; shops, restaurants, and a lively atmosphere are entertaining. And Salt

Lake City is less than 40 miles away, a good day trip. The Children's Museum of Utah is found here; it's a "hands-on, minds-on" place to explore, create, and imagine and is delightfully interactive.

P.O. Box 39
1310 Lowell Avenue
Park City, Utah 84060
(435) 658-5560, (800) 222-PARK (7275)
www.parkcitymountain.com

# SNOWBIRD SKI AND SUMMER RESORT
## Snowbird, Utah

Snowbird, along with Alta, have been named the "#1 Ski Resort in the U.S." by *Skiing* magazine for four years running. Snowbird's diverse terrain includes some of the most challenging skiing in the world. Yet surprisingly, the size of its intermediate, novice, and beginner areas is greater than the total terrain of many notable resorts. Every night more than half the slopes and trails are groomed, paving the way for beginner and intermediate skiers, while leaving the rest for those who seek the light, dry Utah powder. Whatever your proficiency and desire, Snowbird accommodates you with more than 2,500 acres of wide-open bowls, gladed tree runs, steep chutes, nightly groomed trails, and cruising boulevards. From the 500 acres of terrain on Mineral Basin to the terrific novice and intermediate terrain off the Baby Thunder Chair, you'll be amazed by the sheer excitement of skiing the "Bird."

More to know about Snowbird: a vertical rise of 3,240 continuously skiable feet; average annual snowfall of 500 inches; yes, 500 inches, and it's that "dry" Utah powder known worldwide. Snowbird enjoys one of the finest ski seasons in the world. Beginning in mid-November, the ski season regularly extends through mid-May. In fact, skiers have even been known to celebrate the Fourth of July on the slopes.

Snowbird offers ideal family vacations, with accolades from *Skiing* magazine and the Family Channel's Seal of Quality. Family Travel Forum selected Snowbird as one of the "Top Ten Getaways for Tiny Travelers."

**Accommodations:** A cozy slopeside pedestrian village, Snowbird harmonizes fittingly with the rugged, natural beauty of Little Cottonwood Canyon. And everything at the resort—accommodations, restaurants, shops, skiing, and activities—is within easy walking distance.

Snowbird has three distinctive condominium properties: the Inn, the Lodge at Snowbird, and the Iron Blosam Lodge. Each offers homelike features, such as fireplaces and kitchens; pools, saunas, exercise facilities, and other services are included or easily accessible. Snowbird's flagship accommodation, the Cliff Lodge and Cliff Club, offers easy ski-in, ski-out access along with North America's foremost Persian and Oriental rug collection. Three restaurants, two lounges, and the world-class Cliff Spa and Salon make it the perfect place to retire after an exhilarating day on the slopes.

Winter rates for a room in the lodge range from $189 to $389; summer rates drop to $79 to $169. One-bedroom condominiums with full kitchen are $279 to $569; two bedrooms are $409 to $869; summer rates are lower. Call Central Reservations at (800) 453-3000 to help find the best accommodations for your family. Also, the Web site has a helpful calendar of rates and availability.

**Dining:** The dining at Snowbird is diverse, with more than fifteen restaurants and lounges to please a variety of tastes and styles. Snowbird dining offers everything from Niçoise-style striped sea bass to mountain-grilled burgers to coconut beer-battered shrimp. The Aerie Restaurant is Snowbird's flagship of fine dining. Try the Lodge Bistro for cozy dinners, buffet, and the wonderful view from the Atrium, or great steaks at the Steak Pit. Casual dining is found at the Birdfeeder, El Chanate (Mexican), and Wildflower (Italian); and families enjoy the Forklift for breakfast and lunch, and, of course, Pier 49 Sourdough Pizza. The Rendezvous serves burgers and sandwiches, and Superior Snacks is just that. Children's menus are available at all sit-down restaurants. Find après-ski at the Aerie Lounge, Cantina, Wildflower Lounge, or Lodge Bistro Lounge; nightlife with weekly jazz at the Bird; and live music, dancing, pool, and thirteen TVs at the Tram Club. Again, the Web site is extremely clear, with listings for each time of day you may feel hunger pangs.

**Children's World:** From family ski zones to the Mini Mining Town kids trail, Snowbird is certain to please young skiers. And remember, on Snowbird only, children under six ski free, while up to two children seven to twelve ski the chairs for $10 . Tram upgrades are complimentary for nightly rate lodging guests; $15 for others.

Snowbird's youngest guests, six weeks to three years old, are well cared for in a safe, fun environment at Camp Snowbird, a state-licensed child-care facility where an open-door policy allows parents to drop in, with picture ID, of course. Registration is required at least two weeks in advance. A full day from 8:30 a.m. to 4:30 p.m. costs $90.

Day Care Camp for ages three to twelve includes snow play, arts and crafts, table games, and free play; lunch and snacks are included. A full day is $85; half day, morning or afternoon, is $70, only if available.

SMILE stands for Snowbird Mountain Integrated Learning Experience, and it's what happens at the ski school as kids gain confidence and skills on the mountain (801-933-2170). For three-year-olds, Chickadees has just the right mix of one-hour one-on-one lessons each session, snow play, and indoor play. Fee of $120 per half-day session includes lunch and equipment. Full day is $190, from 8:30 a.m. to 4:30 p.m. For Kinderbirds, ages four to six, the cost is $160 for a full day with lunch and supervision. It meets from 9:15 to 3:00 p.m. Seven- to twelve-year-olds join Mountain Adventures for fun in developing their skills on either skis or snowboards. Grouped by age and ability, the challenges are shared with peers. A full day from 9:15 a.m. to 3:00 p.m., including lunch, is $125. Snowbird is a Snow Monsters resort, so kids can expect to bump into them around the school (www.snowmonsters.com).

Wednesday and Saturday nights the Kids Club is open from 6:30 to 10:00 p.m. for kids ages four to six. Admission to the "nightclub" is $45 ($55 on Saturday) and includes dinner, entertainment, and craft projects. Adventures After Dark takes seven- to fifteen-year-olds out and about; even the most blasé are excited by the Zip Rider, snowshoe treks, pool parties, tubing, action movies, or ski and snowboard jaunts. Times and cost are the same as above. Babysitting in your room is available at $15 per hour, with a three-hour minimum.

Summer brings different activities for Camp Snowbird (ages four to twelve, $60,

$50 for second child). Kids explore the canyon with nature hikes and science experiments; work on sports skills and arts projects; and swim every day. Children are divided by age into groups of eight to ten campers. Open early June through late August, from 8:30 a.m. to 5:00 p.m.; all days must be preregistered (a one-time $25 fee) and campers get a T-shirt.

**Recreation:** Snowbird's Mountain Host program offers free guided skiing tours every day to acquaint guests with the runs and lifts best suited to their skiing abilities. All you need is a lift ticket and a smile to join the group and get better acquainted with the incredible mountain. Snowbird and Little Cottonwood Canyon neighbor Alta offer one lift ticket for both resorts. Made possible by Snowbird's second Mineral Basin chairlift, the Alta-Snowbird ticket provides two of the world's top resorts in one day of skiing.

Almost as famous as the snow, and every bit as great, is the ski school. More than 300 professional instructors offer all-day or by-the-hour private and group lessons. Or, if you want to take your vacation to new heights, try one of Snowbird's specialized seminars that address the specific interests and needs of women, seniors, snowboarders, and experts.

The Activity Center will fill you in on all that goes on: ice-skating, tubing, snowshoeing, and luging. Children must be twelve to book the luge sleds on Tuesday, Thursday, and Saturday evenings on Chickadee. Want to be the first to make tracks in all that powder? For $50 extra, expert skiers take the first tram with experienced guides, and history is made. Also on the agenda are night skiing, summit snowmobiling, back-country tours, swimming, and hot tubs to warm you up after all that snow. Cliff Spa at the Cliff Lodge has a staff of forty just waiting to pamper you. Evenings are filled with après-ski, live music, free ski and snowboard movies, or adventure lectures.

In summer the focus of activities is still on the great outdoors. Snowbird has tennis courts on-site; an extensive program is found at the Snowbird Canyon Racquet and Fitness Club, a short drive away, which offers ten indoor and thirteen outdoor tennis courts, racquetball and squash, yoga, and kickboxing, along with aerobics classes and a weight room. Golf is less than fifteen minutes away at the championship Old Mill golf course designed by Gene Bates. Another six courses are within a thirty- to forty-five-minute drive.

Try the Oriental rug tours, stargazing, and murder mystery dinner theater; or spend the day pampering yourself at the Cliff Spa. Off-site, you can visit the Winter Sports Park, tour Antelope Island, check out downtown Salt Lake City, or shop in Park City.

---

**P.O. Box 929000**
**Highway 210 Little Cottonwood Canyon**
**Snowbird, Utah 84092**
**(801) 742-2222, (800) 232-9542**
**www.snowbird.com**

# VAIL/BEAVER CREEK RESORTS
### Vail, Colorado

Lots of folks talk of Vail and Aspen in practically the same breath. Granted, several similarities between the two come to mind: Both rank right at the top in excellent skiing, both are high in the Rockies west of Denver, both are chic and sophisticated, and to both have been appended newer developments that are upscale and family friendly—Beaver Creek at Vail and Snowmass at Aspen.

Unlike Aspen's history as an old mining town, Vail grew up in the 1960s. The modern-day careful planning and systematic development based on European resorts give Vail its atmosphere; it is a well-laid-out, Alpine-style village designed with the pedestrian in mind (it's nice that so few cars spoil the scenery). Actually, there are three village areas at the base of Vail Mountain—Golden Peak, Lionshead, and Vail Village—each with its own lodging, restaurants, and facilities, and each within walking distance of base lifts. In practical terms, though, since each abuts the next, most folks think of the tripartite as one friendly town. Over the past ten years, Vail Resorts has spent $125 million improving Vail Mountain. Vail Village and Lionshead are now receiving the same attention. Construction began in spring 2005 with new lodging at Gore Creek Place and in Lionshead, The Arrabelle at Vail Square, a luxury RockResort. A new skier bridge connecting the mountain and the square is complete, and additional plans for the plaza include more shopping and dining, a larger ice-skating rink, and spiffy new facilities for skiers plus enhanced streetscapes and landscaping—Vail is on the move and is calling it Vail's New Dawn.

Beaver Creek is just 10 miles farther down the road. Opened in 1980, Beaver Creek, too, has been planned around a pedestrian village; in addition to the accommodations in the village, lodges and condominiums are tucked among the grand spruce trees on the mountain. Shuttle-bus lines service the Vail Valley, within each village and between mountain bases. A year-round resort area, the Vail Valley also boasts of its summer beauty and offers art and music festivals, hiking, mountain biking, and more from June through October.

**Accommodations:** Lodging at Vail can be right at the mountain base a couple of skips from the chairlift and dripping with amenities, or back a few paces and not so loaded with extras, or most economically, a shuttle ride away. Of course, these options are reflected in the rates. Vail Valley's Lodging Quality Assurance program is designed to provide guests with just that: information and quality assurance. A Platinum rating represents the finest accommodations; Gold is upscale, inviting, and stylish; Silver offers comfortable accommodations; and Bronze is acceptable, with no frills. The LQA ratings are for the rooms themselves, not location, costs, or amenities. Vail/Beaver Creek Central Reservations at (800) 525-2257 can help sort it all out for you. The Lodge at Vail is the closest to a ski-in, ski-out hotel in the village itself; additional Gold properties include Lionshead Inn, Lodge Tower, Lion Square Lodge, Manor Vail, and Christiania. Vail Visitor Services at (800) 525-3875 also can assist with reservations and information, or go to www.vail.com.

With deluxe accommodations and a car-free village, Beaver Creek is a favorite of families. The Park Hyatt, Trappers Lodge, the Inn at Beaver Creek, the Pines Lodge, and Beaver Creek Lodge (all suites) are all beautiful ski-in, ski-out village-based properties. The Park

Hyatt offers Camp Hyatt, their own daily, year-round child-care program for ages three to twelve (970-949-1234). The Ritz Carlton also has their own program for children, called The Ritz Kids (970-748-6200), for ages five through twelve. The Charter at Beaver Creek and loads of condominiums and townhomes offer a wide range of lodging and amenities. Nearby Arrowhead and Bachelor Gulch also offer ski-in, ski-out options. Beaver Creek supplies complimentary shuttle service between areas. Call (800) 427-8308 or (888) 830-7669, or visit www.beavercreek .com for more information and reservations.

Winter is divided into value season (late November to December 21 and again in April), regular season (January 5 to mid-February), and high season (Christmas and mid-February to early April). Summer rates can be as much as 50 percent lower than winter rates. Discounts for children are just about universal, and package plans are often a good value. The "Travel Deals" section of www.vail.com offers guests lodging discounts, and more than 150 properties in the Vail Valley are listed with Vail/Beaver Creek Central Reservations at (800) 427-8308.

**Dining:** Hungry for a hamburger? Eager to savor a juicy steak? Or is Mexican fare your idea of the perfect après-ski dinner? In the Vail Valley all this is possible, plus Italian, Asian, French, German, and, of course, American food. With more than 110 restaurants and bars, there are lots of choices. Many restaurants are right in the lodges, such as the Lodge at Vail, Lion Square Lodge, the Landmark, and the Charter at Beaver Creek. Others are in the villages at the base of the lifts or in the pedestrian areas. Larkspur, at the base of Golden Peak, is listed by *USA Today* as a "don't miss while in Vail."

More restaurants are on the mountains and not just quick, cafeteria-style mountainside rest stops: Some hit gourmet standards. Whenever weather permits, outdoor

barbecues are planned at the midmountain points. Many of the restaurants have children's menus—just ask.

**Children's World:** Vail and Beaver Creek both have similar high-quality programs for children. Prices and hours may vary slightly, and reservations are highly recommended for both. At Beaver Creek and at Golden Peak in Vail, the Small World Play School entertains little ones two months to six years old from 8:00 a.m. to 4:30 p.m. daily. The toddlers and preschoolers enjoy games, songs, crafts, and indoor and outdoor play in a colorful nursery/schoolhouse atmosphere. Separate playrooms for ages two to eighteen months, nineteen to thirty months, and preschoolers offer closer supervision. The cost varies by season: from $87 to $97 at Vail, and from $97 to $107 at Beaver Creek. Beaver Creek has half-day sessions from noon to 4:00 p.m. if space is available. At Vail, afternoon child care from 12:30 to 4:30 p.m. costs $65 to $72. For an additional fee Vail offers a thirty-minute ski/snow-play program for toddlers twenty months and older. For more information, contact Small World at Vail at (970) 479-3285 or Beaver Creek at (970) 845-5325.

For guests only, the Park Hyatt at Beaver Creek has its own Camp Hyatt children's program for ages three to twelve, with activities offered daily from 9:00 a.m. to 10:00 p.m. when the mountain is open. Indoor and outdoor play (nonskiing) are featured, and kids can attend for an hour, the evening, or an entire day. The price is $16 per hour; lunch or dinner is $10 additional. Spring and fall, Camp Hyatt may be available but "on-call," and reservations must be made twenty-four hours in advance (970-949-1234; www.beavercreek.hyatt.com).

Youngsters ages five to twelve years staying at the Ritz Carlton can join the Ritz Kids, a daily program in winter and summer season. Hours are 8:00 a.m. to 4:00 p.m., with full-day sessions for $125, mornings only at $60, and afternoon with lunch for $75. From 4:00 to 6:00 p.m. is Munchies and Movies ($18), and then Kids Night Out runs from 6:00 to 10:00 p.m. with dinner included for $75. Kids have a great time with the themed activities such as talent shows or secret agents. A nice bonus is socializing with Bachelor, the dog. Children under five are welcome to join the sessions with an adult or babysitter, at half price. Children may also attend for hourly sessions ($18) when the activities are on-site (970-748-6200; www .ritzcarlton.com/resorts/bachelor_gulch/).

The Children's Ski and Snowboard Center operates out of three locations—Lionshead, Golden Peak, and the Village Hall at Beaver Creek (convenient no matter where you're staying!) and divides children into groups (three- to six-year-olds and seven- to twelve-year-olds for skiing and up to fourteen for snowboards) for daily lessons from 8:00 a.m. to 4:00 p.m. Both groups have some indoor activities as well as skiing; the older children's schedule concentrates more on skiing. At Vail, programs are $103 to $139, depending on the season, and include lesson and lunch. Lift tickets are free to age five; youths pay $17. Snowboarding lessons are available for ages seven to fourteen; cost is the same. At Beaver Creek, programs are $114 to $153. More information on both children's programs is available at (970) 476-3239 (Vail) or (970) 845-5464 (Beaver Creek). Teens can meet new friends, explore the mountain, and perfect their ski and snowboard skills at Vail. Lesson only is $120; lesson/all mountain/lift is $147. Simply "too cool for school."

Adventure Zones are special areas on the slopes designed just for kids. Chaos Canyon has bumps, jumps, twists, and tunnels. At others, an old fort, a tepee village, and ancient Indian burial ground await exploration. On Tuesday, Wednesday, and Thurs-day, Night Owls provides a supervised evening of fun at Adventure Ridge. Seven- to twelve-year-olds enjoy dinner and activities atop Vail Mountain from 4:30 to 8:30 p.m. during regular season ($62).

In summer Small World Play School is at Beaver Creek only and starts at two months of age with infant and toddler programs, and special minicamp programs for four- and five-year olds. Hours are Monday through Friday from 8:30 a.m. to 4:30 p.m.

The town of Vail has many programs for youths, open to all (www.vailrec.com). Imagination Station, in Lionshead, is an interactive museum for children ages two to twelve, operating select hours during winter and summer. Admission is $5 per child; free for adults and infants. Children three and older can stay with staff for fun activities ($10 per hour; three hours maximum). Kids Nights Out are also scheduled—check with them at (970) 479-2292. Camp Vail operates from Red Sandstone Elementary, Monday through Friday, from mid-June to mid-August. The Pre-Kamp for ages thirty months to pre-kindergarten balances the desire for fun with the limits on "little legs and big spirits." A 6:1 ratio ensures individual attention, and it's structured around a weekly theme. Hiking, gondola rides, tours of local businesses, and arts and crafts fill the day from 8:00 a.m. to 5:00 p.m.; the cost is $65 daily or $300 for five days.

Camp Vail, for ages five (and entering kindergarten) to twelve, runs from 7:30 a.m. to 5:30 p.m. and utilizes the whole Vail Valley for fun. Enthusiastic young counselors guide kids in a variety of activities that they can often choose, and Friday is a wild card, break-out day. Ratio is 12:1, and the cost is $62 per day or $290 per week. Campers participate in caving, orienteering, swimming, golf, fishing, and climbing as well as art, drama, and nature discovery. On Friday in July and August, Extreme Adventure

Camp offers an extra bit of excitement. Rock climbing, rafting, river tubing, caving, and amusement and water parks challenge youths ages eight to thirteen years. Fee is $20 to $40 in addition to Camp Vail. Call (970) 479-2290 for details.

At Beaver Creek, Discovery Camp ($80) is for ages five to seven; and Adventure Camp ($90) for ages eight to twelve. Pony rides, canoeing, panning for gold, river rafting, mountain biking, ropes course, and miniature golf are some of the activities, all geared toward each age group. Field trips and special evening activities are also planned. Camp runs Monday through Friday, 8:00 a.m. to 4:30 p.m. For a true Rocky Mountain adventure, the 5-Star Camp ($95) for ages five to twelve, with age restrictions on some activities, does more unusual activities such as kayaking, rock climbing, Jeep tours, horseback riding, or go-karts. Call (970) 845-5464 for details and reservations.

**Recreation:** The name of the game is skiing, and the Vail Valley has all the ingredients for an excellent ski holiday. In the middle of the White River National Forest, Vail Mountain rises to 11,570 feet; at Beaver Creek the summit is 11,440 feet. The vertical drop is more than 3,450 feet at Vail and 4,040 feet at Beaver Creek. An average annual snowfall between 300 and 350 inches (and an artificial snowmaking system) accounts for a season lasting from late November to mid-April.

Vail and Beaver Creek skiable terrain totaling more than 6,900 acres (lift tickets for the two mountains are interchangeable) provides variety for all levels of skiers, from gentle beginner slopes to challenging intermediates to exciting mogul and bowl skiing. Vail's Blue Sky Basin provides a unique wilderness ski experience, featuring 645 acres of natural, gladed terrain in two world-class bowls.

In addition to the typical group and private lessons for all ability levels, the Vail/Beaver Creek Ski School offers free classes with videotaped analysis and high-powered workshops in mogul and powder skiing. Meet the Mountain introductory tours are scheduled daily; this is a morning ski tour with guest-services staff who acquaint you with the area's history and topography. Or enroll in lessons in cross-country skiing, which is so refined here that distinctions are made between backcountry skiing, telemark skiing, and track skiing.

Other wintertime sports include ice skating at Dobson Ice Arena, Black Family Rink in Beaver Creek, or Nottingham Lake; snowmobiling at Piney Lake; and ice fishing. Snowcat tours to above 10,000 feet offer spectacular views, and if you can walk, you can snowshoe, for an up-close view of winter. The Colorado Ski Museum is here, or relax in one of the three cinemas. An evening outing in a horse-drawn sleigh may be the right way to finish off a perfect day, or enjoy a brisk horseback ride in the snow. Indoor evening entertainment includes nightclubs and movie theaters; favorite haunts for kids are the video arcades, the Game Garage Arcade, and the Vail Youth Center.

Even after the last skier comes down the mountain in late spring, fun in the Vail Valley continues. As in the winter, summertime activities focus on the beautiful outdoors. Hiking through stands of aspens along the trail systems up Vail Mountain and Beaver Creek Mountain, biking on paths through wildflowers, and fishing in mountain streams get you back to nature. Ride horseback at Eagle Ranch, Beaver Creek Stables, and Piney River Ranch, or muster your courage for river rafting.

Vail Valley has thirteen golf courses, suited to all abilities and pocketbooks. Some are public, some are private or semiprivate, and some are connected to various lodging in the Valley. You're sure to find the one that's just right for your skills. With 300 days of sunshine each year, tennis shines here. For a little Mozart with your game, schedule one of the free Ford Park courts at concert time. Fancy a spa experience? There are at least ten in the area, including the natural Yampah Spa and Vapor Caves in nearby Glenwood Springs. And Beaver Creek hosts weekly rodeos—great fun for the whole family.

Summer Adventure Ridge starts with a scenic ride on the Eagle Bahn Gondola to the Ridge, where you can spend the entire day. In addition to laser tag, trampoline, orienteering, hiking, disc golf, sledding, guided tours, and mountain bikes, the kids can even hunt for buried bones at the Dino Dig. Cost varies for each activity. The Ridge is open select dates June to September; it is also open in winter, with different activities. The Discovery Center, at the top of the Eagle Bahn Gondola, teaches about our environment through fun, interactive displays and nature hikes. The seven-acre Vail Nature Center is a favorite place for birds and wildflowers and to sample a wide variety of programs. Cultural events are plentiful: the Arts Festival in June, Vail Valley Music Festival all summer, International Dance, and the Vail Jazz Festival in August. At Beaver Creek, the Vilar Center for the Arts has children's theater, stand-up comedy, Broadway shows, and musicals. Free movie nights for kids twelve and under, plus costume contests add to the fun. Sunday afternoons, Vail Valley chefs demonstrate their skills.

Hot summer nights come alive at Vail Valley—actually, the entertainment is hot, not the weather. Hot Summer Nights concert series are on Tuesday night, with covered seating and picnics allowed. Gondola rides are free on Friday after 5:00 p.m. to Eagle's Nest on the top of Vail Mountain; drink specials, games, free live music on the deck, and the best sunset views are all here. Add piano bars, live music venues, sports bars, and dance clubs to the mix; and for the younger crowd, pool, foosball, music, and movies. For a weekly entertainment schedule, check the Web, or kiosks and flyers in the Village. All in all, Vail/Beaver Creek is a tasty resort!

---

**Vail, Colorado 81658**
**(800) 525-2257, (800) 525-3875**
**www.beavercreek.snow.com**
**www.vail.snow.com**

# WEST

California
Idaho
Nevada
Oregon
Wyoming

# THE ALISAL GUEST RANCH AND RESORT

Solvang, California

Okay, so cattle ranches are not the first thing that comes to mind when you think of southern California or Solvang. Nevertheless, it is the West, and at least one does exist. In the Santa Ynez Valley of southern California is a real working cattle ranch—the Alisal (from the Chumash Indian word meaning "grove of sycamores"). Some things just don't change—cattle have been grazing here for almost 200 years, and century-old sycamore trees line the private entrance road. Some sixty years ago the current owner's father, a cattleman himself, decided to open the ranch to guests. Today visitors enjoy the atmosphere of an active ranch with the facilities of a resort on this 10,000-acre spread. This is California, after all, so one would expect golf, tennis, first-class accommodations, fine dining, and wine tasting, along with horses and wranglers. And that indeed is what the Alisal delivers. Named a "Family Resort of the Year" by *Family Circle; Sunset Magazine* also ranked it one of the "50 Best Dude Ranches in the West." Only forty minutes from Santa Barbara and two hours from Los Angeles, the Alisal is a welcome haven to harried city-dwellers that is open year-round.

**Accommodations:** In classic California ranch design, seventy-three cottages accommodating up to 200 guests are clustered near the swimming pool and tennis courts or overlooking the golf course. Either studios or two-room suites, all have a wood-burning fireplace, covered front porch, flower gardens in front, and refrigerators. There are no in-room telephones or television—how relaxing! Suites offer a sitting room and soaring ceilings. Based on double occupancy and a Modified American Plan, studio rates are $465 to $510 daily; two-room suites are $525 to $595. Children two and under stay free, ages three through six are $55, and six years and older are $85. Cribs are $15 per night. There's a two-night minimum, and Saturday check-ins are not allowed. Weekdays between early September and early June, a Round-Up vacation package is offered. For the price of a room, the Alisal includes unlimited golf, horseback riding (two-hour rides), tennis, and fishing for two people. The package is also available weekends from November through March.

**Dining:** The Ranch Room serves breakfast from 7:00 to 10:00 a.m. (a lavish buffet or a la carte) and gourmet dinners from a ten-item menu that changes every evening. Dinner is a dress-up affair; jackets are required for gentlemen sixteen and older (ties optional), and ladies and children dress appropriately for fine dining. Reservations are requested. Parents with small children are encouraged to have dinner early, before the peak hours. Children's menus are available on request. Alisal requests that children's behavior be monitored, especially at meals. In all fairness, they request the same of people with cell phones! Lunch is not included in the room rate but can be ordered from the Chuckwagon Grill (poolside snack bar) or at the Ranch Course Grill (open from 11:30 a.m. to 3:00 p.m.) on the golf course. The River Grill is also a public restaurant, open daily for breakfast, lunch, and dinner. You may also order a box lunch. In summer you can saddle up early for a breakfast ride to Adobe Camp or enjoy a haywagon ride to your breakfast. Try the seafood barbecue at the lake or a Cal-Mex barbecue at the rodeo arena in the evening. Saturday brings an all-ranch barbecue at the pool lawn. The Oak Room Lounge, an inviting room with a large fireplace, is decorated with warm colors, rustic Western artifacts, and Native American–style rugs. Open at 4:00 p.m., cocktails and complimentary appetizers are served, and stories of the day's activities are shared. It's adults-only after 9:00 p.m., with live entertainment and dancing that begins at 6:30 p.m. During the summer and holidays, the Waggin' Tongue Lounge by the pool is open daily from 11:30 a.m. to 4:00 p.m. and reopens at 8:30 p.m. after the Saturday night barbecue. The General Store is happy to deliver snacks, beverages, wine, beer, and other goodies to your room.

**Children's World:** All summer long and at holiday times, counselors conduct an active schedule of arts and crafts, scavenger hunts, volleyball, hikes, croquet, and other outdoor games.

From age seven and up, children can participate in horseback riding on the trail rides ($75 per ride) or in private lessons. Younger children get corral rides and equestrian-care lessons ($30). Everyone learns more about ranch animals at the Alisal Barn Yard. Children's golf and tennis lessons are also available. Tennis lessons are given for ages five to fourteen, twice a week for a half hour. Young Tigers golf lessons are also twice a week for a half hour for ages seven to sixteen. Children love the private lake, where they can participate in fishing, boating, or canoeing. Summer evenings may include campfires with sing-alongs and stories, which are always better at the lake setting. A Family Rodeo is staged weekly in the summer—this is every kid's dream of being a cowboy come true. After watching wranglers perform, they get to participate in branding (on leather or wood), roping, and rodeo-style games; a Western barbecue completes the evening.

The arts-and-crafts room is open daily year-round from 9:30 a.m. to 5:30 p.m., where activities are ongoing. One-hour activities such as disc golf, chalk art, relay races and lawn games, dodge ball or kick ball, face painting, and various water games are scheduled during the day—children can drop in and out as they are interested in the activity.

L'il Wrangler Club has afternoon sessions (1:00 to 4:00 p.m.) for children ages four to ten, on Tuesday and Thursday from mid-June to the end of August; cost is $25 per session. There's a price reduction for two children. Activities include indoor and outdoor fun. Ages four to six are grouped together, as are ages seven to ten, and may have the same activity, such as Fish Fun, but each suited to their age; for example, the older children will go boating on the lake while younger ones fish from the shore. Wacky Water Days, on Thursday, are for everyone. Kiddie Korral is the ranch's program for children ages three to five and is offered Sunday through Friday from 6:00 to 9:00 p.m. for dinner and evening fun ($25 per child). Kids ages six to ten have their nature cookouts, a pool bash, barbecues, and movies.

Tweens (eleven to twelve years old) share some things, like movies, but have their own dinner activities at the Chuckwagon Grill, lake, or Adobe Camp as well. Late night they may have bingo, talent shows, country dancing, or an adventure at the Adobe Camp. The summertime activities for teens involve their favorite things: eating, music, movies, and sports. Teens have their own section of the weekly barbecue dinner events, plus off-property movies, late-night campfires, or movies at the ranch.

During the winter the arts and activities room is open from 10:00 a.m. to 4:00 p.m., but supervision is intermittent. Golf, tennis, and horseback-riding lessons fill in the other times. Children's and family activities are scheduled on holidays, but less frequently than in the summer. Check the daily program. Some are complimentary; others have a fee, such as archery, creative beading, or guided mountain biking.

**Recreation:** Most recreational activities at Alisal have fees. Family Times allow sharing of two-hour nature walks, archery, a ropes course, and crafts such as tie-dye and creative beading. Evening entertainment begins at 8:30 or 9:00 p.m. Family bingo, talent night, storytelling, country dancing, and more are offered. Tweens and teens have their own programs. Kids and family activities are pretty much nonstop from early morning to late night, with lots of choices. A daily recreation guide is placed in each room.

Be sure to saunter over to the barn to be matched with the perfect mount for the twice-daily trail rides ($75 per two-hour ride). A breakfast ride is offered three times a week in summer, twice a week during the rest of the year. On summer evenings (Tuesday and Thursday), extend the day with evening rides from 5:00 to 7:00 p.m., or participate in the weekly summer rodeo. More than 50 miles of trails meander through oak and sycamore groves in the rolling hills and along the lake. Wranglers are happy to share a bit of advice about riding, information about the ranch, or maybe even some tall tales along the way.

Trading trails for tees, the gently rambling fairways of two eighteen-hole golf courses are graced with eucalyptus as well as oak and sycamore trees and occasionally a deer or two. Each of the two championship golf courses, the River Course and the Ranch Course, has distinct characteristics shaped by its unique terrain. The driving range, putting green, and practice trap can keep you so busy you'll ride off into the sunset on a golf cart rather than a horse! The resident pro and the pro shop can help with anything from lessons to new equip-

ment. On the tennis courts (seven in all, located in one of the most scenic areas of the ranch), you're likely to find a good game from 8:00 a.m. to 5:30 p.m., and the resident pro conducts private and group lessons.

If your interests are more wet-and-wild, you might swim in the large outdoor heated pool (certain times for adults only) or head to the lake and hop on board a sailboat, rowboat, paddleboat, canoe, or kayak. Even beginners find lots of enjoyment in the sailing and fishing lessons offered. The spring-fed lake—man-made, but mature and encompassing one hundred acres—is stocked with bass, bluegill, and catfish, much to the delight of every angler. A catch-and-release policy protects the fish.

Mornings bring yoga, Pilates, and aqua exercise for those energetic people over sixteen. After riding, golfing, playing tennis, swimming, sailing, and fishing, you can always jog, bicycle, join a guided nature walk, play volleyball, badminton, horseshoes, shuffleboard, croquet, or bocci ball, or take on the new challenge course. Tired yet? Indoors you might play pool or table tennis in the recreation room or relax in the adults-only library with a good book or board game by the fireplace. Be sure to save energy for the evenings, filled with square dancing, cookouts, and movies as well. Every summer Wednesday brings a country fair and rodeo. And strolling through the quaint town of Solvang is always a treat. You are in wine country, so enjoy a tour of the vineyards, a little wine tasting, and the spectacular beauty of the Santa Ynez Valley.

---

**1054 Alisal Road**
**Solvang, California 93463**
**(805) 688-6411, (800) 4-ALISAL**
**www.alisal.com**

# COFFEE CREEK RANCH

## Trinity Center, California

Coffee Creek Ranch, northern California's only three-diamond dude ranch, is located approximately 300 miles north of San Francisco. Surrounded by National Forest and the Trinity Alps Wilderness Area, the ranch covers 367 acres along Coffee Creek and is home to wranglers and dudes alike. In 1877 Old Charley Henseley staked three claims along Coffee Creek; in 1900 he lost them all in a poker game to Ben Pinkham for $1. Mrs. Pinkham started a boardinghouse for the miners, and it all began then, evolving into a dude ranch in 1946. The ranch has been in the Hartman family since 1976, being handed down to the next generation, current owner/managers Alicia and Shane Ryan. Alicia and Shane are parents of young children themselves, and they've made their ranch into a truly family-friendly place.

Whether you are an old pro at horseback riding or a greenhorn mounting up for the first time, the ranch hands will ensure that your horse and your excursion match your abilities. You can roam this territory all day long or ease into your new cowboy lifestyle more slowly with a half-hour lesson or a two-hour trail ride. Coffee Creek Ranch is open from Easter to Thanksgiving.

**Accommodations:** The sixteen cozy cottages are scattered among the trees, both in the central ranch house area and in the Grove, along the creek; some of the paths may be a little steep. Rustic on the outside, modern on the inside, each cottage is decorated according to its name: Circle B has butterflies, bears, and Bigfoot, A is for apples, Flying F is a fishing motif, and the Branding Iron has a wall of brands. Many have wood stoves; all have decks or patios. Spring and fall are geared toward adults; kids are welcome, although there's no specific program or activities for them. In summer, however, families rule. One-week stays are required, beginning on Saturday. Per-person rates for a one-bedroom are $1,175 for adults ($1,057.50 for ages fifty-five and up, a nice touch), teens are $1,155, children three to twelve are $1,055, and the under-three set is $360. Infants under one year stay free. Cribs, playpens, and highchairs are also complimentary. Satellite TV is in the main lodge only. The rates increase by only $10 to $20 per person for two-bedrooms, so book early! Rates include your private cabin in the woods, daily maid service, three meals daily, all activities and entertainment, the children's program—just about everything except horseback riding, which has extra fees in the summer. A two-hour ride is $40, breakfast and picnic rides are $45, a half-day ride is $50, an all-day ride is $85, gymkana is $25, and the overnight pack trip is $150. Now, here's the real deal: A weekly rate of $350 gives you all rides (at least four hours daily) *and* the overnight trip! Junior riders, ages six to eleven, receive one complimentary lesson. Friday is departure day, and the horses' day off.

**Dining:** The food at Coffee Creek is outstanding. Recognizing the healthy appetites that fresh air and exercise can generate, the main dining room serves up hearty, nutritious meals with fresh fruit and vegetables, Black Angus beef, and homemade bread from old family recipes. Dining is family style, so you get to meet your fellow guests, and of course the children strike up immediate friendships. Wednesday nights bring a six-course menu with accompanying wines; outdoor barbecues and poolside cookouts are fun events while Mexican and Italian buffets please everyone. For an adventure, ride out to a cowboy breakfast or a picnic on the trail. Beer and wine are served in the Pony Room.

**Children's World:** The youth program is also quite flexible. For all ages, it's included in the rates, daily from 9:00 a.m. to 5:00 p.m. However, counselors are usually around and available as needed. For instance, if you're going on an early morning trail ride, they will take your kids as early as 7:30 a.m. On its fun-filled schedule are archery, nature walks, pedalboating, gold panning, games, and crafts. Ages three to five are designated Cowboys and Cowgirls and get free pony rides, playtime with the Corral Critters (rabbits, lambs, pigs), lawn games, and story time. Junior Wranglers, for ages six to eleven, branch out into paddleboats, swimming in the creek, fishing in the pond, and one free horse clinic. Bronc Busters (twelve- to seventeen-year-olds) get to do it all plus their own special roping lessons, overnight campout, orienteering, rifle and trap shoot instruction, plus hiking to the lake. Although there's no formal program in the evening, counselors are generally present at the evening family activities. For children under three, care is provided during the day. If additional babysitting is required, you can make arrangements for $7.50 an hour.

**Recreation:** Saddle up and head into the wilderness for an all-day or a two-hour ride. You'll venture up into the mountains and through the wooded landscape along a clear fresh stream; maybe you'll spot a deer or a bear. Even "dudes" will soon experience the friendly spirit of a trail ride. Riding is included in spring and fall; a fee is charged in summer.

Try your hand at fishing; you've a choice of stream, river, pond, lake, or wilderness—fly fishing or bait casting. The locals say that Coffee Creek yields up some mighty fine trout, so an afternoon with rod and reel may turn into a fresh-fish supper. If fishing's not for you, how about panning for gold in the creek? Perhaps you'll test your keen eye on the archery or rifle range. Hiking trips are an option, and mountain bike trails run through the wilderness area. When not out and about, enjoy the heated swimming pool, volleyball, shuffleboard, basketball, or pedal boating. A small cottage houses various games; kids under eighteen need to be accompanied by an adult. Doing a lovely bit of nothing is also an option—just let the mountain air work its magic.

Evenings are lively at the ranch, with more activities than days of the week. Hayrides, bonfires, dancing, bingo and talent shows, karaoke and a live band, and even a rodeo liven things up after dark.

If you have the time and energy to leave this idyllic ranch, venture out to gold mines and museums, a winery, a National Scenic Byway, historic Weaverville, Hodges Cabin, or Joss House State Park.

---

**HC 2, Box 4940**
**Trinity Center, California 90961**
**(530) 266-3343, (800) 624-4480**
**www.coffeecreekranch.com**

# HOTEL DEL CORONADO

## San Diego, California

Soft sand, endless sunshine, surfing . . . California beaches do conjure up an image. The Travel Channel chose Coronado as the best beach for families and named the Hotel del Coronado as the "main attraction." And so it is. Here you'll find 18 miles of broad beach, a boardwalk, a 15-mile bike trail along Glorietta Bay, and, at the center, the magnificent Victorian hotel that is San Diego's most famous landmark. Set on twenty-eight acres, it's southern California's only beachfront hotel, strange as that sounds. From its beginning in 1888, the Del has become legendary, visited by celebrities, presidents, princes, and plain people. Rand McNally recognized the Hotel del Coronado for enjoying "more fame and historical significance than perhaps any hotel in North America," and the Del is a National Historic Landmark. The Del is very proud of its history and offers lots of tips to include this history in your vacation. Before your trip, visit the Web site for lots of insider information, or go to your library for books on the area and the era when the hotel was built. Kids love the fact that in the 1890s people spent months at a time vacationing at the Del. Even your teen might like the Web site article "Before There Were Teens," a brief history of teens from then until now. During your visit, take part in the special historical programs offered, talk with hotel employees, seek out those vintage spots for photographs, and be sure to check the gift shop for *The Loveliest Hotel You Can Imagine,* a collection of actual letters from a real girl, Noel, who stayed here in 1892 for three months. Beautifully illustrated with original watercolors, it's a delightful memento of your stay. If you're movie fans, *Some Like It Hot* was filmed here. And of course, there's a resident ghost. In 1892 a beautiful young girl, Kate Morgan, checked in—and never checked out. History can be fun here.

Founded in 1769, San Diego is California's oldest city and the first settlement for twenty-one Franciscan missions established along the coast. But it's not all about the past. Today, San Diego is a great vacation spot, with excellent weather, a vibrant downtown, and many attractions for families. And to its credit, the Del has also come into the twenty-first century well equipped to make your vacation a delightful experience. Coronado means "the crowned one," certainly very fitting in view of the multiple accolades the hotel has received: "Top 10 Resorts in the World," *USA Today;* "500 Greatest Hotels in the World," *Travel + Leisure;* "Top 100 U.S. Resorts," *Travel + Leisure Magazine Readers Poll;* "Best Resort Getaway," *Los Angeles Magazine;* "Best Resort in San Diego," *Orange County Register Readers Poll* and *Travel + Leisure en Español;* and finally, "Top 15 Family Resorts," *Travel + Leisure Family Magazine* and "America's 10 Best Family Resorts," *Family Life Magazine.*

**Accommodations:** A wide range of rooms exist; rates are based on size and view. Rooms in the Victorian building are charming and traditional, blending nineteenth-century elegance with modern comforts. The Ocean Towers and California Cabana rooms are more contemporary, with ocean-themed decor. Recently remodeled, all 679 rooms have all the usual amenities. All three areas contain rooms and suites from small (200 square feet) to large (more than 600 square feet), from no view to full oceanfront view. Premium options allow you to upgrade within a category: Victorian, Resort, Premier, and Suites. Rates, as always, are variable but begin at $395 for a resort room with no view or $610 for an oceanfront view. Children under eighteen stay free in the room, and there is a $22 per room per day resort fee. With a three-night minimum, a summer Beat the Heat package begins at $335 per night and gives a $150 credit to use during your stay. Bed-and-Breakfast packages start at $285 (weekdays) and $325 (weekends) per night and include accommodations and breakfast buffet for two adults at Sheerwater. A Spa package (two-night minimum) begins at $350 per night and includes a $175 spa credit. The Best of San Diego package (starting at $1,210) includes four nights' lodging; two adult admissions to Sea World, the Zoo, and Wild Animal Park; plus a welcome gift.

**Dining:** The Crown Room is an experience in itself. Designed by Wizard of Oz author L. Frank Baum, the chandeliers, in keeping with the name, are glowing crowns. Windows circle the room, with amazing California views. All in all, it's a delightful setting for the award-winning Sunday brunch. For oceanfront dining and giant fireplaces, Sheerwater serves breakfast, lunch, cocktails, light fare, and dinner daily. Regional specialties, an exhibition oven, and an innovative children's menu make this a favorite with families—and those views! Open nightly for dinner, 1500 Ocean is the newest addition. Casually elegant and completely California, it features Southland Coastal cuisine, a signature glass sunset-hued wall, and terrace seating overlooking the Pacific. During the day, stop by the Bakery for coffee and pastries. Seasonally, the poolside Splash Bar, the Boardwalk Café, and the Cabana Bar (right on the beach) all feature light fare and tropical drinks. The Sun Deck Bar & Grill has great views and seasonal live entertainment.

Named for the hotel's founders, the Babcock and Story Bar is also an oceanfront setting for wine, drinks, and light fare.

**Children's World:** Fun is planned for children of all ages, and it's cool enough that even teenagers join in. Tent City was the center of most activities from 1900 to the 1940s, and the tradition carries over for children. Tent City Kids' Camp for ages four to twelve operates year-round, Tuesday through Saturday. Throughout the day, Kids' Crafts offers one-hour programs featuring, you guessed it, crafts. Cost is $15 per hour, and children may pick and choose the activity that interests them. Supervised camp programs are on Saturday from 12:30 to 3:30 p.m. and every evening from 6:30 to 9:30 p.m. Kids may make binoculars and then go on a safari through the grounds, have sand-castle competitions or seashore scavenger hunts, or fly kites. Cost is $45 and includes dinner. Surfing lessons with wetsuit and board for ages six and up are $80 in a group or $105 private. The whole family likes Sunday S'mores, with a beach bonfire. In summer and holiday times, more activities are available, like *Radical Reptiles and Friends,* a live show.

The Coast Club Teen Lounge is the Del's spot strictly for teens, ages twelve to seventeen. The Coast Club features video games, foosball, food and drinks, music, TVs, omnipresent and essential-to-life computers, and the chance for teens to meet. The Coast Club is open throughout the summer and during the holidays. The Del is actively wooing teens with year-round biking tours, surfing lessons, boogie boards, and volleyball. MooTime Creamery is a popular gathering spot. "The Teen Survival Guide" lists suggestions for activities such as Flick and Float (a movie viewed from an inner tube in the pool) and bike or boat rentals. It's all very loose but identified as being for teens. The Spa offers special facials for teens, and, of course, all the shops attract them like bees to honey. Coronado Island offers several surf and skate shops, plus fun apparel stores; Orange Avenue and the Ferry Landing also feature dozens of eclectic eateries for hanging out. A world-class skate park is irresistible to aficionados of the sport. What's not here for them?

**Recreation:** A full-time recreation center has you covered for just about any activity. Beach chairs are complimentary. Everything else can be rented: boards, wetsuits, umbrellas, or cabanas. This is California, so surfing lessons are practically required, and you must make a regular appearance on the beach. Explore Coronado Island by bike on your own or take the two-hour Coronado on Wheels Bike Tour. Rent a kayak, paddleboat, sailboat, or water ski next door at the Boathouse. Golfers simply cross the street to the Coronado Municipal Golf Course for a putting green, a driving range, and an eighteen-hole course. Or you may wish to stroll

the lush gardens, take fitness classes, or join a yoga session on the beach, and then relax by one of the two pools or the hot tub with a summer novel. Of course, you'll want to take advantage of your oceanfront location. A sunset sail tops the day off nicely. San Diego is a great destination for families. Sea World, the world-famous San Diego Zoo, Birch Aquarium, Wild Animal Park, and Balboa Park are worthwhile attractions. Just across the bridge, downtown San Diego offers hundreds of trendy cafes and shops in the historic Gaslamp Quarter, Seaport Village, and Horton Plaza. And Old Mexico is just a ninety-minute train ride and a short border crossing away.

---

**1500 Orange Avenue**
**Coronado, California 92118**
**(619) 435-6611, (800) HOTEL-DEL**
**www.hoteldel.com**

# LA COSTA RESORT AND SPA
## Carlsbad, California

Everyone should have at least one spa experience in their life. La Costa is a luxurious resort, a serious spa, and somewhat of a legend. In fact, it was the first establishment to revive the spa regimen as Americans became more health-conscious in the 1960s. Today you can pursue a program of exercise and sound nutrition, redefining your lifestyle after years of sedentary executive matters; or you can indulge in a program of sheer pampering, relieving the stress and tensions of the everyday world. La Costa also has a focus on families and was named the "#2 Most

Family Friendly Resort in the U.S." by the Travel Channel.

Located in Carlsbad, just thirty minutes north of San Diego and ninety minutes south of Los Angeles, La Costa enjoys lovely southern California weather and a picturesque setting of rolling hills. The 400 lush green acres of this four-diamond resort provide an oasis of relaxation.

**Accommodations:** More than 400 guest rooms and suites are all decorated in a Spanish style and situated around courtyards, near the tennis facilities, adjacent to the spa, and along the golf courses. Casual elegance prevails, and rooms were all redesigned in 2006 to be even more comfortable. Roughly twelve room types exist, from standard Plaza to Presidential Suite, so rates vary. Daily rates for Plaza rooms are $325 to $350; deluxe rooms are $500 to $525; and suites begin at $625. Children under eighteen staying in their parents' room are free. For infants, ask for complimentary padded cribs, playpens, high chairs, baby-proofing supplies, and special children's bath products. A souvenir stuffed animal accompanies the crib. Rental strollers are also available. And for older kids, ask about Nintendo Game Boys. All children receive a "goody bag" on arrival. Packages can provide a savings. For example, Legoland is just minutes from the resort and has partnered with the hotel to provide Plaza accommodations, breakfast, and tickets to Legoland. The package begins at $475 for two adults and one child; extra children are $45 each. Kidtopia Experience offers your family accommodation, daily breakfast for four, and a half-day Kidtopia program for two children, beginning at $405 per room, per night. A $21 per night resort fee is assessed for incidentals.

**Dining:** Just because this is a spa, don't expect diets and tasteless tofu. Oh, no. Dining here is gourmet and still healthy. Legends California Bistro features classic California cuisine, along with vegetarian selections from the Chopra Center. It's open daily from 6:30 a.m. to 9:00 p.m.; 10:00 p.m. on weekends, when a jazz trio plays. Dine indoors or out in the California sunshine. At the Marketplace you'll find your Starbucks morning coffee, TCBY treats, and an Internet cafe, if you need a technology fix. Fire and water combine nicely in the Bluefire Grill; fountains, a fireplace with handblown glass wall, and grills set the stage for scrumptious dining at dinner Tuesday through Sunday. If you choose the outdoor patio, another firepit warms and cheers you. Seafood is featured; coastal specialties and fresh vegetables are the base, while California is the inspiration. Fresh juice drinks, smoothies, and light, healthy food are served alfresco in the garden courtyard at the Spa Café. Weather permitting, lunches and drinks are served poolside at the Splash Bar & Café. A Healthy Kids menu is available at restaurants and for in-room dining.

**Children's World:** Kidtopia is active year-round and operates from 9:00 a.m. to 4:00 p.m. daily. For three- to twelve-year-olds, the fun includes arts and crafts, indoor and outdoor games and activities, an arcade, a playground, water slides, and seven (yes, seven) swimming pools. Kids not only enjoy themselves, but they often learn something too, as they experience the surroundings in imaginative and entertaining ways. One of fourteen daily themes sets the stage, whether it's sports, science or adventure, pirates, or Hawaii. The fee is $80 for a full day; $45 for a half day. Lunch is included.

Infants and toddlers ages six months to three years have their own special area and age-appropriate activities, from 9:00 a.m. to 4:00 p.m. Rates are $15 per hour, with a two-hour maximum. It's OK to return after a break. Individual babysitting can be requested through the concierge.

On Friday and Saturday nights, dinner and entertainment are offered from 6:00 to 10:00 p.m.; the fee is $45 a night. Vibz Teenspace for ages ten and up provides 6,000 square feet of fun and a place to gather. Children's tennis and golf clinics are also offered, along with that quintessential California sport, surfing.

**Recreation:** La Costa's awards are many: fifteen accolades for spa, golf, and tennis, and voted the "#1 Spa in the West" by *Travel + Leisure* in 2005. The spa programs and facilities are extensive.

Facials from deep cleansing to mud packs, massages of the shiatsu and Swedish variety, herbal wraps, body scrubs, exfoliation, aromatherapy, reflexology, and hydrotherapy baths are just some of the methods utilized to revive weary guests. Athletic Club facilities include swimming pools, a weight room, a cardiovascular room, Pilates, spinning, and a jogging track. You can join one of the many exercise classes offered throughout the day, or, with an exercise physiologist, you can devise a personalized fitness program. Individualized analysis also extends to dietary counseling and menu planning. This is, after all, California, and some of the special lectures and workshops have included Tai Chi, Intuitive Solutions, Goddess Retreat (for women only, of course), or Creating a Life Plan. Check to see if there's something of interest to you during your visit.

The Chopra Center is a unique place for healing and deep rejuvenation. Yoga and meditation are offered, along with Ayurvedic treatments and three- to five-day programs. Deepak Chopra, a Western-trained physician from India, has done much to introduce principles of this ancient Indian health system to the West. Ayurveda refers to the "knowledge of life" and has been practiced for over 5,000 years.

Golf enthusiasts find their exercise on the two eighteen-hole championship courses. At the Golf School the latest technology is used to scrutinize and improve your game. Tennis players have seventeen courts at their disposal and can choose clay or hard-court surfaces. Clinics are held daily, and private instruction is easily arranged. The golf and tennis pro shops offer a wide range of equipment and apparel.

With seven swimming pools and the Pacific Ocean minutes away, kids are in water heaven. The new Splash Landing features three pools, three water slides (with height requirements of 36 to 46 inches), and a water play zone. Spend time at the family pool with a sandy beach for the younger set, and drop in for the weekly evening family "dive-in movies." If you simply can't leave your laptop, reserve a poolside cabana, with wireless access of course. In summer La Costa runs a beach shuttle from 10:00 a.m. to 6:00 p.m. Half-day Surf Camps for ages six to twelve include equipment and lunch. While the exercise potential at La Costa is extensive, the rejuvenation potential is unlimited.

San Diego is a paradise for children; among other attractions are Birch Aquarium, San Diego Wild Animal Park, Seaworld Adventure Park, and the famous San Diego Zoo. Old Town San Diego and Carlsbad, or Village by the Sea, are day excursions the entire family will enjoy. Legoland is just minutes away, and irresistible for kids (and many adults!).

---

**2100 Costa del Mar Road**
**Carlsbad, California 92009**
**(760) 438-9111, (800) 854-5000**
**www.lacosta.com**

# LOEWS LAKE LAS VEGAS RESORT

Henderson, Nevada

In this twenty-one-acre gloriously natural setting of mountains, desert, and lake, it's hard to believe you're only 17 miles from the glitz and glitter of the Las Vegas Strip. It's also just a short day trip to Lake Mead, Hoover Dam, Red Rock Canyon, and the Valley of Fire. Who says you can't have everything? The resort is comfortably terraced into the hillside and reflects the best desert architecture. A Moroccan flavor is apparent in the high arches and deep loggias, the grilled ironwork, and the relaxed, open feeling engendered by mountains in the desert.

In December 2006 Loews Hotels purchased Lake Las Vegas from Hyatt Hotels. Luxurious upgrades are planned, and $5 million will be invested to bring Loews services and amenities, which exceed AAA four-diamond standards. Guest rooms, suites, and casitas and all bathrooms will be enhanced; the pool decks and cabanas, lakeside fire pit, and terraces are being renovated. Most important, Loews promises their signature excellent and intuitive service.

**Accommodations:** The 493 guest rooms and 46 suites reflect the open-air style of the Mediterranean, and most have views of the lake, mountains, or golf course. The theme is Moroccan and features imported furnishings; most rooms have small balconies, and all have refrigerators. A real pleasure is that the windows actually open, so you can enjoy the wonderfully clear desert air. Rates are based primarily on occupancy, not season, and range from $199 to $395, rack rates. They may be less, if the hotel is under 60 percent occupancy. Ask about the special when you book three nights and get one free, or five nights and receive two free nights. The

Something for Everyone package includes one night's lodging, two half days in the Kids Club, breakfast for four, resort fee, and, for Mom and Dad, a spa treatment and two complimentary drinks. Cost is around $500. A resort fee of $15 per room per night covers incidentals. If you desire a second room for the kids, there is a 50 percent discount, based on availability.

**Dining:** Breakfast at Loews is a big deal, with emphasis on local flavor, along with some healthy items. Enjoy juices custom-blended at the table or a hot chocolate bar (or frozen hot chocolate bar when it's warm). Marssa, the showcase restaurant, features a full sushi bar (rated best in the valley by *Zagat*), a presentation kitchen where you can watch the culinary artistry, and a menu inspired by the Pacific Rim and exotic Asian flavors. Inspired by the Moroccan tradition of cooking in an earthenware pot, Café Tajine, open for breakfast, lunch, and dinner, serves New American cuisine with an international flavor. Dine indoors or out, with the ever-present scenic views. The poolside Sandsabar & Grill keeps you well fed and watered. The twenty-four-hour Marrakesh Express is the place to have that special coffee, shop for the unusual delicacy to take home or enjoy in your room, or indulge in a late-night dessert in the desert. People-watch, as a change from the scenery, while sipping a drink at the Arabesque Lounge in the lobby. Restaurants have a children's menu.

**Children's World:** Loews loves kids—of all ages. Special children's menus (with healthy options), a lending library of games, Fisher Price welcome gifts, and unique programs are always available. Kids Club is open daily year-round; hours are from

10:00 a.m. to 5:00 p.m. and again from 6:00 to 10:00 p.m. for an evening session. Advance reservations are required. A good-size room is dedicated to camp activities that are diverse and related to the unique aspects and location of each property. Boating and swimming in the lake, scavenger hunts, water slides, and arts and crafts occupy children; as much time as possible is spent outdoors with active games and playground free time. The cost is $40 per session from 10:00 a.m. to 1:00 p.m. and 2:00 to 5:00 p.m. Extending the morning session to 2:00 p.m. to include lunch is $55; the all-day session (10:00 a.m. to 5:00 p.m.) is $80.

Evenings bring stargazing and a starlight dinner along with games, movies, drumming, and karaoke contests. Planned for ages three through twelve, the cost is $55 and includes dinner.

Teens receive VIT treatment (but low-key so that they're not embarrassed) and a backpack upon check-in. Even better, there's a special closet of DVDs, Game Boys, and other hot items that can be borrowed for the duration of the stay.

Loews prides itself on taking care of all members of the family—hence, Loews Loves Pets, for discerning animals on the road. Pets are not only allowed but they are welcomed with a personal note from the general manager, all kinds of local information just for them, toys and treats, special pet place mats with bowls—even hand-prepared meals. A "puppy pager" and DO NOT DISTURB/PET IN ROOM sign complete the pet package, and the concierge is happy to arrange for walks. Some dog's life!

**Recreation:** Golfers are delighted to discover two Jack Nicklaus Signature Golf Courses, plus the Falls, a course designed by Tom Weiskopf, with dramatic elevation changes from desert to mountainous landscapes. The Falls has been voted "Best New

Upscale Public Course" by *Golf Digest* and one of the "Top Ten You Can Play" by *Golf Magazine.* All the courses take advantage of the dramatic desert scenery and the largest privately owned lake in Nevada; the Falls even overlooks the famous Las Vegas Strip, seen in an amazing natural setting. Reflection Bay Golf Club is home to the Nicklaus/Flick Game Improvement School if your game needs a boost.

The heart of the resort is the 320-acre lake, with 10 miles of shoreline and beaches for water play and sunning. Take a spin in a pedal boat or kayak, sail, relax, and go fishing in an electric boat or rent a bicycle and ride along the lakeshore.

The daily Spa Moulay membership is included with the resort fee, so take advantage of the twenty-four-hour fitness room. You'll find eleven treatment rooms to pamper you (extra cost for treatments). After a workout at the fitness center or a yoga class, two outdoor pools and a swimming lagoon beckon you to relax in the tented cabana shaded by palm trees. The children's pool with water slide and sandy "beaches" keeps youngsters happy for hours. Sport Court is the place to play volleyball, short court tennis, or basketball; a putting green, croquet, and horseshoes help you while away an afternoon. If you want to try your hand at the slots, a complimentary shuttle will take you to the Strip. Actually, during the day, and in small doses, Las Vegas is an exciting place for kids too. The various hotels outdo each other for exciting attractions: Walk under and around lions in a glass den at MGM Grand; acrobats fly through the lobby at Circus Circus Adventuredome; an outside roller coaster circles New York–New York; at the Luxor, learn about ancient Egypt through IMAX movies and ride an elevator almost sideways to the top of the pyramid; knights joust at the Excalibur; Atlantis falls at Caesars; and the waters dance to music at the Bellagio—the list goes on and on. This is just a sample, so you see why making several trips is not a bad idea. If you need a different excitement from gambling, an adventure concierge will arrange treks to the Grand Canyon, kayaking on the Colorado River, or Hummer tours of Nevada's Valley of Fire.

Closer to home you'll find MonteLago Village, connected to the resort by walkways and water taxis, and offering dining, shops, and entertainment along the water's edge.

It's reminiscent of an ancient Mediterranean village. You can stroll the narrow shaded streets or shop on the two-level bridge as if you were promenading on Florence's Ponte Vecchio in Italy.

---

**101 Montelargo Boulevard**
**Henderson, Nevada 89011**
**(702) 567-6000, (800) 23-LOEWS**
**www.loewshotels.com**

# MONTECITO LAKE RESORT
## King's Canyon National Park, California

How about vacationing with Earth's largest living thing? No monsters or even whales here—we're talking about the giant sequoia trees. Set on forty-two acres within the Giant Sequoia National Monument, the Montecito Lake Resort is in partnership with the Sequoia National Forest to protect these incredible trees and give people a chance to play and appreciate nature in this wonderful area. Between King's Canyon and Sequoia National Parks, the resort sits at 7,500 feet elevation, on Lake Homavalo. Not only do they have a children's program, but they cover the entire gamut from toddlers to seniors. Yes! Kids, take your parents to camp! Parents, this is your chance. Be honest, now. Sometimes, as you send your precious child off to frolic and play all day, don't you wish you could go to camp too? Is there maybe just a tinge of envy, a nostalgic remembrance of summer days of your own youth, when nothing stretched before you but time and fun? Well, rejoice! Montecito Lake Resort has more than thirty varied activities and programs for everyone! This resort epitomizes our philosophy of family travel—time together and time apart. Kids

and parents can join each other's activities or do their own, or both.

Be sure to fill your gas tank in Fresno or Visalia as no gas is available near the parks. Stop at the park's Lodgepole Visitor Center on your way up and brush up on your Sierra Nevada and sequoia natural history, see the Crystal Caves, and take the short drive to visit the General Sherman and the General Grant Giant Sequoia Trees—the Earth's largest tree and the official Christmas Tree of America. Then on to the resort for a rollicking good time and quintessential camp fun. The resort is open 365 days a year and is uniquely beautiful in each season. In January 2007 the Dally family became new owners of this sixty-year-old camp. Rated one of the "Top Ten Family Resorts" in the country by *Travel Smart* newsletter and Family Travel Forum, it has also been featured in *National Geographic Traveler, Travel + Leisure,* and *Food & Wine* magazines. In 2006 *Good Morning America* rated it as one of the "Top Ten Family Camp Resorts."

**Accommodations:** Approximately 206 guests can be accommodated. Four lodges contain thirty-six lodge rooms with private baths that can accommodate two to eight people; four two-room suites suit larger families. All rooms have either king- or queen-size beds and deluxe bunks, with "country inn" decor and daily housekeeping included. For the really hardy, there are five lakeside cabins (propane heating) and eight mountain-view cabins (wood-burning stoves). Decor is comfortable and similar to lodge rooms, except there are no facilities in the cabins. Two bathhouses are nearby.

From mid-June until Labor Day, Montecito Family Camp is in high gear. Four- or eight-night stays are available before and after those dates; during summer only six-night stays are available, with Sunday arrivals. A six-night all-inclusive package in the cabins is $925 per adult, $885 for teens, $835 for youths two to twelve years, and $125 for infants six to twenty-three months. Package cost in the lodge is $1,045, $1,005, $975, and $125. Rates are per person. In summer, one-night stays are allowed only on Saturday; rates are $179 to $189 based on double occupancy, plus $20 to $30 for each additional person regardless of age. Summer Family Camp rates include all meals, the children's programs, and most activities for the entire family (horseback riding and waterskiing are extra). Fall rates include lodging, buffet meals, evening activities, and snacks available twenty-four hours daily. Rates are $149 to $189 for two adults, $30 for each additional person. Cabins are $10 less. Winter rates are $139 daily, based on two adults; $30 for each additional person. Holiday rates are higher, and the cabins are closed in winter. Rates include all meals, snacks, and the children's program for ages five to eleven. There's no program for the under-five set in winter. Spring again includes all meals and some evening activities; rates are $129 to $189 for two; $30

for each additional person. Cabins are $99 to $179; $20 for each additional person.

**Dining:** Guests consistently rave about the food at the lodge. The staff takes care to prepare only the freshest and finest selections, and the choices available are impressive. California cuisine, vegetarian specialties, and kid-friendly dishes are all part of the package. Mothers especially are delighted to dine so well, with no cooking or dishes! Meals are hearty and served buffet-style. Breakfast choices include eggs and cereal, along with waffles, pancakes, bacon, and sausage. Fresh fruit is served at every meal. Lunch offers not only sandwiches and salads, but hot entrees as well. Dinner features fresh vegetables, a salad bar, and a choice of several delicious entrees. And guess what? Dessert is available from lunchtime on into the evening, along with hot soups and snacks. Good thing there's all those activities. And heaven forbid anyone should ever be hungry; fruit, cereal, snacks, and do-it-yourself sandwiches are available twenty-four hours daily in the main lodge, along with hot and cold beverages, including Starbucks coffee.

**Children's World:** In summer separate programs divided by age for Minnows (two years), Tadpoles (three and four years), and Chipmunks (five and six years) have two adventure cabins and two play yards, a gymnastics area, and their own space on the lake. Summer activities include pony rides, dock fishing, insect safaris, kiddie Olympics, swimming, artistic fun, boating, and more, depending on age. In winter, it's for ages five to eleven years. Sessions are for two hours in the morning and two hours in the afternoon, but the activities are nonstop; there's snow play, snowshoeing, skiing, and indoor activities. Montecito's philosophy is that learning is fun, and children love to learn. The programs for youths and teens are always "free choice," where kids tell the counselors what they want to do—their favorite activity or stay with the group. When they do, they are then fully committed to the activity and get excited about it, regardless of age. Age groups are Marmots (seven to eight years), Bobcats (nine to ten years), Cougars (eleven to twelve years), and Bears (thirteen to seventeen years). All have separate leaders and KILTS (teens in training for leadership) who help with choices. Parents may join at times, and evening activities are for everyone. A typical day includes the morning Pow Wow planning, four activity sessions, the evening program, and nightly campfire.

**Recreation:** Summer has about thirty-five listed activities, and in winter, count on at least twenty. Most recreation is included in the rates; there are additional charges for horseback riding, mountain bikes, and waterskiing; instruction and guided tours outside of summer camp are extra, but very reasonable. Children's programs are always included in the rate, when they're offered (summer and winter). And of course, parents can do as many or as few activities as they wish. Forests, lakes, and mountains provide the backdrop for learning and fun. Waterskiing, wakeboarding, canoes, paddleboats, sailboats, stream and lake fishing, the swimming pool, and hot tub are starters for water experiences. Twenty horses and two teaching are-

nas, scenic trail rides, hiking, and mountain biking range over the mountain; at the resort try archery, trampolines, tennis, a golf cage, fencing, a rock-climbing wall, and the rifle range. The list just goes on and on. In summer some activities are weekly, like the Artist of the Week program, which teaches watercolor and oils; and there are once-a-week "happenings" like carnivals, variety shows, and theme nights. Evening activities have something for the whole family to share and have fun: games, karaoke, night hikes, stargazing an amazing sky, Casino Night, or movies. Traditional camp activities for adults, even grandparents, are as exciting as for the kids. Whatever your skill level, the staff is ready and able to instruct and help. Winter brings snowshoeing, dog-sledding, tubing, ice-skating, snow bikes, skiing, and snowboarding. Montecito Lake Resort has been voted the number two cross-country ski resort, with 82 kilometers of trails.

---

**8000 General's Highway**
**King's Canyon National Park, California**
**93633**
**(800) 227-9900, (800) 843-8677**
**www.montecitosequoia.com**
**www.mslodge.com**

# NORTHSTAR-AT-TAHOE
## Truckee, California

Tahoe has long been known for the clear deep waters of a 200-square-mile lake, the majestic mountain peaks of the Sierra Nevada, and its proximity to the entertainment and nightlife of Nevada casinos. Northstar-at-Tahoe enables vacationers to partake of all of these. Open year-round, it

is a 2,420-acre mountain resort just 6 miles from Lake Tahoe that offers winter and summer family sports activities. Lake Tahoe straddles the California/Nevada state line and at 6,223 feet is the largest alpine lake in North America. It is the second-deepest lake in the U.S. (1,645 feet at its deepest point) and so clear you can see a dinner plate at 250 meters. And who do you suppose figured out that if you were to tip Lake Tahoe over, the water would be 14.5 inches deep over all of California?

With the Nevada state line only 7 miles away, side trips to gambling casinos are manageable excursions for grown-ups. But it's not all about glitz. Northstar has long received accolades as one of the top family ski resorts in the United States. *FamilyFun, Ski Magazine, Child* magazine, and *Family Life* magazine have all recognized Northstar for its family programs and children's ski and snowboard school. The resort was featured as a top family destination on NBC's *Today Show*. Northstar is dedicated to the environment, and their mission is to treat it with respect. The championship golf course is a certified Audubon Cooperative Sanctuary, and the resort promotes environmental planning, water quality management, and revegetation practices. Northstar participates in Sustainable Slopes, an environmental charter for ski areas.

A new project, The Village at Northstar, combines lodging, shopping, strolling, and dining in a village ambience with retail stores and restaurants, plus a 9,000-square-foot ice-skating rink. More shops and ninety-three condominium units will be added in 2007. So right now, there's a lot of redoing and renaming going on, but it's all for a better mountain.

**Accommodations:** The lodging facilities include hotel-type rooms, condominiums ranging in size from studios to four-bedroom units, and three- to six-bedroom homes. With the exception of the lodge rooms, all have a fully equipped kitchen and fireplace; many units have a private balcony overlooking the wooded landscape and the mountains. The wooden facades and rustic designs of the buildings blend well with the natural setting.

Village rooms start at $159 in summer and begin at $236 in winter. Two-bedroom condominiums start at $275 in summer, $339 to $395 in winter. The Ski Trails lodging is closest to the slopes; ski-in, ski-out on-trail condominiums begin at $315 for a one-bedroom and $415 for a two-bedroom. Rates do not include a $5 per night resort fee. Cribs are provided at no additional charge. Package plans are available throughout the year and provide a savings. The on-site transportation system is complimentary for Northstar guests. Guests also have complimentary access to the Swim and Racquet Club with swimming pools, fitness center, tennis courts, and outdoor hot tubs. A Teen Center is located here as well.

**Dining:** The restaurants at Northstar mean time off for the family cook. The Martis Valley Grill, at the golf course, is open holiday weeks in winter, and daily for breakfast, lunch, and dinner in summer months. Themed family-style buffets (Italian, Southwest, Mediterranean, etc.) are offered. In summer the Turn, at the golf course, has patio dining for lunch and afternoon snacks. Or call your order in while teeing off at the ninth hole, and pick it up as you play through.

The two winter restaurants on the mountain are the Lodge at Big Springs, open for breakfast and lunch, and the Summit Deck and Grill, open for lunch. Each offers an informal atmosphere and allows skiers to get back on the slopes quickly. The Summit Deck is really that—set at 8,600 feet on top of Mount Pluto, it has wonderful views of Lake Tahoe and the Pacific Crest from the outside deck. However, to dine here you must be able to ski or ride intermediate runs. At the top, barbecue is the order of the day, and Chilly Pepper's at the Day Lodge is a hot new spot with tasty specials.

In the Village, Timbercreek provides casually elegant dining, with all-natural and fresh ingredients. Opening in 2007, Mikuni at Northstar features Japanese cuisine and sushi. Earthly Delights and Big Wave Burritos and Wraps offer quick-prep, tasty foods, while Euro Snack, at three locations, delights kids with Belgian waffles and French hot dogs. Also catering to kids, S'mores Kiosk at the ice-skating rink has hot chocolate and kits to create your own s'mores at the special fire pit. And finishing off the list for families is Rubicon's, with pizzas, pasta, and salads. Two cabana bars on either side of the rink offer libations at the end of the day, and the Patio Bar is a great place to unwind at night. Grapes and Grounds is just what the name implies— stay or go.

**Children's World:** The Minors' Camp Child-Care Center is fully licensed for child care and nonskiing outdoor play. In the winter it is open daily from 8:30 a.m. to 4:30 p.m. Under the guidance of an experienced staff, two- to six-year-olds paint, learn songs, listen to stories, play in the snow, and take walks; with snacks and a hot lunch, the full-day fee is $99 to $109; half-days are $79 to $89. Pagers are given to parents for added assurance.

In the past, *Ski* and *Family Life* magazines have ranked Northstar's kids' ski and snowboard school as among the best in the nation. The new Children's Center, located in the center of the Village, makes it easy to get kids set up for the day's ski experience. Children ages three to six may be dropped off at the Children's Center in the Village as early as 8:00 a.m. for all-day lessons, which run from 10:00 a.m. to 3:30 or 3:45 p.m., or from 9:45 a.m. for ages seven to twelve years. Parents should accompany older children to the Village Ski School Area, on the deck directly above the Village Children's Center.

Lucky Stars (age three) and Super Stars (ages four to six) have all classes outdoors on the snow, but with lots of breaks, snacks, and variety to keep children interested and energized. All-Stars, skiing or snowboarding for ages seven to twelve, groups children by age and ability and offers something for everyone. All-day rates are $119 to $139 for all ages and include lift ticket, five-hour lesson, equipment, and lunch. The afternoon package does not include lunch and is $92 to $102. Register early, as availability is limited. If your children need lessons only, the full day costs $109 to $129; $75 to $85 for a half day. On all programs holiday prices are higher.

Parents receive special attention too. Northstar has devised an interchangeable Parent Predicament lift ticket that allows them to share a lift ticket for the day and tag-team child care. The "Mommy, Daddy, and Me" program couples parents with an experienced instructor to give them tips on teaching their three- to four-year-olds how to ski. The complimentary forty-five-minute lesson is offered at 1:30 p.m. Sunday through Friday, excluding peak periods.

Star Parks are six terrain parks for kids, just their size and designed with jumps, bumps, and secret snow play areas to kick off skis or boards and just play. Patrolled by ski patrol, they're close to main runs as well. Look for star prints on the trail map.

While Northstar has many activities for children in summer, there is currently no supervised camp program or child care offered. Check with the resort to see if this changes.

**Recreation:** For downhill skiing at Tahoe, you can look forward to 2,280 vertical feet and an average snowfall of 350 inches. The Northstar Village is at the base of Mount Pluto, which rises to a summit of 8,600 feet. There are seventy-nine runs and sixteen lifts, and locals boast of sunshine 80 percent of the season. The ski school, with its 200-plus instructors, offers lessons for beginners through experts to help all visitors meet the variety of this mountain. Fifty kilometers of groomed trails attract cross-country skiers; lessons, guided tours, and snowshoe rentals are available at the Nordic Ski Center. Superpipe, half-pipe, five terrain parks, and six adventure parks please skiers and boarders alike. Tubing and snow bikes are also popular. At Burton Progression Park the entire family can experience terrain park action together. Rails, low fun boxes, and gentle jumps let you test gravity at your own speed.

Après-ski activities may mean taking a sleigh ride or a trip to the Swim and Racquet Club, where you'll find saunas, spas, an adult lap pool, a fitness center, and a teen center, or enjoying a stroll through the Village, stopping at shops, restaurants, and bars.

During the summer other activities lure visitors outdoors to the sunshine and clean mountain air. Northstar fully promotes the concept of "recess," that precious time dedicated to the sole purpose of running around outside and playing that unfortunately is disappearing from our too-busy lives. Well, here's your chance to bring it back. Enjoy golf on an eighteen-hole course that wanders over meadows, past mountain streams, and through groves of tall pines and aspens. The Golf Course Clubhouse includes a pro shop and a restaurant. To work on improving your game, check with the resident pro for tips, or practice solo on the driving range and putting green.

At the Swim and Racquet Club, play tennis on one of the ten courts, take a swim in the adult lap pool or junior Olympic-size pool, or just soak up the sunshine on the poolside deck. No one over six years old is allowed in the Kiddie Pool, and families have their own hot tub, one of three. A fitness center is open to guests fourteen and older. The Arcade and Youth Center is a favorite place for kids to "just hang" and have some fun, with foosball, table tennis, and video games—plus the usual suspects of TV and vending machines. June through August, Northstar has teen and children's two-day golf clinics for kids, as well as Junior Tennis Camps, rated as a best value.

The Northstar stables provide wellgroomed horses for riding the mountain trails and offer lessons and guided trail rides. Hiking and biking are also favorite sports in High Sierra country. The latest sports addition features bungee trampolines and a mountain-bike park. Take a scenic chairlift ride, and bring your bike along. For adventures in boating and fishing, the clear blue waters of Lake Tahoe await you. And music fills the air every summer Sunday afternoon with free outdoor concerts. Several festivals highlight food, jazz, wine, and beer. The Lake Tahoe Shakespeare Festival begins in July.

---

**P.O. Box 129**
**Truckee, California 96160**
**(530) 562-1010, (800) GO-NORTH**
**www.skinorthstar.com**
**www.northstarattahoe.com**

# SEVENTH MOUNTAIN RESORT

### Bend, Oregon

A vacation in the woods and mountains of the great Pacific Northwest, the serenity of hiking in the forest, and the excitement of exploring the Deschutes River whisk you away from city life and everyday routines. The Seventh Mountain Resort, located on the sunny side of the Cascade Mountains of central Oregon, is a year-round family resort that boasts a cool forest setting and warm hospitality. Nearby Mount Bachelor is the seventh peak in the chain of mountains running south from the Columbia River and the border with Washington State, hence the name. The resort aims to be "a place where you can interact with nature in a hundred different ways, and interact with your family in the only way that really matters." Encircled by peaks, lakes, and meadows, and set in the midst of tranquil beauty with all the necessary amenities, the resort makes it easy to accomplish that goal.

**Accommodations:** You can choose from a variety of accommodations, from a room to a three-bedroom suite. The architecture is modern yet rustic, and natural-wood facades blend well with the wooded landscape. Condominium decor includes rich textures and earthen colors, brick tiles, and folk art. Improvements are ongoing, and the inn has recently renovated "everything but the scenery." Standard units are comfortable and more economical, while premium units provide a bit more luxury. Many room types may feature fireplace, deck, and kitchen; all rooms have free wireless Internet connection and access to the fitness center. Rates for standard units begin at $99 for winter, spring, and fall, going to $109 in summer. A one-bedroom suite starts at $129 to $149. Premium one-bedroom suites begin at $179

to $199. Specials are always changing, but as an example, the Three and Free package offers the fourth night free; a High Desert Summer Family Special provides two nights' lodging, four breakfast vouchers and museum passes, taxes, and the 7 percent recreation fee for $389 to $419 for standard and $499 to $529 for premium. The Whitewater Summer Family Getaway includes two nights' lodging, breakfast, and rafting for four. Packages range from $479 to $639. Hang on, 'cause that's a good deal!

**Dining:** The resort's signature restaurant, Seasons, is open daily for dinner. Using local products, the menu is quintessential Pacific Northwest, creatively prepared. Big Eddy's Café and Provision Company is open all day for breakfast, lunch, dinner, and light snacks. Reminiscent of a 1950s diner, kids love sitting at the counter. A walk-up window opening to the swimming pool is convenient if you want to maximize your time in the sun. Rimrock Bar is open nightly for drinks, pub food, and socializing.

**Children's World:** In addition to individual babysitting, which the staff can help you arrange, events are scheduled all day long for your child's enjoyment. In summer and winter the recreation office publishes a flyer, *This Week at the Inn,* to help you keep track of all the activities. From the end of June to Labor Day and on holidays, Kids' Quest is a supervised play program for children ages five to twelve. A daily charge of $40 covers lunch, arts-and-crafts classes, movies, and more from 9:00 a.m. to 4:00 p.m. each day. Half-day programs are also available for $25 each session, from 9:00 a.m. to noon and 1:00 to 4:00 p.m. Themed activities may feature pirates, mad scientists, or who knows?

Your child might also participate in a tennis clinic, search out treasures on a scavenger hunt, or take a field trip. There are also two playgrounds, and a wading pool and two swimming pools for water recreation.

In winter Mount Bachelor Ski School offers day care and ski/board lessons for children.

The West Village Lodge at the base of the mountain has a state-licensed day-care center for little ones six weeks to ten years old; age-appropriate activities such as crafts, videos, naps, story time, and circles are planned from 8:30 a.m. to 4:30 p.m., and 8:00 a.m. to 4:00 p.m. on weekends. Daily rates are $50 for children thirty months and older; $55 for children younger than that. An hourly rate (limited space) is $14, with a two-hour minimum. Children may bring their lunch, or a box lunch is available for $7, and parents are welcome to eat with their children. For an additional $30, Snowplay is a one-hour outdoor introduction to skiing that can be added for three-year-olds.

Little Rippers is for ages four to six years and has a maximum of three children per class. Cost is $125 for a full day; $105 for a half day. Mountain Masters, for ages six to twelve, is grouped by age, ability, and ski or board. Lesson, lift, and lunch are $95 for a full day; $80 for a half day (no lunch). For more details, visit www.mtbachelor.com, or call (541) 382-1709 or (800) 829-2442.

**Recreation:** The recreation department at the inn plans activities for every member of the family, concentrating on water sports, swimming, tennis, and raft trips on the river in the summer; and ice-skating, cross-country skiing, and sleigh rides in the winter. Wintertime also means the thrill of downhill skiing at nearby Mount Bachelor, only 14 miles from the inn.

In summer you just have to discover the beauty of the Deschutes River. Take a relaxing canoe ride and get back to nature, or join a moonlight raft trip. Twice-weekly evening float trips with a barbecue are family favorites. For more daring souls, there are guided white-water raft trips through the rapids. If you prefer to take in the scenic river from land, horseback riding is a great alternative; group trail rides run along the river and into the Deschutes National Forest. The National Forest is also a picturesque haven for hikers and joggers. For the fisherman, the recreation office arranges trips to the favorite spots with a naturalist guide. For a rock-climbing challenge, Smith Rock State Park is one of the best places in the West. Golfers enjoy that the resort is next door to Widgi Creek, one of central Oregon's most popular courses.

Back at the resort, take a dip in one of the two pools, rent a bicycle, play a good game of tennis on one of the four Plexipave courts (group clinics and private lessons are offered), work out in an aerobic-exercise class at the nearby Athletic Club, try your talents in an arts-and-crafts class, go in-line skating, or get lucky in a bingo game. The rec office organizes all sorts of ball games—softball, volleyball, football, and soccer. Play table tennis, take in a poolside movie, or head to the video-game room. Then relax in the sauna or one of the hot whirlpool baths.

The Oregon High Desert Museum, just 6 miles south of Bend, discloses the natural and cultural history of this region. The museum makes for a fun as well as educational afternoon.

This part of Oregon experiences beautiful Indian summers, so activities continue well into the fall. During the winter months special treats include ice-skating, sleigh rides, cross-country skiing (with lessons for novices), and horseback riding through the snow-covered landscape.

The resort is the closest lodging facility to the Mount Bachelor ski resort (800-829-

2442; www.mtbachelor.com) and provides daily transportation to the mountain base. With 3,365 vertical feet, 71 runs, 3,683 skiable acres, and plenty of dry powder (an average of 350 inches yearly), Mount Bachelor means excellent downhill skiing for all levels of ability. You'll also find snowboarding, cross-country and telemark skiing, snowshoeing, tubing, and more. The five lodges at the mountain have restaurants for breakfast, lunch, snacks, and cocktails; ski shops; and the ski school, which offers group lessons for all ranges of expertise as well as private lessons. The season is long here, attracting many visitors late into spring.

**18575 Southwest Century Drive**
**Bend, Oregon 97702**
**(541) 382-8711, (800) 452-6810**
**www.seventhmountain.com**

# SNAKE RIVER LODGE AND SPA

## Teton Village, Wyoming

In the early 1800s a lone trapper named John Colter inadvertently discovered much more than the beaver he was hunting. After wandering in the Northwest Territory for some months, he returned home with tales of vast untouched forests, thermal pools, and sulfur springs, of catching a fish in a fresh stream and cooking it in a nearby boiling one. Everyone laughed and dubbed it "Colter's Hell." Then other mountain men found the same phenomena, and gradually, the Jackson Hole valley became the crossroads of the Western fur trade. Today, two centuries later, this land is protected by Yellowstone and Grand Teton National Parks and has become the crossroads for travelers searching for grandeur and wilderness, trading their tame existence for adventure, but with comfort and luxury—a far cry from a tent, a few blankets, and a campfire. The Snake River Lodge and Spa is definitely luxurious; a member of Preferred Hotels & Resorts Worldwide, it is also Jackson Hole's first AAA-rated four-diamond award resort and is also a Rock Resort. It is located 50 miles from the south entrance to Yellowstone, 10 miles from Jackson Town Square, and only 1 mile from the southern entrance to Grand Teton National Park.

**Accommodations:** Completely renovated in 2001, the Snake River Lodge is snuggled into the mountain at the base of the Jackson Hole Ski Resort, with eighty-eight guest rooms and fifty-seven condominium/suites. The decor is Western; the feeling is one of comfort—leather, warm wood, and stone fireplaces. Rooms have many amenities, from plush robes to wireless connections, cable TV, and minirefrigerators. Luxury rooms add a gas fireplace, and executive rooms feature a comfortable sitting area with sofa bed and a jetted bathtub. Views vary; all standard rooms have a partially obstructed view, while deluxe rooms overlook the village; some rooms have balcony with valley views. Room rates April through November begin at $139 to $385. December through March begin from $249 to $489. Children fourteen years and younger stay free in the same room with parents. The concierge can arrange everything prior to your arrival—groceries, dining, child care, and spa services. Use the online request form. In April and November, much of the area is closed; at the hotel, the restaurant and spa are not operative.

In summer the Family Float and National Park package brings nature and luxury together for a family of four: three nights' lodging, a scenic float trip, a National Park Pass valid for one year, breakfast daily, and one boxed lunch for four. Cost varies depending on date and accommodation, ranging from $1,088 to $1,880 for two rooms or $1,452 to $2,319 for a two-bedroom suite. The Cloud 999 package is a great deal—three nights' lodging and a credit at the Spa, for $999—available May and June and October through mid-December.

Opened in 2003, Crystal Springs Condominiums are located right next to Snake River Lodge, offering one to three bedrooms. Rates for a one-bedroom unit are $260 to $370 in summer; winter rates for two-bedroom units begin at $795.

In the heart of Teton Village, the lodge is still only 20 yards to the lift, so it's ski-in, walk-out access, with heated walkways and hiking trails literally out the back door.

**Dining:** The GameFish restaurant features regional favorites and an extensive wine list for dinner, plus an expansive breakfast buffet to start your day off right. The Fireside Bar is a great place to unwind, sample a regional beer, and meet friends. The restaurant closes in April and November. One of the pleasures of being in the village is the wide choice of nearby restaurants. Kids like Billy's Burgers for "the best hamburger in Jackson Hole"; Nani's Genuine Pasta House, a comfortably cozy place; and Mountain High Pizza, of course. Lots of restaurants feature steaks, seafood, and game; the Alpenhof Bistro, Blue Lion, Gun Barrel Steak and Game House, Off Broadway Grill, and the Million Dollar Cowboy Steakhouse are good places to begin. Cadillac Grille has

been a local favorite for twenty-four years, and Merry Piglets is the oldest and most popular Mexican eatery. Breakfast and lunch at Jebediah's, microbrews at Snake River Brewery & Restaurant, Austrian specialties at Stiegler's, a raw bar at Rendezvous Bistro, contemporary Asian and Latin with over 900 wine selections at Koshu Wine Bar, and Sweetwater's lunches at the log cabin—there's something memorable for everyone!

**Children's World:** The winter and summer programs for children at Snake Lodge utilize the Jackson Hole Mountain Resort facilities at The Kids Ranch (307-739-2779). The Cody House is a 106,000-square-foot children's facility housing day care for ages six months and up, as well as all youth rentals and Mountain Sports School. Fort Wyoming, a Western playground, is adjacent, and in winter, a magic carpet and gentle protected slope is perfect for little first-timers.

The Kids Ranch Summer Day Camp operates mid-June to Labor Day from 9:00 a.m. to 4:00 p.m., combining recreation, nature, history, and science. In June, camp is open Monday through Friday, then daily in July and August. For older children, mornings are active, spent hiking from the aerial tram or at the climbing wall; after lunch and free play, science projects and arts and crafts are followed by water play or an afternoon activity. Wranglers are from six months to two years, Rough Riders encompass three-year-olds to kindergarten, and Explorers are first to fifth graders. Teen Extreme is for middle and high school students. Their activities include mountain biking, rock climbing, orienteering, hiking, environmental education, horseback riding, soccer, kayaking, bungee trampoline, and other outdoor sports. Lunch is included, and all ages are $85 for the day.

In winter, little Wranglers are looked after and entertained with indoor and outdoor play. This licensed child-care facility provides lunch, but parents may need to bring any special foods. Cost is $120 for full day, 8:30 a.m. to 4:30 p.m.; $100 for morning, and $90 for afternoon. Pioneers program is for ages three and four, with two outdoor ski sessions on the magic carpet and ski-oriented indoor play. The full day is $137; half-day afternoon is only $100.

For Ski School, a full day is from 9:00 a.m. and pick-up is at 3:15 p.m.; half day is 12:45 to 4:00 p.m. Rough Riders (ages three to six) have small class size with specially trained instructors, lunch, and lesson/lift ticket for $120; half day is $100. Little Rippers (ages five to six) have beginner snowboard semiprivate lessons with maximum of three children for $185. Explorers (ages seven to fourteen) do just that—explore the mountain and scout for moose and eagles while improving their skills on skis and boards. Lesson/lift is $140 or, afternoons only, $125. Teen Extreme for twelve to seventeen years is a unique skiing/riding program for advanced youths who often ski/board with the Athlete Team. The Terrain Park and Superpipe are perfect for kids to practice as it's not too small and not too big—just right. At all levels, Scavenger Hunts have kids sliding all over the mountain to combine skiing and riding skill building with fun and educational mountain exploration. Ski-cology is an interactive program that combines environmental awareness with ski/board lessons. Kids find secret trails with native plant and animal life—this hands-and-skis-on experience is so much fun that they don't even know they're learning! Special events include Kids Night Out and the New Year's Eve Glo-Worm Parade, a real highlight. Kids Night Out is scheduled on specific dates year-round for ages three to fourteen. Grouped by age, kids enjoy indoor games, movies, and dinner or maybe ice-skating on the pond or sledding. Sometimes Owlie the owl and Petey the Peregrine falcon come for an interactive demonstration with live birds of prey. From 6:30 to 9:30 p.m., it's $60 per session.

**Recreation:** At the lodge, the five-story Avanyu Spa offers body and mind restoration; Avanyu is the Tewa Native American name for the mythical water serpent representing the life-giving powers of water, used extensively here. The Fitness Center features Cybex strength training. Indulge and entertain the whole family in the stunning indoor/outdoor swimming pool with cascades of waterfalls, large boulders, warmed walkways, sauna, and hot tubs hidden in caves (open 8:00 a.m. to 10:00 p.m.).

Winter in Jackson Hole means snow, lots of snow—often more than 500 inches! With three ski areas and some of the most accessible back-country skiing, that's a lot of fun as well. Skiing here can be ranked big (Snow King, vertical rise 1,571 feet, 400 skiable acres), bigger (Grand Targhee, vertical rise 2,400 feet, 2,000 skiable acres), and biggest (Jackson Hole, with a vertical rise of 4,139 feet, 2,500 acres of skiable terrain and 50 percent expert). Check out each of their Web sites for all the information, and to see which one fits your needs. Snow King has ice-skating and a tube park, and there's snowmobiling and snowshoeing in the Parks. Horseback riding is offered at Goosewing Ranch, a year-round guest ranch; half day, full day, and even overnights are offered. Dogsledding combined with swimming and a barbecue lunch? Now that's a new twist! It helps that it's in the Granite Hot Springs area, though. Sleigh rides or a snowcoach tour of Yellowstone puts a whole new face on winter.

Summer brings all those wonderful mountain activities of hiking, mountain biking, fly fishing, kayaking—outfitters throughout the area offer all mountain diversions. And at Jackson Hole Trail Rides, in Teton Village, from June through September, you have a chance to ride into Grand Teton Park. Other summer "to-dos" include rafting on the Snake River, a hot-air balloon ride, or fishing at Crystal Springs Pond behind the hotel. Snow King Resort at the south end of Jackson has a 2,500-foot Alpine slide; ride the chairlift to the top, and they say you control your own speed down. Uh-huh. Next to the slide is Alpine Golf, an eighteen-hole miniature golf course with waterfalls, ponds, and great views. Plus the events in the Parks—for example, Colter Bay Marina in Grand Teton has scenic boat cruises to Elk Island and canoe rentals. Everything around here is scenic, whether it's an adventure on air, land, or water. Redesigned by Robert Trent Jones, the Jackson Hole Golf and Tennis Club is rated by *Golf Digest* as one of the top ten resort courses in the nation. Like everything else here, it's very beautiful, with views of the snowcapped mountains and water hazards provided by the Gros Ventre River. Movies on the Mountain are family films shown outside on the base of Jackson Hole Mountain Resort. Monday through Saturday for the entire summer, you can witness frontier justice in a shoot-out at Jackson Town Square. The longest-running in the country, it's been happening for forty-five years—guess justice is kinda hard to come by. Music and arts also fill the summer days and evenings.

**7710 Granite Loop Road**
**Teton Village, Wyoming 83025**
**(307) 732-6000, (866) 975-ROCK**
**www.snakeriverlodge.com**

# SQUAW VALLEY USA

## Olympic Valley, California

Squaw Valley—the name itself is synonymous with skiing. From the earliest days (would you believe 1949?), the sunny California weather, six high alpine peaks, and 4,000 acres of lift-served terrain have made this a world-class ski area. From its beginning with one chairlift, a rope tow, and a lodge to hosting the 1960 Olympics, Squaw Valley is now a premier destination resort with year-round recreation and a strong commitment to environmental programs as a member of Sustainable Slopes. Mother Nature deposits an average of 450 inches of snow between mid-November and April, which means upper-mountain skiing into May. The Sierra Nevada and Lake Tahoe provide a spectacular backdrop, and the vastness of the area contributes to a wide variety of skiing. Squaw Valley is located near the north end of Lake Tahoe.

**Accommodations:** A central reservation office (800-545-4350) will work with you to find the most appropriate lodging for your family and your needs. Hotels, motels, lodges, and condominiums all have various rates and package plans. Among the closest to the slopes are Squaw Valley Lodge, a four-diamond ski-in, ski-out condominium ($215 to $1,025); three-day ski packages are available from $414 per person. The

PlumpJack Squaw Valley Inn ($199 to $769), located next to the tram, has sixty rooms and includes a mountain breakfast. The luxurious, four-diamond Resort at Squaw Creek nestles at the base of its own private Squaw Creek lift with valet ski-in, ski-out service—and no lines. Renovated in 2005, the rooms and suites are generous, and the views of the valley are stupendous. A full-service spa, year-round children's program, private ice rink, and three swimming pools make this an ideal place for families. Connected to Squaw Village by a short shuttle, the resort is convenient to the hustle and bustle but deliciously secluded and self-contained as well. Rooms range from $249 to $349; fireplace suites run from $299 to $419; and one- to three-bedroom penthouses are $449 to $2,000.

**Dining:** Squaw Valley is certainly the place to eat, drink, and be merry, and choices are plentiful. In the base village, start your day with coffee and home-baked goodies at Wildflour Baking; try a French hot dog or Belgian waffle at Euro Snack; or enjoy microbrews and good food (with lots of sunshine vitamin D) at the Sundeck Tavern. The kids won't be able to walk past Northern Lights, offering ice cream and refreshments. Dave's Deli has take-out meals, supplies, and sundries; pizza at Le Chamois has been a tradition for thirty years. Blue Onion Café boasts the best breakfast in the Squaw Valley, served all day. Village restaurants to sample include Balboa Café, for "American Bistro" style; Mamasake Sushi Bar, where you can "eat raw at Squaw"; or Fireside Pizza Co., always a staple. In the mood for French cuisine? Try PlumpJack Café, an offshoot of the San Francisco eatery. See what other wonderful places your family will discover.

On the mountain, Gold Coast, at the top of the Funitel, has a food court on the lower level and the Crossroads Café on the upper level, with wraps and salads and a wonderful view from the outside deck. The Mermaid or Waterfall Bars may call you over for a short stop at day's end. As always, many eateries close or have limited hours in spring and summer, so do check beforehand.

The Sunset Dinner at Alexander's is delightful. Ride the Cable Car to High Camp, winter and summer, and savor views of the valley and Lake Tahoe with your three-course dinner. The Terrace Restaurant and Bar also offers panoramic views, lunch, and a place to relax at day's end. The Poolside Café, overlooking Lagoon & Spa, has a fun kids' menu, soup-and-salad bar, and hot sandwiches; eat indoors or on the open sundeck. In summer the poolside barbecue and umbrella bar really shine.

The casinos and showrooms of Nevada are accessible for dining and evening pleasures. If you want to stay in the neighborhood, however, try the après-ski at or evening fun at Bar One; Plaza Bar; Blue Coyote, for the sports bar experience; or Zenbu Tapas Lounge, with dining and dancing late into the night. The Loft Bar is a local favorite, with vintage photos. Most unusual may be the Auld Dubliner, an Irish pub actually built in Ireland, dismantled, and shipped to Squaw. Can't argue with authentic tradition on this one!

**Children's World:** SquawKid's Children's Center is 12,000 square feet of comprehensive programs, all for kids ages three to twelve. KT the Bear presides on most days, to the delight of little ones. Adjacent to the lifts at the base of the mountain, it's designed to be a one-stop center for families with everything kids need and special parking. Parents can even buy their own lift tickets there to save time. Squaw Valley no longer has a daycare program for toddlers. Snow Cubs is a ski-snowplay program for three- and four-year-olds and includes one-hour ski lesson, arts and crafts, using snowshoes, a walk around the village, and active play. Snow Sliders, for ages four to six, enhances learning and keeps kids smiling. The full-day program includes several hours on the snow, snack, and lunch; a new magic carpet lift helps with tired little legs. This is a physically demanding program, and if youngsters choose not to ski in the afternoon, they may join the snow play, movies, and other activities with the Snow Cubs. Junior Mountain is for ages seven to twelve, with more focus on safety, skill development, and skiing etiquette—and still keeping the kids smiling. The Snowboarding program for ages seven to twelve has the same goals. For all programs, nonholidays, the cost is $109 for a full day and $79 for a half day. Holiday times go to $139 for all day, and $108 for a half day. All children receive lesson and all-day lift ticket; lunch is included in the full-day session. Sessions run from 8:30 a.m. to 3:45 p.m.

The Resort at Squaw Creek offers guests a daily, year-round program for children ages four to twelve, with appropriate winter or summer activities. Mountain Buddies runs from 9:00 a.m. to 5:00 p.m., with half-day ($50, plus $5 for lunch) or full-day ($90, including lunch) sessions. Each day offers a theme, such as Olympics, Wet & Wild, Colors, or Gold Rush, with a nice mix of outdoor activities and indoor creativities. The child/staff ratio is a maximum of seven to one. Evening sessions ($60), from 6:00 to 10:00 p.m., include dinner. In summertime Squaw Valley also organizes events and activities for families: Old West Weekend, Village Movie Nights, Sunday Family Kite Flying, or Hiking with a Ranger.

**Recreation:** The definite wintertime focus of Squaw Valley is skiing and snowboarding. Squaw Valley receives 450 inches of snow every year—that's over 37 feet! One of the unique aspects of skiing here is that one wonders, where are the trails? Squaw Valley has thousands of acres of open bowl skiing rather than traditional trails. Instead of trails being rated, the lifts are rated beginner, intermediate, and advanced based on the type of terrain they serve. Add this to sunny California days, and you can see the attraction. Squaw Valley has three dedicated terrain parks and two half-pipes, plus a 525-foot super-pipe—enough to keep huckers and jibbers happy.

Imagine yourself on an uncrowded run. The sun is shining, and you kick up some powder as you stop to check out the scenery. Take off your goggles and look out over glistening white snow to the blue waters of Lake Tahoe. Seventy percent of the runs are for beginner/intermediate skiers. Moreover, Squaw Valley is one of those rare places where this group is not confined to the lower elevations but can ski all day above 8,000 feet in the sunny, sheltered bowls. The vertical drop is 2,850 feet, and challenging slopes for expert skiers are not lacking, as the 1960 Winter Olympics were held here. In fact, Squaw Valley considers itself the birthplace of the American Extreme Skiing Movement. Squaw's six peaks are interconnected by thirty-three lifts that include a 110-passenger cable car, a 28-passenger Funitel (the first of its kind in North America), four high-speed detachable quads, and three 6-passenger chairs. The ski school organizes classes and clinics for all levels, from beginners to racing competition. A special timed race course allows skiers to perfect their racing styles (and keeps them off the regular slopes!). High Camp is the base for night skiing and riding under the stars, the most extensive at Lake Tahoe. Your day or afternoon lift ticket is valid.

Cross-country skiing, offered at the Resort at Squaw Creek, augments the snow diversions of Squaw Valley; the Olympic Ice Pavilion and snow tubing round it out. The Ice Pavilion also operates in summer, if you find yourself pining for winter sports.

In the summertime the cable car operates for scenic tours, hiking, swimming, full-moon hikes, stargazing, mountain biking, and many more events. The High Camp Bath & Tennis Club has a spectacular mountain location at 8,200 feet, surrounded by the beauty of the Sierra's peaks. The Headwall, on the mountain, offers wall climbing, bungee trampolines, and a new experience that promises a thrill, the Skytrek. Climb up a tree, and then trek among the treetops through a series of twenty-five platforms connected by cables, bridges, and zip lines. Tennis, fishing, biking, horseback riding, and nature trails are popular pastimes. At the Resort at Squaw Creek, an eighteen-hole Robert Trent Jones Jr. golf course winds through mountain and meadow. Also available here are fly-fishing classes for beginners to more skilled anglers and two well-stocked ponds for practice. The Truckee River and Lake Tahoe entice you to float, raft, or boat or simply sit by the edge and enjoy a cool drink. The *Tahoe Gal,* a restored steamboat, departs Tahoe City on brunch, lunch, sunset, and dinner cruises— even a monthly full-moon cruise to fulfill the romantic in you.

**P.O. Box 2007**
**1960 Squaw Valley Road**
**Olympic Valley, California 96146**
**(530) 583-6985, (800) 403-0206**
**www.squaw.com**

# SUNRIVER RESORT

## Sunriver, Oregon

Nestled in the pines between the towering Cascade Mountains and the high desert, Sunriver Resort encompasses 3,300 acres on the dry side of the Cascade Mountains and enjoys nearly 300 days of sunshine each year. This four-diamond resort has earned numerous awards, including *Condé Nast Traveler's* "Top 50 Ski Resorts in North America," *Family Circle's* "Top 10 Vacation Destinations," and "#1 Family Resort in the Northwest" from *FamilyFun* magazine; at least eight golf awards, including top one hundred golf resorts in the world and one of the one hundred best women-friendly courses; plus dining and wine awards. It's a unique blend of natural beauty, resort comforts, personal service, and great recreation that makes for a memorable vacation. Sunriver has three championship golf courses (and *Golf Magazine's* coveted Gold Medal) and offers one of the most complete lists of recreational activities to be found, including organized children's, teen, and family programs. In the winter enjoy world-class skiing at nearby Mount Bachelor. Sunriver Resort has its own shuttle to the mountain that will have you on the slopes within minutes.

**Accommodations:** Accommodations at Sunriver Resort include deluxe rooms and suites, featuring stone fireplaces and private decks; the suites accommodate two to six people and have a kitchen and dining/living room. River Lodges are close to the main lodge and offer great views; four two-story buildings house deluxe rooms featuring Northwest decor. Lodge Village rooms and suites are also just steps from the Sunriver Lodge and underwent a $3 million renovation in 2005. Summer rates range from $199 to $249 for rooms and $259 to $345 for suites in Lodge Village; River Lodges are $199 to $359. Higher rates apply on weekends and in summer. Winter rates at Lodge Village average $155 (room) to $288 (suite). Guests at Sunriver enjoy access to the resort and club membership privileges for golf, fitness center, and dining.

Approximately 400 private homes and condominiums can be rented with a two-night minimum and one-time cleaning fee. With one to five bedrooms, these can easily sleep up to ten people comfortably. All include a well-equipped kitchen, living and dining areas, and fireplace; some have hot tubs and deck. They are strategically located along the golf course, tucked in among the pines, facing the Cascade Mountains, or overlooking the Deschutes River. Prices for a two-bedroom range from $179 to $279 per night, size and season being the determining factors.

**Dining:** The Meadows at the Lodge specializes in Northwest cuisine and is open for breakfast, lunch, and dinner daily. Enjoy great views and an imaginative children's menu. The Merchant Trader Café, located on the lower level of the lodge, features snacks and lighter fare for breakfast, lunch, and family dinners and is open daily. As the name suggests, while you dine you can shop the unique merchandise here. In summer, dine outdoors and enjoy dinner and stargazing, with live music on weekends. McDivot's at the Woodlands brings casual food to the putting greens. The Grille at Crosswater Club is open during the summer months for lunch and dinner and has limited winter hours. A private club atmosphere, it's open to resort guests and members only.

In addition, Sunriver's Village Mall has a number of restaurants and a grocery store. Whether you cook in or dine out, the variety from quick sandwiches to gourmet fare satisfies almost any mood. For late-night fun, the Owl's Nest Pub in the lodge offers cocktails nightly and live entertainment every Friday and Saturday night.

**Children's World:** Fort Funnigan gives children ages three to ten a chance to develop new skills and friendships as they create, discover, and experiment in Sunriver's unique environment. A 3,400-foot fenced playground with ceremonial tepees is all for them. It's a state-certified program with a low child-to-adult ratio. Each session revolves around a theme and includes nature study, adventure, crafts, and games. Sample themes are junior detective, pirates of the high desert, fish and fun, rodeo, or twistin' tropics. Details of all programs can be found on Sunriver's Web site, along with a helpful parent handbook. Fort Funnigan operates daily except Sunday from mid-June through Labor Day, and on holidays and some weekends. Spike, the porcupine mascot, hangs out daily at Fort Funnigan; he often makes surprise appearances at other events. Costs are $70 for a full day, 9:00 a.m. to 4:00 p.m. with lunch. Half days are $35 (9:00 a.m. to noon or 1:00 to 4:00 p.m.) and are available on Monday, Wednesday, and Friday.

Evening programs are also themed—kids enjoy clown school, south of the border, weird and wacky science, Oregon Trail campout, and safari expeditions. Monday and Friday evening sessions are 5:00 to 9:00 p.m. with dinner for $45; and Tuesday, Thursday, and Saturday from 6:00 to 9:00 p.m. without dinner for $35. No night programs are offered on Sunday or Wednesday.

Guided Adventures is designed for preteens and teens (ages eleven through fifteen) and is held during the summer months. On Monday, Tuesday, Wednesday, and Friday from 9:30 a.m. to 3:30 p.m., activities are geared toward the more independent and adventurous nature of this age group. Prices vary according to the scheduled activity: Wrangler Day features horsemanship and trail rides; Challenge Yourself is safe but thrilling and involves ropes, cables, tall trees, bikes, and more; an excursion to the top of Mount Bachelor via chairlift, a day playing on glaciers, and hiking back down the mountain; and River Adventure, bike riding and canoeing along the Deschutes River. Also on Friday night is Cosmic Bowling from 9:00 p.m. to midnight in Bend. Kids are advised to bring their bike, helmet, and lunch every day.

Teens ages thirteen to nineteen have their own summer schedule, generally two to three hours in the afternoon and evening (much their preference!). Night Spiker Volleyball, with the unique effect of black lights and neon body paint; indoor rock climbing in Bend; dodgeball at the resort; white-water rafting; and cosmic bowling 'til midnight in Bend are some of the scheduled events. Often a dance is scheduled weekly. During the rest of the year, loose activities are offered for teens, such as dances or pizza parties. The Outpost is a gathering place for teens and also a "meet-up" place for families.

In addition, youth summer activities include bicycle riding, swimming lessons, balloonology, canoe or white-water raft rides, games, and tennis. The resident naturalists at the Sunriver Nature Center introduce children to the magic and mystery of the local environment and animals; the Nature Center is open year-round. There's an extensive list on the Web site with all the details.

In winter the rink at the Sunriver Village Mall makes a great spot for ice-skating. Wintertime also means that all the services of Mount Bachelor are available. The West Village Lodge at the base of the mountain has a state-licensed day-care center for little ones six weeks to ten years old; age-appropriate activities such as crafts, videos, naps, story time, and circles are planned from 8:30 a.m. to 4:30 p.m., and 8:00 a.m. to 4:00 p.m. on weekends. Daily rates are $50 for children thirty months and older; $55 for children younger than that. An hourly rate (limited space) is $14, with a two-hour minimum. Children may bring their lunch, or a box lunch is available for $7, and parents are welcome to eat with their children. For an additional $30, Snowplay is a one-hour outdoor introduction to skiing that can be added for three-year-olds.

Little Rippers is for ages four to six years and has a maximum of three children per class. Cost is $125 for a full day; $105 for a half day. Mountain Masters, for ages six to twelve, is grouped by age, ability, and ski or board. Lesson, lift, and lunch are $95 for a full day; $80 for a half day (no lunch). For more details, visit www.mtbachelor.com, or call (541) 382-1709 or (800) 829-2442.

**Recreation:** The Sage Springs Spa and Club is the venue for Sunriver's golf and tennis. With fifty-four holes of outstanding championship golf, set amid rivers, meadows, wetlands, pine forests, and spectacular Cascade Mountain views, the Sunriver golfing experience offers incredible variety. Crosswater was designed by Robert Cupp and John Fought and offers play exclusively for resort guests and Crosswater Club members. It is designated a certified Audubon Sanctuary. The Woodlands was designed by renowned architect Robert Trent Jones Jr. and consistently ranks among the top twenty-five resort courses nationwide. The Woodlands' tree-lined fairways, seven lakes, and strategically placed sand traps challenge players. The Meadows, playing to more than 7,000 yards, has four sets of tees, meticulously prepared bent grass greens, and spectacular Cascade Mountain views; it is also home to the Sunriver Resort Golf Learning Center. No wonder *Golf Digest* rates the golf resort as one of "America's 100 Greatest."

Tennis at the Sage Springs Spa is a year-round sport with three indoor courts and four outdoor courts. Indoor court fees are $24, and you can stay after your game for the steam room or hydrotherapy spa. Outdoor court fees are $10, and another twenty-seven courts are to be found scattered throughout the Sunriver Community. If your serve or backhand needs some polishing, you can always sign up for lessons. Sunriver Resort offers their own year-round tennis program.

Two swimming centers are operated by and open to the community; each has a heated Olympic-size pool, a diving pool, and a wading pool, providing plenty of variety. The south pool also has a water slide and hot tubs. The Lodge Village pool and three outdoor spas are for guests only. An indoor three-lane lap pool is available at Saga Springs Club.

The Deschutes River provides hours of enjoyment for fishermen, who snag brookies, rainbows, and German browns. The Sunriver Marina offers canoe, raft, and kayak float trips down the scenic and calm Deschutes. Marina staff will pick you up downriver and bring you back to the marina; the trips are offered mid-April to mid-October, weather permitting. For the more adventurous, local outfitters offer half-day and full-day white-water rafting trips down more turbulent portions of the Deschutes, leaving from the resort daily during the summer months.

For the landlubbers in your party, just about any type of rental bikes are available for excursions on the 30 miles of paved paths; guides at the Sunriver stables are ready to show off the scenery in rides along the river; the wilderness beckons interested backpackers. Trails past meadows and through the woods await joggers and nature lovers. Surrounding Sunriver Resort is the Deschutes National Forest, offering additional opportunity for back-to-nature serenity and elbow room. The Sunriver Nature Center, a private, nonprofit organization, has been offering extremely comprehensive, very reasonably priced programs for more than twenty-five years. Many nature walks, lectures, and programs are free; there are also archaeology tours, combined biking/bird-watching excursions, spelunking in Lava River Cave, and much more. See galaxies, nebulas, and all of space at the Sunriver Nature Center & Observatory; a nature trail and botanical garden provide earthly fun and learning.

Sage Springs Club and Spa features spa services and hydrotherapy spas; a fitness club with extensive classes in yoga, aerobics (water and other), Pilates, and more; and personal trainers who are available to help with your regimen.

Sunriver Village has restaurants and interesting shops and boutiques. The Sunriver Music Festival takes place in August; orchestral programs are presented in the Great Hall, originally constructed as an officers' club when what is now Sunriver Resort was Camp Abbot, a training center for the Corps of Engineers during World War II. The Great Hall is composed of 511 logs, totaling 150,000 board feet of lumber, and is the only original building that remains. Completely restored to its original beauty, it serves as Sunriver's most popular entertainment venue.

Lots of activities are available for families, from the fairly sedate Vacation Creations to the challenge ropes course. Vacation Creations is scheduled daily and offers the joy of creating in a different medium every time: ceramics, body art, candles, tie dye, soap making. Children must be accompanied, and prices vary. Black-light volleyball is another event the entire family can enjoy. For ages ten and up, the challenge ropes course involves zip lines, a trapeze, cables, and trees. Pony rides for kids under six; hayrides and carriage rides for everyone; night golf under the full moon with flashing golf balls; rock climbing; spin fishing; biplane and glider rides; canoe, cave, and volcano tours—we could go on and on.

The High Desert Museum, 8 miles from the lodge, is a terrific educational introduction to the cultural and natural history of the Northwest, and a big attraction for kids and adults alike. The otter pond, where you can watch playful otters, is a favorite highlight, as is watching the birds of prey in action.

At Sunriver you'll find a dozen ways to enjoy winter. Mount Bachelor (800-829-2442; www.mtbachelor.com) is one of the West's top-rated ski areas. You'll find breathtaking views, plenty of deep powder, and slopes to challenge skiers and snowboarders of all abilities—from beginners to Olympic champions. You can head cross-country on miles of groomed forest trails or break your own path through snowy meadows. Trek the mountain outback by snowshoe, snowmobile, or dogsled, or take a leisurely tour in a horse-drawn sleigh. And at day's end back at the resort, slip into a steaming outdoor spa for a relaxing soak.

---

1 Center Drive
P.O. Box 3609
Sunriver, Oregon 97707
(541) 593-1000, (800) 801-8765
www.sunriver-resort.com

# SUN VALLEY
## Sun Valley, Idaho

---

Just saying "Sun Valley" calls to mind fantastic downhill skiing, beautiful powder, and gorgeous sunshine. Located in south-central Idaho, Sun Valley is a Tyrolean-style village perched high in the Sawtooth Mountains. With a ski season that runs from late November to late April, spectacular scenery, and mountain air, Sun Valley is indeed a skier's paradise. In 1935 the Union Pacific Railroad sent Count Felix Schaffgtosch to search for the perfect spot for a grand American resort to draw rail travel west. After months of finding nothing that met his strict criteria, he happened upon Ketchum, an old mining town in central Idaho. His response? "This place combines more delightful features for a winter resort than anyplace I have ever seen in Switzerland, Austria, or the U.S." Averell Harriman, then chairman of the railroad, determined to build a resort worthy of the majestic setting, and Sun Valley was born in 1936. The new resort was instantly successful, and European nobility and Hollywood royalty flocked here, creating the first destination resort in America. That standard of excellence and style continues today, as families from around the world continue Harriman's vision of "roughing it in style." Sun Valley introduced the world's first chairlift and began the long-running affair between Americans and skiing.

You won't need your car at Sun Valley, as it's a walking village. Even the condominiums are close, but if they seem too far, just hop on the complimentary bus. Continuous round-trips to Dollar and Bald Mountains are offered by both the resort and KART, the Ketchum Area Rapid Transit; service is free throughout the Wood River Valley.

**Accommodations:** The historic, original Sun Valley Lodge provides upscale lodging and fine dining in an imposing four-story hotel. Each of the lodge's 148 rooms and suites has a French Country decor with marble-appointed baths. The Sun Valley Salon & Day Spa, massage center, heated swimming pool, and bowling alley are located here. Room sizes vary, and Family Suites are one option, with three beds in two rooms with one bath. July and August are the highest season, and rates range from $269 to $469; winter rates drop by approximately $10 to $20; spring and fall are even lower. The chalet-style Sun Valley Inn is set in the midst of the village and contains meeting spaces, rooms, and suites. There are workout and laundry facilities, open to all resort guests, and the super-heated Inn Pool for year-round swimming in the crisp mountain air. Summer rates are $249 to $289 for a standard room and $309 to $319 for a suite; $249 to $299 in winter. Deluxe condos are located near the lodge and inn; rates range from $199 for a studio to $449 for a two-bedroom. Standard condos form a horseshoe around the village, all within a ten-minute walk of the inn or lodge; rates range from $179 to $289. Both include daily maid service, fully equipped kitchens, and spacious living areas. There is no additional charge for cribs, and children stay free in the room with parents. Ages fifteen and under ski free—one child per adult, with purchase of adult lift ticket.

**Dining:** Thirteen restaurants at the resort please almost any mood from fancy to family-style. Though many families cook meals in their condominium units, occasional nights dining out mean a real vacation for the family chef too!

The Lodge Dining Room, open for dinner and Sunday brunch, combines excellent service, fine dining with a French flair, and live music in an elegant setting. Also in the lodge, Gretchen's is open for breakfast, lunch, and dinner with a warm, family atmosphere. In summer enjoy the gourmet buffet on the terrace overlooking the famous outdoor ice rink.

In the village, Konditorei and Sun Valley Deli have sandwiches, pastries, and ice cream; kids love the Bald Mountain Pizza & Pasta. The Ram Restaurant at the Inn is open evenings only for steak, seafood, and fondues.

On the mountain, Sun Valley's owner considers "Baldy" a "regal mountain, wearing a crown with three jewels"—the award-winning day lodges of Warm Springs, Seattle Ridge, and River Run Lodges. A fourth jewel, Dollar Mountain Day Lodge, has just been added. Cluster stations ensure that your food is fresh and prepared exactly to your order—baked potatoes, soup, salad, and grills are above-average mountain fare. Lookout at the top of the mountain is cafeteria-style; Roundhouse is more intimate, with seating around a four-sided fireplace—it's the first original day lodge and open for lunch only. Dollar Cabin suits youngsters just fine and offers their all-time favorites of hot dogs, hamburgers, and fries.

In winter, for an unusual adventure in dining, take a horse-drawn sleigh ride to a rustic cabin nestled in the woods; at the Trail Creek Cabin, enjoy prime rib or Idaho trout near a warm fire. Après-ski haunts include the Duchin Lounge, in the lodge, known for its "HBR" (hot buttered rum) and a favorite for socializing, live music, dancing, and entertainment. The Boiler Room, open only in winter, most evenings features après-ski entertainment and early evening performances of live comedy or music. *Forever Plaid,* a family musical, generally plays once a week. First-run movies show in the Opera House in winter and summer.

**Children's World:** While Mom and Dad are schussing down Bald and Dollar Mountains, children are not left out of the fun in this winter wonderland. At Dollar Mountain, Tiny Tracks starts three- and four-year-olds off with an introductory one-hour class for $70. Dollar Mountain Camps are tailored to the needs of four- to twelve-year-olds and emphasize sound fundamentals. Supervision begins at 8:30 a.m. and ends at 4:00 p.m. The "Bald Eagles" Camp strengthens technique for the six- to twelve-year-old intermediate to expert skier and snowboarder on Baldy (levels 5 to 9). Classes begin and end at River Run Plaza, and supervision goes from 8:45 a.m. to 3:45 p.m. The day includes four hours of on-snow instruction along with supervised breaks and lunch for both groups. Cost is $120 per day and does not include lift ticket; children may ride the lift alone. Consecutive day rates are lower. The Beginner Camp for four- and five-year-olds is $150. Snowboard clinics for ages seven to twelve are also at Dollar Mountain; same hours and rates apply.

The licensed Sun Valley Playschool in the village entertains nonskiing little ones five years old and younger, including infants. The school has games, toys, arts and crafts, and a nap room for tots who grow weary of all the excitement. There are opportunities for ice-skating and an outdoor playground for romping in the snow. Rates and schedule are the same as in summer.

In summertime Playschool activities for the five-and-under group turn to swimming, arts and crafts, paddleboating, hayrides, and walks around the village. Hours are

Monday through Saturday from 8:30 a.m. to 4:30 p.m. Rates are for a full day or half day and depend on age: three months to two years, $95/$75; potty-trained and older children (two to five years), $85/$67. Pony rides ($79) and hayrides ($15) are extra.

For youngsters ages six to fourteen, from mid-June through early September, the day camp can be enjoyed daily. Fishing clinics, hayrides, paddleboating, swimming, ice-skating, and lift rides fill the days. Some activities are extra, such as horseback riding or barbecue ($15). Full day is $88, half day is $67, and lunch is $8.

**Recreation:** Suitable terrain for all levels of skiers is provided at Sun Valley. With its wide-open spaces and gentle trails, Dollar Mountain (628 vertical feet), known as "the finest teaching mountain in the world," is favored by beginners and those who want a few warm-up runs. Bald Mountain, with 3,400 vertical feet, is a challenge and caters to intermediate and expert skiers. Combined, these mountains offer seventy-five runs, twenty-one lifts, and 2,054 skiable acres. Sun Valley prides itself on lots of good skiing, from well-groomed terrain to unpacked powder and short lift lines—the combination every downhill skier seeks. A complimentary bus service operates continuously throughout the day, shuttling guests to the base of both mountains.

The Nordic and Snowshoe Center grooms 40 kilometers of well-marked trails for cross-country skiers through aspen trees, along the creek, and over sloping meadows. There are also 8 kilometers of designated snowshoe trails. Sun Valley was a pioneer in providing Nordic skiing specifically for children. Machine-set tracks designed for a child's stride cover 3 miles of the Nordic Ski Center and in some places parallel adult tracks, allowing an easy family cross-country-skiing experience. Backcountry skiers can tour the mountain from yurt to yurt (Siberian-style huts), finding a warm, welcoming meal and bed at each.

Private and group lessons are available in both downhill and cross-country skiing at beginner, intermediate, and advanced levels. With indoor and outdoor rinks, another favorite wintertime sport has become a year-round one here. Ice skates can be rented, and just behind the lodge is an Olympic-size skating rink where such greats as Sonja Henie, Peggy Fleming, and Dorothy Hamill have practiced. Saturday night ice shows are presented throughout the summer and have been a tradition for over sixty-five years.

Another year-round activity is swimming; there are two glass-enclosed indoor heated pools (one at the lodge and one at the inn), one outdoor Olympic-size pool, and a kiddie pool. Relax in the sauna or the Jacuzzi, or make an appointment with the masseur in the lodge to ease your overworked muscles. The game room in the lodge offers pool tables, video games, and bowling alleys; or perhaps you'd like to take in a movie at the Opera House. The shops in the village might tempt you with their selections of books, gifts, fashions, jewelry, pottery, and toys.

Summer brings music festivals, parades, antiques and crafts fairs, bicycle races, and much more. Tennis and golf enthusiasts are in their heyday, for there are eighteen outdoor tennis courts, as well as clinics and private lessons with video-taped analysis. An eighteen-hole championship golf course, redesigned by Robert Trent Jones Jr., rolls over gently sloping terrain. Two nine-hole courses provide another option. At the pro shop, you can arrange for lessons and pick up extras in equipment and clothing.

Fishing in Silver Creek makes a pleasant afternoon for novice fishermen as well as experienced anglers; Sun Valley Lake is stocked with trout. The mountain trails are open to you for horseback riding and hiking in the wooded wilderness; chairlifts give access to "Baldy's" Summit. Trap and skeet shooting (instruction available) are also popular with summer visitors. Try white-water rafting on the Salmon River, take a rowboat or paddleboat out on the lake, line up rentals at the bike shop, or take a hike from the chairlift. Whether winter or summer, you'll be captivated by the majestic mountains and the warm, friendly atmosphere of Sun Valley.

---

1 Sun Valley Road
Sun Valley, Idaho 83353
(208) 622-2001, (800) 786-8259
www.sunvalley.com

# THE WESTIN
# MISSION HILLS RESORT

Rancho Mirage, California

Palm Springs is another name associated with Hollywood stars and elegant living. Its prestigious neighbor, Rancho Mirage, is newer, but making its own name as "the Playground of the Presidents." Set on 360 acres next to the Mission Hills Country Club, this four-diamond Westin welcomes guests to the California desert. The lush landscaping and verdant golf courses belie its desert location, but the surrounding mountains and canyons, which reflect the sun and shadow and the clear starry nights, are stark and wondrous reminders of what lies beyond the resort's boundaries.

Shopping and art galleries vie with golf as diversions, and natural sightseeing is varied. Indian Canyons have indigenous flora and fauna in dramatic contrast to the rocky gorges and barren desert; Joshua Tree National Park's 8,000 acres encompass some of the most interesting geological displays in the California desert; and the Living Desert's magnificent botanical gardens provide a fascinating and educative journey. Palm Canyon Drive and El Paseo have all the glitz and glamour you might crave. Casinos, hot mineral springs spas, and shopping are pleasant diversions.

**Accommodations:** Southwestern adobe mixed with classic Moroccan design provides a distinctive architectural achievement. Blue domes reflect the cloudless skies; warm brown arches repeat themselves down a long pathway, framing the desert palms and mountains. The 472 guest rooms are scattered in sixteen low-rise pavilions interspersed with meandering walks, gardens, lagoons, and waterfalls. Guest rooms are of generous size and feature a private patio or balcony. Thirty suites each have a separate parlor. Westin has become noted for their "heavenly beds and baths." Westin's rates are totally based on occupancy levels, so it's difficult to define a range. December, January, and March through June is high season; rack rates are $400 to $450. That would be the maximum, if the hotel were completely full. During the off-season, rates may begin as low as $149. Packages are also offered—for example, a nightly rate of $199 with a $200 spa gift certificate. Being flexible with your dates may be helpful. Children under eighteen stay free in their parents' room. Often there are specials for families, too; for example, children stay, play, and eat free, or families enjoy a complimentary buffet breakfast for two adults and two children plus an in-room movie. Ask about Westin Fun, where two children join the Westin Club and eat free.

**Dining:** Bella Vista features continental Mediterranean cuisine and is open for breakfast, lunch, and dinner. Typically Californian, it blends a sunlit atrium with palm trees. Indoor/outdoor dining is available; with views of waterfalls and colorful gardens, it hardly seems like the desert. Season's Grill, open from 11:00 a.m. to 9:00 p.m., offers fun and fresh food for families. If you can't tear yourself or your kids out of one of the three swimming pools, Las Brisas Café serves light poolside snacks and drinks; Caliente is the poolside cabana area. When the ice-cream urge strikes, head to the Cafe and Ice Cream Parlor. For evening cocktails the elegantly casual Lobby Lounge offers drinks and a tapas menu. Sit inside or on the patio with its circular fire pit. Westin has prepared a nice list of family restaurants in the area for those who want to venture out.

**Children's World:** Westin Kids Club is a basic program at Westin resort properties, designed to make family travel safe, convenient, and enjoyable. Children get special age-appropriate gifts upon check-in; parents get a safety kit, if desired (electric-outlet covers, adhesive strips, ID bracelets, and local emergency numbers); and the room is ready with cribs, potty seats, or bed rails if needed. High chairs and bottle warmers are complimentary, jogging strollers are available to rent, meals can be ordered in advance from a children's menu so that they are ready upon arrival at the restaurant, and a lot of information about local things of interest to families is available. It's a really comprehensive approach, and during the summer, special rates and "Kids Eat Free" promotions are generally available.

Discovery Room is the hub of children's activities, filled with games, movies, and fun and educational activities. On their first arrival kids are presented with a Discovery Pack filled with goodies: maps, compass, disposable camera, canteen, and membership bracelet.

The Cactus Kids program for ages four to twelve bills itself as "the coolest thing in the desert." Operating daily year-round from 9:00 a.m. to 4:00 p.m., it costs $45 per three-hour session (9:00 a.m. to noon and 1:00 to 4:00 p.m.) or $15 per hour. Lunch is additional. Reservations are requested at least one day in advance, and the program will be run for even one or two children. Activities include arts and crafts, volleyball, lawn games, movies, nature walks, and bicycle riding. On Friday and Saturday, kids gather for dinner and more action from 5:00 to 8:00 p.m.; cost is $50.

**Recreation:** Two championship golf courses, two practice ranges, and six greens and sand traps keep golfers happy. The Pete Dye Resort Course has his trademark deep bunkers and undulating fairways, while the Gary Player Signature Course is a mosaic of waterfalls, ravines, and lakes. Take lessons from the resident pros, or sign up for a Golf Digest School. Play tennis in the cool of the evening on the seven lighted tennis courts, or join the Reed Anderson Tennis School. Forget something? The pro shops have everything you need. Las Brisas is the largest of the three swimming pools; it was made to resemble the surrounding canyons and has a 60-foot water slide, two whirlpools, and spacious sundecks. Treat yourself to massage, herbal wraps, and facials at the new Spa at Mission Hills; work out at the fitness club; or follow a more leisurely pace with traditional lawn games such as croquet and shuffleboard. Westin's evening ritual, "unwind," eases the journey from day into night. Enjoy food, drink, and something unique to each resort—at Mission Hills it's Native Indian storytelling in the Lobby Lounge.

If you need more action, Oasis Waterpark is nearby as well as Camelot Park, where you can enjoy miniature golf, bumper boats, go-karts, or batting cages. Take the Palm Springs Aerial Tramway 8,516 feet to the Mountain Station for a bird's-eye view, and hike through Mt. San Jacinto Wilderness State Park. Weather permitting (meaning when there is snow), Nordic skiing operates from November to April. At the opposite end of the environmental spectrum, explore the desert by four-wheel drive with experienced guides who can show you the secret life of the desert, or have a real Old West experience in a two-hour covered-wagon tour. As a contrast to all this nature, any teenagers in your party might gravitate toward the Palm Desert Town Center, the area's largest indoor shopping mall. Palm

Springs and El Paseo shopping are just minutes away.

Also in the vicinity you'll find the Children's Discovery Museum of the Desert, the Uprising Outdoor Adventure Center, the Desert Museum and the Living Desert, Moorten Botanical Gardens, and the wineries of Temecula Valley. Indian Canyons make an interesting hiking excursion, and Joshua Tree National Park (100 miles), with its fascinating trees and vegetation, is a good, but long day trip.

---

**71333 Dinah Shore Drive**
**Rancho Mirage, California 92270**
**(760) 328-5955, (800) WESTIN-1**
**www.westin.com**

# CANADA

Alberta
British Columbia
Ontario
Quebec

# DEERHURST RESORT

Huntsville, Ontario

The Muskoka region is Ontario's most popular holiday area. With its clear lakes and beautiful woodlands, it attracts visitors in summer and winter. Deerhurst Resort encompasses 800 acres on the shores of Peninsula Lake and allows guests to experience all the beauty of the area. And yes, there are still deer at Deerhurst.

The original lodge at Deerhurst was opened in 1896 by Charles Waterhouse, with just eighteen guest rooms. Three generations of Waterhouses oversaw the expansion of the property, and today it is one of the largest resort complexes in Canada. It was voted the "Best Summer and Winter Resort in Ontario" by e-kidstoronto.com; and the *Toronto Sun* has voted it the Bronze Award in the "Best Resorts" category. It's a place where families can share the fun together as well as share the stories about their own adventures.

Deerhurst is two-and-a-half hours by car north of Toronto, or only forty minutes by air from Toronto to the resort's private airstrip.

**Accommodations:** Today's accommodations are a far cry from the lodge rooms (without baths) of the early days. At that time the resort was accessible only by steamboat, and the first guests paid $3.50 per person for a week's lodging, with three meals daily! Today, low-rise accommodations for 400 guests are located throughout the resort's landscaped acres. The guest rooms and suites are well appointed and comfortable and are grouped in condominium-style buildings with views of the lake, woods, pools, and golf course. Rates include complimentary access to a wide array of leisure activities, and are higher in summer. A variety of styles suit every need. For families, the junior one-bedrooms are

quite popular; a separate sitting area, kitchenette, and patio or balcony allow for more space. Deluxe and Luxury suites have full-size stove and refrigerator. In the main building, the simplest Traveller's rooms begin at C$99; Pavilion rooms and suites are C$129 to C$799 nightly. It's a ten-minute walk to the beach. Bayshore rooms are only two minutes from the beach, overlooking the lake; rates are C$159 to C$339. Junior one-bedroom suites are near the pool and Pavilion; rates are C$169 to C$369, an excellent value. Deluxe one- to three-bedroom suites range from C$259 to C$799. You may obtain groceries in Huntsville, 13 kilometers from the resort. A daily resort fee of C$7 per room provides parking, shuttle service, fitness center, squash, tennis, racquetball, swimming pools, whirlpool and saunas, hiking/biking trails, and children's playroom. In summer, it covers golf putting and practice area, pedal boats, kayaks, water bikes, and wind surfing; in winter, cross-country skiing, ice-skating, and tubing. Children under eighteen stay free when occupying their parents' room.

**Dining:** In the Eclipse Restaurant, no less than eight chefs display their talents with regional bounty; venison, fresh fish, wild mushrooms, and wild berries are often featured in creative dishes. The cuisine is matched by the decor of lake and trees viewed through huge picture windows and set under soaring Douglas fir ceiling beams. Open for breakfast and dinner, it's all family friendly. The signature restaurant, Steamers, is pure Canadian, with intimate dining rooms in a romantic log-house atmosphere designed for adult dining. The Pub at the Pavilion is casual and well suited for families; soups, sandwiches, pastas, and salads are typical fare here, served all day, from 11:00 a.m. to 11:00 p.m. The Poolside Deck, with views of the lake, serves barbecue favorites in the summer; a golfers lounge is also available for all-day summer dining.

A Modified American Plan is available for adults only. This includes a buffet breakfast and three-course table d'hôte dinner or a la carte selections from the three resort restaurants. Cost is C$62 per person per night and must be purchased for each day of your stay. There is no meal plan for children, but children's menus are available in the Pub and the Eclipse Dining Room.

Just off the lobby, the Landing Lounge is a good place to meet, unwind, and start the evening. Deerhurst keeps reinventing the critically acclaimed nightly entertainment, which is also Canada's longest-running stage show. This lavish performance of music, dance, and exciting visuals is where Shania Twain started performing, so who knows what future superstar you may see? CW's Lakeside Bar & Dance Club, open seasonally in the original lodge by the lake, is the place to end the evening with deejay, dancing, laser lights, and arcade. Special shows are performed three times a week.

**Children's World:** Deerhurst has partnered with the YMCA to entertain your children. From 9:00 a.m. to 5:00 p.m., year-round on Saturday and Sunday, and daily during summer and public school holidays, something cool is always happening. For children five and under (beginning at eighteen months), crafts, games, story time, and indoor/outdoor play are on the menu; ages six to twelve have team games, science experiments, scavenger hunts, and outdoor adventures like snow tubing or nature walks. Bambi Club, for younger children, meets in its own area, especially

suited to little ones; cost is C$35 for full day or C$25 for a half day. Deer Club (for school-age kids) fees are C$30 per day or C$20 per half day. Lunch is available from 12:30 to 1:30 p.m. for an additional C$10. Make reservations at (705) 788-5040.

**Recreation:** The eighteen-hole Deerhurst Lakeside Golf Course was built in 1966 and redesigned in 1988 with many enhancements. Built in 1991, the top-rated Deerhurst Highlands is a magnificent eighteen-hole course winding atop a ridge above the lake, resulting in a combination of challenging play and beautiful scenery. Golf awards are numerous. Highlands Course is included in *Golf Digest's* Planet Golf rankings of the best courses in one hundred nations, along with being the only Ontario resort course to be in the top twenty list of Canadian courses. A driving range, practice tees, and target greens make up the seven-and-a-half-acre instructional facility. A team of professionals direct private lessons and group clinics.

The Pavilion, a complete sports complex, consists of two indoor tennis courts, a racquetball court, a squash court, a fitness room, a U-shaped swimming pool with wading area, and a whirlpool. Also available here is the Spa, where you can relax in the steam and sauna rooms or schedule a massage, facial, body wrap, or hair-styling service.

If you prefer to exercise in the open air, three more swimming pools await you, and six more tennis courts are outdoors (tennis lessons are available). Water sports on the lake abound: sailing, waterskiing, kayaking, fishing, and sailboarding. And you can hike and jog along the nature trails in the beautiful Muskoka Woods. Horseback riding or a horse-drawn carriage or hayride lets the horse exercise, and you simply enjoy, while mountain biking puts you back on the pedal. New adventures include a Hummer Tour or paintball.

Included in the accommodation rates are tennis, squash, racquetball, the swimming pools and beach, hiking trails, and the fitness room. In summer, kayaks, pedal boats, and sailboards are all complimentary to guests. Canoes, sailboats, and waterskiing are available for a fee. Four lakes mean over 60 kilometers of waterways to explore, and replica boats tour where grand steamships used to travel. Fish for lake trout and northern pike, or just sit by the water and take it all in.

Something is scheduled just about every hour from 8:00 a.m. until 2:00 in the morning. Start the day with power walks, yoga, or aquafit in the pool; then try basketball, road hockey, or volleyball; junior golf lessons or tennis lessons; watercolor and funky folk art; and all kinds of dance, such as adult ballroom, Dance! Dance! for ages three to eight, and Hip Hop for nine- to fourteen-year-olds. Afternoon and early evening are for family activities such as Kids R Krafty, stuffing a teddy bear, building a birdhouse, nature hikes, and treasure hunts. After dinner, a guided sunset canoe trek, family movie, teen movie, or bingo may beckon, wrapped up with a beach bonfire and marshmallows. Set one evening aside for the musical review, and another for the magic show, and at least one party night at CW's Lakeside Bar and Dance Club, to put all those dance lessons to use. Fees vary for these activities.

In winter, cross-country ski trails and equipment, outdoor ice rink and skates, hockey and broomball equipment, and snow tubing, plus indoor racquet sports, pool, and fitness room are complimentary to guests. Deerhurst is the gateway to more than 2,000 kilometers of groomed trails and is right on the Trans Ontario Provincial trail system that connects the entire province, so snowmobilers are in snow heaven. Just next to the resort is Hidden Valley Highlands, open on weekends for a little taste of downhill skiing and snowboarding on eight slopes and thirty-five acres of runs. Group sleigh rides or a spin in an old-fashioned cutter will have everyone singing "Jingle Bells." For something a little more unusual, try dogsledding.

**1235 Deerhurst Drive**
**Huntsville, Ontario**
**Canada P1H 2E8**
**(705) 789-6411, (800) 461-4393**
**www.deerhurstresort.com**

# DELAWANA INN RESORT
## Honey Harbour, Ontario

The Delawana Inn Resort is situated just ninety minutes north of Toronto in Honey Harbour, a natural safe harbor of Georgian Bay often called the "sixth great lake" and known for its warm water and sandy beaches. The Georgian Bay Islands National Park consists of fifty-nine islands; the largest, Beausoleil, is a short boat ride from the resort and an easy day trip. This area is steeped in history dating back to the 1600s, when the Jesuits and fur traders began establishing stopping points on the route to Sainte-Marie Among the Hurons. The area is rich in natural beauty, with several national and provincial parks, two UNESCO Biosphere Reserves, and Wasaga, the world's largest freshwater beach. Resort guests have access to seven beaches. Tourists have been coming to this area since 1897, when Victoria House Hotel was built; the only access was by boat, and the fare was a whole 15 cents. In the 1920s it became the Delawana Inn, named after the legend of a local chief and expanded gradually over the years. Destroyed by fires in 1952 and 1973, it has been rebuilt to be even better. In 1996 it was sold to a Toronto development company, whose principals had vacationed there as children. Going into its third century with enthusiasm and dedication to families, it's easy to see why "The Del" has been voted Canada's "Top Summer Family Resort" in 2005 and 2006 and is a Gold Member of the City Parent Hall of Fame, having been chosen by readers for five of eleven years. The Hotel Fun 4 Kids Web site ranked it a "5-star facility for families." Open from mid-May to mid-October, the Delawana Inn is totally about families.

**Accommodations:** The style throughout is classic Ontario lake resort, and the rooms are generally spacious and family-friendly, with a variety of bed types. Five types of accommodations span rooms to houses; Parkview, Lakeview, Edgewater, Suites, and Chalet have varied accommodations and styles within each group, and six houses are on-site. Rates are per person. In spring and fall, daily rates range from C$130 in Parkview to C$205 in Chalet; children under two stay free, and rates for ages three to eighteen-plus range from C$30 to C$95. Rates include all three meals, all resort facilities, and a daily boat cruise. In July and August arrival dates are Thursday, Friday, or Sunday for stays from two to seven nights. Mid-July through mid-August is high summer, when rates are roughly C$30 to C$50 more per adult per day than the rates listed here. The great news is that up to two children under fifteen stay and eat free all

summer when parents are on a meal plan; during two special weeks, two children under seventeen stay free. Single parents have special rates as well. One child stays free with no single supplement when staying in the Beeches or when paying a 25 percent single supplement charge in the Birches or Spruces. Rates include just about everything: lodging, two meals daily, all resort facilities, supervised day care, a full social program for everyone, golf, pool and beach parties, pontoon cruises, nature programs, and evening entertainment. Two-night packages begin at C$395 per person in Parkview, up to C$595 per person in Chalet. Seven-night packages are C$1,095 at Parkview up to C$1,775 in Chalet. Children's rates are per day, based on age: C$30 for ages six years and younger; C$60 for ages seven to twelve; C$75 for ages thirteen to fifteen; and C$85 for ages sixteen through seventeen. Rates for children through age twelve include all meals; rates for teens and adults include breakfast and dinner only. Check the Web site for all the specials and packages the resort offers.

**Dining:** The main lodge is rustic fieldstone and fir, with a huge lobby fireplace. Coffee and tea are available 24/7 in the fireplace lounge. The Royal Dining Hall is trimmed in exposed wood beams, with large windows overlooking the Georgian Bay. Meals are lavish and part of the package. The breakfast buffet includes as much or as little as you want—roll and fruit, or pancakes, sausage, and eggs to order. In spring and fall a lunch buffet is available. Kids have their own evening buffet, hot dog and pizza parties, and early-evening movies. Parents can dine at their leisure and may select from four entrees, soup, salad, and dessert; a buffet; or, on Barbeque Nights, steak right off the grill. Dress code is smart casual. The Mackinaw Grill is a good option for lunch, with wraps, sandwiches, pizza, and light fare—lunch is not included in the summer packages for adults and teens. In spring and fall the Marine Deck Bar has light snacks, music, and neat views. The Boathouse Bar is open nightly to guests only. It's the place to gather for darts, video games, and shuffleboard; to listen to music; or to watch the game. Weekly events during summer happen here, so check the social calendar.

**Children's World:** From toddler to teen, Delawana covers every age and interest. Kids can't wait to join the VIK (Very Important Kids) Club, and everyone receives a welcome gift bag. A playground, a splash pad, sprinklers, and even a resident clown amuse kids. The Delawana Daycare has both an indoor and an outdoor dedicated space. With a three-to-one ratio, cribs, and playpens, their concern for safety is evident. Hours are from 10:00 a.m. to noon and from 1:00 to 5:00 p.m. For ages three to twelve, summer camp runs daily from 10:00 a.m. to 5:00 p.m. Sunday afternoon is free time, due to arrivals and departures. Days are not long enough for all the activities, and the variety is amazing. Divided into age groups of caterpillars, fireflies, crickets, dragonflies, and hornets, activities are geared to each group's abilities. Junior geologist is a favorite, and activities are balanced between active games and arts and crafts, with break times for the littlest and more adventures like canoeing and capture the flag for the older kids. Kids have lunch together, and afternoon activities such as a beach or pool party or contests are often for the entire VIK Club. From 5:00 to 7:00 p.m., you might get to see your child, but then they're usually back at the VIK Club for evening fun—beach campfires, color wars with water balloons, carnival games, or a gold rush. Teen Squad is also daily from 10:00 a.m. to 5:00 p.m., with an evening activity after dinner. The difference is that they plan really cool things

that teens actually want to do, like half-day hiking or canoeing excursions, evening ice-cream cruises or outdoor movies, basketball tournaments, rock climbing, bonfires, water-skiing, trips to local attractions, and much more.

**Recreation:** In addition to the summer camp, daily nature programs allow the entire family to learn about and explore the incredible natural abundance of this area. Explore the wetlands, learn about bugs and insects, get up close and personal with reptiles and amphibians, learn GPS survival, watch birds of prey, go on rock hunts, or track furry critters. Evenings are just as exciting, with two-hour programs that are just plain fun. Take a guided painting tour, grab a flashlight and explore the night, watch the stars, learn history from a canoe or kayak, or really "bug" someone searching for all sorts of live specimens! Junior naturalists can earn a Delawana Nature Certificate for completing three nature adventures. Kids seven to sixteen may participate in a daily, all-day junior golf clinic (C$135). Want to learn to sail or just sharpen your skills? The three-day sailing clinic is for you (C$75). The Adventure Course challenges all ages with climbing walls, and sophisticated team or group exploits involve ringing Mr. T's bell, swinging from vine to vine, the stairway to heaven, or the high-wire bridge. Water, water, everywhere: You can choose from a swimming pool or seven beaches in the area. Two beaches are on the property; North Beach, the largest, is supervised. Rent a motorboat or sailboat, take a forty-five-minute cruise around Georgian Bay, or boat over to Beausoleil Island for the day. Summer guests can frolic on the water trampoline and the "iceberg," a giant inflatable that doubles as a climbing wall and slide. Take out a paddleboat, canoe, or water bike; kayak or windsurf; or learn to water-ski. Fish off the docks or shoreline (you need a license), build a sand castle, or simply read a book. Do check out the social itinerary—we couldn't possibly list all the things to do, as there's literally two to four activities every hour. Sign up at the social kiosk, next to the pool. Golf here is low-key, with a nine-hole pitch-and-putt and an iron range, but there are lessons and a pro shop. Two tennis courts, minigolf, table tennis, hiking, biking, pool parties, basketball, volleyball, bocci ball, guided WaveRunner safaris—stop me! At this point, it's off to the Wanakita Wellness Spa, where the sauna, Vichy shower, and ten treatment rooms will soothe and relax. Of course, they also have yoga and pre-breakfast walks. Then get ready for the evening entertainment shows, featuring music, comedy, hypnotism, magic, acrobats, and jugglers. And tomorrow is another day, filled with more and more and more—what a vacation! If there's time and energy, lots of local sights can draw you—Sainte-Marie Among the Hurons, the Martyr's Shrine, Discovery Bay, and Wye Marsh Wildlife Center are all nearby.

**P.O. Box 279**
**42 Delawana Road**
**Honey Harbour, Ontario**
**Canada POE 1E0**
**(705) 756-2424, (800) 627-3387**
**www.delawana.com**

# FAIRMONT CHATEAU LAKE LOUISE
## Lake Louise, Alberta

The Fairmont Chateau Lake Louise is located 100 miles west of Calgary in spectacular Banff National Park. Banff National Park was the third in the world, and the first in Canada, founded in 1885 after the accidental discovery of a hot springs on Sulphur Mountain. Starting out as a 26-square-kilometer reserve, it is now 6,641 square kilometers of incredible beauty, part of the UNESCO Rocky Mountain World Heritage Site and the most visited park in Canada. Glaciers, snowcapped peaks, meadows of mountain flowers, wilderness, wild creatures, and the impressive Icefields Parkway make this area well worth many visits.

Is there anyone who has not seen an aerial photo of an amazingly colored lake surrounded by mountains, always with that stunning castle-like structure in the foreground? The Fairmont Chateau Lake Louise is generally referred to as the "Diamond in the Wilderness"—four diamond, to be exact. Views from the hotel across this magnificent glacier-fed lake are truly breathtaking, as the eye takes in the expanse of the lake's turquoise water, the blue ice of the Victoria Glacier, and the majestic peaks of the Canadian Rockies that form the Continental Divide. The mountains provide excellent opportunities for skiing in winter and endless exploration into the wonders of nature in summer. Luxurious and inviting, the elegance of another era blends with the natural wonders that surround you. The resort is open all year.

**Accommodations:** Original accommodations on this site, built in 1890 by the Canadian Railway, were rather modest, welcoming a mere dozen adventurous guests at a time and during summer only. Following two devastating fires, which left only the Painter wing standing, the main structure of the current hotel was built in 1925. An additional wing was created in the late 1980s. From the elegant lobby to the helpful staff, careful attention to the needs of guests is evident everywhere. The resort's 489 rooms, ranging from standard bedrooms to suites, are all comfortably and pleasantly decorated. Carved wood, curved lines, an Alpine flavor, a hint of a splendid past—it's all here. Some even offer the luxury of a private Jacuzzi. Rooms facing the lake are preferable, but it's difficult, if not impossible, to find a bad view anywhere. Rates depend on occupancy at the Fairmont, so the following is only a guide. June, July, and August have the highest rates; for families deluxe rooms are preferable for longer stays, as standard rooms are rather small. A standard hill-view room could be C$279 in winter, going to C$499 in summer; a lake-view room begins at C$649 in August. Deluxe rooms' estimated range is from C$375 to C$799. Promotions, packages, and occupancy can create lower rates; again, flexibility with dates is always advantageous. Children under eighteen stay free in the same room.

**Dining:** The Fairmont prides itself on a truly unique Canadian cuisine. For fine dining at its best, the gracious and elegant Fairview Dining Room presents a lovely selection of Alberta beef, Tataki of Bison, and lamb and fish dishes as well as a wine list of more than 400 labels from around the world, including wonderful British Columbia wines. Old-world tradition prevails at the Walliser Stube, with a classic Swiss menu featuring their famous fondue. In summer, dine in the grand manner in the opulent Victoria Room, where table-to-ceiling windows overlook lush flowers and the blue, blue lake. Stone fireplaces and wooden beams enhance the setting. Get an early start on your day at the Poppy Brasserie, or stop by for lunch or dinner (7:00 a.m. to 8:30 p.m.)—delicious international specialties are the order of the day. The Chateau Deli is open twenty-four hours a day, and you can leisurely eat there or get it to go. Want a gourmet lunch to go or have a craving for a decadent dessert in the middle of the night? This is the place for you. Afternoon Tea in the Lakeview Lounge is a nice tradition, and not at all stuffy. A pot of specially blended tea, sparkling wine, exquisite finger sandwiches and pastries—ummm, quite civilized. At the other end of the day, sink into the thronelike chairs of the Lakeview Lounge and revel in the glacier, forested slopes, and other glorious views while you sip a sunset. Step through the doors of the Glacier Saloon and into the Old West. Shoot a game of pool, dance to live music, and meet and mingle; it features pub meals, light snacks, après-ski, and a patio in summer. Warmth and hospitality are what's really served throughout the hotel.

**Children's World:** A staff-supervised children's playroom is available daily in ski season only. Here kids from age three can do crafts, watch movies, play games, or (literally) hang out on the climbing wall. A C$20-per-day fee applies. It's open from 9:00 a.m. to 10:00 p.m. Parents may leave their children for a maximum of four hours while they pursue other activities within the hotel; they cannot, however, leave the grounds, as this is not licensed day care. At other times, babysitting can be arranged; rates are C$14 per hour for up to two children. A nice touch is that all sitters have undergone the Royal Canadian Mounted Police security check. Yes, the "Mounties" do still exist!

Five minutes away at the Lake Louise ski area, Telus Play Station and Daycare looks after infants from as young as eighteen days to six years, in a bright, warm environment.

Hours are from 8:30 a.m. to 4:30 p.m. Rates vary by age: C$59 for children up to nineteen months; C$49 for toddlers to thirty-six months (C$29 for a half day); C$39 for preschoolers to six years (C$25 for a half day). Lunch is C$8 extra. Add a one-hour introduction to ski lesson for C$20; two one-hour lessons for C$29; or a half-hour "Moms and Tots" lesson for C$10. Kids Ski for ages five to twelve explores the mountain and increases skill through fun and games. Snowboarding is for ages seven to twelve; both groups have instruction in small groups divided by age and abilities. A full day (five and a half hours) is C$89 with supervised lunch and progress card at day's end. Design Your Own package allows you to add lift (C$18), equipment, or lunch (C$13). The Discover package for first-timers is C$79 for full-day lift, equipment, and lesson.

**Recreation:** Lake Louise boasts 4,200 skiable acres, with 139 named runs, the longest of which is 8 kilometers (5 miles). Forty-five percent of the runs are intermediate, and 30 percent are expert. A nice feature is that every chairlift has an easy and a more difficult way down, opening the mountain to all levels of ability. With a vertical rise of 3,250 feet and a top elevation of 8,650, the annual 200-inch snowfall is respectable. Whether on a long run from the top of the mountain or in the middle of acres and acres of open bowls, everyone in the family will find his or her favorite terrain.

Cross-country skiing is a big feature at the Fairmont, with a wide variety of picturesque trails leading right from the hotel. Ice-skating on Lake Louise, snowshoeing, dogsledding, and horse-drawn sleigh rides add action to the wintertime picture. Evenings are filled with stargazing and stories by the fireplace. The resort has an indoor swimming pool, a hot tub, and a well-equipped exercise room; visit the spa for a variety of therapeutic treatments.

In May the resort sponsors a wine and food festival. In summer the Lake Louise Gondola and Interpretive Center does truly special programs. Ride to an elevation of 6,850 feet, where two ecosystems meet and the Rockies are spread before you in a majestic panorama as you learn about grizzly bears in their own habitat. Excursions that range from four to eight hours, with professional mountain guides, reveal the nature and history of the Canadian Rockies in a national park that is home to elk, bighorn sheep, moose, and mountain goats. Canoeing on the lake and biking the many trails open up to visitors the natural splendors of this region. Every imaginable mountain sport, winter or summer, is here. A special Mountain Adventure Concierge will help you plan—many activities sell out far in advance, so be sure to book when you make your reservation (403-522-1601). Torchlight dinners on the mountain, soaking the day away in the mineral hot springs, or heli-skiing the glacier—Lake Louise guarantees to live up to your expectations. *Skiing* magazine voted Lake Louise number one for scenery and number two for value in all of North America. And the wonders of a great national park surround you; in Banff, don't miss the drive through the Bow Valley, or a day trip on the scenic Icefields Parkway.

---

**111 Lake Louise Drive**
**Lake Louise, Alberta**
**Canada T0L 1E0**
**(403) 522-3511, (800) 441-1414**
**www.fairmont.com/lakelouise**
**www.skilouise.com**
**www.canadianrockies.net**

# FAIRMONT LE CHÂTEAU MONTEBELLO

## Montebello, Quebec

You don't have to travel all the way to Europe for a vacation in a French chateau. Voilà! The Fairmont Le Château Montebello is a luxury resort in a peaceful woodland setting located on the shores of the Ottawa River between Montreal and Ottawa.

Built of more than 10,000 massive cedar logs by a team of craftsmen in 1930, Fairmont Le Château Montebello served as an exclusive private club for forty years. In 1970 it became a resort open to the public year-round. Today the Château's old-world charm and contemporary elegance come together as a lovely holiday destination, with the distinction of being one of the world's largest log structures. Le Château Montebello is a CAA/AAA four-diamond resort with a five-star rating from Quebec Lodging. Awards are numerous—in 2007, *Travel + Leisure*'s top 500, in 2006 *Travel + Leisure*'s "#1 Family-Friendly Resort in Canada," in 2005 *Condé Nast Traveler* Gold List, and one of Family Travel Forum's "Top 10 Getaways for Family Togetherness."

**Accommodations:** The central log chateau shelters all 211 guest rooms and suites, combining rustic elegance with a Swiss chalet–inspired decor. Guests can gather around the huge six-sided fireplace sitting in the center of the soaring three-story atrium for warmth and socializing. The chateau has four wings radiating from the center, affording the guest rooms views to the river, gardens, and forest. Yield management is the rule for rates at most Fairmont hotels. This means that rates depend more on availability than season—room rates seem to range from C$215 to C$309 in general. However, if occupancy were low, rates could drop. Most Fairmont hotels have Only One Way summer rates starting at C$199. Bed-and-breakfast packages include one buffet breakfast, access to the sports center, squash, indoor pool, and tennis courts; rates start at C$289 per room, based on double occupancy in summer to C$249 off-season. Between the end of May and late September, Family Fun two-night packages start at C$439 per night (two adults, two children under twelve; inquire for rates on teens) and include lodging, daily buffet breakfast and dinner, bike rental, miniputt, a pontoon boat cruise, half-day canoeing at Fairmont Kenauk, and the Children's Activity Program. With any stay, a children's rate of C$39 for ages six to twelve, and C$22 for ages four and five includes buffet breakfast and dinner, welcome gift, three hours of children's program or day care, evening films, crafts, and other activities. Promotion is good daily in summer, and on weekends at other times of the year. Other packages offer more nights and more "goodies"; inquire about the Montebellissimo, or Summer Magic, beginning at C$419 per night, with a minimum five-night stay and lots of extras. The Summer Family Adventure offers your very own wilderness cabin on a private lake, with boats, guided nature walk, and all sports facilities at Le Château Montebello, beginning at C$897 for three nights. Children eighteen and under stay free in the room with parents.

**Dining:** For dinner, Aux Chantignoles is the rustic yet gourmet dining room of the resort. Menu items such as rack of caribou with juniper berries enhance the feeling of a hunting club; the French flavor shows in the cassoulet of snails. The breakfast buffet gives a jump-start of energy to your day; this is also the venue for the Sunday brunch. The Golf Club Terrace is popular for light lunches; a food cart makes the rounds of the greens if you just can't wait. The Igloo Bar is a summer restaurant for outdoor barbecues, ideal for lunch or dinner. The Bistro-Bar la Seigneurie is the place for gathering at the end of an active day; enjoy cocktails at the bar, "pub grub," or a light repast at one of the small tables or the central gazebo-like area while kids are entertained with video games and pool tables; a house band plays on weekends.

Rue Notre-Dame, where the hotel is located, has many popular eateries. Try the charming Café Terrasse la Lanterne, an ivy-covered roadside inn in Montebello's commercial district with river views and delectable desserts. For lunch, Le Bistro feels like dining at a friend's home; Le Zouk Resto-Pub is a rustic-looking joint that's a favorite with locals and tourists alike. At night, the bar is a favorite hangout. For international dining Le Mar-Lyn, in a beautiful old home, is great for romantic dinners, while Le Pot au Feu serves up an eclectic and creative menu in a homey ambience.

**Children's World:** Daily during July, August, and school holidays, fun rules at the Children's Activity Center, from 9:00 a.m. to noon and evenings from 7:30 to 9:00 p.m. Appearances by Monte the Beaver create even more excitement. Year-round, the program operates only on Friday and Saturday evenings, Saturday from 9:00 a.m. to noon, and Sunday from 9:00 a.m. to 1:00 p.m. Outdoor activities such as hiking and group games are mixed with toys, games, and arts and crafts based on the ages and number of children in the program. The program, for ages three to twelve, is included in the Summer Family Fun

package; otherwise, cost is C$35 per session. Outside of regular program hours, day care or babysitting is available at an hourly cost of C$9 for one child, C$10 for two children, with a three-hour minimum.

**Recreation:** Le Château Montebello is quite proud of its golf course, ranked as Quebec's second toughest by *Canada Golf Magazine*. It features a wide range of difficult holes and natural obstacles, so golfers need to be alert with a few tricks in their bag. The golf school provides lessons and organizes clinics. At the Health Club and Sports Complex, you can work out in the exercise room, play squash or tennis, swim laps in the indoor pool, or relax in the saunas or whirlpools. The outdoor pool is a beautiful setting for relaxing, sunning, and swimming. Referee the kids in volleyball and badminton games, then round up the whole crew for bike riding or miniputt. Other activities include water sports, cruises, riding a Jet Ski, and horseback riding.

The Ultima Spa offers professional services, including full-body massage, facials, body wraps of mud or algae, body exfoliation and polishing, and therapeutic baths using either relaxing pine and rosemary milk or stimulating mineral salts. What a treat after a full day of activity!

The whole family can discover the beauties of Fairmont Kenauk, a 100-square-mile plant and wildlife preserve within 6 miles of the resort, with scores of activities—bird watching, picnics, hikes with or without a naturalist, mountain biking, or fishing. Explore White Fish Lake by rowboat or canoe, float down the Kinonge River, or rent a motorboat at the marina. It's a great place to laze away summer days enjoying nature. Omega Park provides a slightly different approach to nature. Drive along a 10-kilometer road through 1,500 acres of a woodland corral where native animals small (raccoons, wild boar, and deer) and large (bison, black bears, and wild sheep) roam free. Don't forget your camera! About 10 miles west of Montebello is the Plaisance Waterfall, cascading more than 200 feet within the Papineau-Labelle Wildlife Reserve; it's a great spot for a picnic and hike.

Snow brings enchantment to the woods and hills and is the focus of wintertime fun. The familiar activities of ice-skating, ice-fishing, sleigh rides, and snowmobiling compete with the more exotic: dogsledding, curling, snowshoeing, broomball, and deck hockey. More than 27 kilometers of cross-country ski trails beckon, or you may prefer just a walk in the snow and curling up with a good book in front of the huge six-sided fireplace in the chateau.

---

392 rue Notre-Dame
Montebello, Quebec
Canada J0V 1L0
(819) 423-6341, (800) 441-1414
www.fairmont.com/montebello/

# FAIRMONT LE MANOIR RICHELIEU

## Charlevoix, Quebec

In Quebec's Charlevoix County, near Quebec City, the mountains and forests stretching along the great St. Lawrence River create a vista of magnificent scenery and quiet charm. In this rural area, where farming and agriculture are part of daily life, Fairmont has created a historically splendid resort, blending the quiet charm of the countryside with the sophistication of a three-star, four-diamond resort. The hotel was one of *Condé Nast Traveler's* top seventy-five hotels in North America and is on the Gold List of "World's Best Places to Stay." Tourism in Charlevoix dates back to 1761, when sportsmen came for the salmon fishing and wilderness. The original Le Manoir Richelieu was built in 1899, atop a cliff overlooking the majestic St. Lawrence River. Destroyed by fire in 1928, it was rebuilt in the style of a French castle and opened again in 1929. A $140 million renovation and expansion was completed in 1999, bringing the hotel back to its original glory, as the "Castle of the Cliff."

The Charlevoix region was granted status as a World Biosphere Reserve by UNESCO in 1988 and is the first biosphere reserve to be populated in the world. Within its boundaries are historical gardens, art galleries, a marine museum and eco-center, and many working studios for pottery, papermaking, and fabrics; an amazing variety of wildlife also calls this area home.

**Accommodations:** Comfort and luxury are offered by 405 guest rooms and 17 one- and two-bedroom suites, and kids love the idea of staying in a castle. Rates depend on occupancy at the Fairmont, so the following is only a guide. Summer is high season, when a Fairmont room with garden view is C$269; river view is C$319. Those same rooms in winter are C$149 and C$189; and in spring the rates drop even more. Bed-and-Breakfast packages begin at C$100 per person, with extra charges for children. Only One Way Summer rates start at C$179, May to September, based on double occupancy. Children under eighteen stay free in the room with parents. A summer family fun package includes breakfast and dinner, miniputt, a horse-drawn carriage ride, bike rental, tennis, and the kids' club; rates vary according to number and ages of children.

**Dining:** For fine dining, the four-diamond restaurant Le Charlevoix, overlooking the St. Lawrence, showcases antiques, local art, and fresh produce from the region. Also overlooking the river, Le Saint-Laurent, the hotel's main dining room, is open for breakfast and dinner and is famous for its buffet. Fresh fish and grilled specialties will tempt you. Families enjoy Le Bellerive, with a relaxed bistro atmosphere, which serves a casual menu and light buffet; in summer dine alfresco on the sunny terrace. Enjoy breakfast, light snacks, and local micro-brews at the Clubhouse restaurant; even if you don't play golf, the view of this famous fairway between mountain and sea is spectacular. At 6:00 p.m. the Golf Clubhouse magically turns into Le Point Cardinal, another dining option featuring Canadian beef and fresh seafood, enhanced by fresh, local, hand-picked produce. Arrive there in style from the hotel in a hostess-driven power cart. Sip a cocktail at La Brise Lobby Bar or stroll over to the Bar Le Marie-Clarisse or Salon Murray at the Casino. For a romantic evening, the French cuisine at L'Auberge sur La Cote in nearby La Malbaie is a favorite of townsfolk.

**Children's World:** The Kid's Club is a friendly place for children to gather. In summer the club operates daily from 8:00 a.m. to 10:00 p.m. for ages four to twelve. Fees are C$16 per hour (C$9 each additional child) or C$100 for the entire day (C$85 for second child, C$75 for the third), including meals. Daytime (8:00 a.m. to 5:00 p.m.; C$80) and evening (5:00 to 10:00 p.m.; C$40) or morning (8:00 a.m. to noon; C$40) sessions are also available. Children

participate in aquatic games, swimming, sports, arts and crafts, treasure hunts, and nature excursions. A mini-cinema for kids has shows all day, with popcorn. A giant beanbag and children's playground are always popular.

In winter, weekends for kids begin at 5:00 p.m. Friday and continue almost non-stop until noon on Sunday. Friday and Saturday nights until 10:00 p.m. and all day Saturday are filled with the same pursuits as summer, plus the outdoor thrill of snow-shoes, ice-skating, and sledding. Babysitting is available for C$9 per hour, with a three-hour minimum.

**Recreation:** Golf at the Fairmont Le Manoir Richelieu began in 1925, when President William Taft opened the eighteen-hole award-winning course. As well, at least three public courses are nearby, so golfers can't get complacent. At the resort itself, enjoy saltwater swimming indoors or out, a wading pool, and water volleyball and basketball. A game room provides evening entertainment for the family. An evening spent at the Casino de Charlevoix, next door to the hotel, may be rewarding—if your luck holds. Horse-back riding with gorgeous views, pony rides for the youngsters, and carriage rides at sunset are found at the equine center. Tennis, aqua-aerobics, hiking, a fitness room, sea or river kayaking, and mountain biking will keep you in shape, while a whirlpool soothes you at the end of it all. Lawn games and French Bowl are delightful ways to pass an afternoon. AmeriSpa can pamper you with twenty-two treatment rooms, and even a seven-day rejuvenation.

Winter snows bring wonderful outdoor opportunities such as sleigh rides, dogsledding, ice-fishing, horseback riding, and all those sports that require snowshoes, skates, or cross-country skis. Plus you can give the traditional Canadian sport of broomball a whirl. The Multi-Sports Center can arrange it all. Snowmobiles are so popular that the resort provides parking, if you want to bring your own! Skiers have a choice of Mont Grand-Fonds (15 kilometers from the hotel), with a 335-meter vertical drop and cross-country skiing; or Le Massif, at 770 meters (2,536 feet) the highest vertical drop east of the Canadian Rockies, with an average snow-fall of over 250 inches (80 kilometers away). The hotel has shuttles to both ski areas.

For foreigners, shopping at the hotel or nearby local craft shops and art galleries can be a bargain with the exchange rates and tax regulations. The Route des Saveurs (Flavor Trail) showcases the region's excellent products: lamb, migneron cheese, and mini-vegetables. The circuit includes restaurants that use regional products in their cuisine and also a tour of the farms that produce them. It's an authentic glimpse into another way of life, and a great way for kids to make the connections with where food originates other than the grocery store. The Park of Hautes-Gorges-de-la-Rivière-Malbaie follows the Rivière Malbaie as it winds through some of the most extraordinary valleys between the highest cliffs east of the Canadian Rockies. Here you can participate in biking, canoeing, hiking, and kayaking; or the more sedate can enjoy a glass-bottom boat cruise. A cruise to the mouth of the St. Lawrence to witness migratory whales is a thrilling experience for all; between June and October at least six species of whales also visit. Charming villages dot the coastline. The Tourism Office (800-667-2276) has loads of information.

---

**181 rue Richelieu**
**La Malbaie, Quebec G5A 1X7**
**(418) 665-3703, (800) 257-7544**
**www.fairmont.com/richelieu**

# GRAY ROCKS RESORT
## Ville de Mont-Tremblant, Quebec

Just 75 miles northwest of Montreal, in the Laurentian Mountains, you will find a charming four-season, four-star lakeside family resort with a definite French flavor. Right in the middle of French-speaking Canada, Gray Rocks welcomes American visitors, and both French and English are spoken here routinely. You might choose to take the opportunity to brush up on your French, but rest assured that your interests uttered in English in the dining room, on the tennis courts, or during a ski lesson will be well received with warm French-Canadian hospitality.

Since its beginning in 1906, Gray Rocks has developed into a renowned ski, golf, and tennis resort with hotel and condominium accommodations for all tastes. The hotel sits on the shores of Lac Ouimet. Gray Rocks's own ski mountain, Sugar Peak, rises right behind the hotel; beautiful views of Mont-Tremblant are also impossible to miss. Golf was the first sport in this area, followed by skiing. Today recreational pastimes also include tennis, water sports, horseback riding, mountain biking, or nature hikes. In 2006 Gray Rocks celebrated one hundred years of fun.

**Accommodations:** Fifty-one lakeside rooms with private balcony are available in the hotel's Pavilion and Chalet Suisse; fifty-four regular rooms have lake or mountain views; rooms and suites have various bed arrangements. Fifty-six one-, two-, and three-bedroom condominiums are tucked in among the trees ¾ mile from the hotel, with free shuttle-bus service. All condos have fireplaces, full kitchen, and balcony or patio. As usual, rates depend on the size of the accommodation, the number of people, the location, and the season. Hotel rates generally include meals (dinner and breakfast); condominium rates do not. Spring and fall hotel rates are lowest, from C$115 to C$155; summer is considered the end of June to Labor Day, when rates are C$145 to C$185. Hotel rates are per person, based on two adults, while condominium rates are per unit. Condominiums are C$165 to C$255 in spring and fall; C$225 to C$435 in summer. At the hotel, children up to five years old receive free meals and lodging; special rates for older children in the hotel vary by season and age. In spring and fall rates are C$35 for children ages six to ten and C$45 for ages eleven to seventeen. In summer, the rate is C$95 for all children over five years. Ask about special one- to three-night packages when you book. If you're renting a condo and want a meal plan, daily rates are C$62 for adults, C$50 for ages eleven to seventeen, and C$40 for ages six through ten. Under-fives always eat free.

In winter guests can enjoy a bed-and-breakfast package, which includes one night's lodging, one breakfast, a one-day lift ticket, entertainment, and access to the indoor pool; the value-season rate is C$99 to C$129, and the regular-season rate is C$119 to C$139. Ski A La Carte packages include the above, plus one dinner and two days' lift tickets. Lift tickets are valid for both Gray Rocks and the nearby sister resort, Mont Blanc. Per-person package rates in regular ski season are C$150 to C$190; holidays are C$20 more. Children's rates apply. This package is for hotel guests only. Condominium rates during regular season range from C$268 to C$469 per unit per day, with no extras. Weekly rates in regular season are C$1,560 to C$2,400.

The most popular winter package is the all-inclusive ski or snowboard week from Sunday to Saturday morning. You will enjoy six nights of lodging; twelve full-course meals; twenty hours of ski instruction or ten hours of snowboard instruction with the renowned Snow Eagle Ski School; video critique; seven-day lift ticket; races and awards; and a welcome party. In the regular ski season, the package is C$1,349 to C$1,699 per person based on double occupancy. Inquire about adding ski week amenities to the condos. Skiing can be an affordable sport, after all. And Gray Rocks is family-friendly during both winter and summer.

**Dining:** The main dining room, with its fireplace and picture windows overlooking scenic Lac Ouimet, provides a pleasant ambience during meals. Continental and French-Canadian cuisines are featured; four-course table d'hôte dinners and lavish breakfast buffets keep guests satisfied. Cozy lounges with fireplaces and lake views are perfect to relax and mix with old and new friends; the Thirsty Eagle Bar, with a circular fireplace, has evening entertainment in season. In summer, twice-weekly barbecues are scheduled on the outdoor patio. There's also a cafeteria at the Chalet Lucile Wheeler, located midmountain and accessible by car, shuttle bus, or skis. Both golf courses have a clubhouse with snack bar and lounge area.

**Children's World:** In summer during July and August, the daily children's activity program is in high gear. Youngsters join other children their own ages for supervised morning and afternoon events. Preschoolers ages three to five head to the playground, go on treasure hunts and hayrides, or frolic on the private beach. Kids ages six to nine go swimming and horseback riding, try their talents in arts and crafts, and join hayrides. Preteens (ten to twelve) and teens (thirteen and older) enjoy volleyball, tennis, hiking, canoeing, sailboarding, fishing, and various excursions. For all children ages three to five, the cost is C$35 per child per day and includes lunch. The 9:00 a.m. to 3:00 p.m. programs are included for hotel guests ages six to seventeen as part of the package. Camp is available to condominium guests' children for C$35. Day care for ages six months to two years is also offered and promises "vigilant supervision and experienced staff"; the ratio of children to supervisor is 2:1 and cost is C$60 per day. Private babysitting may be arranged, with a three-hour minimum.

Junior Golf clinics for ages six and up run Monday through Friday, for a total of ten hours. The teaching ratio is 5:1, and the fee is C$35 per day; C$160 for five days. Junior tennis clinics are offered for ages six to ten and eleven to sixteen; C$25 per one-hour session. For more serious aspirations, the one- or two-week resident Junior Camp programs in golf and tennis will definitely improve skills.

In winter Gray Rocks's philosophy is to put children on skis as much as possible. Given that the resort's own gentle mountain is just out the back door, this philosophy is easily practiced. The children's ski classes are divided along age lines as well as ability; heaven forbid your first-time thirteen-year-old skier should be in a class with four-year-olds! Camaraderie in a peer group is important in the learning experience. Children and teens can also meet their friends in a variety of après-ski activities, such as cookie baking, face painting, treasure hunts, arts and crafts, table tennis tournaments, parties, movies, water polo, and sleigh rides or bingo with Mom and Dad. You want to have some fun with your kids, too!

Day-care service is also available in winter for ages six months to two years, as well as private babysitting. Snow Eaglets combines day care and snow play with an introduction to skiing. Three-year-olds spend one to two hours (as tolerated) in outside play and ski familiarization; four- and five-year-olds have more stamina and therefore more ski time. It's very personalized for your child's abilities and desires. Daily rates are C$85 for a full day with lunch, and C$35 for a half day; C$400 for a week includes 8:30 a.m. to 4:00 p.m. daily, with lunch. In addition, Monday evening from 5:00 to 6:00 p.m., children gather while parents have wine and cheese; and again from 6:00 to 10:00 p.m. on Friday, for the awards and ski dinner. On the mountain an exclusive snow park for beginners is close to the day lodge and children's services and is kept secure with an easy-ride "magic carpet" lift and fenced outdoor play area.

The Junior Ski and Snowboard weekly program is designed for ages six to thirteen; it's included with hotel vacation packages, C$400 for condo guests. Two-hour ski lessons in the morning and afternoon (snowboarding is morning only), plus the special evening hours, have kids schussing down the slopes by the end of the week.

**Recreation:** Think of Gray Rocks as a university for sports. Its qualified ski, golf, and tennis instructors combine expertise with a sincere enthusiasm for teaching. Improvement of skills and self-confidence go hand in hand, and both are better achieved with ample doses of encouragement and humor. More than 250,000 ski-weekers have enjoyed Gray Rocks's unique teaching methods in a safe, uncrowded ski environment.

The Snow Eagle Ski School has a fine reputation (rated by *Ski* magazine as one of the top-ten ski schools in North America) and more than fifty years of experience. The resort boasts a number of third-generation families who have learned to ski on these slopes and continue to return for their winter holidays. Though Gray Rocks has a modest 620-foot vertical drop, there's variety on the twenty-two runs. Snowmaking facilities cover 95 percent of the slopes, ensuring a ski season from Thanksgiving through early April. Mont-Tremblant ski resort is less than 5 miles from Gray Rocks, so intermediate and advanced skiers can seek additional challenges there. The ski boutique can meet your needs for rentals, repairs, fashions, and accessories. Cross-country skiing is a growing favorite at Gray Rocks. Nearby Domaine St. Bernard offers well-maintained trails through the woods, next to the river. A tour around the area is a lovely way to spend a winter morning, and a sleigh ride with the kids caps off a perfect day.

Summertime opens another whole realm of outdoor sports and activities. There's a private sandy beach along a section of the lake. This is Canada, but summers are hot, so swimmers will be happy. The complete marina near the beach offers opportunity for canoeing, sailboarding, sailing, taking out a paddleboat, or enjoying an afternoon of fishing.

A classic eighteen-hole golf course (La Belle) will take you through lush fairways over diverse terrain framed by the rugged beauty of the Laurentians. Three learning holes are reserved for Eagle Golf Academy players. The combination of time-proven teaching strategies and small class ratios helps players take strokes off their game and turns newcomers on to the joys of the sport. In 2001 Gray Rocks opened an eighteen-hole championship course (La Bête) designed by renowned golf architect Graham Cooke. The course winds its way along Devil's River, offering superb views of the surrounding mountains. With bent grass tees, greens, and fairways, four sets of tees to choose from, and eighteen distinct and challenging holes, you will leave knowing you have played one of Canada's best courses. In fact, it was voted the best family golf resort in Quebec by *Golf Ranking Magazine.*

Tennis buffs enjoy the largest outdoor complex in Canada with twenty-two Har-Tru courts (ten near the hotel and twelve at the golf club). Tennis lessons with videotaping can help you isolate the improvements necessary for a good game. Gray Rocks's golf and tennis academies offer acclaimed two-and five-day clinics, plus junior camps.

Jogging along the lake or hiking and horseback riding in the hills are excellent ways to explore the countryside and revel in the clean mountain air. You can enjoy a nice afternoon next to the beach playing lawn games or get in shape at Le Spa fitness center. Le Spa features an indoor swimming pool, an exercise room, hot tubs, a sauna, and a professional massage service. Many activities are offered free of charge; some, such as golf, tennis, and horseback riding, carry additional fees.

Family activities are many at Gray Rocks. Visiting the playground, sharing the putting green or croquet, evening barbecue and bonfire, bingo, karaoke night, and hay (or sleigh) rides are just some of the ways families share fun.

---

**2322 rue Labelle**
**Ville de Mont-Tremblant, Quebec**
**Canada J8E 1T8**
**(819) 425-2771, (800) 567-6767**
**www.grayrocks.com**

# SEVERN LODGE

### Port Severn, Ontario

Severn Lodge is beautifully located in the midst of the Georgian Lakelands of Ontario, only 90 miles from Toronto. Georgia Bay forms the northeastern part of Lake Huron and is named in honor of England's King George IV. The area's piney woods, fine fishing, and clear waters attract many vacationers. The geographic features of the Cambrian Shield area where the lodge is located are unique. Spectacular rock formations created during the Ice Age, granite outcroppings, windswept pines, and hardwood forests dot the many islands and inlets. And the Severn Lodge, on the shores of Gloucester Pool, adds to the natural features with its warm pride of being "owned and operated by the same family, for families, since 1937." The Severn Lodge location dates back to the mid-1800s, when the lodge building served as one of the headquarters for the Georgian Bay Lumber Company. At that time the trip from the Waubaushene train station took nearly half a day; today, it's only a ten-minute trip via highway. Severn Lodge is a special place, where the everyday hustle and bustle quiets, and one has time to breathe the fresh air, relax, and do as much or as little as you want. Set in a sheltered cove, the resort encompasses one hundred acres of waterfront property, with over 2,000 feet of private shoreline. The lodge is open from mid-May to mid-October only.

**Accommodations:** Severn Lodge's early-twentieth-century ambience remains preserved in the many white clapboard buildings, log crisscross railings, and cobblestone sidewalks. All accommodations and facilities, however, are very modern.

Grouped in about a dozen individual buildings surrounding the main lodge and set among the trees and along the lake, the accommodations are in three styles. Hotel-style rooms have two double beds with a view of the waterfront; family-size rooms are one large room with two sleeping areas separated by a dividing wall and a sitting area with sofa bed; and two-bedroom units offer more privacy. Three different rate groups reflect location and different amenities. Two- to seven-day packages are fully inclusive and include lodging, baggage handling, two or three meals daily (according to the season), the children's activity program, evening entertainment, and use of the recreation facilities. Children's rates are based on age, and some weeks during summer (June especially) are designated "kids free" (under twelve) and 50 percent off for teens. Stays for children two and under are always complimentary. Adult rates are per person and range from C$349 to C$514 for spring and fall (two to three days). Seven days in July and August run C$1,045 to C$1,274 for adults; C$389 for children ages two to four; C$459 for ages five to eight; C$616 for ages nine to twelve; and C$729 for teens to age seventeen. Cottages and suites are located on the water both on-site and off-site, about five minutes by boat or car from the resort. These rates are per unit and include the entertainment, activities, and recreation at Severn Lodge, but no meals or daily maid service. Weekly rates in summer range from C$1,759 to C$2,329. Remember, that's less in U.S. dollars, depending on the current exchange.

**Dining:** The charming, elegantly rustic main lodge dining room serves a view of the waterfront with food, wine, and warm hospitality. The Heritage Room, with its log-beamed ceiling, takes you back to an earlier time, while the Lakefront Room is light and airy, with soaring ceilings and window cupola. The Canadian cuisine is accompanied by freshly baked breads and pastries. Severn Lodge has a reputation for delicious foods, and children always have special choices (including vegetables and fruit) and even their own summertime buffet. A weekly excursion takes all the children to a nearby island for a picnic. Some summer days feature a poolside barbecue with grilled foods; you can dine either inside or outside. Usually you have four or five choices for dinner; one night each week there's a barbecue; another may be a deluxe buffet. Fresh, high-quality, healthy foods are always used, and vegetarians are not forgotten. Picnic lunches can be prepared for guests who are off hiking or canoeing during the midday meal.

**Children's World:** The summer activities program seems to combine the best of all worlds, flexibly structured with lots of freedom. The folks at Severn Lodge appreciate the fact that families also want time together on their vacations, so kids can come and go, joining parents for picnics, island explorations by canoe, or other family activities, and then returning to fun-filled time with their peers. Children gather after breakfast, break for lunch with parents, and after that they're off again until about 5:00 p.m. Daily from late June to Labor Day, the camp includes hikes, crafts, volleyball and baseball games, swimming, diving and boating lessons, picnics, and movies. Add waterskiing, Indian Night, Talent Night, a Fish Derby, corn roasts, and bonfire sing-alongs, and you know you have happy kids. No additional charges are applied for these events, and children of all ages are welcome to participate.

Every effort is made to include even very young guests, and a supervised toddler activity program provides pint-size fun, with specially designed indoor and outdoor play areas for two- to four-year-olds. The program is complimentary and includes arts and crafts, sand-castle building, and other beach and playground activities. This program runs daily, and kids eat most meals with their parents. The lodge staff can also arrange an individual babysitter for an extra cost. Favorites among the younger set are the sandy beach; the playground, with its swings, slide, sandbox, and climbing equipment; and the dock, for "just fishin'." The Junior Program (ages five to eight) has supervised activities around themes of history, culture, or nature. Kids are kept busy with fishing derbies, waterskiing and tubing, island picnics, beach bonfires, and scavenger hunts. Ages nine to twelve are in the Youth Program, filled with age-appropriate fun, and teens have just what they like—many things to do and not too much structure. Programs for older children are daily in high summer, but all ages eat most meals with parents; occasionally a pizza party or picnic is scheduled "for kids only."

**Recreation:** Severn Lodge also knows that creating family memories is an important part of the vacation. Lots of family activities such as picnics, canoeing the coves, horseback riding, and just exploring can be fit into the flexible schedules of the kids' program. Evening entertainment in the Regatta Room is geared toward all ages and often includes children. Severn Lodge is really a family operation, and programming is eclectic and interesting. Sometimes it may be a nature "show and tell," where local experts with reptiles or falcons will come, bringing "friends" to demonstrate their stories. Or an early "explorer" will land on the lakeshore during the bonfire and tell stories about the early days of discovery. There's a sense of camaraderie about Severn that makes a memorable vacation.

Water sports are an important part of Severn Lodge. Wonderful swimming can be had either in the lake or in the heated swimming pool; perhaps you'd like to try the whirlpool spa at the deepwater dock. Maybe you would prefer to stay on top of the water in a fishing boat reeling in walleye, bass, muskie, and northern pike. Also on top of the water (with any luck, you will stay on top) is the waterskiing instruction offered several times a week. Free use of the lodge's sailboats, paddleboats, kayaks, and canoes can make an afternoon lazy or exciting, depending on your skill. The resort has a unique collection of antique runabouts and motor launches. Rental fees are charged on a daily or weekly basis for outboard boats, motors, and Jet Skis; the lodge offers island cruises on board the 37-foot vintage 1922 mahogany motor launch for an extra charge.

On land you can jog or hike on the trails around the lodge's one hundred acres, explore on mountain bikes, or play a game of tennis. The recreation building, with its library and large stone fireplace, is quite inviting if relaxing is a favorite pastime; here you will find table tennis, a wide-screen TV, card and board games, and a pool table.

Nearby sightseeing (15 to 20 miles) takes you back in history; Sainte-Marie Among the Hurons, a Jesuit Mission, and the Huron Indian Village are reconstructions of seventeenth-century settlements. You will also find horseback riding, golf, live theater, museums, casino gambling, and fabulous shopping in nearby lakeside villages. Canada's Wonderland, a major theme park, is one hour away.

---

**Box 250, 116 Gloucester Trail**
**Port Severn, Ontario**
**Canada L0K 1S0**
**(705) 756-2722, (800) 461-5817**
**www.severnlodge.on.ca**

# SUNSHINE VILLAGE
## Banff National Park, Alberta

High in the Canadian Rockies in Banff National Park is Sunshine Village, one of the best ski destinations in Canada. Perched along the Continental Divide, the peak elevation at Sunshine is 9,200 feet. Located only 85 miles west of Calgary and just 5 miles from the town of Banff, Sunshine is a three-mountain (Goat's Eye, Mount Standish, and Lookout) ski resort that is constantly being improved. Back in the 1920s and 1930s, Banff was a summer destination. Those skiers that did come were usually from Europe and were referred to by the locals as "those people with wooden heads and feet to match." Most had to ski over from Banff—hardly a day trip!

In summer White Mountain Adventures in Canmore provides day trips only, starting you out on the mountaintop for hiking and mountain pleasures. Follow the clearly marked trails on your own, or take a free interpretive walk led by experts. Uncrowded and incredibly scenic, Sunshine Village is a good example of man and nature in harmony.

**Accommodations:** The Sunshine Inn, constructed in the 1960s and 1970s, is still the only on-slope accommodation in the Canadian Rockies; it's right in the middle of the ski area, at an elevation of 7,082 feet with access via gondola. A three-story complex consisting of eighty-four rooms and suites, the inn affords its guests ski-in, ski-out access and a chance at making those coveted "first tracks." The inn is open from

November to May only. Accommodation options include rooms and suites in the main hotel and older terrace rooms in an adjoining wing. Terrace rooms have separate sleeping areas with doors, but showers only and no TV; inn rooms have full bath, TV, and a queen and sofa bed. Rates include lift tickets, and children six and under always stay and ski free. Children over six pay C$25. In value season, standard inn rooms begin at C$350 to C$400. The inn was recently renovated, so the pricing structure for the 2007–2008 season may change. Packages offer four days of skiing and three nights' lodging in peak season, starting at C$494 per person; rates for April spring break start at C$359.

Getting to the inn is easy. Check in at the base area, take the gondola to the village, and start skiing. Your bags will magically arrive at your room, and your car will be parked. If you arrive outside of gondola hours, you'll have the thrill of taking "Sunshine Suzy," a cross between an SUV and a tank. She's also available for a fee if you want to escape the mountain at an odd hour, say for an evening in Banff. In the world's longest and fastest gondola, the trip takes twelve minutes; gondola hours begin at 8:00 a.m. and weekday closing is at 5:30 p.m., 7:00 p.m. on Saturday, and 10:30 p.m. on Friday and Sunday. If you want to ski Sunshine but don't fancy staying on the mountaintop, central reservations has lots of options in Banff. A shuttle bus operates between Banff and Sunshine Village.

**Dining:** Three locations on the mountain offer amenities. The mountaintop village, where the inn is located, has the largest selection, with six restaurants, bars, and lounges. The inn's dining room, the Eagle's Nest, offers fine dining, from rack of lamb to fantastic sirloin steak. The Chimney Corner is a lounge offering cocktails, well-priced food, and entertainment in the evenings. In the Daylodge, the Deli and the cafeteria-style Alpine Grill offer soup and sandwiches. The Lookout Bistro is a full-service restaurant for midday dining. The new Mad Trappers Saloon, located in the original 1928 Sunshine Lodge, is the place to go for lunch, drinks, and après-ski. Goat's Eye is the midstop; the gondola connects to the village at the top and the base area. Goat's Eye Gardens has hot food and drinks as well as snacks, beer, and wine. The gondola base area is where you first arrive, and it has a great restaurant. The Creekside Bar and Grill has just about everything—a to-go breakfast so that you can hit the slopes early, sandwiches and pizza for lunch, a full sit-down menu, and, at the end of the day, an après-ski bar.

When you feel like escaping the mountain, nearby Banff has one hundred–plus restaurants, many of them family-friendly. Joe Btfsplk's Diner is a 1950s-style diner, complete with jukebox, neon, and red vinyl booths; what better than a burger and a shake, unless it's homemade meatloaf and apple pie. Casual dining on hearty, traditional Italian food is the order of the day at the Old Spaghetti Factory, where portions are so large you might consider sharing. In an original 1928 building, Melissa's has served Alberta steak and a great kids' menu for three decades—locals say the breakfast is *huge*. Speaking of breakfast, Phil's serves it all day, with free dollar-size pancakes for kids under eight. Coloring books, toys, and baby utensils—and, on the other end, a 10 percent discount for seniors—make this a favorite with families. Craig's Way Station has an extensive menu, with specials for kids, including fourteen different chicken dishes. Have breakfast here at any time of day, with fireplace and view.

**Children's World:** Day care and children's ski schools are in the village at the base of the Clock Tower, where children are carefully supervised in a variety of programs. Be sure to check exactly what is included in the five-day packages, as you may want to adjust the kids' programs to fit what is complimentary into a coherent day for your youngster. Tiny Tigers Daycare is a safe, licensed facility for ages nineteen months to six years, with indoor and outdoor play, lunch, and snacks. Cost is C$30 for a half day, C$60 for a full day with lunch. Three- to six-year-olds have all the advantages of day care, plus one hour of skiing in the morning and afternoon—it's popular, so reserve early. Cost is C$50 for a half day, C$100 for a full day with lunch.

Children from six to twelve years old have the Kids Kampus program, where laughter and play go hand-in-hand with learning to be better skiers or riders. A full day (ski or board) is C$90, including lunch. Discovery Club, an introductory program for first-timers (ages six to twelve), provides everything needed to get kids started enjoying the snow with skis or boards. A full day is C$160; add-on days are also available. We all know that different ages have different notions about what's fun. Sunshine Mountain Riders for thirteen- to eighteen-year-olds knows what this group wants. Small teams spend the day exploring the mountain with peers, grouped by age and ability; lunch and easy socializing are included for C$100 daily. Three, four, and five days are available at all levels.

**Recreation:** There are three mountains to ski: Goat's Eye, Lookout, and Standish. Once a day Snowhosts give a tour of the mountains. Sunshine Village is located on the Continental Divide, where you can ski the provinces of both British Columbia and Alberta off the same run. The top elevation at Sunshine is almost 9,000 feet, and the base elevation is 5,440 feet, yielding skiers more than 3,500 vertical feet. Mother Nature drops more than 10 meters (33 feet) of snow here each year, which results in good skiing from mid-November through the end of May. Of the 107 named runs currently open, 55 percent are intermediate; the remainder are split evenly between beginner and expert. Many of the runs are above the treeline, giving skiers that top-of-the-world feeling. Sunshine Village boasts North America's largest new ski terrain, Goat's Eye Mountain (elevation 9,200 feet), offering extreme-expert-only (Double Black Diamond) chutes and glades, runs, and free fall with an 83-degree pitch. Two snowboarding parks (one half-pipe and one terrain park) keep snowboarders happy. Delirium Dive is the ultimate in extreme skiing.

When not skiing, you may want to pursue less rigorous activities in the family games room or relax your weary muscles in the sauna or the Sunshine Inn's giant outdoor hot pool, rated Canada's best by *Ski Canada* magazine. Mad Trapper's is the gathering place to down a few and grab a bite, to trade mountain adventures and tall tales of the trails, and to make new friends from all over the world.

---

**Box 1510**
**Banff, Alberta**
**Canada TOL OCO**
**(403) 762-6500, (877) 542-2633**
**www.skibanff.com**

# TIGH-NA-MARA RESORT

## Parksville, Vancouver Island, British Columbia

Tigh-na-Mara is Scottish for "house by the sea," an apt description of this lovely, secluded resort on Vancouver Island. Encompassed by twenty-two acres of forest, heavy with Douglas fir and arbutus, it's bordered by 3 kilometers of sandy beaches and the Pacific Ocean. The climate is temperate, considered sub-Mediterranean, and the water is allegedly the warmest in Canada. The land has changed hands many times and has grown from one log cabin in 1946 to the present 192 log buildings. The current owners have had the property since 1981 and continue to improve, renovate, and redefine the vision. After a recent C$1.5 million expansion, the Grotto Spa is now the largest resort spa in British Columbia. Families have been coming for more than twenty years and always receive a royal welcome. Tigh-na-Mara claims the largest summer recreation program on Vancouver Island and works in conjunction with several local companies. It is an island, so in getting here you have a chance to appreciate the gorgeous views and wild coast. Many roads lead here: You can take the BC Ferry from Vancouver (Tsawwassen); there's a small airport at Comox, about fifty minutes from the resort, and shuttles can be arranged; or Harbor Air can take you from downtown Vancouver to Nanaimo in twenty minutes, if you're traveling light. Parksville is about a two-hour drive from downtown Victoria. A ferry also departs from Port Angeles, Washington.

**Accommodations:** All lodging is handcrafted construction, built with fir and cedar logs. In total, 192 units are located throughout the property; styles fit into the surroundings and include spa bungalows, ocean-view condominiums, and rustic log cabins. All units have a gas fireplace; some have a kitchenette or balcony; most suites are one-bedroom. The log cottages are the most popular with families. Standing alone in the forest, they have privacy, wood-burning fireplaces, full kitchens, and patios with a barbecue area. Jedediah, the newest, is a two-story log building in a forest setting, with studio units. While a studio unit might be a bit small for families, it does have a Murphy bed and kitchenette and is the best priced, at C$199 per night. Rates listed are for July. Tigh-na-Mara does set rates based on occupancy, so they may vary. Each style has its unique benefit, so it could be hard to choose. Ocean-view suites are in a three-story log condominium with private patios overlooking spectacular views of the Georgia Strait and Coast Mountains, full kitchen, and dining area; rates are C$279. Spa bungalow suites feature a full kitchen, large Jacuzzi tub, and private patio in a forested setting near the Spa; rates are C$319. One-bedroom cottages are C$279 per night; two-bedrooms are C$339. Children under five stay free; rates for children to age eighteen are C$10. A Bed, Bath, and Breakfast package allows a C$16 credit for each person for breakfast and gives a complimentary mineral bath for each adult; room rates may also be lower.

**Dining:** With cuisine inspired by the surroundings, the Cedar Dining Room changes menus with the season. A weekly "fresh sheet" takes advantage of fresh local ingredients. Expect scrumptious seafood specialties as well as more traditional meats and vegetarian choices. It's open for breakfast, lunch, and dinner. A full children's menu is available year-round, along with high chairs and booster seats. At the Spa the Treetop Tapas and Grill is open daily for lunch and is quite unique. Enjoy light, crisp, and unique "bites," all in the comfort of your robe. Have just a few, or order the "Endless Tapas" for C$40 and spend the entire afternoon indulging yourself. The Copper Lounge is open from 11:00 a.m. to 10:00 p.m., offering West Coast appetizers and daily specials. In the evening, start off with a cocktail and a little something from the tapas-style menu. End with liqueurs, cigars, and weekly live music to round out the evening.

**Children's World:** Tigh-na-Mara knows how important it is for parents to feel secure about where their kids are and what they're doing so that parents can enjoy their own pursuits. Playpens and high chairs are available to rent. Two playgrounds, with swings, slides, and a fort, offer an outlet for all that energy. Summer here is July and August, when the recreation staff shifts into high gear. Daily from 1:00 to 4:00 p.m. is "drop-in time" for ages five and up. Activities by age groups include crafts, games, and beach and pool time; for the older (eleven and up) tweens and teens, more active sports like volleyball, tennis, and croquet are on the agenda. This program is complimentary to guests. Parents can enjoy a leisurely, if early, dinner while kids are entertained with their own themed dinners and activities. Children are happily occupied from 4:30 to 7:30 p.m.; cost is C$15. For the tweens and teens, off-site trips (from C$15 to C$25) include pizza and a movie in Nanaimo, laser tag or go-karts, minigolf in Riptide Lagoon, or minigolf and bumper boats (like bumper cars, only wetter!). For younger children, babysitting is done by local people of all ages who have been interviewed and have their Babysitting Certification and own transportation. Book at least twenty-four hours in advance.

**Recreation:** A recreation staff of seven people and nearly eighty scheduled activities ensure that there is something for everyone to enjoy here. Six golf courses are located within five to twenty minutes of the resort, so golfers have variety and convenience. Adults can sample from yoga on the beach, acquafit and Pilates classes, tennis, guided meditation, wine tasting, Latin dancing, or a trip to the Grand Canadian Casino. For kids, swimming lessons, playing with new friends, horseshoes, volleyball, basketball, and table tennis are available. For the family, beach barbecues, campfire stories, and movies are fun activities. Try a little bonding with father-son golf or mother-daughter jewelry making or manicures. The staff is happy to customize activities for your family, such as an excursion to nearby Horn Lake Caves for a little spelunking or a tour of Milner Gardens. One swimming pool is right next to the main lodge, and a second pool is indoors for winter or inclement weather, along with a whirlpool and steam room and weights. Just a five-minute walk from the resort is Fitness Connection, where workouts are complimentary to guests. Rathtrevor's Beach, a tidal beach, is sandy and flat. What this means is great fun when the tide goes out, because warm tidal pools are left behind, filled with fascinating creatures like starfish, sand dollars, and your kids. At high tide you can rent a paddleboat. Another fun activity is digging for clams at Craig Bay, one of the best clam beaches around. Ask the staff for some buckets and the chef for some recipes. Mountain bikes and children's bikes are available to rent for a ride through Rathtrevor Provincial Park or Top Bridge Trails for spectacular scenery and a swim in the river. A marine biologist conducts tours and lectures on native species and habitats, beach walks, and more. For art instead of nature, Reader's Theater gives youngsters a chance to "star" in a stage production—if they're shy, they may want to help with sets and costumes or sit in the audience. Designed as a natural grotto, the Grotto Spa is all about feeling good. A 2,500-square-foot mineral bath with a 20-foot waterfall starts you off right. Add eighteen treatment rooms with all sorts of therapies, two relaxation lounges, and an outdoor balcony with a lavender and herb garden—even a spa concierge for all your needs. And don't forget those delicious tapas. Perhaps instead of eating the caviar, you'll have a facial with it!

If all that's not enough action, local excursion companies offer rain-forest visits, nature tours, or whale watching. Summer is the season, and the orcas are on the east coast (like Tigh-na-Mara), while gray whales are seen on the west coast. Local family attractions and parks include Paradise Mini Golf and Bumper Boats and Arcade, Lions Adventure Playground and Waterpark, Cyber City (go-karts and paintball), skate parks, horseback riding, and Coombs Market. The Parksville Beach Festival is in August.

---

**1155 Resort Drive**
**Parksville, British Columbia**
**Canada V9P 2E5**
**(250) 248-2072, (800) 663-7373**
**www.tigh-na-mara.com**

# WHISTLER/BLACKCOMB
## Whistler, British Columbia

---

If you're lucky enough to hear the whistling call of the indigenous marmots, you'll easily recognize how Whistler Mountain got its current name. Originally known as London Mountain, on the old Caribou Gold Rush Trail, this area saw its first settlers in 1914, when an adventurous couple built a fishing lodge on the shores of Alta Lake. Though still attracting fishermen in the summer, Whistler is famous today as an outstanding ski destination. The village has a permanent population of approximately 10,000 people.

Skiers first schussed these slopes in the mid-1960s, and the early 1980s witnessed considerable expansion and development, primarily the opening of Blackcomb Mountain. The two mountains, Whistler and Blackcomb, are serviced by three base facilities. In the Coastal Mountains, Whistler/Blackcomb is just 75 miles north of Vancouver.

Here's just some of what people are saying about Whistler: *Ski* magazine calls it the number one ski area in North America and the "#1 Dream Vacation Destination"; the *Daily Telegraph* has rated it the number two ski resort in the world. It has the longest ski season in Canada; and in North America it boasts the most skiable terrain (more than 7,000 acres), the greatest lift-serviced vertical (5,280 feet), the most slopeside accommodations, and the most qualified ski instructors. *Family Travel Forum* rated it the "Top Family Getaway" and it was *BC Parent*'s "Families Favorite Ski Resort." Whistler is constantly adding new awards, including best mountaineering, best late season resort, *Condé Nast*'s Hot List, and best new expert terrain. And finally, *USA Today* called Whistler one of the top ten places to chill while enthusiasts ski. Whew, that's a lot of mountain! Better go soon and beat the crowd, as Whistler has been chosen as the site of the 2010 Olympics and Paralympics games. Whistler will host the Alpine, Nordic, sliding, and all Paralympic events, while Vancouver will host the ice events, freestyle skiing, and snowboarding. The Olympics Information Center is near the marketplace in the village.

**Accommodations:** Hotels and condominiums are found throughout Whistler Resort in all price ranges. Five Whistler hotels were named on the *Condé Nast* reader's poll of the top fifty ski resorts in North America: The Westin Resort, the Fairmont Château Whistler, the Pan Pacific Lodge, the Summit Lodge, and the Delta Whistler Resort all garnered acclaim. The larger facilities are the Fairmont Château Whistler at the base of Blackcomb, with ski-in, ski-out convenience, 550 units, indoor and outdoor swimming pools, a health club, and indoor tennis courts; the Delta Whistler Village Mountain Suites, an all-suite facility; and the Westin Resort, one of the locations for day-care facilities and child care with ski-in, ski-out options and 419 suites, in the heart of the village. Midsize properties are the Marriott Residence Inn, with 184 units slopeside on Blackcomb Mountain, or the Crystal Lodge in the village, with 134 rooms. For condominiums, consider Stony Creek, Glaciers Reach, and Aspens; smaller complexes such as the Hearthstone Lodge, Powderview, Whistler Resort and Club, or Whiski Jack Condos might also be the perfect choice for your family. Contacting Central Experience at (800) WHISTLER or Central Reservations at (888) 882-8858 is the first step in sorting out all these choices. Tell them your priorities, and they'll help find the perfect lodging for your family. You might want to consider one of the available packages, or book a "hot deal" online. Inquire about the PEAK rating system to help with consistent, reliable information.

Most everything is within easy walking distance, and pedestrian-only spaces mean real freedom of movement and less worry about the children. Upper Village is located at the foot of Blackcomb Mountain—here you'll find the chairlift, and in summer, the Farmer's Market and Kid's Adventure Zone. It's a short five-minute walk to Whistler Village. The Whistler Activity Centre at the Conference Center is a good resource for maps, activities, tours, restaurant recommendations, and information. Hours are 9:00 a.m. to 5:00 p.m. daily, and 10:00 a.m. to 10:00 p.m. in summer. The free Village Shuttle runs from 8:00 a.m. to midnight daily and makes a loop from Marketplace (Village North) to the Upper Village—the front of the bus says Village Shuttle, so you can't miss it.

**Dining:** With almost a hundred restaurants and cafes, you'll never have trouble indulging your palate's whim, whether you crave French, Italian, Japanese, Mexican, Thai, or Greek cuisine or even fast food. Five restaurants on Whistler and eight on Blackcomb serve hearty soups and stews, burgers, pizza, waffles, sushi, quiche, and pasta to skiers reluctant to leave the slopes for very long. Christine's at the top of Blackcomb Mountain lets you enjoy fine dining in your ski boots, with a view as superb as the menu. At Blackcomb Base II, 18 Degrees Below is the breakfast and lunch spot for teens, with their kind of food—burgers, fries, and pizza. Blackcomb has several log cabins scattered around the mountainside, with tasty treats like waffles or barbecue. A special evening snowmobile adventure to the Crystal Hut for a cheese fondue makes a nice family memory. The Dubh Linn Gate Pub at mountains' base is an authentic Irish pub, perfect for day's end. In a ski resort known for fine dining, The Bearfoot Bistro is not just a meal but an experience—five courses served with five different wines. Some of the restaurants favored by families are Black's Restaurant, the Old Spaghetti Factory, Monk's at Blackcomb, Dusty's at Whistler Creek, and the Keg Steakhouse. Caramba, Earl's, the Mongolie Grill, Milestones, and Wildwood are more family favorites. Après-ski is also family-friendly here; children of all ages are welcome until 7:00 p.m., so you can enjoy a drink with friends while the kids have hot chocolate.

**Children's World:** Whistler Kids' instructors are highly trained ski and snowboard professionals, specializing in kids' needs. Teaching more than 140,000 kids every winter, Whistler Kids is Canada's premier recreational operation for children. No wonder the kids keep bringing their parents back!

Whistler Kids offers a broad range of programs catering to kids as young as three months; kids first take to skis at three years. Daily rates for full-day day care at three locations are C$98, and ski programs for three- to four-year-olds are C$109 with lift and lesson; five- to six-year-olds are also C$109 for lesson and lift, either ski or snowboard (available for ages six and up only). Seven- to twelve-year-olds can choose ski or snowboard programs for C$130; and Ride Tribe! for ages twelve to eighteen gives them lots of action and informal lessons with no standing around (C$144). Twelve-year-olds can choose either Whistler Kids or Ride Tribe. If time permits, consider one of the Adventure Ski Camps, available at all levels. Packed with fun activities, kids stay with the same group and instructor, building friendships and confidence and increasing learning and skills. Two-day camps run on the weekend, three-day camps are from Monday to Wednesday, and five-day camps are Monday through Friday.

Saturday Night Out, from 6:00 to 10:00 p.m., is for kids ages five to twelve and gives everybody a break. The mountain and the village are the stage for themed nights with dinner and experiences they can't wait to tell you about (C$45). On Thursday, mid-December to mid-March, weather permitting, Whistler Kids Jib Sessions provides an evening introduction to tricks and jibs on the Magic Carpet and Magic Chair (ages five to twelve, minimum Level 3 ability). From 5:30 to 9:30 p.m., kids should be ready to jump, jib, jive, and have dinner too!

But Whistler is not just about winter. Unlike most ski resorts, Whistler has children's programs year-round, although this may change, so please check. In the spring, programs are daily from late April to late June, for ages eighteen months to twelve years. Running from 9:00 a.m. to 4:00 p.m., activities are similar to the summer, with two age groups (eighteen months to four years and five to twelve years). Cost is C$59 including lunch and snacks; half day is C$39. Fall is a similar program, but details were not available at press time. The Meadow Park Sports Centre and the Whistler community also have summer camps and activities for children and families. Late June to Labor Day, daily summer programs for children are packed with activities that build skills and self-confidence and are just plain fun. Located at various venues throughout Whistler, there's something for kids of all ages.

In fact, camps and activities are so plentiful that it's almost impossible to describe them. Go to www.whistlerisrecreation.com and spend a few hours choosing. In July and August camps swing into full gear for children ages thirty months to seven years. Camp Tiny Tyke, for ages thirty months to four years, is on Tuesday and Thursday mornings (C$21); activities include nature walks, visits to the fire hall, painting, theme days, and cooking. Camp Action Adventure, for four- and five-year-olds, goes to the water park, miniputt, and climbing wall, and kids also make kites and tie-dye; it meets on Monday, Wednesday, and Friday from 9:00 a.m. to 3:00 p.m. (C$32). Camp Summer Sunsations is Monday through Friday from 8:30 a.m. to 5:30 p.m. (C$39) for grades one and two; it features biking, swimming, canoeing, and field trips. Camp Sunsations Breakout is more advanced and offers Adventure with a capital A, taking it to the next level. Specialty Camps, also for older youths, include kayaking, wakesurfing, acting, soccer, martial arts, and Broadway musicals; you may have to schedule your vacation around a particular camp!

For eight- to twelve-year-olds, the Mountain Bike Program is a comprehensive, skill-based program allowing specific progression. Daily or two- and three-day camps go from beginners level through trials park, descents, and trail rides for intermediate and advanced riders. Cost depends on equipment needed, and ranges from C$83 for full day, including lunch, to C$133 to C$148, including bike and safety equipment.

Maurice Young Millennium Place is Whistler's Centre for Arts, Culture, and Inspiration. There's a little bit of everything here; check it out at www.myplacewhistler .com. The Whistler Blackcomb Foundation Childcare Centre, known as Teddy Bear Daycare, is here and offers quality care for children ages thirty months through school age. Visitors are welcome, seven days a week, 7:00 a.m. to 7:00 p.m. (604-935-8415). At the other end of the age spectrum, MY Youth Centre allows twelve- to eighteen-year-olds their own space with all their favorite things, like DVDs, Nintendo 64, air hockey, pool, and table tennis (604-935-8187). It's also the center for some planned events such as hikes and overnight excursions.

**Recreation:** Get introduced to Whistler/ Blackcomb in free morning or afternoon guided tours, and you'll begin to appreciate the mountains. More than 200 trails, twelve bowls, and three glaciers provide all the variety any skier could hope for. Choose chutes filled with powder, steep runs through trees, broad trails perfectly groomed, or mogul monsters. The average annual snowfall of 360 inches is complemented by sophisticated snowmaking capabilities. Both mountains open in late November, and skiing continues to late April on Blackcomb and to mid-June on Whistler. Blackcomb opens again in mid-June for glacier skiing through August for those who can't get enough of winter. Both mountains average 55 percent intermediate terrain; Blackcomb has about 5 percent more expert trails.

When taking a break from skiing, try ice-skating, snowshoeing, and snowmobiling, or organize a sleigh ride. Cross-country skiers take to the 10 miles of track-set trails through the forest and valley. Or try indoor rock climbing. Summer or winter ecotours are available. For just a little less strenuous exercise, visit one of the many spas, or stroll through the village to discover its more than 200 shops.

Summer or winter, family activities abound. It would take pages and pages to begin to outline all there is to do at Whistler/Blackcomb; we encourage you to check the extensive Web site so that you can find your favorites and plan ahead. Activities range from aerial sightseeing to zip lining; there's even a list of twenty things to do for under C$25. Especially for the ski and ride programs in winter and adventure camps in summer, advance reservations are a must.

In summer golf is a premier sport, with four eighteen-hole courses, each with fine credentials. The Whistler Golf Course was designed by Arnold Palmer, and the Château Whistler Course was designed by

Robert Trent Jones Jr. Jack Nicklaus was responsible for Nicklaus North, which opened in 1994, and the Big Sky Golf and Country Club was designed by Robert Cupp.

Hiking and biking across the Alpine terrain are favorites with summertime visitors. Whistler's intent is to become a mountain-biking mecca, and they are well on their way. For family fun, the Meadow Park Recreation Center has an indoor pool outfitted for kids, an outdoor playground and water park, and an indoor ice rink for those who miss winter. You'll also find a lap pool, hot tub, fitness studio, weights, and squash court. Adventure Zone is one of those places where you can do everything—wall climbing, minigolf, luge, trapeze, kiss-the-sky trampoline, and horseback riding. Zipline Ecotours gives a twist to outdoor adventure by having you spend two and a half hours flying through the trees over a series of cable cords and suspension bridges with a bird's-eye view over gaping gorges and rushing rivers. The five lakes provide fishermen, swimmers, and boaters with ample fun. Two movie theaters, art galleries, a museum, an art studio with fun workshops, and three Internet cafes may draw you indoors for a while. A variety of festivals and special events are available throughout the year, and actually, more visitors arrive in summer.

---

**Tourism Whistler**
**4010 Whistler Way**
**Whistler, British Columbia**
**Canada VON 1B4**
**(604) 664-5625, (800) 944-7853**
**www.tourismwhistler.com**
**www.whistler.com**

# INDEXES

## Alphabetical Index of Resorts

Weekapaug Inn, Weekapaug, Rhode
   Island, 25
The Westin Mission Hills Resort, Rancho
   Mirage, California, 238
Whistler/Blackcomb, Whistler, British
   Columbia, Canada, 265
Wild Dunes Resort, Isle of Palms, South
   Carolina, 65

## Resorts by State/Province

### UNITED STATES

**Alabama**
Marriott's Grand Hotel Resort, Golf Club &
   Spa, Point Clear, 93

**Arizona**
Enchantment Resort, Sedona, 141
Hyatt Regency Scottsdale Resort at Gainey
   Ranch, Scottsdale, 147
Los Abrigados Resort and Spa,
   Sedona, 151
Pointe South Mountain Resort,
   Phoenix, 153
Tanque Verde Ranch, Tucson, 156

**Arkansas**
Horseshoe Canyon Ranch, Jasper, 123

**California**
The Alisal Guest Ranch and Resort,
   Solvang, 204
Coffee Creek Ranch, Trinity Center, 207
Hotel Del Coronado, San Diego, 209
La Costa Resort and Spa, Carlsbad, 211
Montecito Lake Resort, King's Canyon
   National Park, 216
Northstar-at-Tahoe, Truckee, 218
Squaw Valley USA, Olympic Valley, 227
The Westin Mission Hills Resort, Rancho
   Mirage, 238

**Colorado**
Aspen/Snowmass Village, Aspen, 164
Breckenridge Ski Resort, Breckenridge, 170
The Broadmoor, Colorado Springs, 174

C Lazy U Ranch, Granby, 177
Keystone Resort, Keystone, 185
Vail/Beaver Creek Resorts, Vail, 197

**Florida**
Amelia Island Plantation, Amelia Island, 70
The Breakers, Palm Beach, 73
Cheeca Lodge and Spa, Islamorada, 78
Club Med/Sandpiper, Port St. Lucie, 83
Hawk's Cay Resort, Duck Key, 86
Marco Island Marriott Resort, Marco
   Island, 91
The Resort at Longboat Key Club, Longboat
   Key, 95
South Seas Resort, Captiva Island, 97
Sundial Beach Resort, Sanibel Island, 99
TradeWinds Island Resorts/Island Grand,
   St. Pete Beach, 101

**Georgia**
Callaway Gardens, Pine Mountain, 75
The Cloister, Sea Island, 80
Jekyll Island Club Hotel, Jekyll Island, 88

**Idaho**
Sun Valley, Sun Valley, 234

**Illinois**
Eagle Ridge Resort & Spa, Galena, 108

**Kansas**
Great Wolf Lodge, Kansas City, 118

**Maine**
Sugarloaf/USA, Carrabassett Valley, 21

**Maryland**
Hyatt Regency Chesapeake Bay,
   Cambridge, 53

**Massachusetts**
The Lighthouse Inn, West Dennis, 9

**Michigan**
Grand Traverse Resort and Spa, Acme, 114
The Homestead, Glen Arbor, 120
Grand Hotel, Mackinac Island, 112
Mission Point Resort, Mackinac Island, 128
Shanty Creek, Bellaire, 132

# Children's Programs by Season

As an aid in planning your vacation, resorts are listed according to when the children's programs operate: Daily Year-Round, Summer, or Winter. Some resorts, such as ski areas, may be listed under both Summer and Winter. Many resorts may also have children's programs during other times of the year; for example, major holidays or year-round on weekends. We have marked these resorts with an asterisk (*) to indicate that there is more available than just summer or winter; check the entries for details. It is always safest, however, to contact the resort to ensure that the children's program is running when you want it. Please note that other resorts not listed are considered family-friendly but have limited or no supervised children's programs: Great Wolf Lodge, Highland Lodge, and Ludlow's Island Resort. Again, please see resort descriptions for details.

## WINTER PROGRAMS

# ABOUT THE AUTHORS

JANET TICE was born and reared in Oklahoma and then spent just as many years in New York City. Always a gypsy (although her mother denies it), she considers herself a citizen of the world. She earned a Bachelor's Degree in Psychiatry from the University of Oklahoma and a Master of Science degree from New York University in the same field. With more than twenty-five years spent in the travel business, she was there in the infancy of family travel. From 1985 to 1995, she was the director of Families Welcome!, one of the first tour companies for families. She currently resides in Chapel Hill, North Carolina.

JANE WILFORD was born and reared in New Orleans, Louisiana. She earned a Bachelor of Arts degree in Art History and History from Duke University and a Master of Science degree in Library Service from Columbia University. After living for several years in New York and London, she currently resides in Charleston, South Carolina, with her husband, D. Sykes Wilford. The Wilford family travels extensively throughout the United States and Europe.

# HELP US KEEP THIS GUIDE UP TO DATE

Every effort has been made by the authors and editors to make this guide as accurate and useful as possible. However, many things can change after a guide is published—establishments close, phone numbers change, facilities come under new management, and so on.

We would love to hear from you concerning your experiences with this guide and how you feel it could be made better and kept up to date. While we may not be able to respond to all comments and suggestions, we'll take them to heart, and we'll also make certain to share them with the authors. We'd love it if you'd like to share *your* favorite family vacation spot! Please send your comments and suggestions to the following address:

The Globe Pequot Press
Reader Response/Editorial Department
P.O. Box 480
Guilford, CT 06437

Or you may e-mail us at:
editorial@GlobePequot.com

Thanks for your input, and happy travels!